TITO AND THE RISE AND FALL OF YUGOSLAVIA

Tito and the Rise and Fall of Yugoslavia

RICHARD WEST

ff

faber and faber

This edition first published in 2009
by Faber and Faber Ltd
Bloomsbury House, 74–77 Great Russell Street
London WC1B 3DA

A CIP record for this book is available from the British Library

ISBN 978–0–571–25581–8

Contents

Foreword

My interest in Yugoslavia dates back to the year I spent as a teenage national service soldier in Trieste, the former Austro-Hungarian port whose population is largely Italian but partly Slovene. Although Tito had broken with Stalin by the time I arrived, he was still making noisy claims to Trieste as well as parts of Austria. During my pleasant sojourn, I met many Yugoslavs and started to learn Serbo-Croat as well as basic Italian and German.

On going to Cambridge University after my army service, I studied the history of the Balkan people and, during the summer vacation of 1951, I visited Yugoslavia for the first time, staying in Zagreb. Its famous archbishop Alojzije Stepinac was then serving a sentence in Lepoglava prison. In October 1953 I went on an eight-month postgraduate visit to Belgrade and Sarajevo, making a special study of the period around the assassination of Archduke Franz Ferdinand in 1914, the most momentous event in twentieth-century history. From Sarajevo, in June 1954, I wrote my first article for the *New Statesman*, to mark the fortieth anniversary of the crime.

On the strength of more articles about Yugoslavia, I got a part-time job with the then *Manchester Guardian*, becoming its Yorkshire correspondent during the winter months, but spending the summers in the Balkans. During the 1960s, when I was spending much of my time in Africa, Latin America and South-East Asia, I kept returning to Yugoslavia for holidays and occasional journalistic work.

From the start of the 1970s, there were warning signs of renewed Serb–Croat tensions, and worries about what might happen when Tito finally went. From 1975, the new editor of the *Spectator*, Alexander Chancellor, frequently subsidised my visits to central and south-east Europe, as he did during the last years of Yugoslavia, when he was editor of the *Independent Magazine*. It was thanks to him that I got the chance to witness some of the tragic events of 1989–91 in Serbia, Croatia and Bosnia-Hercegovina.

My view that the breakup of Yugoslavia would lead to a civil war, first in Croatia and then in Bosnia-Hercegovina, did not conform to the popular wisdom, so that I found it difficult to get articles on Yugoslavia published, let alone acquire the financial means to return there. I therefore decided in the autumn of 1991 to write a book of Balkan memoirs. This would also include a historical study of what really happened in Yugoslavia during the Second World War. This book was a rather uneasy mixture of memoir and history. However, in early 1993 the publisher Christopher Sinclair-Stevenson came up with the simple but brilliant idea of writing a life of Tito, the very personification of Yugoslavia.

Whereas, when I first came back from Yugoslavia during the 1950s, people would almost invariably ask, 'Is Tito a Communist or a Yugoslav nationalist?', today they ask quite different questions: 'Was Tito a Serb or a Croat?' and 'How did he hold these people together?' These are some of the questions that this book is intended to answer.

Normally, in a foreword like this, I would mention by name some of the many people who have offered me hospitality, advice and criticism over the years. However, in view of the atmosphere of suspicion and bitterness now pervading the former Yugoslavia, I thought it best not to associate anyone else with views that are really my own.

However, I should like to thank my dear wife, Mary, who has supported me and borne with my moods of anger and gloom during the last few years, when it must often have seemed to her that the problems of Bosnia-Hercegovina were flooding her kitchen.

1 The South Slav Lands 1815

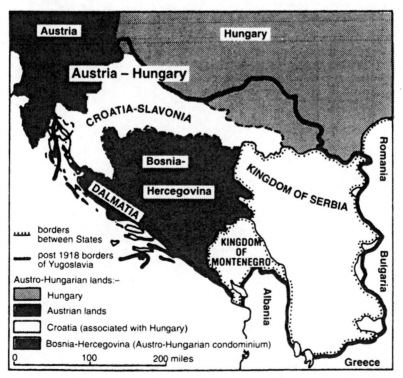

2 Yugoslavia on the eve of the First World War

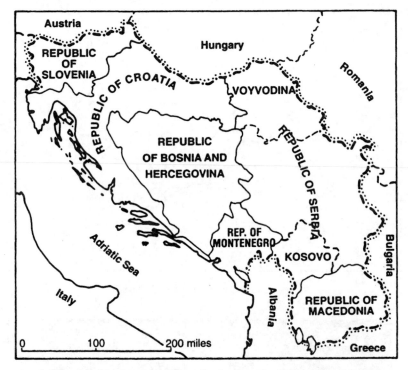

3 The federated units of Yugoslavia after the Second World War

Pronunciation

The pronunciation of Serbo-Croat words was, until recently, rather mysterious to the foreign reader. Nowadays we are all too familiar with the pronunciation of names such as Sarajevo, Karadjić, and Milošević. I have everywhere adopted the Serbo-Croat spelling in Latin script except for the names of the Serb and Croat paramilitary organisations, the Chetniks and Ustasha (pronounced oostasha). Although the second of these should strictly be declined, I have preferred to use it unchanged as a singular, collective and plural noun, and also as an adjective.

The following simple notes on pronunciation are borrowed from Anne Kindersley's *The Mountains of Yugoslavia*, in turn adapted from W. A. Morison's *The Revolt of the Serbs against the Turks*.

c	*ts* in *ts* in ca*ts*
č	*ch* in *ch*urch
ć	between *ch* in *ch*urch and *t* in *t*une
dj, dž	*j* in *j*ug
g	*g* in *g*et
j	*y* in *y*es
lj	*lli* in mi*lli*on
nj	*ni* in mi*ni*on
r	always rolled; between consonants it becomes a vowel; *ur* in Scottish b*ur*n

s	*s* in *s*ad
š	*sh* in *sh*in
ž	*s* in pleasure
a	*a* in f*a*r
e	*e* in b*e*d
i	*i* in g*i*ve
o	*o* in for
u	*u* in p*u*sh

I

The History of the South Slavs

Josip Broz, the future Marshal Tito, was born in 1892 at the village of Kumrovec in Croatia, north-west of the provincial capital Zagreb, or Agram as it was then called. Although it had been a kingdom during the early Middle Ages, by the late nineteenth century Croatia was ruled from Budapest and belonged to the Austro-Hungarian Empire. Hungarian was the official language, used even for buying a railway ticket; the middle classes in Agram spoke German; only the peasants were monoglot in their South Slav language, now known as Serbo-Croat. Josip's mother came from across the River Sutla and therefore belonged to the Slovene branch of the South Slav people, speaking a different though closely related language. The Slovenes had never aspired to independence and now belonged to the Austrian province of Carniola, whose population was largely German or Italian.

As a young man, Tito acquired the Austro-Hungarian lingua franca of German and went to work in Slovene Carniola, the mainly Italian port of Trieste, Czech-speaking Bohemia and then the capital, Vienna. He joined the Austro-Hungarian army, and when the First World War broke out he went off to fight the Serbs, his fellow South Slavs. It was not until after the war, and the breakup of the Austro-Hungarian, Turkish, German and Russian empires, that Kumrovec became part of the Kingdom of Serbs, Croats and Slovenes, or Yugoslavia as it was later called.

In April 1941, after the Axis conquest of Yugoslavia, Kumrovec became part of the Independent State of Croatia, under the Ustasha terrorists, but the Slovenes across the River Sutla were swallowed up in Hitler's Reich or Mussolini's Italy. During the next four years of civil war between Serbs, Croats and Muslims, Tito emerged as the one man offering unity to the South Slav peoples. In 1945 he set up a federation embracing the six republics of Serbia, Croatia, Slovenia, Montenegro, Macedonia and Bosnia-Hercegovina.

In 1991, eleven years after Tito's death and one year before the centenary of his birth, Slovenia and Croatia declared themselves separate, sovereign and independent states, with their own armies, customs and excise, and immigration control. The River Sutla, separating the homes of Tito's father and mother, was now the frontier between two not very friendly states. The breakup of Yugoslavia in 1991, as in 1941, led first to a rising of Serbs in Croatia, and then to a three-way slaughter in Bosnia-Hercegovina. In spite of what has been said by the foreign press and even by some of the South Slav demagogues, there is no 'ethnic' difference between the warring factions in Bosnia-Hercegovina, all of whom are alike in blood, appearance, language and bellicose nature. All that divides them is their ancestral religion, so that the Greek Orthodox call themselves Serbs, the Roman Catholics call themselves Croats, while the unhappy Muslims, who used to describe themselves as Yugoslavs or Bosnians, are now known by a faith in which many of them do not believe.

In order to understand the career of Tito and how he tried to unite the South Slav people, we have to go back to the Middle Ages to see the origins of the great divide between the two Christian churches and Islam. Modern political commentators too often try to explain human conflict in sociological terms such as class struggle, racialism or male oppression of women. They either ignore or discount the influence on the human heart of history, myth and religion. As soon as one looks at these things, the once bewildering conflict of Serbs, Croats and Muslims becomes as clear as do the analogous conflicts in Northern Ireland and India.

Anyone who approaches the Yugoslavs without some knowledge of their religious history is like a chicken trying to understand a ladder, as the Spanish proverb goes.

The South Slavs were one of a series of peoples who moved into Southern and Western Europe to fill the vacuum left by the breakup of the Roman Empire. At the height of their power, the Romans had colonised the Balkan region as far as the Black Sea, where modern Romanians still honour their name and speak a derivative of their language. Latin was used as the lingua franca down to a line running from northern Albania, through Niš in Serbia, east to the present Sofia. Beneath that line, Greek was the language of writing and civilisation.

With the establishment of the Eastern Empire at Constantinople in AD 330, and the steady decline in the power of Rome, a series of hordes from Asia and north-east Europe came south and west to prey on a feeble population. Some, like the Huns and Vandals, came only to burn, plunder and then withdraw, while others settled the land and adopted the Christian religion. Such were the Goths in Spain, the Magyars in Hungary and the Avars in Bulgaria.

The origin of the various Slavs such as the Russians, Ukrainians, Poles, Czechs and Slovaks is still a matter of argument, but it seems that the South (or Jugo) Slavs came from what is now Poland, north of the Carpathian Mountains. During the sixth century AD, they started to cross the River Danube, continuing south towards Greece and west towards the Adriatic. In the course of their progress along the wide river valleys, into the Balkan mountain range and down to the Dalmatian coast, the South Slavs drove out or absorbed the existing people, known to the Romans as the Illyrians. Although some historians disagree, popular wisdom holds that these Illyrians were the ancestors of the modern Albanians, whose language does not resemble any other spoken in Europe.

The eastern wing of the South Slav migration gave a variant of its language to the Bulgarians, who are mostly an Avar people, and to some of the Macedonians, who are today a mixture of Slavs, Avars, Greeks and Albanians. The Slavs first tried to conquer and

then were absorbed by the Eastern Empire, and such leading men
as Emperor Justinian and the general Belisarius may well have
been Slav in origin. The Slovenes, a smaller branch of the South
Slavs, settled in the Carinthian and Julian Alps among the Germans
and the Italians.

The great majority of the South Slav people, speaking the
language now called Serbo-Croat, settled in what came to be called
Serbia, Croatia, Montenegro and Bosnia-Hercegovina. It seems
that the first political entities were established in what are now
northern Albania, Montenegro and parts of Croatia just inland
from the coast. In about the ninth century, foreigners first noticed
that some of the South Slavs called themselves Serbs or Croats,
though it is not clear whether these names derived from the people
or from the places they inhabited.

In spite of later division, both political and religious, the
language spoken by most of the South Slav people has stayed the
same to the present day. A foreigner learning Serbo-Croat may
notice peculiar dialects spoken in country districts such as eastern
Serbia and the Dalmatian coast, but unless one is a linguistic expert
one will notice little difference between the languages spoken in
Belgrade, Zagreb and Sarajevo. The word for 'what' may vary; the
vowel 'e' is shorter in Serb than it is in Croat; 'bread' is *hleb* in
Belgrade and *kruha* in Zagreb. In the obscene and often blasphemous oaths that punctuate all South Slav conversation, the word
for 'vagina' is *pička* in Serb and *pizda* in Croat. The Serbs have
retained a few Turkish words such as *varŏs* (town) and *para*
(money), besides borrowing others from English and French. The
Serbs listen to *muzika*, the Croats to *glazba*; the Serbs play *futbol*,
the Croats *nogomet*. Many Serbs disapprove of the Western names
for the months, such as *Oktobar*, regretting the old Slav words such
as *Listopad*, literally 'leaf fall', still used by the Croats. The Greek
monks Saints Cyril and Methodius brought the Cyrillic script to
the Serbs as well as the Russians and Bulgarians, but the Croats
adapted the Latin script, so that for instance the sound *ts* became
c, *ch* became *č*, and *tch* became *ć*.

The difference in alphabet shows that, from early on, the South

Slavs were divided by the influence of the Pope in Rome and that of the Patriarch of the Eastern Church in Constantinople. By the eighth or ninth century, the Slovenes were following the customs and doctrines of Rome, while the Bulgars were just as firmly devoted to Constantinople. The main body of South Slavs were not yet committed. Today the Croats boast of their 1,300 years of loyalty to Rome but their first little dukedom during the tenth century owed its secular allegiance to Constantinople, which then controlled much of the Adriatic coast. In those days the Eastern Church was able to use the Latin rite, while the Roman Church was ready to use the Slavonic rite devised by Saints Cyril and Methodius. The little dukedoms in what are now southern Serbia and Montenegro were loosely divided by the influence of Rome and Constantinople.

The division among the South Slavs really began with the Great Schism of 1054 when, in the words of Edward Gibbon in *The Decline and Fall of the Roman Empire*, the papal legate placed on the altar of Santa Sophia 'a direful anathema, which enumerates the seven mortal heresies of the Greeks, and devotes the guilty teachers and their unhappy sectaries to the eternal society of the devil and his angels'.[1] The main theological difference, then as now, was whether the Holy Spirit of the Trinity proceeded from God the Father alone, or from the Father and the Son (*filioque*). Besides its difference of opinion concerning the '*filioque* clause', the Eastern Church also disapproved of some of the Roman innovations, such as the celibacy of the clergy and the shaving of priests' beards.

In the Kingdom of Croatia around the time of the Great Schism of 1054, no clear distinction arose between the Greek and Latin churches. When the Bishop of Split was asked in about 1050 why he had a wife and children, he answered that marriage was authorised by the laws of the Eastern Church. A few years later, in 1060, the synod of Split forbade the use of the Slavonic liturgy and language in church, insisting that services could be held only in Latin or Greek. However, from a letter written by Pope Alexander II in 1067, we find that the Roman Church authority at Bar, in present-day Montenegro, allowed the use of Slav as well as Latin and Greek in its monasteries.[2]

At times the Eastern and Western churches united against the common threat from Islam, but resentment flared in Constantinople in 1183, as Gibbon tells us:

> Neither age, nor sex, nor the ties of friendship or kindred, could save the victims of national hatred, and avarice, and religious zeal; the Latins were slaughtered in their houses and in their streets; their quarters were reduced to ashes, the clergy were burnt in their churches, and the sick in their hospitals; and some estimate may be formed of the slain from the clemency which sold above four thousand Christians in perpetual slavery to the Turks.[3]

At the beginning of the thirteenth century the French knights and Venetian merchants leading the Fourth Crusade turned aside from the purpose of freeing the Holy Land to vanquish and plunder Constantinople.

> In the Cathedral of St Sophia, the ample veil of the sanctuary was rent asunder for the sake of the golden fringe; and the altar, a monument of art and riches, was broken in pieces and shared among the captors . . . A prostitute was seated on the throne of the patriarch; and that daughter of Belial, as she is styled, sung and danced in the church, to ridicule the hymns and processions of the Orientals.[4]

When the Latins seized temporal and spiritual power at Constantinople, the Serbian ruler Stefan Nemanja took the chance to throw off his vassal status. He pledged his support in arms to the Roman Catholic King of Hungary, then asked the papal legate to baptise him under the Roman rite. Thanks to this opportune change of faith, which does not appear in Serbian history books, the Nemanja dynasty built up a Serbian state that came to include most of

Greece. However, Stefan Nemanja's younger son, Sava kept to the Eastern faith, creating a Serbian Orthodox Church independent of Constantinople. Saint Sava, as he is known to his people, invented the slogan 'Only Unity Saves Serbs' ('*Samo Sloga Srbina Spasova*'), which is symbolised by a cross between four Cyrillic esses:

$$\begin{array}{c|c} \mbox{\textcyrillic{э}} & \mbox{c} \\ \hline \mbox{\textcyrillic{э}} & \mbox{c} \end{array}$$

The Serb and Croat kings in the Middle Ages had no permanent capital, court, administration or legal system. They were heads of a loose alliance of military chieftains who roamed the Balkans exacting tribute from their defeated rivals. Serbia and Croatia were not nation states but provinces like Wessex or Mercia in eighth-century England. At about the time of the Norman Conquest of England, the Magyars started to challenge the power of the South Slav rulers. In 1102 the Croatian nobles agreed to a *Pacta conventa*, pledging obedience to the King of Hungary, in return for which they were free from taxation, held equal status with their Hungarian counterparts, and retained their own feudal assembly, the Sabor, and their own governor, or Ban. The *Pacta coventa* remained formally valid until 1918.

During the Middle Ages the idea arose that Croatia comprised not only the geographical heartland around Zagreb but all Roman Catholic Slavs who spoke Serbo-Croat. The Catholics in Slavonia, Dalmatia and Bosnia-Hercegovina who had previously thought of themselves simply as Slavs, or took their name from the clan or region, began to identify with the kingdom that ceased to exist in 1102.

Both the Serbian Orthodox Church and the Croatian Catholic Church tried to impose their faith on the South Slavs in Bosnia and its adjoining dukedom of Hercegovina (from *Herzog*, the German for 'duke'). To add to the problem, the mountains of Bosnia-Hercegovina had also afforded a refuge from persecution to a fanatical sect of Manichaean heretics whose creed had come from Bulgaria. They called themselves Bogomils, ('dear to God') but

because of the origin of their faith, and the fear and hatred that it
inspired, their name was perverted into a synonym for wickedness.
In one of his famous footnotes, Gibbon pointed out that the French
word *bougre* derived from a Bulgarian or Bogomil heretic, as does
the English word, 'bugger'.

The Bogomils were in fact a peaceful sect who believed in the
equal power of God and the Devil, rejecting the Cross, the
sacraments, the Virgin Mary, the Church's hierarchy and its
liturgy, except for the Lord's Prayer. The elect, or 'perfect', had
to forswear the things of the flesh but the Bogomil masses enjoyed
the pleasures of love, music and wine. The rulers of Bosnia-
Hercegovina, who were sometimes sovereign kings and sometimes
Bans, or governors, owing allegiance to Hungary, attempted to
keep the peace between their Bogomil, Orthodox and Roman
Catholic subjects. In 1168 Governor Culin refused to obey the Pope
and the King of Hungary when they told him to stamp out the
Bogomil heresy.[5] However, at that time the papacy was much
disturbed by a wave of similar Manichaean heresies in western
Europe, such as the Albigensians in the South of France, against
whom Simon de Montfort led a crusade in 1209.

In 1238 the papacy launched a first crusade into Bosnia-Hercegovina under the leadership of the King of Hungary's brother,
Coloma. Pope Gregory IX congratulated Coloma on 'wiping out the
heresy and restoring the light of Catholic purity', but he spoke too
soon, for in 1241 the Tatars invaded, and all the crusading soldiers
were called back for the defence of Hungary.[6] In 1246 Pope Innocent IV Ordered Archduke Colocz to lead another crusade, which
slaughtered many Bogomils but did not destroy their faith.

The Franciscans went into Bosnia-Hercegovina in 1260, building
monasteries in the remote mountain regions where the Bogomils
had gone to escape their tormentors. The Franciscans set up an
inquisition in 1291, and also tried to impress the peasants with
wonders such as these described by a papal chronicler.

> One stepped into a large fire and with great hilarity stood in the
> middle of the flames, while he recited the fiftieth psalm . . .

Upon the Eve of St Katherine in 1367, a mighty heavenly flame appeared in the East with an intense light apparent to the whole globe. At that time they say that the loftiest mountains, with all the rocks, cattle, wild beasts and fowl of the air, were miraculously consumed.[7]

All such efforts were unsuccessful, as can be seen from a letter written by John XXII in 1325 to Stephen, the Ban of Bosnia.

Knowing that thou art a faithful son of the church, we therefore charge thee to exterminate the heretics in thy dominion, and to render all assistance to Fabian, our Inquisitor, for as much as a large multitude of heretics hath flowed together into the principality of Bosnia . . . These men, armed with the cunning of the Old Fiend, and armed with the venom of their falseness, corrupt the minds of Catholics by the outward show of simplicity and the sham assumption of the name of Christians, their speech crawleth like a crab and they creep in with humility, but in secret they kill.[8]

The Bosnian rulers, if they were not themselves Bogomils, were tolerant to the heresy. King Tvrtko (1353–91), who threw off Hungarian rule and exercised partial sway over much of Serbia, Croatia and the Dalmatian coast, was even-handed in dealing with all three religious groups under his rule, and has since been acclaimed as a proto-Yugoslav. Bosnia-Hercegovina, in the fourteenth century, was an example to Europe of how people of different religions could live together in harmony.

As the popes crusaded against the Bogomils, a deadlier enemy of the Christian faith was advancing into the South Slav lands from Asia Minor. The Muslim Turks had not yet captured the ultimate prize of Constantinople but they were moving through Greece into the realm of the Serbs. On St Vitus's Day, 28 June 1389, a Turkish army confronted a grand alliance of Serbs, Bosnians, Hungarians, Greeks, Bulgarians and Albanians at Kosovo Polje, the Field of Blackbirds, in what was at that time the largest battle ever fought in Europe. The Serbs were defeated and the Turks became the masters of south-east and central Europe. For the Serbs, St Vitus's Day, or *Vidovdan*, became the symbol of national pride, sorrow and aspiration; on 28 June 1914 a young Bosnian Serb shot Archduke Franz Ferdinand at Sarajevo. During more than five centuries under Turkish rule, the Serbs were determined not to forget the Battle of Kosovo. Bards sang of it to the sound of a one-string fiddle; painters and sculptors depicted the deeds of valour and treachery; churchgoers prayed for the souls of the fallen.

In their romanticising of Kosovo, the Serbs often forget that they were not the only warriors fighting the Turks that day. They also forget that the Turkish army included many Serb converts to Islam, now fighting as janizaries. As Gibbon observes: 'The Janizaries fought with the zeal of proselytes against their idolatrous countrymen; and in the battle of Cossova, the league and independence of the Sclavonian tribes was finally crushed.'[9] The Ottoman Sultan Bajazet completed the conquest of south-east Europe, and then, in the words of Gibbon, 'turned his arms against the Kingdom of Hungary, the perpetual theatre of the Turkish victories and defeats'. After destroying an army of 100,000 Christians at Nicopolis in 1396, Bajazet threatened that he would lay siege to Budapest, then conquer Germany and finally feed his horse with a bushel of oats on the altar of St Peter's in Rome. Gibbon says of Bajazet:

> His progress was checked, not by the miraculous interposition of the apostle; nor by a crusade of the Christian powers, but by a long and painful fit of the gout. The disorders of the moral, are sometimes corrected by those of the physical world, and an acrimonious humour falling on a single fibre of one man, may prevent or suspend the misery of nations.[10]

As the Turks occupied Kosovo and the rest of the Serbian heartland, tens of thousands of Orthodox Christians fled north and west to the realm of the Catholic King of Hungary, most of them settling in what we would now call Croatia. Albanian converts to Islam took the land that had once been farmed by the Serbs and erected their mosques near the Serbian churches at Prizren and Gračanica. Islam also made converts among the South Slavs in the Sandjak region of south-west Serbia and to a lesser extent in Montenegro; but the Turks never entirely conquered the fierce mountain people living there. The city state of Ragusa, now Dubrovnik, and many Dalmatian towns protected by Venice were left alone by the Turks in return for a tax on their trade.

Even when the Turks had entered Bosnia-Hercegovina, the papacy still regarded the Bogomils as more of a threat than Islam. Extraordinary though it may seem to us, the popes in the fifteenth century, and many historians since, regarded Bosnia-Hercegovina as the breeding ground of Protestantism. They saw the Bogomils as the instigators of Huss in Bohemia, the Lollards in England and the Waldensians in France. There is an undisputed connection between the beliefs and practices of the Bogomils and those of the other Christian reformers. The rejection of bishops, liturgies, Holy Communion, the Virgin Mary and even the Cross have all featured at various times among the demands of reformers. Certain Bogomil attitudes – such as preferring St Paul to St Peter, belief in the power of the Devil, and perhaps most of all their sense of being 'the elect' – were to be found in the teachings of Luther, Zwingli and Calvin.

Gibbon was not quite clear about the location of Bosnia, but he was certain that the Bogomils, or 'Paulicians' as he sometimes called them, taught and inspired the Protestants in western Europe:

In the state, in the church, and even in the cloister, a latent succession was preserved of the disciples of St Paul; who protested against the tyranny of Rome, embraced the bible as the rule of faith, and purified their creed from all the visions of the Gnostic theology. The struggles of Wickliff in England, of Huss in Bohemia, were premature and ineffectual; but the names of Zwinglius, Luther, and Calvin, are pronounced with gratitude as the deliverers of nations.[11]

The independent and Protestant voice of the Bogomils comes across in the inscriptions carved on their tombs and reproduced by the modern scholar J. A. Cuddon. Here are three fine examples:

Here lies Radivoj Drašćić. I was a bold hero. I beseech you, touch me not. You will be as I am, but I cannot be as you are.

Here lies Vlatko, who prayed to no man however powerful, and who knew many countries, dying in his own. He leaves neither son nor brother.

Here lies Dragac. When I wished to be, I ceased to be.[12]

Throughout the first half of the fifteenth century, the Bogomils played an important role in the Reformation. They sent delegates to the Council of Basel in 1433 and numerous preachers to talk to the Hussites in Prague. In 1434 the Catholic Bishop of Bosnia-Hercegovina complained that his diocese was 'swarming with Hussites and other heretics'. In 1459 King Stephen of Hungary launched yet another crusade into Bosnia, driving some 40,000 Bogomils into Hercegovina, whose duke at the time was sympathetic to them. King Stephen sent some of the captured heretics to Rome where, it is said, they were 'benignly converted'. Yet still the heresy flourished, so that in 1462 Pope Pius II dispatched a group of scholars to Bosnia-Hercegovina to try to win over the Bogomils by peaceful disputation.[13]

By then it was too late. In the very next year, 1463, the Bogomil leaders made an arrangement with the Turks and in a single week handed to them the keys of twenty towns and fortresses. Although the Hungarians held out for a while at Jajce, which was to be Tito's headquarters 480 years later, the rest of the province quickly became part of the Ottoman Empire. The majority of the Bogomils accepted Islam and were from now on the administrators, the owners of land and the dwellers in elegant towns such as Sarajevo and Mostar. The former Bogomils had the chance to revenge themselves on their former Catholic persecutors. Bosnian troops in the Turkish army that conquered Hungary loved to boast that the hoofs of their horses now trampled enemy earth.

The Christian Bosnians became the *rayahs* (vassals). However, in 1463, the year of the conquest, Sultan Mahomet granted the Franciscan Order an *Atmane* (Charter) exempting their monasteries and their land from taxation, and freeing the monks themselves from the poll tax that weighed so heavily on the other Christians. From then on the Franciscan friars in Bosnia-Hercegovina also enjoyed the right to carry a pistol and cutlass. They took over the duties of parish priests and even of bishops that elsewhere fell to the secular clergy.

By the beginning of the sixteenth century the Croatian nobles were losing faith in the military power of Hungary to resist the Turks, and in 1522 they appealed for help to the Austrian house of Habsburg. In that year Emperor Ferdinand created what came to be known as the Military Frontier, in German *Militärgrenze*, in Serbo-Croat *Vojna Krajina* (pronounced Voy-na-Kry-na). This was a broad buffer zone or cordon sanitaire extending along the borders of Turkish-occupied territory from the Adriatic coast to the Danube. The Military Frontier, which was soon almost as large and populous as civilian Croatia, comprised a network of fortified villages, blockhouses, watch-towers and entanglements, and its centre of authority was the newly created garrison town of Karlstadt, now Karlovac. The Military Frontier was ruled and officered by the Austrian Empire, but it depended upon an army of soldier-settlers known as the *Grenzer*, or Frontiersmen, almost all of whom were Orthodox in religion. Although some had always followed the Eastern rite, the majority were refugees from the Turkish invasion of Serbia. In return for perpetual military service, the *Grenzer* were given allotments of land, the right to choose their captains, and freedom to practise their own religion. The success of the *Grenzer* inspired the Russians to set up a similar frontier force, the Cossacks, to fight off the Turks and their Tatar allies.

As long as the Turkish army threatened, civilian Croatia accepted the Military Frontier, but when the danger receded complaints arose. Croat national pride resented the fact that the Military

Frontier lay outside the control of the Sabor and Ban. The feudal
nobility thought that the *Grenzer*, as freemen, were putting ideas
into the heads of their serfs. The Roman Catholic Church disapproved of the toleration shown to 'schismatics', while almost
everyone thought that the *Grenzer* were brigands.

As the Turks retreated, so the Military Frontier extended south
and east, gaining in size and population. In the early eighteenth
century, the Habsburg armies drove the Turks out of Hungary,
then crossed the Danube deep into Serbia. The Turks fought back
and recaptured Belgrade but no longer threatened to cross the
river. To safeguard his frontier and repopulate his land, the King
of Hungary opened his border to tens of thousands of Serbs who
settled in what is now the Vojvodina. The Orthodox Serbs had
welcomed the Habsburg army to rid themselves of Turkish rule
but the Bosnian Muslims fought the Christian invaders, and even
created their own *Krajina*, or frontier zone, to repel attack. An old
Muslim song from the Hercegovina *Krajina* expresses the character
of the stony region where Tito was later to fight some desperate
battles:

> Such is the way of the bloody Frontier,
> Blood with dinner, blood with supper,
> Everyone chewing bloody mouthfuls,
> Not one day of repose.[14]

During the eighteenth century the Habsburg *Grenzer* came to be
used as crack troops against France or Prussia. When Austria was
allied with England, the Duke of Marlborough's army consisted
largely of 'Croatians', whose passion for rape and plunder horrified
public opinion and fired the rage of Marlborough's enemies such
as Jonathan Swift.

The ideas of the French Revolution reached the South Slavs
during the first decade of the nineteenth century, when Napoleon
conquered Venice and its Dalmatian possessions, the independent
city state of Ragusa and then, in 1809, all of Slovenia and most of

Croatia including the Military Frontier. Calling their conquests *Les Provinces Illyriennes*, after the Roman name for the Balkans, the French emancipated the peasants from forced labour and feudal tax, encouraged the growth of trade and industry, and built proper roads. They also abolished the ancient Croatian Sabor and the office of the Ban as worthless trappings of the feudal past. Because of their abstract, rational thinking and their disregard for religion, history and tradition, the French were the first to see the potential unity of the South Slavs in general, and Serbs and Croats in particular. It was the French who inspired the idea of Yugoslavia.[15]

After the fall of Napoleon and the restoration of Habsburg rule, many Croats and Slovenes looked back nostalgically to the *Provinces Illyriennes*. The Croats especially suffered from the ever-increasing rivalry in the Empire between Budapest and Vienna, which divided them under two separate rules. With the French withdrawal, Austria took over Venice and its territories on the Adriatic coast, but inner Croatia and Slavonia were once more governed by an increasingly nationalistic Hungary. Croat writers such as Ljudevit Gaj protested against the Magyarisation of cultural life and worked towards a revival of national literature and art. The Croatian Catholic clergy also stood out against foreign cultural repression, remembering the days when Croatia was hailed by the popes as *Antemuralis Christianitatis*, the outer bulwark of Christendom. A National Party was formed in the 1840s demanding the unification of all Croatian lands, as well as establishing contact with 'Illyrians' in Belgrade.

Like the Croats, the Serbs were also trying to rediscover or even invent their own cultural heritage. In the early part of the nineteenth century, Serbia and Greece were the first countries to try to free themselves from Ottoman rule, with a series of bloody revolts, followed by still more bloody reprisals. Just as the Greeks looked back to Thermopylae and the conquests of Alexander, the Serbs recalled the Battle of Kosovo. A remarkable scholar and linguist, Vuk Karadjić, brought out a lexicon of the Serbo-Croat language based on the pure dialect spoken in Hercegovina by Serbs, Croats and Muslims alike. Karadjić also roamed through Serbia and Bosnia-Hercegovina listening to and transcribing Serbian poems and ballads, especially those concerning the Battle of Kosovo. These ballads caught the imagination of some of the best-known writers in Europe, including Goethe, and a number of classical scholars who saw in this oral history, sung to the sound of a one-string fiddle, an explanation of how the Greeks came to receive the *Iliad* and the *Odyssey*.

The Kosovo ballads became an issue in the debate on whether the poems ascribed to Homer were written by one man, or woman, or by a number of different bards who added their own embellishments to the story. Those who favoured the second theory continue to seek out old Serb gusla singers, recording their songs in the hope of finding fresh evidence for their argument. The debate on the Kosovo ballads continues still in Homeric circles and in the pages of journals such as the *New York Review of Books*. In a lighter vein, Vuk Karadjić also compiled a collection of funny but wildly indecent Serbian women's songs, which remained unpublished until the 1970s when it appeared in Belgrade under the title *The Red Knight*, one of the many expressions used for the penis.

While Gaj was at work in Zagreb, and Karadjić in Belgrade, the Prince Bishop of Montenegro, Petar Njegoš, was writing his epic poem *The Mountain Wreath*, the expression and inspiration of much that is good and bad in the Serbian national character. The Prince Bishop was six feet eight inches in height, which made him tall even by Montenegrin standards, and he further impressed his subjects with his parlour trick of having a lemon thrown into the air and then drilling it with his pistol. He had travelled widely and filled his mansion at Cetinje with furniture, books and works of art from all over Europe, including a billiard table that had been dragged up the mountain from the sea.

The theme of *The Mountain Wreath*, as of Montenegro's history, was the struggle against the Turks and the South Slav converts to Islam. In particular the poem celebrates an occasion in 1704 when the Montenegrins slaughtered a whole Muslim community. Verse after verse proclaims the message that Bairam, the Muslim feast, cannot coexist with Christmas:

> So tear down minarets and mosques,
> Kindle the Serbian yule logs
> And paint the Easter Eggs.[16]

The political aspirations of the South Slav people were roused by the commotion of 1848 when national, liberal and even socialist revolutions broke out in Germany, France, Italy, Austria and Hungary. Although the Croats had chafed at rule from Budapest and resented efforts at Magyarisation, they disliked even more the Hungarian revolutionary leader Lajos Kossuth, who had said that he knew of no Croat nation and certainly could not find it on the map. At a meeting of the Sabor the Croats appointed as ban Baron Josip Jelačić, a scholar, poet and general commanding the Military Frontier. Asserting his loyalty to the Emperor Franz Joseph, Governor Jelačić led his army of *Grenzer* to crush the rebels in Hungary. Since he was not a good general, Jelačić failed to accomplish the task, which was later performed by the Russian army, so he took his *Grenzer* to crush the liberal rising in Vienna, the home of Franz Joseph. At the same time, *Grenzer* were helping to put down Garibaldi's revolt in Italy. In this way the 'Croatians', as they were generally known, became, like the Cossacks, the bogymen of the Left and the darlings of the Right in Europe. Ironically, Adolf Hitler, who grew up hating the Serbs second only to the Jews, admired the military prowess of the 'Croatians', although they were Orthodox Christians and later came to regard themselves as Serbs.

After the suppression of the 1848 revolution, Austria showered General Jelačić with honours and presents, including the bronze statue of the hero on horseback, with outstretched sword pointing at Budapest, that stands on Jelačić Square in Zagreb. However, the Croats did not for long enjoy the reward for their loyalty to the Emperor. After defeat by Prussia in 1867, Austria had to let

Hungary once more govern the South Slav parts of the Habsburg Empire. Governor Jelačić himself was a kind of proto-Yugoslav and admirer of Serbia. He thought that the Slavs in the Habsburg Empire were looked upon as inferiors by the Germans, Hungarians and Italians: 'I would prefer to see my people under the Turkish yoke than to live under the complete control of its educated neighbours . . . Educated people demand from a people over whom they are ruling also their soul, that is to say their nationality.'[17]

Governor Jelačić's closest adviser during the crisis of 1848 was Ljudevit Gaj, the leader of the Illyrian Movement. In May of that year both men appealed to the Serbian Prince Alexander Karadjeordjević for moral, military and financial help, although with slightly different objectives. According to Gaj's latest biographer, 'Jelačić wanted Serbian co-operation in order to save Croatia and the dynasty. Gaj wanted to create a South Slav kingdom with Serbia at the centre, a plan he had been cultivating since 1842.'[18]

It was the Croats rather than the Serbs who looked to Yugoslavia as a means of finding their own identity. The foremost champion of the idea was the Roman Catholic bishop, historian and linguist Josip Strossmayer, who founded a Yugoslav Academy in Zagreb in 1867. Strossmayer wanted first a union of the Illyrian people of inner Croatia, Dalmatia and Slavonia to serve as a nucleus for a confederation of all the South Slavs. He wanted above all spiritual reconciliation between the Orthodox and the Roman Catholic faiths. At the Vatican Council of 1869–70, Strossmayer opposed to the very last moment the dogma of papal infallibility because he knew the offence this dogma would cause to the Orthodox Serbs. On his death in 1905, at the age of ninety, Strossmayer was mourned throughout the entire Slav world.

A much less admirable character, Ante Starčević, came to be seen as the father of Croat nationalism. An academic philosopher and a journalist, Starčević had moved from an early belief in Illyrianism to outright hatred of Serbs. He based his theories on the continued legal validity of the tenth-century Croat kingdom to which he looked back with romantic ecstasy. He believed in the

Sabor's absolute sovereignty over a state comprising at least inner Croatia, Slavonia, the Military Frontier, Dalmatia and Bosnia-Hercegovina, where the Muslims were to be seen as 'Croatian blood brothers'. Ultimately Croatia would include all Serbia, provided the people there acknowledged themselves to be Croats.

English writers on the Balkans in the nineteenth century frequently wrote the word 'Slav' as 'Sclav' and 'Serbia' as 'Servia', though there is no orthographic justification for either spelling. As Gibbon had pointed out, the enemies of the Serbs employed these spellings to make a connection with *sclavus* and *servus*, the two Latin words for 'slave'. Although Gibbon himself referred to Sclavonia he knew that the word came from *slava* (celebration) and had 'been degraded by chance or malice from the significance of glory to that of servitude'.[19]

Ante Starčević used this play on words to suggest that the 'Slav-Serbs' were doubly slaves, and he used this term to include all people he saw as inferior or of 'impure blood', as well as political enemies. From this he deduced that the Croats were really Goths who had somehow slipped into speaking a Slav-sounding language. Starčević was deft at twisting his own racial theories. For instance he said that the Serbs were an evil, inferior race yet nevertheless included them in the Croat nation. The Serbs were acceptable when they saw themselves as Croats, but as soon as they showed their own national consciousness, they were once again 'Slav-Serbs'. Starčević wrote of the Serbs as 'a breed fit only for the slaughterhouse' and popularised the punning slogan 'Srbe na vrbe' ('Serbs to the willow trees'), meaning 'String them up'. In 1871 his Party of Croatian Rights started an insurrection in the Military Frontier, where there were many 'Slav-Serbs'.

In July 1875, after more than four centuries of Ottoman rule, Bosnia-Harcegovina flared in revolt. The crops had failed in the previous year in the district of Nevesinje, twelve miles from Mostar, and when no taxes were paid the government sent in troops to punish the Orthodox Christian peasants, provoking riot. The rebellion spread to Trebinje, just inland from the Austrian port of Ragusa and close to the independent and Orthodox Princedom of

Montenegro. The events in this obscure province plunged all Europe into a state of crisis that recurred in 1887 and 1908, before the Sarajevo assassination in 1914 led the whole of Europe into war. During the Second World War Bosnia-Hercegovina was the scene of the worst religious massacres in European history, and it was as a result of the carnage that Tito rose to power.

During the first Bosnia-Hercegovina crisis of 1875–8, the two main contenders for taking over the dying Ottoman Empire in Europe were Austria-Hungary and Russia, which also saw itself as the guardian of Orthodox nations like Serbia, Montenegro, Greece, Bulgaria and Romania. The Germans, the French and the Tories in Britain tended to side with Austria-Hungary and Turkey, largely for fear of the Russians advancing on Constantinople.

Allegations of Ottoman cruelty told by Orthodox refugees from Bosnia-Hercegovina fired Serbia and Montenegro into a war against Turkey in 1876. The Turks drove them back, then crushed a revolt in Bulgaria by killing some 12,000 Orthodox Christians. Hundreds of Russians volunteered to fight in the Serbian army, including Tolstoy's fictional Count Vronsky, who set off on a troop train racked by remorse and grief over the death of Anna Karenin, and also by toothache. In London the Tories bellowed for war against Russia and Serbia, chanting the latest music hall ditty:

We don't want to fight, but by Jingo if we do,
We've got the ships, we've got the men, and got the money too.
We've fought the Bear before, and while we're Britons true,
The Russians shall not have Constantinople.

The old Liberal statesman William Gladstone came out of retirement to champion the Orthodox peasants in Bosnia-Hercegovina and Bulgaria, and to call for the Turks to be thrown out of Europe 'bag and baggage'.

A *Manchester Guardian* correspondent, the young Welsh archaeologist Arthur Evans who later won fame and a knighthood as the excavator of Knossos, reported that 250,000 refugees had been driven from Bosnia-Hercegovina, and that 50,000 had died from cold, disease or starvation. When Evans reported that Orthodox women had suffered 'the usual fate' from Muslim soldiers, questions were asked in the House of Commons, and the British consul in Sarajevo made things worse by suggesting that 'in a country like Bosnia, where morality is at such a low point, this last grievance . . . is not their greatest'.[20]

Evans described how the women in Montenegro were hauling ammunition up from the coast to use in the latest twelve-and-a-half-pounder guns. After the Montenegrins captured the Slav Muslim town of Nikšić, Evans found there was 'hardly a house that has not been struck by a shell, and it is not by any means safe to knock too hard on a friend's door when paying a visit'.[21] The Montenegrins took their artillery into Hercegovina to shell the Muslims there as well, but in 1878 the political leaders of Europe ended the war by handing over the province to Austria-Hungary. The Orthodox peasants once more rose in revolt, supported this time by many Muslims. The largely Muslim city of Sarajevo, which had opposed the revolt in 1875, became the headquarters of opposition to Austria. An army of 90,000 men, only one-sixth of whom had any formal military training, took on 150,000 Habsburg regulars. After the pacification, Evans complained that the Orthodox inhabitants of Trebinje were treated by the Austrians 'not as a liberated but as a conquered and inferior race', but he had to admit that Trebinje had 'gained in some material ways from its new drill-masters'.[22]

In his reports to the *Manchester Guardian*, frequently written on mountainsides to the sound of gunfire, Evans displayed a profound understanding of Bosnia-Hercegovina's past, present and future, for his predictions all proved correct. Unlike most modern observers, Evans saw that the South Slavs were alike in blood, language and even appearance:

In an English school there would be a much greater variety of type, physical, moral and intellectual. Suppose the master is a pure-blooded Anglo-Saxon, he may have to deal with scholars whose blood is partly Celtic or partly Norman or partly French, or of other nationalities. But the Bosnian schoolmaster has to deal with a less mixed breed.[23]

Because Evans had studied Bosnian history, especially the Bogomil question, he understood the all-important role of religion in politics. He noted with some amusement that Orthodox peasants were starting to call themselves 'Serbs', in sympathy with the now independent kingdom. He saw the Serbs as the agents of progress towards a union of all South Slavs:

> The silent advance of the Serbian Orthodox Church, borne onwards on a tide of nationality, at the present moment invading Dalmatia, Croatia and Slavonia simultaneously, is fraught with pregnant consequences, and a few generations hence may make the dreams of South Slav union, vain today, easier of realisation than they were in the days of the greatest Serbian Czar.[24]

Evans noted that the Catholic Croats, 'under the denationalising influence of the Romish priesthood', held themselves back from their Serbian kinsmen:

> But – and I have never yet seen this most pregnant fact pointed out – over half the Grenze, the old Military Frontier of Croatia, containing the most warlike and not the least civilised part of the population, is peopled by what is in fact a separate and purely Serbian nationality. By Serbian nationality is meant rather a difference in political tendencies and religion rather than in blood and language.[25]

Although Evans did not believe in an imminent war between Austria and Russia; 'That Austrian interests must eventually clash with Russia seems to me certain . . . And when that day arrives it will be well for Austria, and for Europe, if she has made her peace with her own Slavonian subjects and sapped by conciliatory means the solidarity today existing between the Serbs and Russians.'[26]

Having predicted the First World War, Evans went on to warn against papal intolerance of the Orthodox Church:

> Students of history will point out that in the fifteenth century, Romish bigotry, by throwing Puritan Bosnia into the arms of the more tolerant Turks opened the way for the Asiatic into the heart of Europe. So in this nineteenth century that same intolerance bids fair to escort the Russians in triumph to the Adriatic shore.[27]

This was exactly what happened during the Second World War.

Yet, in his brilliant, uncanny reports for the *Manchester Guardian*, even Evans could not predict that the man destined to bring the South Slav people together after the Second World War would not be a Serb but the son of a Croat father and Slovene mother, born Josip Broz in the village of Kumrovec in 1892.

2

Youth

Tito's own account of his early life, published in *Tito Speaks* by his friend and disciple Vladimir Dedijer, starts with a characteristic blend of frankness and mystery: 'I was born Josip Broz in May 1892, in the Croatian village of Kumrovec, which lies in a district called Zagorje ("the country behind the mountain").'[1] Nine out of ten people reading that sentence will feel frustrated at not having been told the actual day of Tito's birth. Those who were themselves born in May will want to know if they share his birthday. Those who believe in the stars will want to know if Tito was born under Taurus or Gemini. And we need to know the day of Tito's birth to work out his age at the time of his death, which also happened in May.

In fact Tito was born on 7 May but, extraordinary as it may seem to us, he did not celebrate or even remember the day in his childhood and early life. Perhaps it was not the local custom. Towards the end of the Second World War, when Tito was turning into a national hero, his colleagues decided to make his birthday a Day of Youth, and hit on the date of 25 May. So much publicity was given to this official birthday that in 1944 the Germans chose it as the date for their attempt to kill or capture Tito in 'Operation Rösselsprung' ('Knight's Move'). When Dedijer checked with the parish register after the war and found that Tito was actually born on 7 May, it was too late to change the official birthday and Day of

Youth. This was one of the puzzles, gaps and inconsistencies in Dedijer's book that contributed to the persistent rumour that Tito was not the same person as Josip Broz.

Since *Tito Speaks* is almost the only account we have of Josip Broz before he acquired his more famous persona, it is well to examine the weaknesses and far more important virtues of what has become a classic work of biography. It was written six years after the end of the war and three years after the quarrel with Stalin, at a time when Tito wished to assert himself as a Yugoslav national leader, both by reuniting a sorely divided country and by demonstrating defiance of the West as well as the Soviet Union. Most of the gaps in *Tito Speaks* concern what has come to be called the 'nationalities problem', especially the quarrel between Serbs and Croats. But if the book was discreet on domestic matters, it was for its time outspoken and even sensational in its attacks on the Soviet Union. Although in the early 1950s Yugoslavia was itself a police state, running concentration camps, *Tito Speaks* was one of the first and by far the best-informed denunciation of Stalin and by implication the system he had inherited. After the death of Stalin in 1953, and the restoration of Yugoslav–Soviet friendship, Tito wanted to tone down some of the rude things said about Russia in Dedijer's book.[2]

Although Tito glossed over or left out many important matters in what he allowed to be published about his life, he does not seem to have told any serious lies. He was not one of the great majority of politicians and soldiers who tinker with history to show that they were always right. On the contrary, Tito was able to look back on his early life with humour and even self-deprecation. He does not attempt to disguise his weaknesses, such as ostentation in his dress, a certain fecklessness and imprudence with money. Although he does not parade his countless sexual affairs and illegitimate children, he never pretends to have been a respectable married man. The book also reveals Tito's very considerable charm and humour. Above all, the man who comes across in the parts of *Tito Speaks* that are told in the first person singular sounds and behaves like the Tito we know from his greatest biographer, Milovan Djilas, and from the memoirs of others who knew him, such as Fitzroy Maclean.

The Broz, or Ambrose, family came from Dalmatia, fleeing the Turks in the sixteenth century and possibly joining the peasant revolt of 1573. Its leader, Donja Stubica, was executed by having a red-hot crown placed on his head, thereby becoming a hero in Tito's history books. During the insurrection, the serfs at Kumrovec stormed the castle of Cesargrad and cut off the head of the bailiff, but failed to capture the wicked Hungarian Baroness Barbara Erdödy. She later took her revenge by hanging hundreds of serfs from trees in the village. 'Three centuries later,' Tito recalls, 'whenever as children we awoke at night, our mother threatened that the Black Queen of Cesargrad would take us away if we did not go back to sleep at once.'[3]

Tito dwells on 1573 as the only acceptably radical year in Zagorje's otherwise tranquil history; the Turks never succeeded in taking Zagreb. He mentions with pride that one of Napoleon's wounded soldiers took refuge in Kumrovec on the retreat to France. When the Habsburgs won back *Les Provinces Illyriennes* in 1814, they reintroduced the feudal system throughout the South Slav lands of the Empire. Count Erdödy was required to maintain fifty horsemen and two hundred foot soldiers to serve in the Habsburg army, mostly recruited from idlers, according to Tito: 'I have heard tell there were no soldiers from the Broz family except one, and he was a sentinel on the Drava bridge, during the Hungarian rebellion of 1848.'[4] Here Tito is studiedly vague about the occasion when Governor Jelačić led an army from the Croatian Military Frontier to crush the uprisings in Budapest and Vienna. In Communist history books published after the Second World War, Governor Jelačić is shown as a reactionary, and in 1947 his statue was taken away in the night from its plinth in Zagreb.

Although the rebellions of 1848 ended in failure, they led to the abolition of serfdom throughout the Habsburg Empire, and the departure of the Erdödys from Kumrovec. Tito's paternal grandfather, Martin Broz, was one of the serfs to be given his freedom, on the strength of which he married 'a tall, strong woman who was extremely proud of coming from a family of peasants who had been freemen for more than two centuries'.[5] Martin had one son, Franjo, and six daughters, who, under a new Hungarian law, all had a share in the family's land. As a result of this, Franjo was forced into debt in trying to buy out his sisters. However, when he was twenty-four and working as a blacksmith, Franjo married a Slovene girl of sixteen, Marija, the oldest of fourteen children of Martin Javersek, who owned sixty-five acres of farm and woodland across the River Sutla. Tito recollects:

> She was a tall, blonde woman with an attractive face . . . A hard life awaited my parents. Fifteen acres of land, which dwindled as my father's debts came due, were insufficient to feed the family. When the debts became intolerable, the soft and good-natured Franjo gave it up and took to drinking, and the whole burden fell upon my mother, an energetic woman, proud and religious.[6]

Franjo and Marija had fifteen children, of whom Tito was seventh and one of the seven who survived childhood. Although the family's house was the largest in Kumrovec, they shared it with cousins and wanted for space as well as for food. From the age of seven Tito was put to work driving the cattle, hoeing the corn and weeding the garden:

> But the hardest task of all was not physical. It was when my father would send me round the village with the IOU to ask someone to endorse it for him. The other peasants were, like my father, deep in debt, hungry, with many children. I had to listen to curses and complaints and then, at last, almost always, they would endorse the IOU.[7]

Seventy years later, Tito was to take his country's IOUs for endorsement by ever more angry international bankers.

Tito spent much of his boyhood at his maternal grandfather's house in Slovenia, looking after the livestock and horses:

This was the job I liked best, for as early as I can remember, one
of my greatest pleasures was to be with horses. I was already
riding bareback when my head barely reached the horse's
belly. . . . I learned in those days that the better you tend a
horse, the better he will serve you. During the war, I made a
point of dismounting from my horse Lasta (Swallow), when
climbing a hill, and I urged my men to save their horses for the
plain.[8]

Tito was miserable when his father traded their sheepdog Polak
for two cords of firewood. When the dog sneaked back from its
new master, the children hid it in a cave until their father relented
and bought it back. Polak lived to be sixteen and helped to give
Tito his lifelong affection for dogs. 'I had one with me whenever I
could,' he said in *Tito Speaks*, 'and later a dog called Lux saved my
life.'[9] In fact Tito knew perfectly well that Lux was pressing against
him in terror when they were hit by the shards of an exploding
shell, but he did not want to cast doubt on a harmless legend.

Kumrovec was lucky enough to have a school, so that Tito
acquired a basic education, although he was handicapped by
knowing Slovene better than Serbo-Croat, and never got to speak
either faultlessly. His mother made him become an altar-boy but,
according to Tito, the priest gave him a slap and after that he never
went into a church again. This attitude must have upset his mother,
who hoped that Tito would become a priest himself; since Tito
loved his mother, we can assume that the matter troubled him also.
Although we can never know anyone else's feelings about religion,
there are indications that Tito was not such a dogmatic atheist as
he claimed.

The boys of Zagorje started to earn a living at the age of twelve
and Tito became a cowherd for his mother's brother: 'For this I
received my food, and a promise from my uncle that he would buy
me a new pair of boots at the end of the year. But he did not keep
his word; he took my old boots, which had ornaments on them,
repaired them for his son, and gave me a pair which were far worse
than my old ones.'[10] This is the first mention of Tito's lifelong

passion for clothes and footwear, and of his dread that people were trying to rob him. Only a few sentences later, he says:

> My ambition when I was a small boy was to be a tailor, a natural result of the wish of every little peasant in Zagorje to have nice clothes. I remember a baron who used to come to our district, an engineer, big and strong. He had a car that looked like a carriage and could do about fifteen miles an hour. The children would gather around it screaming when he stopped. But he lost every bit of respect in our eyes because the seat of his trousers was mended. We said: 'What kind of baron is he supposed to be with trousers mended like ours?'[11]

The hope of getting some smart clothes led Tito to leave his home at the age of fifteen. A relative of the family was a sergeant stationed at Sisak, a garrison town to the south-east of Zagreb, and he suggested that Tito find a job in the army canteen there. 'Waiters', he said to the eager young cousin, 'are always well-dressed, always among nice people and get plenty to eat without too much hard work.' As Tito admitted to Dedijer forty years later: 'Perhaps it was the point about dressing well that interested me most.'[12]

Sisak was one of the bigger towns in the former Military Frontier, which had ceased to exist in 1881. The Turks had long since left the adjoining province of Bosnia-Hercegovina, and this was annexed to the Habsburg Empire in 1908, causing another crisis and nearly a European war. Tito says nothing of this in his autobiography. As his uncle had predicted, he liked his waiter's uniform but did not take to the arduous work or the extra chore of setting up skittles in the adjoining bowling-alley. With the help of his father, Tito had himself apprenticed to a Sisak locksmith and general mechanic:

> He mended bicycles, shotguns, threshing machines and repaired the handrails on stairs. My friends told me that locksmithing was

a form of engineering and that engineering was the most beautiful
trade in the world; that engineers built ships and railways and
bridges . . . With my family tradition of blacksmithing, this
appealed to me . . .[13]

He qualified as a journeyman in 1910.

When he was not at work on his trade, Tito attended apprentice
school, read Sherlock Holmes stories, bred rabbits and pigeons,
and looked foward to café life with its wine, women, dancing and
smart clothes. In *Tito Speaks* he says that he read the left-wing
papers, admired the Social-Democratic Party and longed to join a
trade union. He does not mention the burning political issue at
Sisak when he was living and working there.

In 1903 Hungary brought in a new system of government for
Croatia which, according to the Balkan expert R. W. Seton-
Watson, 'rested upon a reactionary and narrow franchise, gross
corruption, a packed Diet, press censorship and confiscation,
periodic suppression of trial by jury, a demand for strict subservi-
ence on the part of all officials, the subjection of the judicial to the
executive arm, and a skilful encouragement of the old feud between
Croat and Serb'.[14] In spite of Croatia having the narrowest franchise
in Europe, the general election of 1908 was won by a Serb–Croat
coalition of people favourable to a South Slav union. Because it had
been in the Military Frontier and still had a large Orthodox
population, Sisak was one of the coalition strongholds. In 1909,
the year after the election, the authorities staged the Agram
Treason Trial in which fifty Serbs and Croats were charged with
offences such as using the Cyrillic script and saying that Serbia's
franchise law was more democratic than Croatia's.

Although the Agram Treason Trial excited Croats who had the
vote, and foreign political commentators such as Seton-Watson, it
did not excite the mass of Croats. The idea of a South Slav
federation appealed to some of the Orthodox Serbs in the Military
Frontier region, though many were *kaisertreu* (that is, loyal to the
Emperor). Some educated Croats favoured the 'Yugoslav' ideals of

Bishop Strossmayer. Many younger Croats combined Slav nation-alism with liberal or socialist doctrines from Russia and France, and wanted to overthrow the Habsburg Empire by force. In the years preceding the murder of Archduke Franz Ferdinand by a Serb in Sarajevo, most of the many assassination attempts on Habsburg officials were made by Italians and Croats.

Besides the proto-Yugoslavs there were proto-Croatian national-ists, who wanted to break from the Habsburg Empire but not to join with the hated 'Slav-Serbs'. However, the mass of the Roman Catholic Croats were loyal to their church and emperor. Even Social-Democrats like Tito probably felt they had more in common with factory workers in Austria than with the peasants of 'Yugoslavia'.

With the help of some journeymen he had met in Sisak, Tito got a mechanic's job in Zagreb, at a wage of two crowns and thirty hellers a day. He joined the Union of Metalworkers and the Social-Democratic Party, receiving his membership card and a badge depicting two hands holding a hammer. After a few months' hard work, Tito was able to fulfil his long-standing wish – 'to buy myself a new suit and to return well-dressed to Zagorje and my own people'. For twenty crowns, or just over a week's wages, he bought what he called 'a nice new suit' and left it at his digs before going to the workshop to say goodbye to his fellow workers:

> When I returned the door of my room was wide open, and there was no trace of my new suit. How sad and dejected I was! I had to go to a secondhand dealer to buy an old suit for four crowns, for I did not have the heart to return home to Zagorje in the same clothes I had worn when I worked as an apprentice.[15]

Throughout Tito's early life, the countryside of Croatia was suffering from the impact of cheap American grain and the tariffs erected against it by the Austro-Hungarian government. The result was large-scale emigration to the United States. Tito estimates that 250,000 people left Croatia for America between 1899 and 1913, and many more would have gone if they had had the 400 crowns required for the steamship fare. Tito's father had wanted to send him to the United States in 1907 but could not raise the money. Three years later, Tito was again thinking of America, and bought a copy of Upton Sinclair's *The Jungle*, which describes the life of immigrants in the Chicago stockyards. Although the American dream would remain with Tito until after the First World War, he was ready to settle for second best by joining the thousands of young Croat men who travelled to work through the Austro-Hungarian Empire.

Tito went first to the Slovene city of Laibach, now Ljubljana, the place where he was to die sixty-nine years later. When he could find no work there he continued on foot over the mountains to Trieste. After three days of trudging through the snow, Tito fell prey to his personal jinx: 'In a village where I slept the last night of my journey . . . a cow, looking for salt, tore my suit to bits while I slept. I was not lucky with suits.'[16] He was awestruck by the great port of Trieste, the Hamburg or Liverpool of the Austro-Hungarian Empire, but he did not find any work and remained there only ten days. Forty years later, Tito was almost ready to go to war to drive the Italians out of Trieste, claiming it as a Yugoslav city.

Returning to Slovenia, Tito found a job in a metal-goods factory in the small town of Kamnik. He joined the local Soko ('Falcon') gymnastic club, whose spirit was patriotic and anti-Habsburg. However, the Soko attracted Tito for other reasons: 'I liked their coloured uniforms and feather-tipped caps. I bought one on instalments and took part in every parade, marching at a smart gait behind the band.'[17]

Tito remained in Kamnik until 1912, when the management in Vienna closed the plant and offered the workers money to go to another one of their factories in Cenkovey in Bohemia. When the Slovenes arrived they found that the company wanted to use them as blackleg labour to break a strike by the local Czechs. The two Slav peoples stuck together and forced the plant to take them on at a better rate of pay. 'The Czech workers came to love our people very much,' Tito recalls, 'and I had never felt more welcome abroad than in Bohemia.'[18] He does not mention the strong anti-Habsburg nationalist movement led by Professor Thomas Masaryk, whose lectures drew thousands of young Croats and Serbs to 'Golden Prague' to imbibe the idea of Slav independence. The Communists, who had taken over Czechoslovakia by the time *Tito Speaks* was written, regarded Masaryk as a bourgeois nationalist.

From Cenkovey, Tito travelled widely through Austria-Hungary and Germany, making short stops to work in places of interest. He was not impressed by the Škoda works in Pilsen, nor by the 'sordid' industrial plants in Munich, although he enjoyed the beer in both places. 'I liked the Ruhr much better,' he says, 'what with all the smokestacks sprouting like a forest in so small an area.'[19] He would later cause a forest of smokestacks to sprout in Yugoslavia, without however creating the wealth of the Ruhr.

Tito learned German and adequate Czech, and altogether enjoyed the life of a *Gastarbeiter*, as Croats in Germany came to be called in the 1960s. He recalled the words of his 'good old teacher Vimpulšek from Zagorje, who used to say that a metal worker was the man of the future'. This wandering life brought Tito at last to Vienna, the capital of the Habsburg Empire, and home of his future mortal enemy, Adolf Hitler. Tito went to stay with his brother in the industrial suburb of Wiener Neustadt and found a job at the Daimler factory. There he acquired his love of expensive automobiles: 'I even became a test driver, running the big, powerful cars with their heavy brasswork, rubber-bulb horns and outside hand-brakes to put them through their paces.'[20] On Sunday afternoons he would go to the Orpheum, a music hall with magicians, clowns and light Viennese music. He took fencing lessons and learned to waltz but did not manage to master the quadrille or the polonaise.

On reaching the age of twenty-one, in May 1913, Tito went back to Croatia to do his two-year military service in what he calls in his memoirs 'an army of repression'. Although he complains of the bullying NCOs and the stultifying discipline, Tito thrived on army life, went to an NCO training school and emerged as the youngest sergeant-major in his regiment. He won second prize in the all-army fencing championship in Budapest, and learned to ski on Sljeme Mountain, near Zagreb, where he was stationed during the winter of 1913–14. In his memoirs he says that he was using the army 'to learn as much about military matters as I could', as though he was thinking ahead to his leadership of the Partisans in the Second World War.[21] In reality he was just an ambitious young man who used his army experience to better himself in his later civilian career.

While Tito was doing his military service, the problem of Bosnia-Hercegovina once more brought Europe to, and indeed over, the brink of disaster. Although the Habsburgs had given this once backward province an honest administration, schools, public works, industry, roads and a railway system – much of it tunnelled beneath the Balkan mountains – the Orthodox Christians fretted under Teutonic rule and increasingly came to identify with the Kingdom of Serbia. In Belgrade the corrupt Obrenović dynasty ceased to reign in 1903, when army officers favourable to the rival Karadjeordjević dynasty burst in on the King and Queen, pulled them out of a cupboard and butchered them. The new monarch, King Peter, favoured the Radical Party politician Nikola Pašić and his 'Great Serbia' policy. Although the Serbs at first looked south and east, hoping to conquer territory held by the Turks and Bulgarians, they felt an increasing sympathy with their Orthodox brethren in Hungary, Croatia and Bosnia-Hercegovina. Austria's annexation of Bosnia-Hercegovina in 1908 caused fury in Belgrade and demonstrations of sympathy in Prague. A rebellion by the 'Young Turks' in 1908 still further weakened the Ottoman Empire. Throughout the first decade of the century, foreign opinion was shocked by reports of Balkan atrocities, and in October 1912 Montenegro, Serbia, Greece and Bulgaria embarked on a war to drive the Turks out of Europe.

One of the journalists sent to report the first Balkan War was Leon Trotsky, the Bolshevik theorist and future military commissar but at that time the Vienna correspondent of the *Kievskaya Mysl* (*Kiev Thought*), the largest daily paper in the Ukraine. In late October 1912 Trotsky travelled by train to Zemun on the northern bank of the Danube, then crossed the river by steamboat to Belgrade, just as the war started:

> On the Serbian bank of the Danube and Sava, sentries march up and down. There are members of a home guard, aged between forty-five and fifty-five, wearing peasant clothes with lambskin caps and *opanki* [bark sandals] and with rifles over their shoulders. The sight of these elderly peasants, thus torn from their farmyards, with bayonets protruding from behind their caps, at once created a feeling of disquiet and fear.

Like many foreigners newly arrived in Belgrade, Trotsky began to feel he had entered a strange and alarming country:

> Through one's mind float last impressions of 'back there': the bank official with the neat hair-parting and the black stone on his little finger, the Hungarian colonel with his well-tended fingernails, the snow-white table-cloths in the restaurant car, the toothpicks in rice-paper wrappings, the 'Milka' chocolate on each little table – and then one is irresistibly gripped by the realisation of the tragic seriousness of what is about to happen in the Balkans.

Trotsky observed that the tramlines had been torn up, there were holes in the road, and a vehicle had sunk in a puddle up to the hub of its wheel in front of the new, green-and-white Moskva Hotel. In a stationer's shop he saw huge symbolic pictures of Serbs on powerful horses smashing the Turkish ranks. Crowds had gathered in front of a flower shop to study the latest telegrams from the front. He saw the 18th Regiment marching to war in khaki uniforms, *opanki* sandals, and caps with a sprig of greenery stuck in the top. Trotsky wrote articles on the scandalous gossip, the wily Prime Minister Pašić, and the international press corps:

> In the café of the Moskva, the best café in Belgrade, is the headquarters of the European press correspondents. My dear

colleague *Don-qui-blague* [Don Humbug], wearing a top-hat and carrying a briefcase, rushes like one possessed from table to table, tearing freshly arrived newspapers from other people's hands, and in passing snaps up items of news rather like a dog catching flies. 'Have you heard? Yesterday a reserve officer was shot here for having dealings with Austria.' Three fountain-pens bite frenziedly into writing paper. The Austrian correspondents are depressed. The ministers won't give them an interview.[22]

The four Christian armies drove the Turks out of Macedonia, southern Serbia and Albania, which now became independent. The Serbs captured Kosovo province, kneeling to kiss the ground of the sacred battlefield. The more thoughtful among them may have observed that in the historic 'Old Serbia' the Serbs were now outnumbered by the Albanians (or Arnauts, as Trotsky called them). In the wrangling over Kosovo that has gone on ever since, Albanian historians have asserted that their people formed the majority in the province even before the Ottoman conquest. In 1991, at a history museum in the castle of Kruja in central Albania, I heard the guide explain that the Serbs were not even present at the battle of Kosovo. However, the Ottoman *defter*, or register of land, for 1455 shows that the province was overwhelmingly Slav.[23] Albanians had started to move into the Kosovo in large numbers when the Serbs migrated to Hungary at the end of the fifteenth century. And from 1913 onwards, the Serbs began to move back into the province, expelling and killing many Albanians.

Even Croats like Tito thrilled at the Serbian victory over the Turks, and again over the Bulgars in the second Balkan War. They also envied the wealth of the Serbs compared to the South Slavs in the Austro-Hungarian Empire. Plums grown in the orchards of the Šumadija region, south of Belgrade, provided the basis for Serbia's simple economy. About half the plums were turned into brandy or jam, and the rest were fed to the pigs which were Serbia's principal export. The farmers of Hungary could not compete with the cheap and delicious plum-flavoured pork, and badgered their government into imposing tariffs. In spite of a number of 'pig wars', the Serbian farmers continued to prosper.

The ever more bumptious Kingdom of Serbia now claimed to speak for all the South Slavs in the Habsburg Empire, and set an example as well to the Czechs, Slovaks and Poles. The Habsburgs and their ministers understood that the Serbs were a mortal threat but could not agree on how to contain them. One party hoped to appease the discontent by turning the Dual Monarchy into a Triple Monarchy, giving the Slavs equal status with Austrians and Magyars. It was even proposed that the Kingdom of Serbia should join an Austro-Hungarian-Slavic Empire with three capitals on the Danube, at Vienna, Budapest and Belgrade. The most influential advocate of a Triune Monarchy was the heir to the Habsburg throne, the choleric Archduke Franz Ferdinand, who did not object to the Slavs but detested Italians, Jews and above all Hungarians.

The Archduke and others who hoped to placate the Slavs were outnumbered by those who favoured a pre-emptive military strike at Serbia. The war party in Austria-Hungary had the support of a similar faction in Germany which saw the Serbs as an obstacle to their 'Drang nach Osten' ('drive to the east'). In the new age of oil-powered ships, automobiles and aeroplanes, the Germans were bent on obtaining supplies from Persia, Iraq or the Arabian peninsula, and wanted to guard the route to the East on their Berlin-Baghdad railway. The Germans were also obsessed with the need to make a pre-emptive war against Serbia's mighty protector, Russia, before it developed into a modern industrial, and therefore military, power. Such was the atmosphere in Europe on 28 June 1914 when Gavrilo Princip, a Bosnian Serb, shot dead Archduke Franz Ferdinand and his wife Sophie.

The six young men waiting to kill the Archduke on that Sunday morning were members of 'Mlada Bosna' ('Young Bosnia'), an organisation of Serbs, Croats and Muslims dedicated to South Slav union. One of the six was a Muslim but the remainder, including Princip, came from Orthodox homes and therefore were counted as 'Serbs'. Moreover the murder took place on St Vitus's Day, the anniversary of the Battle of Kosovo. For these reasons, the murder caused an immediate explosion of anti-Serb feeling in Sarajevo, a largely Muslim city with a considerable Croat middle class. Ivan Šarić, auxiliary or co-adjutant bishop to the Roman Catholic Archbishop of Sarajevo, always an enemy of the 'schismatic' Orthodox Church, scribbled a verse anathema calling for God's vengeance to fall on Serbian 'vipers' and 'ravening wolves'.[24] Outside the Sarajevo museum, a clerical orator told the crowd that 'one hundred hangings would not pay for the heads of the two beloved victims'. After a gathering at the Roman Catholic Arch-bishop's palace, a mob of Croats and Muslims attacked the Serb-owned Evropa Hotel. Throughout Bosnia-Hercegovina and in Croatia during the next few days, Serbs were vilified, robbed, assaulted and even hanged. The Bishop of Mostar, Alojzije Mišić, was one of the very few Roman Catholic priests to denounce attacks on the Serbs.

In the wave of arrests that followed the Sarajevo murder, the police found evidence that the assassins had got their pistols and bombs from the 'Black Hand', a secret society dedicated to Serbian expansion. Although the Belgrade government had no part in the plot, it neither cracked down on the 'Black Hand' nor condemned the assassin nor even expressed condolences to the Habsburg family. The Belgrade newspapers crowed over the death of a man they wrongly believed to be anti-Slav.

This all too typical bloody-mindedness led to a wave of *Serbenhass*, or hatred of Serbs, throughout central Europe, with politicians and newspapers calling for violent measures to 'stamp out this nest of vipers'. Such was the popular feeling even in countries that would soon be fighting on Serbia's side. The normally pro-Serb and anti-Austrian *Manchester Guardian* went so far as to say in an editorial: 'If it was physically possible for Serbia to be towed out to sea and sunk there, the air of Europe would at once seem cleaner.'[25]

The Austro-Hungarian government issued an ultimatum to Serbia containing unacceptable demands. When these were refused,

An Austrian Army Awfully Arrayed
Boldly Began Bombarding Belgrade,

as the ditty went. In fact the first shells were fired at the city from
gunboats on the Danube, to which the Serbs replied by dynamiting
the bridge to Zemun, which at that time was in Hungary. During
the next five months the Habsburg armies launched three invasions
of Serbia, first from Slavonia over the River Sava, then from Bosnia
over the Drina and then on Belgrade itself from over the Danube.
All these attacks were repelled by Serbian troops battle-hardened
during the two Balkan wars and led by King Peter, who stood in
the front line with a rifle and forty rounds of ammunition. The
British historian G. M. Trevelyan, who went to Belgrade as a kind
of glorified war correspondent, described the Serb resistance as
'the most thrilling feat of arms that this war had witnessed . . . a
victory in which Washington and Garibaldi would have loved to
take part'.[26] R. W. Seton-Watson, also braving the Austrian shells,
foretold that Belgrade would become the capital of a post-war
Yugoslavia.

In October 1915 the Central Powers (Germany and Austria-
Hungary) finally captured Belgrade, as their ally Bulgaria struck
from the east to sever the railway link to Salonica in Greece, where
the British and French had landed an expeditionary force. The
Serbs retreated over the mountains of Albania, suffering fearful
casualties from cold, disease and the sniping of local guerrillas,
until they arrived at the Adriatic. This fresh disaster, second only
to Kosovo, inspired the haunting and beautiful song that is now
almost a national anthem: 'Tamo daleko, daleko kraj mora . . .
Tamo je Srbija' ('There far away, far away by the sea . . . There is
Serbia').

The remnants of the Serbian army were taken to join the British
and French at Salonica. Meanwhile the Austrians managed to
capture the fortress state of Montenegro, whose king went into
exile in France. The Austro-Hungarians were generous to the
defeated Serbs. They repaired damaged buildings, improved public

health and checked a typhus epidemic. Foreigners working in
Serbian hospitals commented on the 'excess politeness' shown by
Austrian officials. A historian normally critical of the Habsburg
Empire writes: 'When the occupation came to an end in 1918, the
Austrian zone of Serbia was materially better off than before; more
children were at school, and cultural activities had been somewhat
"Europeanised".'[27] This kindly treatment did not appease the Serbs
who fled to the hills in thousands to fight as Chetniks (literally
bandits) and named their babies born in the occupation either
Slobodan (Freeman) or Nadežda (Hope).

The account Tito has given of his adventures during the First
World War is probably true as regards the facts and only becomes
unconvincing when describing his political views. For instance he
claims that on the announcement of the Sarajevo assassination, the
soldiers nudged each other because 'we peasants and workers in
the regiment looked upon war as offering a chance to free our
country from the yoke of the Habsburg monarchy'. Similarly, one
finds it hard to believe that after the declaration of war 'we all
hoped for another heavy defeat like the one the Empire suffered at
Königgratz'.[28]

Tito even went so far as to claim: 'Among the ranks I spoke out
against war. An old Sergeant-Major, loyal to Emperor Franz
Joseph, heard of this and betrayed me. I was arrested, and without
formalities was thrown into gaol in the fortress of Petrovarda on
the Danube.'[29] On other occasions Tito said his incarceration had
been the result of a bureaucratic error. It is inconceivable that, if
he had actually spoken against the war, Tito would have got off
with a few days in prison, or kept his rank. Nor would he have
been sent to fight against Serbia, which is what happened, although
he does not mention this in his memoirs. He belonged to the 10th
Company, 25th Croatian Territorial Infantry Regiment, 42nd
Division, which crossed the Drina to fight in western Serbia before
being driven back. Although the Croatian units contained a proportion of Orthodox 'Serbs' from the Military Frontier, there were
few desertions; indeed these descendants of the *Grenzer* were often
outstandingly *kaisertreu*. Nearly thirty years later, when Tito was

fighting in western Serbia during the Second World War, he liked to point out the sites of his previous battles, until he was warned that these anecdotes might offend the Serbs. For this reason he told Dedijer not to mention this period in his book.

At the end of 1914 Tito's regiment moved to Galicia near the Carpathian Mountains, to try to seal off a Russian advance. Among the Austro-Hungarian troops in the same sector was Jaroslav Hašek, a drunken Czech journalist in civilian life, who later retold his experiences in what is to my mind the funniest novel ever written, *The Good Soldier Švejk*. Tito, however, did not dwell on the humorous side of army life, complaining instead of the bitter cold from which many men died because of inadequate clothing:

> The good uniforms and leather boots we had received when the war broke out were replaced with boots of such poor material that they virtually melted off our feet after three days. The proportion of nettle in the army greatcoats was raised at the expense of wool, and they were useless against the rain.[30]

Tito says that he took good care of his own platoon from the Zagorje region: 'I saw to it that they were not cheated of their food ration, that they had shoes and the best possible sleeping accommodation.'[31] Nearly thirty years later, when Tito sent one of his generals to lead the Partisans in the mountains of Slovenia, he gave him one of his own pairs of thick woollen socks.

Unlike most old soldiers, Tito actually tries to play down his own gallantry and achievements, because these served an empire he later rejected. He even tries to explain away his exploits as having only an academic interest: 'One thing interested me in the science of warfare: that was renonnoitring, because it required a clear head.'[32] On one of these sorties behind enemy lines, Tito's platoon captured eighty Russians and brought them back alive, because he did not approve of unnecessary killing. It was discovered in 1980 that Sergeant-Major Broz was recommended for an award for gallantry and initiative in reconnaissance and capturing prisoners. When one thinks how many dictators have had to invent heroic deeds from their youth, it is pleasant to find one who keeps his courage a secret.

It is interesting to compare the behaviour of Tito and his Croatian platoon with that of the Czech soldiers who crossed over the Russian lines in the hope of being taken prisoner, as did Hašek and his fictional Švejk. The Czechs surrendered in large numbers, sometimes as whole units, whereas there were few desertions from the Croation regiments, even by Serbs who might have felt a sympathy with their fellow Orthodox Russians. It was not through any wish of his own that Tito was captured on Easter Day, 21 March 1915.

> The Russians launched a surprise attack on us. Our officers were at the rear at headquarters celebrating Easter. We held against the infantry advancing frontally against us, but suddenly the right flank yielded, and through the gap poured cavalry of the Circassians, from Asiatic Russia. Before we knew it they were thundering through our positions, leaping from their horses and throwing themselves into our trenches with lances lowered. One of them rammed his two-yard-long, iron-tipped, double-pronged lance into my back just below the left arm. I fainted. Then, as I learned, the Circassians began to butcher the wounded, even slashing them with their knives. Fortunately, Russian infantry reached the positions and put an end to the orgy.[33]

Tito was taken east to a hospital in a former monastery near Kazan on the River Volga. He describes how he developed pneumonia and gives us some insight into his subconscious mind: 'In my delirium, I learned later, I used to accuse the saint on an icon of wanting to steal my belongings.'[34] His suit, perhaps. Tito recovered enough to wander about the hospital, learn Russian and read the novels of Tolstoy and Turgenev.

When he had fully recuperated, Tito was sent to work in a power-driven grain mill near Ardatov in Kuibishev province, which was inhabited by Tatars, Mordvins and Russians. One of the mill owners even suggested that Tito should marry his daughter. In his memoirs, Tito tries to explain why he was not in a POW camp: 'According to the Hague Conventions, as a non-commissioned officer I was not obliged to work. But I was reluctant to sit idle, for there is nothing more killing for a man than a life of idleness.'[35] Or it could be that he was better off as a grain mill mechanic, living comfortably in someone's home, rather than sitting around in a camp eating POW rations.

However, the job at Ardatov did not last long, and Tito became the overseer of a POW camp near Perm in the Urals. The prisoners worked on repairing the Trans-Siberian railway but Tito does not make it clear whether he had to do any manual labour himself. As the man in charge of the prisoners, Tito complained to a Red Cross official that the chief of the railway section was stealing the food parcels. For this he was thrown into a prison cell and flogged by some Cossacks. A few days later, in March 1917, the first wave of revolution broke, and Tito was freed from gaol by local workers. He went back to the POW camp to find the men in a state of excitement: 'The Russian Tsar had been overthrown. We prisoners from Croatia asked ourselves when the day would come for the overthrow of Francis Joseph, the Austro-Hungarian Emperor.'[36]

That statement has the ring of untruth, for if Tito and his fellow Croats had really wanted the end of the Habsburg Empire they would not have remained in a POW camp. Whereas Czechs who gave themselves up to the Russians were treated as enemy soldiers, the South Slavs were encouraged to change sides and join special Yugoslav legions of the Serbian army. Among the many Croats who took advantage of this offer in order to gain release from a POW camp was Alojzije Stepinac, the future Roman Catholic Archbishop of Zagreb, and Tito's main antagonist. The fact that Tito spent two years as a prisoner of the Russians can only mean he was *kaisertreu*, loyal to the Habsburg Emperor.

In the growing confusion of Russia during the spring and summer of 1917, the Austro-Hungarian prisoners found themselves in a kind of limbo, uncertain if they were free or captive. Most of the Czechs and some of the Slovaks wanted to regroup as an army to fight on the side of the French and British to win their country's independence. Later their legions came into conflict with those Czechs who, like Hašek, had thrown in their lot with the Bolsheviks. The Serbs and those among the Croats and Slovenes who wanted a Yugoslavian state after the war supported the army in northern Greece, thereby assisting the Allies. A few of the South Slavs living in Russia during the revolution became active Communists, but Josip Broz was not among them.

In July 1917, while he was helping to repair the Trans-Siberian railway, Tito hid on a train carrying wheat to St Petersburg, where he arrived several days later. He says that he took part in the marches known as the 'July Demonstrations', that he came under machine-gun fire and tried to flee to Finland to avoid arrest. However, in one of his TV broadcasts in 1976, Tito reveals that in fact he went to Finland hoping to make his way to the United States, and adds half-jokingly: 'Had I done it, I would have become a millionaire.'[37]

At the Finnish border Tito was apprehended and sent to gaol in the Peter-Paul Citadel. Three weeks later, he was sent back to Kungur but gave his escort the slip and made his way to Atamansky Hutor, near Omsk in Siberia, where the train was boarded by armed Bolshevik soldiers. The October Revolution had begun.

His experiences in Russia from October 1917 to March 1920 take up less than a page of Tito's memoirs. He writes that the armed workers who boarded the train at Atamansky Hutor told him that he should 'go to the prisoner-of-war camp, where the prisoners had already joined the Bolsheviks and formed the Red International Guard'. Tito enrolled in the Red Guard and also perhaps in the Communist Party, although that is doubtful. He does not even pretend to have been an active Bolshevik:

It has been written on many occasions that I took considerable part in the October Revolution and civil war in Russia. Unfortunately, that is not so. I served several months in the Red International Guard, but I never fought at the front because I was still weak from my wound and from illness, especially after having wandered from Kungur to St Petersburg and back on a meagre diet. Our unit asked constantly to be sent to the front, but Headquarters held us back to do sentry duty at Omsk and to work at the Marianovka railway station.

Reading between the lines, one can guess that the Bolsheviks did not trust the loyalty or the will to fight of foreign prisoners virtually forced to join the Red Guard. Tito does not pretend to have taken much interest in the revolution. He read the Bolshevik newspapers, heard much talk of Lenin, a little of Trotsky and, 'as for Stalin, during the time I stayed in Russia, I never once heard his name'.[38]

Tito does not mention in his memoirs that when he arrived in Omsk in 1917 he met a Russian peasant's daughter, Pelagija Belousova, and married her in the summer of 1919. In 1920, when the railways had started to run again, Tito took his wife to Petrograd (as St Petersburg had now become), then joined with a group of Yugoslavs going to Stettin. After spending six months in Germany, Tito finally returned to Kumrovec in October 1920.

3

The Making of
a Communist

Returning from Siberia in 1920, Tito discovered a Europe transformed by the First World War. The shots fired at Sarajevo on 28
June 1914 had led to the breakup of the Austro-Hungarian,
Russian, German and Ottoman empires, and to the creation of the
independent states of Finland, Estonia, Latvia, Lithuania, Poland,
Austria, Hungary, Czechoslovakia, and the Kingdom of Serbs,
Croats and Slovenes, commonly known as Yugoslavia. Since most
of these new nations won recognition during the peace conference
held by the Allied powers in 1919, they later came to be known to
the losing side as the 'Versailles states'. To the Germans, Austrians,
Magyars, Bulgarians and Soviet Russians, these 'Versailles states'
were artificial entities unjustly created by the victors of the war. Of
all the 'Versailles states', Yugoslavia was most unpopular with its
neighbouring countries and even some of its own population.
Albania, Bulgaria, Hungary and Austria all had territorial claims
on Yugoslavia, as did Italy, one of the Allied powers that was not
content with the Treaty of Versailles. By the time Tito returned to
his homeland in 1920, many Croats were already hostile to the
ruling authority in Belgrade and had come to regret what they too
were calling a 'Versailles state'.

Whatever their later reservations, the South Slavs in the Habsburg Empire had led the demand for the creation of Yugoslavia.
Although the great majority of the Slovenes, Croats and even Serbs

in the Habsburg army were *kaisertreu* at the beginning of the First World War, they soon grew disenchanted because of the horrors of battle and sheer exhaustion. The entry of Italy into the war in 1915 affected the Slovenes and Croats for two distinct reasons. It meant that the Pope, although in theory standing above earthly quarrels, was now the national of a country fighting against the Austro-Hungarian Empire. In May 1917 a papal message encouraged the Slovene and Croat churches to stand on their own.

When the Italians agreed to enter the war at the Treaty of London in 1915, they first extracted from Britain and France a promise to give them all the Austrian territory on the Adriatic coast, with its overwhelmingly Slav population. This meant that in the event of an Allied victory millions of Croats and Slovenes would find themselves under Italian rule, which was still less agreeable to them than belonging to the Austro-Hungarian Empire. With the entry into the war of the United States in April 1917, hundreds of thousands of recent *émigrés* from Slovenia and Croatia became the enemies of the Habsburg Empire and eager to see its downfall. Since there was at the time only a tiny group in favour of an independent Croatia, and no one in favour of an independent Slovenia, the great majority of the South Slav diaspora wanted some kind of Yugoslavia.

Meanwhile Serbia was too concerned with its own fight for survival to pay much attention to plans for the future. By the end of the war, the Serbs and the Montenegrins had suffered casualties two and a half times greater, proportionately, than those of France, which in turn had suffered far worse casualties than had Britain and the United States. Having paid so high a price in war, the Serbs wanted a major share in the fruits of victory, especially since many Croats and Slovenes had fought for the enemy.

During the course of the war, the South Slavs from Austria-Hungary met with delegations from Serbia in neutral Switzerland, but these debates were of less importance than what went on in the Habsburg Empire in 1918, the final year of the war. That summer, anti-Habsburg demonstrations and even military mutinies broke out in the South Slav regions. In September, when French, British and Serbian divisions broke through from Salonica into Macedonia and started the liberation of Serbia, the authority of the Habsburg Empire began to crumble throughout Croatia and Slovenia. The *Grazer Tagenpost* of Carinthia complained:

> All the Slovene areas have been won for the agitation . . . the leaders of the American Slovenes and the Serbians agree in their demands for a single Yugoslav state. In addition to the agitation in representative bodies there is an insidious propaganda from man to man, woman to woman and even from child to child. At church and at school, the creed of the Yugoslav state is taught and the credulous population swears by its principles.[1]

South Slav deputies formed a National Council in Zagreb demanding the implementation of Yugoslavia. On 28 October the Habsburg military authorities handed over to this council all the responsibility for government. On the following day, as the crowds outside shouted for Woodrow Wilson and Thomas Masaryk, Croatia's Diet, or Sabor, formally ended the ancient *Pacta conventa* with Hungary. On 1 December 1918 Alexander proclaimed the Kingdom of Serbs, Croats and Slovenes in the presence of delegates from Zagreb and ministers from the Serbian government. As Stevan Pavlowitch points out:

> Far from being a creation of the Versailles Conference, as is sometimes claimed, Yugoslavia had to impose itself on the international community. It had been proclaimed in December 1918, but the first of the major Allied powers to recognise it – the United States – did so in February 1919, and the last – Italy – in November 1920. Its borders were contested, and almost two years passed by before it felt accepted by the public law of Europe sufficiently to hold elections for a constituent assembly.[2]

It was an unlucky coincidence for the infant Yugoslavia that Germany signed the Treaty of Versailles, effectively making it valid, on 28 June 1919, the fatal St Vitus's Day. To make matters worse, the same date was chosen for the introduction of the Yugoslav constitution in 1921. To Croatian nationalists in the years to come, the new Yugoslavia was not only a 'Versailles' but also a 'Vidovdan' state, imposed on them by foreign powers for the benefit of the Serbs.

In spite of the troubles that lay ahead, the new Yugoslavia was not in fact an artificial state concocted by foreign dreamers. Though long divided by history and religion, the South Slavs were both ethnically and linguistically one of the most homogenous peoples in Europe, very much more so than, for example, the inhabitants of the British Isles. It is salutary to remember that during the years when the Yugoslavs came together after centuries of division, the southern Irish were breaking away from centuries of political union.

When Tito returned home at the end of 1920, Yugoslavia was coming out of the turmoil that had descended on all central Europe after the war, but especially on the defeated nations. In Croatia and Slovenia, the Slav peasants rose in revolt against foreign landlords. Tito says with perhaps a touch of exaggeration that in the Zagorje region 'every night a castle went up in flames, and the next morning saw the distribution of the landlord's estate among the peasants'.[3] As the men of Kumrovec had attacked but failed to capture the castle of Cesargrad in 1573, so at the end of 1918 they made an attempt on Banja Castle, which also belonged to the Erdödy family. This time they succeeded in making an entry, grabbed all they found of value, started a fire and finally dynamited the ancient building. Tito records this exploit with pride. Fifty years later, some of the castles and stately homes that had escaped the wrath of the peasants became his holiday residences.

Tito is contemptuous of the 'bourgeois' National Council, whose members went to Belgrade on 1 December 1918 to 'pay homage' to the Regent, Alexander, and to proclaim the Kingdom of Serbs, Croats and Slovenes. He praises Stjepan Radić, the leader of the Croatian Peasant Party, who warned the delegation as it prepared to leave: 'Look before you leap . . . It is a political error to confront your own people with a *fait accompli* of your own fancy.'[4] In an attempt to explain why the Communist Party opposed the creation of Yugoslavia in 1918 but helped to bring it about in 1945, Tito denounces the greed and profligacy of the Regent, who succeeded his father in 1921. Alexander not only persuaded the Parliament to raise his civil list, or personal grant, but took a directorship in the National Bank and even became a commercial farmer:

> He took over the former state farm at Topčider and sold vegetables and eggs on the Belgrade market in competition with the peasants. Soldiers of the Royal Guard laboured for him without pay, and sold king's vegetables in the market in military trousers and civilian overcoats. The huckster king also opened enterprises for the production of wine and Šlivovica [plum brandy] at Topola and Demir Kapija. All these properties were free from taxes because they were the King's personal possessions![5]

These accusations come oddly from Tito, who would later live like a king at his country's expense, without once submitting a civil list to the vote of a freely elected parliament. And Tito did not share Alexander's thrift and commercial sense in agriculture and banking.

The social unrest in Yugoslavia during the two years after the war had little to do with Alexander, and much to do with the Communist revolutions in Russia, Hungary and Bavaria. In Zagreb, Tito's old regiment joined in a mutiny that had to be put down by Serbian troops, assisted by regiments of the French colonial army, previously serving on the Salonica front. The Vietnamese joined the long list of nations brought in to stop the Yugoslavs killing each other.

Although Yugoslavia refused to participate in the suppression of the Communist revolution in Hungary in 1919, the country's trade unions took part in the international protest strike against intervention. In Zagreb, according to a guide to the city published during the Communist era, the strike was joined by 'the workers of the cigar and chicory factories, bank clerks, the workers of the hat, leather, pencil and fountain-pen factories, waiters, railwaymen, barbers and hairdressers'. As this list suggests, unlike the Ruhr or the industrial north of England, Zagreb did not have a large proletariat. Although the Yugoslav Communist Party won 12 per cent of the votes in the 1920 elections, it did worst in industrial Slovenia, and best in rural Montenegro and Macedonia. In 1921 the Yugoslav Communists turned to terrorist acts, even trying to murder the King, and lost the support of the public. Membership fell from 120,000 in 1919 to 700 in 1924. It was then that Tito began his career as a revolutionary.

When Tito returned to Kumrovec he found that his mother had died and his father had gone to another village, so he and his wife, Pelagija, moved to Zagreb. We know from his memoirs that Tito worked there as a waiter, or rather that he took part in a waiters' strike, and then went back to his locksmith's job; but the pay was a mere three crowns an hour, and scarcely sufficed for the 600-crown monthly rent of a small room. He then got a job as a mechanic in a flour mill at Veliko Trojstvo (Holy Trinity), sixty miles to the east in the Military Frontier region of Slavonia. He made friends with Communists and may have become a Party member. His wife Pelagija lost one child soon after arriving in Yugoslavia, and now lost two more. A fourth child, Žarko, a boy, was born at Velika Trojstvo and survived.

The Kingdom of Serbs, Croats and Slovenes, or SHS (the Serbo-Croat word for 'Croat' is 'Hrvat') was known to the Croats as 'Serbs want it all' (Srbe Hoće Sve') and to the Serbs as 'Only the Croats spoil it' (Samo Hrvati Smetaju'). There was a certain amount of truth in both these interpretations. The Serbs had come out of the war more bumptious, boastful and proud of their military valour than ever. But beneath the self-confidence and the independence of spirit, there lay an abiding fear that the world was against them. This fear dated back to the defeat at the Battle of Kosovo in 1389, when tens of thousands of Serbs had fought on the side of the Turks. During the next five centuries of Ottoman oppression, the Serbs had dreamed of revenge against the apostate Slavs in Kosovo,

Montenegro, the Sandjak and Bosnia-Hercegovina, convincing
themselves that these people were really ethnic Turks who had
learned the Serbian language. Their suffering at the hands of the
Ottoman Empire, then from the threats and attacks of the Austrians and Germans, bred in the Serbs a persecution mania. As in an
individual, so in a nation persecution mania is a self-fulfilling
dread. 'We and the Jews are the victims of Europe,' the Serbs
often say. Because they believe that the whole world hates them,
the Serbs often behave in a way that provokes such a hatred.

In the new Yugoslavia, the Serbs were the dominant people by
virtue of their numbers, their king, their previous independence
and the fact that they had fought on the winning side in the war.
The Serbs were in a majority in the officer corps of the army, in
the civil service and in the police, not only in Serbia proper but
also in Bosnia-Hercegovina, where they were not a majority of the
population. Although the Slovenes got on well with the Serbs, the
rest of the country fretted under centralised government. The tact
and patience needed to weld the country together were precisely
the two qualities that the Serbs were lacking. In the old Military
Frontier, or Krajina, and to a lesser extent in Croatia generally, the
Serb descendants of the *Grenzer* were heavily represented in the
police, and showed little respect for Croatian sensibilities. The
Serbs behaved brutally to the Albanians in Kosovo and to the
Bulgarians in Macedonia.[6] But their conduct was seen at its worst
in the way they remembered the Sarajevo assassination of 1914.

From the outbreak of war through four years of carnage, the
Allies had believed that their cause was just and that the Kingdom
of Serbia had played no part in Archduke Franz Ferdinand's
murder. Then, in 1924, a former Serbian Cabinet minister wrote
in an article that Prime Minister Pašić had known of the plot in
advance. Foreign friends of the Serbs, R. W. Seton-Watson among
them, implored Pašić to make a denial. However, for more than a
year Pašić said nothing, then brushed off the article as a fabrication.
It was beneath his dignity even to answer the calumnies levelled at
Serbia. Worse was to follow.

In 1914, on a bridge near the scene of the crime at Sarajevo,

Austrian officials had erected busts of the murdered couple over a plaque reading: 'On this spot, on 28 June 1914, Archduke Franz Ferdinand and his wife the Duchess Sophie of Hohenburg gave their life and blood for God and country.' Close by was a sign: 'Traveller, Stop' ('Siste Viator'). After the war, Yugoslav officials brutally tore down the busts and memorial. In 1930 a new plaque appeared on the building in front of which Princip had fired his revolver: 'On this historic spot Gavrilo Princip, on St Vitus's Day, 1914, heralded the advent of liberty.' Some of the plotters and their relatives were present at the unveiling ceremony. Poor old Seton-Watson wailed at 'this affront to all right-thinking people'. In his history of the First World War, Winston Churchill wrote: 'Princip died in prison, and a monument . . . erected by his fellow-countrymen records his infamy and their own.'[7]

The plaque was still more offensive to all those South Slavs who had fought in the war on the Austrian side to avenge the Archduke's murder; and it was especially hurtful to Catholics. During the 1920s, the Croatian Peasant Party Leader Stjepan Radić was turning into a powerful tribune of discontent with the Belgrade government, and spent two years in prison for saying: 'We are republicans, but if the Serbs want a monarchy, good luck to them.' Radić was a populist, a friend of the Soviet Union, and an anticlerical Roman Catholic who loved to make jokes about priests keeping concubines and using bad language. Like his hero Bishop Strossmayer, Radić wanted reunion of the Orthodox and Roman Catholic religions, and held up the Church of England as an example.

While Radić spoke for the peasants, the Croatian Church and middle classes were turning towards a narrower, angrier kind of nationalism based on the teachings of Starčević and his disciple Frank. If the Serbs suffered from persecution mania, the Croats were an example of the inferiority complex. For centuries the Croats had been ruled and patronised by the more sophisticated Germans, Hungarians and Italians. Yet because they felt that they belonged to 'western' Europe, the Croats considered themselves superior to the 'eastern', 'Byzantine' and 'primitive' Serbs, even refusing to recognise them as kinsmen. The more the Croats had to acknowledge that the Serbs were like them, the more they hated them. So Caliban hated the face he saw in the mirror. To distance themselves from the 'Slav-Serbs', Croats like Starčević tried to invent a separate ethnography, literary language and history. Yet although the Croats boasted that Zagreb was altogether more civilised and refined than Belgrade, they knew in their hearts it was only a South Slav copy of Budapest and Vienna. Croatia was like a poor country girl reared in the family of a rich city gentlewoman, who now was reluctant to marry a man from her own village.

By 1925 Tito had become a political activist, and his room in Veliko Trojstvo was searched each week by the local police. After the death of his friendly employer, Tito decided to leave his job and, on the advice or instruction of the Party, went to work in the shipyard at Kraljevica, a town on the northern Adriatic. Kraljevica is only just down the coast from the large port known to the Yugoslavs as Rijeka and to the Italians as Fiume (both names mean river), which then was the subject of hot contention between the two countries. Although the Italians had been promised the whole Dalmatian coast when they entered the war in 1915, they were robbed of most of their prize when the Croats opted to become part of Yugoslavia. The fate of Rijeka was still undecided in 1920, when Gabriele d'Annunzio, a writer and Fascist adventurer, took the town with a squad of gunmen. Although these men were soon evicted, Fiume was handed over to Italy along with Zara (Zadar), Pola (Pula), the Istrian peninsula and Trieste (Trst), where Italians were in the majority anyway. Although the Italians on the Dalmatian coast did not try to stop the Croats speaking their own language, as they prevented the Slovenes from doing in Trieste, they tried to Italianise the Roman Catholic Church and treated the Slavs with disdain. Mussolini had the Croats and Slovenes in mind when he told Italian children that they should 'learn to hate' ('imparate a odiare'). In Fiume, Croatian children were made to learn this blasphemous catechism:

What are the Yugoslavs? Serbs. What are the Serbs? Greeks, schismatics, heretics, infidels, enemies of the Church. Can a

Yugoslav be a Catholic? No! What are Italians? Catholics. What
are Catholics? Faithful friends of the Catholic Church and of the
Pope. Where does the Pope live? At Rome in Italy. Therefore
anyone who is a Catholic is also an Italian![8]

Because of the frontier dispute, the shipyard at Kraljevica had
trouble repairing the naval torpedo boats inherited from the
Habsburg navy. From 1918 to 1923 the ships had been in the
hands of the Italians, who stripped them completely before handing
them over to the Yugoslavs, even pouring acid into delicate pieces
of machinery. But Tito and his fellow mechanics worked well: 'We
were all excited when the first torpedo boat started on its trial
journey. The pistons squeaked and we were terrified that the old
iron would fail under pressure. But all went well.' It was characteristic of Tito that, although he was there as a Communist Party
agitator and trade union shop steward, he took pride in his work
on behalf of the Yugoslav navy. As an engineer and mechanic, he
delighted in ships, motor cars, railways, aeroplanes, roads and
bridges, but he wanted them to be used in a Communist Yugoslavia. Towards this end, Tito established at Kraljevica a branch of
the Party, a sports association and a cultural group, to which he
presented guitars from Zagreb and fifty books of his own, including
The Iron Heel by Jack London, *Women and Socialism* by August
Bebel, and *Mother* by Maxim Gorky. He says that his home was a
sort of workers' library.

At Kraljevica, Tito acquired the love of the Adriatic that he was
to indulge in later life by commandeering luxury yachts and a home
on the island of Brioni.

The little free time I had, I spent with a fisherman friend. Once
while we were out in our boat we saw a shark's fin. It cut the
water with such speed that we made haste towards land. A few
days later the shark rushed straight into the nets of a fishing-boat
and was caught. It was twenty-one feet long, and somebody's
boots and quite a collection of other things were found in it.
From then on I never swam far from the shore.[9]

When he was sacked from the Kraljevica shipyard for calling a strike, Tito was sent to organise the workforce of a railway-wagon yard at Smederevska Palanka, about forty miles from Belgrade. In his first published article, for the *Organised Worker*, Tito gave an alarming account of men toiling sixteen hours a day in a freezing shed. When the article was published in March 1927, he was forced to take a job at an engineering works in Zagreb, from which he was also fired.

Tito was then appointed the full-time secretary of the Metal Workers' Union for Zagreb and subsequently for all Croatia. A few weeks later he was arrested and sent to prison while awaiting trial. He was informed that he had broken the law but was not told where the crime was supposed to have been committed. Was it in Velika Trojstvo, Belgrade or Smederevska Palanka? To his surprise, he was taken to Kraljevica, where some of his comrades had been arrested and had claimed that he had given them Communist literature. At the neighbouring town of Ogulin he was kept for so long in prison without coming to trial that he went on hunger strike until persuaded to eat by the kindly judge. Either during or after the trial, Tito appears to have skipped bail, since many years later he had to go back to Ogulin to complete his sentence. Meanwhile, in 1928, the political life of Yugoslavia turned violent.

The Croatian Peasant Party leader, Stjepan Radić, had gone to Belgrade to join with some of the Serb politicians in forming a parliamentary opposition. For this, many Croats accused him of being a traitor, but Radić was no more popular with the supporters of Greater Serbia. On 20 June 1928 a crazed Montenegrin deputy drew a revolver and shot dead Radić and two of his followers. Violent demonstrations broke out in Zagreb and other Croatian towns. Some of the right-wing nationalists, led by the lawyer Ante Pavelić, went into exile to form the Ustasha ('Uprising') terrorist organisation, pledged to achieving an independent Croatia by violence. The Croatian Communist Party called on the population to take up arms to avenge the murder of Radić.

Tito was on the run from the secret police, disguising himself with a pair of thick glasses, and seldom staying two nights at the same address. However, the police caught up with him and claimed to have found some bombs as well as Communist literature in his possession. He was taken to the police cells, chained, savagely beaten up and then kept for three months before coming to trial in November 1928.

Of the five judges at Tito's trial, three were alive and drawing a pension in Communist Yugoslavia twenty years later, so clearly he bore them no malice. He was pleased by the coverage of the case in the right-wing Zagreb newspaper *Novosti*. The paper reported that on the first day of the trial the courtroom was filled by 'young men with long, curling hair, or young girls with bobbed hair, perhaps followers of the new gospel, perhaps acquaintances of the six defendants, who never come to "bourgeois" trials but only attend such propaganda, militant, international-messiah cases'.

The *Novosti* reporter wrote that Josip Broz was much the most interesting person on trial: 'His face makes one think of steel. His shining eyes look over the spectacles in a cool but energetic way ... A large number of spectators no doubt know the stubbornness with which he maintains his beliefs, for a silent attention reigned in court throughout his hearing.' When he gave evidence, Tito admitted possession of Communist literature but said that the bombs had been planted on him by the police.

The finale is told by *Novosti* on 15 November 1928:

> The Communist trial which has become known as the bomb throwers trial was concluded yesterday, with its dominant tone struck once more at the end by Josip Broz. After the sentence was read he rose and turning to the large audience which was already rising to leave the courtroom, shouted three times 'Long live the Communist Party! Long Live the Third International!' ... Thus it was that this unyielding Communist disappeared behind prison walls, for all the world like the captain of a ship who shouts when the ship is sinking.[10]

Prisoners under Tito's regime after the Second World War were not given such friendly write-ups in the press.

As Tito was waiting to start his five-year sentence, King Alexander prepared to end his experiment with democracy. On 6 January 1929 he established a dictatorship, banning political parties, dissolving Parliament and abrogating the constitution of 1921. The dictatorship came at a time of worldwide economic recession. The peasants were getting little for their produce, and actual starvation occurred in poorer parts of the country such as Hercegovina. Tito claimed that the Yugoslav factory workers were getting less than those on unemployment benefit in Britain.

Tito spent most of his years in prison at Lepoglava, a pretty town in the mountains north of Zagreb. The prison itself had orginally been a Pauline monastery for the White Friars in 1300, and during the seventeenth century it became Croatia's first university. At the end of the eighteenth century, Emperor Franz Joseph II dissolved the Pauline Order and the building remained unoccupied until later Austro-Hungarian rulers converted it into a prison, when, according to Tito, it became a synonym for oppression and forced labour.

Although the regime was harsh and the prisoners suffered from the cold in winter, Tito acquired the job of looking after the electricity power plant, and in return was allowed to have books and other privileges, such as meeting his friends at a café in town. He was given an assistant, a prisoner slightly older than himself called Moša Pijade, one of the Communists who became part of his intimate circle of friends and colleagues over the next thirty years. Pijade was a Belgrade Jew, a small, wizened, untidy creature with round, owlish spectacles and a querulous manner that concealed enormous courage and good humour. Having a natural bent towards pedantry and philosophical hair-splitting, Moša Pijade revelled in Marxism, and tried to interest Tito in the same subject. Although Tito later described his time in Lepoglava as like being at university, he never bothered with Marxist literature beyond such basic texts as the *Communist Manifesto* and practical guides to winning power, such as Lenin's *What is to be Done?* In so far as Moša Pijade had a profession other than that of prisoner, he was a painter in the impressionist style and executed portraits of several fellow prisoners, including Tito.

While Tito was in prison, his wife Pelagija went back to her native Russia, fell in love with another man and left the boy Žarko to grow up in institutions. Djilas thinks that Tito was hurt by his wife's infidelity, but in those days the Party did not allow for 'bourgeois sentiment'. Although there was no woman waiting for Tito when he left prison, he nevertheless purchased a smart new suit to wear on the day of his release.

During the years of Tito's imprisonment, from November 1928 to March 1934, the whole world was in crisis. A crash on Wall Street led to economic depression, mass unemployment, a loss of confidence in the capitalist system, and the rise to power of President Franklin D. Roosevelt. In the Soviet Union, Stalin carried out the collectivisation of agriculture, the liquidation of more than ten million peasants, and mass deportations to the Gulag Archipelago. In Germany, Adolf Hitler won a general election and started to build his Third Reich.

Hitler's declared intention of tearing up the Treaty of Versailles posed a threat to the smaller nations of Europe. In February 1934 Yugoslavia joined with Romania, Greece and Turkey in a Balkan Entente to defend themselves against any potential aggressor. Yugoslavia looked to its wartime ally France to offer it protection from countries such as Italy, Hungary and Bulgaria. In June 1934 the French invited King Alexander to pay a state visit later that year.

After a spell of outright dictatorship, King Alexander had established a new constitution in 1931 allowing a modified parliamentary role to the politicians. He was anxious to win over the discontented Croats and held out an offer of compromise to the Peasant Party leader Vlatko Maček, who had succeeded the murdered Radić. King Alexander was worried about the increasingly nationalist and anti-Serbian attitude of the Croatian Catholic Church, exemplified by the new Archbishop of Sarajevo, Ivan Šarić, the poet whose verses had whipped up popular hatred after the assassination in 1914. When the Archbishop of Zagreb died in 1934, King Alexander insisted that his successor should be Alojzije Stepinac, one of the Croats who had volunteered to fight with the Yugoslav legions during the First World War. Although Stepinac was not yet the narrow-minded Croatian nationalist that he was to become during the Second World War, he was already a puritanical zealot.

The new Archbishop of Zagreb brought together under the mantle of Catholic Action all those fighting the evils of Communism, liberalism, secular education, divorce reform, swearing, adultery, fornication and above all the 'white plague', by which he meant all forms of birth control, from abortion to coitus interruptus. In his concern with sexual morals, Stepinac even denounced mixed sunbathing and swimming on the Dalmatian coast. Stepinac's hostility to the Soviet Union was expressed in the semi-official diocesan weekly *Katolički List*, whose views he approved and whose editor he had appointed. His biographer, Stella Alexander, says that 'some of the anti-Communist articles in the early 1930s were unpleasantly anti-Semitic but in a traditional, pre-Hitlerian way, coupling Jews with Communists and Freemasons as enemies of the Church'. She cites an article on the Soviet Union written in 1935, which speaks of the leading role in diplomacy, commerce and government of such men as 'Jew-Radek' and 'Jew-Litvinov':

> No wonder horrors take place . . . Jew-Marxists are aliens, the land is alien to them and they are alien to the people over whom they rule . . . So they run the countryside with great facility. They lightheartedly undertake scientific experiments on peoples. No misfortune which befalls Russia, neither famine nor death touches them. These Jew-Marxists behaved abominably when they built the great canals through which flowed the blood of the poor workers before they were filled with water . . . these canals to the White Sea were built by prisoners under Jewish overseers from Jagoda to Kogan, Behrman, Suka, Rappaport and Transol, the chief engineer . . .[11]

When Archbishop Stepinac went to Belgrade in 1934 to pledge his allegiance to King Alexander, he spoke for the Croat people as well as the Church: 'I told the King that I was not a politician and that I would forbid my clergy to take part in party politics, but on the other hand I would look for full respect for the rights of Croats. I warned the King that the Croats must not be improperly provoked and even forbidden to use the very name of Croat, something which I had myself experienced.'[12]

This complaint was a typical expression of the grievance felt by the Croats, especially their anger at what they saw as job discrimination in the civil service, the army, police, education, the railways and postal service. R. W. Seton-Watson, though generally sympathetic to Croatian demands, has described the Croats as the most quarrelsome Slavs. In her book *Black Lamb and Grey Falcon* another British observer, Rebecca West, offers a long dissertation on the character of the Croats, reaching back to Byzantine history, to explain why they so often talked at the top of their voice. She did not appear to notice that the Serbs as well are inclined to shout out even trivial items of information.

The Croatian grievance against the Serbs was revealed to the world on 7 October 1934, when a Ustasha agent shot dead King Alexander in Marseilles as he began his state visit to France. Since Ante Pavelić, the man who had plotted the murder, lived in Italy, while his Ustasha gang also enjoyed financial support and protection from Germany, Hungary and Bulgaria, the assassination led to a dangerous confrontation between these states and the Balkan Entente, which was supported by Britain and France. Only twenty years after Sarajevo, the quarrel among the South Slavs threatened to spark off another world war. However, on this occasion the Belgrade government was the aggrieved party, and it acted with moderation and dignity, earning the gratitude of the rest of Europe. The German representative at King Alexander's funeral, Reichsmarschall Hermann Goering, was flattered by his reception and came to admire the Serbs who had been such stalwart enemies during the First World War. Alexander's brother Prince Paul was appointed Regent to the young King Peter.

Tito was in Slovenia when he heard of King Alexander's murder. Since leaving prison he had become a full-time party worker, answerable to the Central Committee in exile in Vienna, living and travelling on a series of forged identity cards and passports. It was now that he came to be known as Tito, a quite common name in the Zagorje region.

At a Party gathering near Ljubljana, Tito met for the first time the young Slovene schoolmaster Edvard Kardelj, who in later years was to become one of his three closest friends and lieutenants. With his spectacles, his ink-stained fingers and dowdy clothes, Kardelj looked the part of an earnest, small-town socialist, bringing professional pedantry to his Marxist dialectics, but he was also brave, stubborn and loyal. In any other Communist Party he might have become just a faceless bureaucrat, but under the influence of Tito, Kardelj blossomed into a formidable politician. Although he came across in public as harsh and unsympathetic, he was popular with the other Communist leaders, and Tito always regarded him as his most reliable deputy.

Soon after King Alexander's assassination, Tito was told by the Communist Central Committee to go to Vienna and then to Moscow to work in the offices of the Comintern, where his knowledge of Russian and German would be useful. The officials at the Yugoslav frontier were on the alert for suspicious characters trying to leave the country, but Tito was fortunate. An Austrian woman had asked him to hold her baby, and when it wet itself on his knees, the frontier guards were so amused that they did not bother to check his papers. A few weeks later, Tito was nearly caught by the Austrian police. But as he no doubt realised, the greatest danger was waiting for him in Moscow, where the Communist Party purges and the Treason Trials had already begun.

This was Tito's first visit to Russia in fourteen years, and his first time ever in Moscow. He did not try to rejoin his estranged wife, Pelagija, but led a spartan and probably celibate life at the Lux Hotel in Gorki Street. 'Accustomed in prison to solitude, I went about little in Moscow,' he says, and his only friends while there were other Comintern staff, such as Edvard Kardelj and Georgi Dimitrov, the leader of the Bulgarian Communist Party. In

Moscow and on a visit to the Ural Region, Tito noticed that things
had gone wrong in Russia:

> I witnessed a lot of careerism and elbow-pushing; I talked with
> collective farm members and noticed them nudging each other
> when they wanted to say something. People in Moscow somehow
> avoided each other, hesitated to speak. I was not in Moscow
> when the big purges occurred. But even in 1935 there were no
> end of arrests, and those who made the arrests were later
> themselves arrested. Men vanished overnight, and no one dared
> ask where they had been taken . . . One morning the militia
> summoned a Yugoslav worker who had been living in the Soviet
> Union and working in a factory for many years, with his wife.
> They informed him he was sentenced to eight years' exile in
> northern Siberia. They were not even allowed to return to their
> flat to take their things but were sent to Siberia directly. No one
> dared ask how they had offended.[13]

Hundreds of Yugoslav Communists were to die in the purges,
including Tito's predecessor as general secretary of the Yugoslav
Communist Party, a man known as Milan Gorkić. Although Tito
rose to power in competition with men like Gorkić, it would not
have been in his character to have innocent people sent to their
death, and no evidence against him has been published in recent
studies.[14] The Russians had probably noticed Tito's ability as an
organiser and lack of concern with ideological squabbles.

From 1935 to 1940, when he was finally confirmed as secretary
of the Yugoslav Communist Party, Tito worked as a Comintern
agent in Yugoslavia, Austria and France, where he organised the
dispatch of volunteers to fight in the Spanish Civil War. When the
Yugoslav Party's Central Committee moved from Vienna to Paris,
Tito lodged in the Latin Quarter and liked to stroll in the Père
Lachaise Cemetery, the resting-place of the Communards of 1871.
As caretaker secretary of the Yugoslav Party from 1937 to 1940,
Tito first moved the Central Committee from Paris to Zagreb, then
built up a new, young leadership loyal to him. Although paying

lip-service to Marxist principles, Tito always judged a man by his character:

> Our basic standard . . . was the respect a man enjoyed in his circle; if he was a worker, what his attitude was towards other workers, whether he enjoyed their confidence, whether he was a good comrade, whether he was unselfish, whether he was courageous, what his character was like, what respect he enjoyed with regard to his personal life: whether he was a drunkard, a gambler, what he was like at his trade.[15]

The qualities required of a Yugoslav Communist sound much like those required of a British Boy Scout.

In about 1937 Tito met Alexander Ranković, a Serb from the Šumadija region but uncharacteristically quiet-spoken and even reserved. Like Kardelj, he had come through many years of imprisonment and torture without betraying his Party or friends. Besides ruthlessness and determination, Ranković had a streak of cunning that fitted him for his later role as head of the police and Minister of the Interior. Unlike most people drawn to such work, he was not vindictive or cruel by nature, and never became an ogre in the eyes of the Yugoslavian people. Ranković was devoted to Tito, and knew how to coax him out of his moods of depression or anger.

Having selected Kardelj and Ranković, Tito chose as his third lieutenant a man of far greater talent, amounting to genius: the young Montenegrin Milovan Djilas, who went on to become, with Solzhenitsyn, one of the gravediggers of Marxism. When Tito first met him in 1937, Djilas was a Communist of the most angry, fearless, pigheaded, poetic and thoroughly Montenegrin kind. Almost at once he was chosen as the third and youngest of Tito's lieutenants; later he would be a Partisan of outstanding courage, the leading protagonist in the breach with Stalin, and then a rebel, disgraced and imprisoned. More than anyone, Djilas had seen in Tito a combination of friend, elder brother, beloved uncle, hero and leader in war, so his final rejection by Tito would come as a personal as well as political tragedy. Yet Djilas went on to write a series of memoirs that are by far the truest, fullest and fairest accounts of Tito and Communist Yugoslavia.

Djilas first met Tito in Zagreb early in 1937, and during a talk on Party matters found him to be 'a strong man but not a careful listener'. On the train returning to Belgrade, Djilas was nagged by a memory:

> Tito's image seemed familiar somehow, like something out of a distant dream. I couldn't get it out of my head. Finally I realised that I had seen his portrait in prison, painted by Moša Pijade. That was Josip Broz! At our next meeting I felt it my duty to tell him how I knew his name. He attached no significance to the knowledge, and smiled cautiously. There was something human and beautiful in that smile.[16]

All four leaders had the peasant or working-class background demanded by Communist Party rules, but most of the active support for the movement came from the sons and daughters of the bourgeoisie at Zagreb and Belgrade universities. One of the brightest in Tito's team, and the dearest to him personally, came from this privileged background. His name, Ivo Lola Ribar, is now scarcely remembered because he did not survive the Second World War, but he needs to be mentioned as further proof of Tito's excellent judgement of character. Although his father, Ivan Ribar, stood on the liberal Left in politics, Lola revolted against the whole 'bourgeois' system and flung himself into Communist Party work at Belgrade University. From Djilas's description of Lola Ribar denouncing an older comrade for factionalism and anti-Party activities in 1937, we recognise the same type as the public school Communists active at Oxford and Cambridge: 'Ribar was young and he looked young. He was fashionably dressed and had bourgeois manners – I recall him putting out half-smoked cigarettes.'[17] To the surprise and at first the chagrin of some of the comrades

from humbler backgrounds, Tito appointed this golden youth to
the Central Committee. Tito's acumen is shown by the fact that
Lola Ribar went on to become the most loved and respected man
in the Party after Tito himself.

After another visit to Moscow in 1939, Tito was officially
appointed general secretary of the Yugoslav Communist Party. He
was now living in Zagreb with Herta Hass, an eager and beautiful
student of mixed Slovene and ethnic German (*Volksdeutsch*) origin,
who bore Tito a son, Alexander (or Miša for short), early in 1941.
However, by that time Tito was already falling in love with a girl
less than half his own age; she too was a student Communist, and
had come to Zagreb to take an illegal course in radiotelegraphy.
Her name was Davorjanka Paunović but during the war she came
to be known as Zdenka. She was strikingly beautiful, with an olive
complexion and large, dark eyes. She was also hysterical, self-
obsessed, foul-tempered and deeply unpopular with the Communist leaders, who much preferred the brave and gentle Herta. Tito
however was captivated by Zdenka, perhaps because of her sexual
passion, and during the war he made her his mistress as well as his
radio operator and secretary. Tito got to know both Herta and
Zdenka, later grandly referred to as his 'common-law wives',
between Hitler's invasion of Poland in September 1939 and his
attack on Yugoslavia in April 1941.

Before considering the cataclysmic events of 1941–5, it might be
well to reflect on the Yugoslavia that existed between the two wars.
In the light of what happened afterwards, it is all too easy to say
that Yugoslavia was always an artificial, unworkable 'Versailles
state', imposed on its people by ignorant foreigners. Yet, as we
have seen, Yugoslavia was not created by the Treaty of Versailles,
and came into being against the wishes of some of the countries
signing that treaty. Although the history of the first Yugoslavia was
fraught with unrest and stained by two major assassinations, it was
peaceful compared to that of most of Europe during the same
period. The Soviet Union, Germany, Austria, Hungary, Italy and
Spain all suffered dictatorship and the suppression of civil liberties
between the wars. In fact the 'Versailles states' of Poland, Czecho-

slovakia and Yugoslavia were islands of freedom and tolerance in a central Europe subjected to Fascism and Communism. The quarrel between the Serbs and Croats was not yet as vicious as that between the English and Irish.

During her visits to Yugoslavia in the 1930s, Rebecca West saw few examples of persecution and violence, but many things that were admirable. We know that the Communists and the Ustasha were tortured and imprisoned, but they were after all attempting to break up the state by terrorism. We would not judge a modern British government simply on how it treated the men of violence in Ulster. Foreign friends of the Yugoslavs were often exasperated by their behaviour. As early as 1921, R. W. Seton-Watson wrote that the Serb officials were worse than the Habsburg officials had been, and that Serb oppression was more savage than its German equivalent. In 1928 he was moved to write: 'My own inclination is to leave the Serbs and Croats to stew in their own juice! I think they are both mad and cannot see beyond the ends of their noses!'[18] Yet three years later, Seton-Watson was able to see in Bosnia-Hercegovina a symbol of hope for this turbulent part of Europe:

> The historic mission of Bosnia is still not at an end, though I trust it will never again figure in the forefront of international complications. It has always been the focusing point, and sometimes the battle signal, of the Jugoslav national movement: it is the geographical centre of the race, the dividing line between the religious and cultural influences flowing from Rome and Byzantium. There are some foolish propagandists who regard this as an unbridgeable gulf. I, on the contrary, would fain believe that in the future, Bosnia may prove a source of concord rather than of disunion, and while preserving its high romance, its ancient historic individuality, its very real natural talents, it may become a potent factor in the great cause of national unity.[19]

Seton-Watson's dream of a peaceful Bosnia-Hercegovina was fading even before the end of the first Yugoslavia. In the hope of settling the main nationalities problem, Prince Paul had obtained

an agreement, or *Sporazum*, between Vlatko Maček, the leader of
the Croatian Peasant Party, and Dragiša Cvetković, a Serb politician sympathetic to non-Serbs. Under the *Sporazum* the Croats
were given a semi-autonomous province under a governor, while
Maček became the deputy of the Yugoslav Premier Cvetković.
This separate Croatia also included the south-western region of
Bosnia-Hercegovina where Roman Catholics outnumbered Orthodox Christians. It was understood in the *Sporazum* that the rest of
Bosnia came under the rule of Belgrade, and therefore Serbia.

This agreement between the Serbs and Croats was quite unacceptable to the Muslims who made up a third of the population of
Bosnia-Hercegovina, and outnumbered the Christians in most of
the towns. Because they belonged to the ancient land-owning and
governing class, the Muslims were also more prominent than the
Christians in the political life of the countryside. This attempt by
the politicians of Belgrade and Zagreb to clear up Serb–Croat
differences at the expense of the Muslims foreshadowed the dire
events of 1941 and 1991.

The *Sporazum* and an earlier concordat with the Vatican were
part of Prince Paul's strategy to unite his people in the face of the
threat from neighbouring countries with designs on Yugoslav
territory. Hitler's annexation of Austria and occupation of Czechoslovakia, followed by Mussolini's conquest of Albania in April
1939, had led to the fear that Yugoslavia might be next on the list.
By giving autonomy to Croatia under the moderate Peasant Party,
Prince Paul hoped to remove the threat from the Ustasha terrorist
organisation, which was supported by Italy, Germany, Hungary
and Bulgaria. After Germany's conquest of most of northern
Europe, and the Soviet Union's annexation of eastern Poland, parts
of Finland and Romania, as well as the three Baltic states,
Yugoslavia felt increasingly isolated and vulnerable. Although
Prince Paul himself and most Yugoslavians were sympathetic to
Britain, prudence dictated appeasement of the Axis powers.

In early 1941 Hitler was engrosssed in preparing 'Operation
Barbarossa', his plan to invade his ally the Soviet Union, and had
no intention of being diverted by a Balkan war. The reason he did

in fact turn his attention to the Balkans had nothing to do with Yugoslavia. On 28 October 1940 Hitler's ally Mussolini had used Albania as a base for an ill-considered and ill-timed invasion of Greece, from which he was soon in retreat and calling for German help. In December 1940 Hitler gave orders for the invasion and conquest of Greece, before the launching of 'Barbarossa' in May 1941. For both these operations his armies would have to pass through Romania and Bulgaria, and he would need at least the acquiescence of Yugoslavia.

In February 1941 Hitler summoned the Yugoslav Premier and Foreign Minister to Berchtesgaden, treating them to a characteristic blend of charm and threats. Under ever more bullying pressure, Yugoslavia joined Romania and Bulgaria in signing a Tripartite Pact on 25 March, with the assurance that Germany would respect its sovereignty and would not ask for military help or the free passage of *Wehrmacht* troops. Common sense, caution and an instinct for self-preservation were all on the side of accepting the pact; but these are not Serbian characteristics. The Serbian response to a threat, especially a threat in the German language, has always been rude defiance. On the day that the pact was signed, the Serbian Orthodox Patriarch Gavrilo Dožić protested to Prince Paul, then went on Belgrade Radio with an appeal to the Serbs to rally behind their faith. His address was relayed from Ljubljana but not from Zagreb.

On 27 March, one of the doom-laden dates of the Yugoslav calendar, a group of junior army and air force officers mounted a *coup d'état* in Belgrade, deposed Prince Paul and put in his place the young King Peter. As the new government formally cancelled the Tripartite Pact, immense crowds gathered in Belgrade, chanted slogans in favour of Britain, smashed all the windows in the German tourist board building, which also served as Gestapo headquarters, and solemnly tore up the swastika flag.

In London Winston Churchill announced: 'Today, Yugoslavia has found its soul.' His tribute still further heightened the mood of jubilation and pride in Serbia. However, in Zagreb Archbishop Stepinac wrote in his diary for 27 March: 'In the end, the Croats

and Serbs are two different people, a north and a south half which
cannot be joined except by a miracle of God. Schism is the greatest
curse of Europe, almost greater than Protestantism. Here there is
no morality, no principle, no truth, no justice, no honesty.'[20]

In Rome Mussolini welcomed the *coup d'état* because it would
give him the chance to destroy Yugoslavia and win some of its
territory in Slovenia and Dalmatia. He compared this outburst by
the 'incorrigible' Serbs to the Sarajevo murders that started the
First World War.[21] In Berlin Hitler at first refused to believe
reports of the *coup d'état* and the insult shown to the German flag.
He thought it was some kind of joke. Then doubt gave way to
tempestuous rage. He ordered a massive air attack on Belgrade 'to
cauterise the Serbian ulcer', followed by 'Operation Enterprise 25',
a two-pronged invasion from Austria and Bulgaria.

During the last nine days of peace, the Yugoslavs do not seem to
have understood the horror in store for them. Tito, having rushed
to Belgrade after the *coup d'état*, went back to Zagreb apparently
thinking the crisis was over. The new Prime Minister, General
Dušan Simović, arranged for his daughter's wedding to take place
on 6 April, the Orthodox Palm Sunday. The Communists also looked
forward to Palm Sunday, the date of a new Soviet-Yugoslav pact.

Early on the morning of 6 April the streets of Belgrade were
crowded with worshippers going to church and shoppers attending
the open markets. Just before seven o'clock, the first wave of
German bombers came in from across the Danube to attack the
military airport, the anti-aircraft guns and the water system serving
the fire brigade. As flames and smoke appeared all over the city,
Stuka dive-bombers descended almost to rooftop level, demolishing
blocks of flats, hospitals, churches, schools and the National
Library, wiping out its collection of medieval manuscripts. In *Tito
Speaks* the journalist Vladimir Dedijer, who had reported the
Spanish Civil War, describes the destruction of the city where he
was raised and went to school:

> In the very centre of Belgrade, a bomb hit the Church of the
> Assumption and a shelter in its immediate vicinity, where a

wedding party sought refuge, with the bride in white, the groom with rosemary in his buttonhole, the priest in his gold-embroidered robes – two hundred persons in all . . . Nobody emerged alive from the shelter . . . At 11 a.m. came the second attack, more violent than the first. Anarchy in the city was complete. Gipsies from the outskirts penetrated the centre of town and broke into shops, dragging away expensive furs, food, even medical instruments. A bomb hit the zoological gardens, and the wild animals started roaming through the burning city; a polar bear made his way to the River Sava, groaning painfully.[22]

Four hours after the start of the bombing, Tito, who was in Zagreb, heard the news on a German broadcast – Radio Belgrade had ceased to function. Hurrying into the centre of town, he passed the headquarters of the Croatian Peasant Party, hearing from its militiamen that they welcomed the German invasion. German tanks entered Zagreb on 10 April, and Belgrade two days later, while the Italian army advancd down the coast. The young King Peter and the members of his Cabinet drove into Bosnia and then into Montenegro, from where they flew to Jerusalem on 12 April. Tito compares the King's behaviour with that of the latter's grandfather, who had joined his troops on the retreat through Albania, then adds a malicious jibe: '. . . the King and the Government did not forget to take part of the gold of the National Bank with them, and loaded ten cases into one of the planes. When they were flying over Greece, through a storm, one of the cases fell on one of the ministers and killed him.'[23]

Although Tito and his Communist Party played no part in the *coup d'état* of 27 March, he tried to take some of the credit for having delayed the start of 'Barbarossa'. Some historians now deny that the Yugoslav incident spoiled Hitler's plan for the invasion of Russia. The fact remains that the operation scheduled for May did not begin until 22 June, and the German army ended up being caught in the Russian winter on the outskirts of Moscow and Leningrad.

After the conquest came the division of Yugoslavia. The Third

Reich incorporated northern Slovenia, while Italy took the southern part, the Dalmatian coast and Montenegro. Italy's vassal state Albania was given the province of Kosovo. Bulgaria 'redeemed' the parts of Thrace and Macedonia lost to Greece and Serbia during the second Balkan War of 1913. Hungary took the fertile lands of Bačka, Branje and Medjimurje. A rump Serbia was placed under the *Wehrmacht* High Command, 'to be treated exceptionally badly'. Inner Croatia, Slavonia, Srem (between the Sava and Drava rivers), those parts of Dalmatia that had not been ceded to Italy, and all Bosnia-Hercegovina were recognised on 10 April as the Independent State of Croatia (Nezavisna Država Hrvatske), or NDH under the Ustasha leader, or Poglavnik, Ante Pavelić.

4

Wartime

When the Axis occupation of Yugoslavia began in April 1941, Josip Broz was a middle-aged and undistinguished Comintern agent hiding in Zagreb under a false name, with his true identity known only to a handful of comrades. Within four years he was to become the internationally famous and glamorous Marshal Tito, the peer of Stalin, Roosevelt, de Gaulle and Churchill. The story of Tito's rise to power is one of the most extraordinary in the modern age, and also one of the most obscure.

Tito and his historians later tried to explain the eventual Communist victory in Yugoslavia as a national liberation from the Axis occupation. Many British writers, especially those who served in the Allied military mission to Tito, have tended to back this version of events. Others, especially those who were dropped into Yugoslavia to fight on the side of the royalist Chetnik forces under Draža Mihailović, have blamed the Allies for helping Tito to crush his democratic and Serb opponents.

Both the Titoist and the British accounts have tended to concentrate on events from 1943 onwards, when Italy was dropping out of the war and Germany had begun a fight for survival. In that year Tito established power in most of the mountainous regions of Bosnia-Hercegovina and Croatia, and, although the Chetniks were still unchallenged in Serbia proper, they were coming under increasing threat from the Partisans to the west and from the Soviet Red Army battling its way from the east.

Tito's historians and most of the foreign writers on Yugoslavia have underplayed or simply ignored the catastrophic and fearful events that took place as early as April 1941, six months before Tito went into action and more than two years before Britain entered the scene. In virtually all the memoirs and history books, the Independent State of Croatia, or NDH, appears if at all as a vague and shadowy puppet regime, and its leader, Ante Pavelić, as an insignificant quisling. It is only during the last few years, since Croatia again became independent, that foreign or even Yugoslav scholars have paid proper attention to the NDH.

Far from being an unpopular alien state, the NDH had the undoubted support both of the great majority of the Roman Catholic Croat population and of the Church itself. Far from being a docile puppet regime subservient to its Axis allies, the NDH was incomparably more determined, more ambitious and more independent than Mussolini's Italy, and more violent than Hitler's Reich. The NDH policy towards the almost two million Orthodox Serbs of 'convert a third, expel a third and kill a third' was conceived without the support of the Axis powers, and was executed with a ferocity that horrified the Italian army, and shocked even the German SS.

The Serbs in the NDH who escaped the Ustasha massacres and extermination camps went on to become the toughest troops of Tito's Partisan army. Other Serbs took their revenge by massacring their Catholic or more often Muslim neighbours, and by trying to set up a Greater Serbia. These Chetniks were also the deadly enemy of the Partisans, so that some of the bloodiest fighting was really a civil war among the Serbs. As Tito admitted late in life, he came to power because of the carnage among the Yugoslavs. Ironically Ante Pavelić's policy towards the Serbs led to the very two things he most feared and detested: a Communist government and a reunited Yugoslavia.

Yet even late in the war, when the Partisans held most of the mountainous regions of Bosnia-Hercegovina and Croatia, the Pavelić government still held Zagreb and Sarajevo, as well as the populous northern plain. Archbishop Stepinac and the entire

Catholic Church stayed loyal to Ante Pavelić and the NDH. After the war almost all the leading Ustasha escaped into exile, to keep alive the dream of a resurrected Croatia. Archbishop Stepinac remained behind to lead the resistance to Tito, for which he was tried and sent to prison and later put up for canonisation. The hatred and bitterness roused by the Ustasha in the NDH lived on throughout the years of Communist Yugoslavia, foiling all Tito's efforts to introduce 'Brotherhood and Unity'. Fifty years after the NDH was founded, Croatia once more became independent.

Those very few foreigners who have studied the NDH see it as one of the most horrendous regimes in history. The Irish essayist Hubert Butler, who was also an amateur archaeologist, called the archives of the Croatian Catholic Church, 'the Rosetta Stone of Christian corruption'.[1] The Italian Carlo Falconi wrote in *The Silence of Pius XII* that the Ustasha were in some ways worse than the German Nazis: 'Only in Croatia was the extinction of at least half a million human beings due more perhaps to hatred of their religion than of their race, and was sacrilegiously bound up with a campaign for rebaptism.'[2]

The Cambridge historian Jonathan Steinberg, who has examined the Roman Catholic attitude to the Jews in Hitler's Germany, Pétain's France and Tiso's Slovakia, has this to say on the NDH:

> In all these studies, religion and churches react; they do not act. Even those who criticise the silence of Pius XII, never suggest that the Vatican caused the massacres; the issue is whether the pope and the clergy did enough to stop them. The Croatian case will not fit such comfortable secular categories. Croatian fascism, the Ustasha movement . . . combined Catholic piety, Croatian natonalism and extreme violence.
>
> The terrible evidence of those years and the terrible revenge claimed in ours reminds us of the religious wars of the sixteenth century. The Croats were Catholics the way that the people of South Armagh are Catholic; religion, nation and self merged into an explosive, unstable mixture.[3]

In the chapter that follows, concerning the first three months of the Independent State of Croatia, Tito does not make an appearance, although the events described were the cause of his ultimate rise to power. These same events, and the hatred and passion they engendered, were also the cause of Tito's failure to build a Yugoslavia that would remain united after his death.

5

The Ustasha
Terror

On 10 April 1941 a Zagreb newspaper published the text of King Peter's speech on the German bombing of Belgrade four days earlier: 'On the morning of Palm Sunday, while children slept their innocent sleep and the church bells were ringing for prayer to God, the German airplanes without warning let fall a rain of bombs on this historic town.' The King went on to describe how low-flying German planes machine-gunned fleeing women and children. The next morning, Good Friday, the same newspaper welcomed the German panzer divisions to Zagreb: 'God's providence in concord with the resolution of our allies had brought it about that today on the eve of the resurrection of the Son of God our Independent State of Croatia is also resurrected . . . all that is right and true in Christianity stands on the side of the Germans.'[1] On the day the Germans entered Zagreb, the Ustasha veteran Slavko Kvaternik proclaimed the Independent State of Croatia on behalf of its leader, Ante Pavelić, who came back from exile in Easter Week, wearing a black Fascist tunic.

After thirteen years in exile as a criminal wanted for murder and treason, Pavelić was a mystery figure to most of the citizens of the Independent State of Croatia. And although over the next four years his photograph would appear in all the newspapers, on public buildings, proclamations and even the postage stamps of the NDH, his square, heavy features were to remain unimpressive and unmemorable. He had one of those faces that always seem to be blurred and out of focus in photographs.

Pavelić's writings and speeches were as characterless and grey as his face. His surviving daughter has given a pious account of Pavelić as a family man but he comes across as lacking in warmth, humour or any particular personality. The German Plenipotentiary General in Zagreb, Glaise von Horstenau, detested Pavelić but does not bring him to life in his otherwise witty and savage account of the Ustasha leaders. We know that Pavelić went to Mass each day in his private chapel but not if he had any strong Christian devotion. His only recorded interests outside politics were philology and philately. He had taken from Ante Starčević the absurd idea that the Croats were really Goths who had fallen by accident into speaking a Slav-sounding language, and had recently published a Croat lexicon, cutting out all 'Serb' words, an ambitious task since the languages are almost identical. He stole for himself the stamp collections of some of the Jews and Serbs he murdered.

Like many extreme Croat (and Serb) nationalists, Pavelić came from the harsh limestone mountains of Hercegovina, where Muslims, Roman Catholics and Orthodox Christians live together in mutual fear and suspicion. 'A pure racial Croat both in name and blood,' wrote one of his clerical sycophants in 1942, describing how Pavelić went to the Jesuit school at Travnik, then to Zagreb University.[2] He did not mention that Pavelić's wife was Jewish.

From the Jesuits, as from his fellow law students, Pavelić picked up the viciously anti-Serb views of the nineteenth-century theorist Ante Starčević and his follower Josip Frank, as well as a loathing of Bolshevism and Yugoslavia. After fleeing the country in 1928, Pavelić found havens in Hungary, Mussolini's Italy and Hitler's Germany, all of which wanted to overturn the Treaty of Versailles. For most of the 1930s, Pavelić ran an Ustasha training camp at Siena, from which he sent back agents to Yugoslavia to plan the uprising, carry out bomb attacks and swear in recruits. Many of these recruits were novice Franciscans, as the novelist Evelyn Waugh discovered when he served in the military mission to Yugoslavia in 1944–5.

Although Pavelić and his Ustasha were both helped – and used – by the Italian Fascists and German Nazis, the Croatian nationalists do not seem to have borrowed any coherent political ideology from them. Aleksa Djilas has done his best to explain the Ustasha creed: 'They were at once a modern totalitarian and terrorist organisation, conservative traditionalists, Roman Catholic Clericalists (struggling against Orthodox Christianity, Jews and Communist atheists), and primitive, peasant-populist rebels.'[3] In dealing with his Axis allies, Pavelić was respectful and eager to please, provided they let him exterminate the Serbs. When Mussolini objected, Pavelić turned to the more understanding Hitler, who in June 1941 advised him that if he wanted a truly lasting NDH he must pursue 'a fifty-year-long policy of intolerance'.[4]

Among Pavelić's colleagues, the most important were Slavko Kvaternik, the head of the armed forces; Andrija Artuković (also known as 'the Yugoslav Himmler'), the Minister of the Interior; and Mile Budak, the Doglavnik (Deputy Leader) and Minister of Religion and Education. The Kvaterniks were hereditary right-wing terrorists. One had died in an armed attack on the Serbs in the Military Frontier as early as 1871. Slavko had married the daughter of Josip Frank.

Soon after Slavko Kvaternik proclaimed the NDH in Zagreb on 10 April, his younger brother Peter was killed by the Serbs for sabotaging the Yugoslav army's defence of its country. At the state funeral held in Easter Week in Zagreb, the German General Glaise von Horstenau met Slavko Kvaternik and earnestly warned him not to accept the 'comic-opera title' of Croatia's first Field Marshal. Later von Horstenau came to detest Field Marshal Kvaternik and still more his son Eugen-Dido, the head of the secret police and the concentration camps.

Artuković was one of the Ustasha leaders educated at Široki Brijeg, a Franciscan seminary near Mostar that became the command post for the extermination of Serbs in Bosnia-Hercegovina. After leading an unsuccessful armed revolt in the Velebit region in 1932, Artuković went to England in 1934, to organise a contingency plan for murdering King Alexander, if the attempt in France should fail. The historian Hubert Butler devoted an essay to Artuković, who stayed for a year in Ireland after the war while on his way to California. Describing Artuković as a bureaucrat and a 'desk murderer', Butler concluded: 'Very few people have heard of him, yet if his story were told with remorseless candour, we would have a picture not only of Croatia forty years ago but of all Christendom in our century.'[5]

Deputy Leader Mile Budak, a writer of popular novels with a nationalistic and pious theme, provided the NDH with culture. He made it his business to win over fellow novelists, poets, artists and sculptors, especially those who had not been Croat separatists. Among those bullied or buttered up was the world-famous sculptor Ivan Meštrović, who was persuaded, after a few weeks in prison, to take an NDH art exhibition around Europe. The leading Croatian poet Vladimir Nazor eventually joined the Partisans, but in 1941 he composed verses very acceptable to Budak:

> This is no time for music and mandolins
> Now is the time for each of us
> To live as wolves and lions,
> In other words as Croats.[6]

The country's leading surrealist writer, Miroslav Krleža, who had been a Communist in the 1920s and later supported the Tito regime, was allowed to remain in Zagreb throughout the war, thanks to Budak's protection.[7] Soon after the liberation in 1945, a single-issue magazine appeared in Zagreb, reproducing the various odes, declamations, paintings and busts by well-known Croats who had praised the Ustasha and the Germans during the previous four years. The editor pointed out that most of those named were now vociferous for the Partisans.[8]

As Minister of Education, Budak ensured that the young were taught to honour the medieval Kingdom of Croatia, whose red-and-white chequerboard emblem now appeared on the flags of the NDH and the sleeves of the Ustasha troopers. In one of his speeches, Budak likened the Ustasha to the crusaders in the Holy Land: 'It should be remembered that the Catholic Church, which is neither a terrorist organisation nor stupid, led six crusades to recover Christ's grave. This went so far that even the children joined in crusading wars. If this was so in the eleventh and twelfth centuries, we can be sure that the Church understands our Ustasha struggle.'[9]

Whereas the medieval crusaders went out to fight the Muslims and only occasionally clashed with the Eastern Christians, the Ustasha wanted the Muslims to join them against their principal foe, the Orthodox Serbs. In his effort to win the support of the Bosnian Muslims, Budak frequently claimed that the Croats belonged to two religions, the Roman Catholic Church and Islam:

The NDH is an Islamic state wherever our people belong to the Islamic faith. I emphasise this because it is necessary to know that we are a state of two creeds, Catholic and Muslim. We know how big is the role our church has played in our history and therefore we cling to it. We would have held to it even only for political reasons, for it has been the only bulwark that Belgrade could never surmount . . . We Croats must be happy and proud that we have our faith and at the same time we must be aware that our brother Muslims are also the purest Croats, as our revered leader Ante Pavelić has already declared.[10]

Pavelić had also established a mosque at Zagreb by adding three minarets to the arts pavilion designed by Meštrović.

At mass meetings throughout the spring and summer of 1941, Budak railed at the 'Vlachs' (strangers or foreigners) in the NDH, by which he meant followers of the Orthodox Church. At Vukovar, in eastern Slavonia, he said that the Serbs in the NDH were not real Serbs but 'wandering beggars from the east whom the Turks had brought as servants and porters'. He reminded his audience of the folk-saying: 'Give a Vlach half the food from your plate, and use the other half to hit him over the head and kill him, or else he'll do it to you.'[11]

On a few occasions Budak abandoned these rustic expressions to expound his policy towards the Serbs with brutal precision. In a speech at Gospić on 22 June, reported four days later in the official NDH newspaper *Hrvatski List*, Budak made the comment referred to earlier, that a third of the Serbs would have to convert to the Roman Catholic Church, a third would have to leave the country, a third would have to die. No reference has been found for the saying attributed to Budak in the same speech: 'For the Serbs, Gypsies and Jews, we have three million bullets.'[12]

As the Minister for Cults in the Independent State of Croatia, Budak executed its policy towards the Orthodox Christians, Jews and Gypsies. But in so far as this policy involved the direct participation of the Roman Catholic Church, notably in the rebaptism of converts, responsibility passed to the Croatian hierarchy, above all to Archbishop Stepinac. He was not only head of a Church preparing to take in some 600,000 converts, a third of the Orthodox population, he was also one of the priests and father-confessors to men such as Pavelić, Budak, Kvaternik and Artuković, all pious Catholics who looked to the Church for moral and spiritual guidance. If Archbishop Stepinac disapproved of any action taken by the government of the NDH, especially if that action was taken in the name of the Catholic Church, it was his duty to speak out. The behaviour of Archbishop Stepinac under the NDH, was not only controversial at the time but led to his trial in 1946, and became still more contentious after his death in 1960, contributing to the breakup of Yugoslavia. He was, in his lifetime, the major opponent not only of Tito but of the concept of South Slav unity, and since he is due for canonisation he may be remembered when Tito and Yugoslavia have been forgotten.

Since becoming Archbishop of Zagreb in 1934, Stepinac had developed into an ardent, almost obsessive, Croatian nationalist whose bigotry was softened only by his piety and a measure of human kindness. Like many in whom religion combines with love of country, Stepinac gave special devotion to Mary the Mother of God and also 'Queen of Croatia', making an annual pilgrimage to her shrine at Marija Bistrica, about forty miles north of Zagreb.

After a visit to the Holy Land in 1937, Stepinac began a campaign for the canonisation of Nikola Tavelić, a Franciscan from the Dalmatian coast who died in Jerusalem in 1391. Stepinac believed that the fame of Saint Nikola, and the monument he proposed to build for him on the Velebit mountains overlooking the Adriatic, would draw attention away from the thirteenth-century Serb Saint Sava, whom Roman Catholics did not recognise. Saint Nikola would make a special appeal for the Ustasha and other extreme Croatian nationalists who in the late 1930s were waiting for their chance to seize power. Before going to the Holy Land, Nikola Tavelić had served for fourteen years in Bosnia-Hercegovina, stamping out heresy by fire and the sword, as members of the Franciscan Order were to do in the 1940s. The bare Velebit mountains where Archbishop Stepinac wanted to build a monu-ment to the saint had been the site of the unsuccessful Ustasha rising led by Artuković in 1932.

The year 1941, which witnessed the birth of the Independent State of Croatia, had long since been chosen to mark the 1,300th anniversary of the Roman Catholic Church of Croatia. Historians such as Viktor Novak cast doubt on the authenticity of this claim, suggesting that the first connection with Rome probably took place in the ninth century. Moreover the people who lived on the Dalmatian coast and other regions now claimed by the NDH had stronger ties with Constantinople, and therefore the Eastern Church, than they did with Rome. The 1,300th anniversary celebrations should be seen as an affirmation of Croat pride in the past and hope for the future, rather than as the marking of a historical event.

Its coincidence with the anniversary may explain why the Indepen-dent State of Croatia was greeted by Stepinac as a gift from God. On 12 April, only six days after the bombing of Belgrade, the Archbishop called on Slavko Kvaternik to pledge his loyalty to the Ustasha regime, and four days later went to see Pavelić, who by then had arrived from Italy. Both these visits, together with a radio broadcast made by Stepinac, took place before the surrender of Yugoslavia, a fact which friends of Stepinac put down to inadvertence.

In a circular letter to his priests on 28 April 1941, Stepinac expressed his joy at the new regime introduced by Adolf Hitler and Ante Pavelić:

> Our people has come face to face with its age-old and ardently desired dream. The times are such that it is no longer the tongue which speaks but the blood with its mysterious links with the country, in which we have seen the light of God, and with its people from whom we spring. Do we need to say that the blood flows more quickly in our veins, that the hearts in our breasts beat faster? . . . It is easy to see God's hand at work here.[13]

Neither in public nor, as far as we know, in private did Archbishop Stepinac, either in April 1941 or for at least a year to come, voice any doubts concerning the men who had given Croatia independence. The official Catholic newspaper *Nedelja* praised them by name in an article published on 27 April:

> God, who directs the destiny of nations and controls the hearts of kings, has given us Ante Pavelić and moved the leader of friendly and allied people, Adolf Hitler, to use his victorious troops to disperse our oppressors and enable us to create an Independent State of Croatia. Glory be to God, our gratitude to Adolf Hitler, and infinite loyalty to our Poglavnik, Ante Pavelić.[14]

In the middle of April, Ante Pavelić went to Rome to offer the crown of Croatia to the Duke of Spoleto, a cousin of the King of Italy, who accepted the honour but never actually went to Zagreb. At the same time Pavelić was granted an audience with the Pope, who gave the NDH his *de facto* but not his *de jure* recognition, and sent Monsignor Ramiro Marcone to Zagreb as his apostolic visitor. Since Archbishop Stepinac did not go to Rome with the Poglavnik, it has been suggested that they were not in agreement. If there was any dissension, it may be because the Archbishop, like many patriotic Croats, was angry with Pavelić for having ceded much of the coast to Italy. Stepinac wept when he heard the news.

The supposed quarrel had already taken place when Stepinac wrote the pastoral letter already quoted. The same letter goes out of its way to praise the leadership of the NDH:

> Knowing the men who today govern the destinies of the Croatian people, we are deeply convinced that we will go forward with full understanding and help. We are convinced and expect that the Church in the resurrected state of Croatia will be able to proclaim in complete freedom the uncontestable principles of eternal truth and justice.

Whereas Stepinac was courteous and formal in his praise of the new regime, the Archbishop of Sarajevo, Ivan Šarić, was a fanatical Ustasha supporter who hero-worshipped Ante Pavelić. A big, hearty and boisterous man of passionate likes and dislikes, Šarić often broke into verse when be became excited. He had been auxiliary Bishop of Sarajevo in June 1914, when Archduke Franz Ferdinand was assassinated, and he had immediately penned an anathema on the Serbs:

> Lord, turn thy eyes from heaven . . .
> Eternal Judge, condemn the savage beasts and vipers . . .
> Protect and guard thy humble people,
> Lest they be torn apart by the ravening wolf.[16]

In those pre-war days Šarić had been loyal to the Austro-Hungarian Empire and therefore at variance with those of the clergy, especially Franciscans, who wanted an independent Croatia. After the fall of the Habsburg Empire and the emergence of Yugoslavia under Serbian domination, Šarić came round to the theories of Ante Starčević and his modern disciple Pavelić. Whether or not Archbishop Šarić swore the Ustasha oath on a gun, a bomb and a dagger, he had been in touch with the organisation

in exile as early as 1934. In that year Šarić attended the Eucharistic
Congress in Buenos Aires which at that time, as after the Second
World War, was the favourite refuge of Croat nationalists. In an
article published in the Ustasha newspaper *Sarajevski Novi List* on
11 May 1941, Archbishop Šarić recalled the encounter of seven
years earlier:

> I was with our Ustasha in North and South America. The bishops
> there, Americans, Germans, Irish, Slovaks and Spaniards, with
> whom I came into contact, all praised the Croat Ustasha as good,
> self-sacrificing believers, as godly and patriotic people . . . How
> many times have I heard the Ustasha ask where they would be
> without their priests . . . I sang with the Ustasha with all my
> heart and voice 'Our Beautiful Homeland', all with big tears in
> the eyes. And with eager hope in its beautiful, sweet and golden
> freedom, uplifting ourselves to God, we prayed to the Almighty
> to guide and protect Ante Pavelić for the freeing of Croatia. The
> good God heard and, behold, he answered our cries and suppli-
> cations. 'God, we thank Thee; Lord, we acknowledge Thee.' . . .
> And we shall always join belief in country with our religious
> belief. Croats for ever! Catholics for ever! God and the Croats![17]

While Šarić and the Ustasha were meeting in Buenos Aires, their
leader and hero Ante Pavelić had planned, though he did not
personally carry out, the murder of King Alexander of Yugoslavia
in Marseilles. The Yugoslav authorities, who had no doubt kept an
eye on Šarić in Buenos Aires, complained to the Vatican that its
Archbishop in Sarajevo had not expressed condolences on the death
of the King. On his way back to Yugoslavia, Šarić stopped off in
Rome, where Cardinal Pizzardo took him to task for this negli-
gence, pointing out that the Pope himself had sent condolences.
Šarić replied that, 'on the Pope's part, that was merely an act of
diplomacy'.[18]

Archbishop Šarić returned to Rome in 1939 as one of the
delegation sent to request the canonisation of the medieval Franciscan Nikola Tavelić. There, in St Peter's Basilica, the Archbishop

first met his hero Ante Pavelić. He described the occasion in some
of the twenty-two verses of his 'Ode to the Poglavnik', which was
printed on Christmas Day 1941 in *Katolički Tjednik*, with a signed
portrait of Pavelić and a decorative border of Christmas-tree
candles and little silver bells:

> Embracing thee was precious to the poet
> as embracing our beloved Homeland.
> For God himself was at thy side, thou good and strong one
> so that thou mightest perform thy deeds for the Homeland . . .
> And against the Jews, who had all the money,
> who wanted to sell our souls,
> who built a prison round our name,
> the miserable traitors . . .
> Dr Ante Pavelić! the dear name!
> Croatia has therein a treasure from Heaven.
> May the King of Heaven accompany thee, our Golden Leader.[19]

Like Stepinac in Zagreb, the Archbishop of Sarajevo thought
that the Mother of God protected his country:

Above the new, young and free Croatia, the image of the Virgin
Mother, the beautiful shining image has appeared in the heavens
as a sign – *signum in cielo*. The Lady comes to visit her Croatia,
within her maternal mantle she wishes to enfold her young,
reborn Croatia exactly in the thousandth year of the Catholic
Jubilee. Again she descends on the flags of our freedom to occupy
her ancient place; in order to protect us and to defend us as she
did at the time when our Bans and Princes went into battle under
the flag bearing her image.[20]

In the summer of 1914, when Šarić was writing inflammatory
verse that helped to provoke attacks on the Serbs, the Bishop of
Mostar in Hercegovina, Alojzije Mišić, issued a pastoral letter
reproaching those who were sowing hatred. More than a quarter of
a century later, in 1941, Dr Mišić was still the Bishop of Mostar

and still preaching friendship towards the Orthodox Christians. As we shall see, he was to become the only senior churchman to speak out against the Ustasha regime. The rest of the dozen Croatian Catholic bishops were loyal and even enthusiastic followers of the Poglavnik. Archbishop Stepinac was the most guarded and cautious in his support, especially when Germany started to lose the war. Archbishop Šarić of Sarajevo was to the end of the war, and for many years after, the most vehement Ustasha.

Some of the bishops imitated the seventeenth-century Vicar of Bray in England who changed his politics and his religion according to who was in power. The ablest trimmer in the NDH was Antun Aksamović, the Bishop of Djakovo, the see once occupied by Josip Strossmayer, the world-famous scholar and a believer in Yugoslav unity. While Yugoslavia remained in existence, until April 1941, Aksamović stuck by the principles of his nineteenth-century predecessor and was the most 'Yugoslav' of all the Croatian bishops. When Ante Pavelić came to power, the Bishop of Djakovo suffered a change of heart and threw himself into the task of converting Serb 'schismatics', even praising the sixteenth-century zealots in France who had massacred the Protestants on St Bartholomew's Day. Bishop Aksamović's letters to Ante Pavelić called the latter 'the Great Son of the Croats', 'the Hero of our Blood' and the 'Giver of Freedom'. In June 1945 the Bishop of Djakovo invited the Central Committee of the Croatian Communist Party to lunch, made speeches in praise of Tito, and the next year played host to an international peace delegation in Zagreb.[21]

On 26 June 1941, the day that *Hrvatski List* published Budak's 'Convert a third, expel a third and kill a third' policy towards the Orthodox Serbs, the Catholic hierarchy met in Zagreb. Present at the conference, which was presided over by Archbishop Stepinac, were Archbishop Šarić of Sarajevo, Bishop Aksamović of Djakovo, and the bishops of Belgrade, Banja Luka, Split, Hvar, Šibenjik and Senj, while the Bishop of Mostar sent a friar as his representative. The assembled bishops decided to go in a body to Ante Pavelić, in order to show their devotion and trust. At the reception Archbishop Stepinac greeted Pavelić and, having explained that love of religion and country spring only from God, went on to declare: 'The consciousness of this has brought us today before you so that we, the legitimate representatives of the Church of God in the NDH, give you, its Head of Government, our heartfelt greetings, with the promise of our loyal and true co-operation towards a better future for the homeland.' In his equally warm reply, Pavelić thanked the bishops and was photographed for the press, surrounded by churchmen.

Two months before he met the bishops, Pavelić had begun to put into action his plan to wipe out the two million Orthodox Christians, Jews and Gypsies within the NDH. In April 1941 the government issued decrees forbidding the use of Cyrillic script, closing the Orthodox schools and making the Serbs wear blue armbands, with the letter 'P' for 'Pravoslav' (Orthodox). In May and June the government passed laws depriving the Jews of the right to property or marriage with gentiles.

The state authorities took the lead in the mass conversion of Orthodox Christians to the Roman Catholic Church, waiving the need for instruction and granting a rebaptism virtually on demand. Throughout the spring and early summer of 1941 Roman Catholic priests, attended by armed Ustasha, carried out mass baptisms in Orthodox villages throughout the Military Frontier and in Bosnia-Hercegovina. A Bosnian newspaper boasted that by September 1941 more than 70,000 Serbs had converted in the Banja Luka diocese alone.[23] By 1945 the number of converts in the NDH amounted to more than 300,000.

Those who joined the Catholic Church, often literally at gunpoint, were without exception poor and ignorant peasants, because the laws of the NDH expressly refused conversion to anyone with a secondary education, teachers, merchants, rich artisans and peasants, and above all Orthodox priests. These groups were all considered to have a 'Serbian consciousness' and therefore to be incapable of becoming true Croats. Such people would have to leave the country or die. Many educated Serbs and Jews, especially those in the cities and towns, became aware of the danger and fled of their own accord to Serbia or to those parts of the coast that had been ceded to Italy. The government of the NDH, in order to hasten the exodus of the Serbs, arranged with the Germans to have them transported by train to Belgrade, meanwhile forcing them into concentration camps, where many died of disease, hunger and brutal treatment. Even during the summer of 1941, some of these transit camps were already turning into the death camps that later became a feature of the Independent State of Croatia.

Among the Serbs who prudently left the NDH before the terror and killing turned to frenzy was Bogdan Deanović, an Orthodox priest at Borovo on the Danube, in eastern Croatia. While Father Deanović was living in exile near Belgrade, he received a letter with news of home from his Roman Catholic opposite number Father Andelko Gregić clearly a good-hearted man and no friend of the Ustasha. Borovo lay in the see of Djakovo, whose bishop, Aksamović, was keen on mass conversion as a way of enlarging his flock as well as saving the lives of the Orthodox peasants. The letter conveys the fear and moral corruption pervading the Independent State of Croatia:

> With pain in the soul and great disapproval we have condemned the happenings and the policies to the Orthodox Church, but this was a furious storm against which we were powerless to act. People looked on helplessly at what was happening, and everyone in his heart condemned it, but at the same time we had to let it happen. Many others [Orthodox Christians] have gradually come to share your fate. Above all the intelligentsia. They [the authorities] have tried to deal with the peasants in another way by making them say that they feel and call themselves Croats. And indirectly they've tried to get them to join the Catholic faith. They began understandably with people of mixed marriages. A mass of people followed, many of them state functionaries who feared for their lives. It was no use saying that it wasn't right to convert without personal conviction or understanding of the faith. They were frightened.
>
> I know that you abroad have observed what's happening here, and that it's detrimental to the Orthodox Church. However, my

dear colleague, if one considers the human beings involved, it has done them good and a favour. If we hadn't done [the conversions], God knows what might have happened in the village. Seen from a spiritual point of view, we've accomplished that unity of the faith that has always been our ideal. In fact they [the converts from Orthodoxy] have stayed with their own beliefs. All they've had to do is acknowledge the supremacy of the Pope in Rome, and for ordinary people that's of no significance. I know it hasn't been done in a legal fashion, for there have been moral pressures, but the responsibility for that doesn't lie with individuals. It's been done under orders. The Church officially condemns forced conversions because they're done for material advantage, but to have stuck by the rules would have been hard and damaging.

The [Orthodox] church at Borovo now has Catholic services and the church's goods now belong to the [Catholic] Church. Your vineyard and orchard have gone to some Dalmatians and I fear they'll ruin [the land] unless it goes back into good hands. That's how the revolution has been, and God alone knows what might happen.

I don't know whether you blame and curse me but, my dear colleague, as far as your personal things and property are concerned, the Franciscans haven't got hold of or spent a single dinar. I've saved everything that could be saved. The icons and pictures are in a secure place. I've had the gold and silver plate cleaned. Do you want to know what it looks like now? Tiptop![24]

Father Deanović who got away with his life and kept his icons, was one of the fortunate Orthodox priests in the Independent State of Croatia. At least 130 priests perished in the Ustasha massacres that began in April 1941, when raiding parties from Zagreb swooped down on villages in the Military Frontier, near to such towns as Osijek, Glina, Karlovac, Sisak and Knin. In a village near Bjelovar, the Orthodox priest, the teacher and 250 peasants, men and women alike, were forced to dig a grave in which they were buried alive with their hands tied behind their backs.[25] At Otošac, early in May, the Orthodox priest was made to watch as his son was literally hacked to death, along with 350 other villagers. Then the Ustasha turned on the father, pulled out his hair and beard, gouged out his eyes and then tortured him to death.[26]

At the small town of Glina, the Ustasha butchered 1,000 Serb men, women and children inside the Orthodox church, which they then set on fire, burning alive a further thousand Serbs including the priest. Near Drvar, the Ustasha took the Orthodox priest and seventy of the faithful into the hills, where they cut their throats and hurled the bodies into a ravine. At Osijek, in eastern Slavonia, a Franciscan ordered the death of an Orthodox priest, who was seized by the Ustasha and then had his nose, ears and tongue cut off before he was stabbed in the stomach. Of the 577 Orthodox clergy, 131, including three bishops, are known to have been murdered in cold blood, while sixty or seventy others died in the fighting. The Ustasha burnt down or dynamited a third of the Orthodox churches, frequently with the faithful inside.

The Franciscan Order played a leading role in the slaughter in Bosnia-Hercegovina, where they had first arrived in the thirteenth century to wipe out the Bogomil heretics. The centre of operations was the monastery at Široki Brijeg, the Alma Mater of many leading Ustasha. Its most famous old boy, Minister of the Interior Andrija Artuković, ordered the massacre of 4,000 Serbs in his native district in May 1941. A law student from Široki Brijeg won a competition by cutting the throats of 1,360 Serbs with a special knife, for which act he was given the prize of a gold watch, a silver service, a roast sucking pig and some wine.[27]

A local Ustasha, Viktor Gutić, had sworn in many Franciscans during the existence of the former Yugoslavia, and as a reward was appointed Prefect of Western Bosnia. On 27 May, while on the way to Banja Luka, Gutić became indignant because there were no Serbs on the public gallows at Prijedor, whereas in Sanski Most twenty-seven bodies were to be seen hanging. On the orders of Gutić, the Ustasha seized the Orthodox Bishop of Banja Luka, shaved his beard with a blunt knife, gouged out his eyes, cut off his nose and ears, then lit a fire on his chest before dispatching him. A few days later *Hrvatska Krajina* reported a ceremony at a church near Banja Luka: 'Blessings upon the first national Croatian banner in Bosnia took place in the convent of Nazareth before the Sisters of Christ's Precious Blood . . . The standard-bearer was Viktor Gutić.'[28]

In the district of Livno, a Franciscan preacher told his flock: 'Brother Croats, go and slaughter all Serbs, and first of all slaughter my sister, who is married to a Serb, and then kill all the Serbs in a row. When you have finished, come to me and I'll hear your confession and give you forgiveness for your sins.'[29] Another Franciscan chided his congregation: 'You are old women and you should put on skirts because you have not yet killed a single Serb. We have no weapons or knives and we must forge them out of scythes and sickles so that you can cut the throats of Serbs whenever you see them.'[30]

The Ustasha newspaper *Hrvatska Krajina* carried a long report of the visit by Viktor Gutić to the Franciscan monastery at Petrićevac, where he delivered a rousing address:

> Like an angel with a fiery sword, Prefect Dr Gutić raised his voice which had been muted until now, declaring emphatically: 'Each and every Croat who takes the side of our enemy of yesterday [the Serbs] is not only not a good Croat but an opponent and hinderer of our previously thought-out and calculated plan for the cleansing from our Croatia of unwanted elements. Let us call on the mercy of God if that patriotic labour sometimes oversteps the usual bounds of religious morals and ethics, knowing that Almighty God, the most stern but also the most good and charitable, will approve the struggle to guard the independence of the long-suffering but God-loving Croatian people.'[31]

Gutić was one of the first on record to use the term 'cleansing' (in Serbo-Croat 'čišćenje', pronounced cheesh-chen-ye) to mean the elimination of Serbs or Orthodox Christians from the NDH. It later became the semi-official euphemism, occurring constantly in the documents of the administration.

The Ustasha had already converted, expelled or murdered hundreds of thousands of Serbs by 26 June 1941, when the Catholic bishops met to pledge their support to Ante Pavelić. Within forty-eight hours, on St Vitus's Day (28 June), when Serbs gather in solemn memory of their ancestors who fell at the Battle of Kosovo in 1389, the Ustasha started a second and even more ghastly round of mass murder. Whereas the first atrocities took place largely in the Military Frontier region of Croatia, the second wave struck at the larger Orthodox populations of Bosnia and Hercegovina, the stony and mountainous hinterland of the Adriatic coast. During the first two months of the NDH, the Ustasha had been inhibited in their task of killing the Serbs by the presence of German and Italian occupation troops, who did not understand or approve this fratricidal hatred. However, after the launching of 'Operation Barbarossa' on 22 June 1941, most of the German units left to fight on the Eastern Front, while the Italians withdrew to their new territory on the coast.

On the morning of St Vitus's Day, which was also the anniversary of the Sarajevo assassination, the Ustasha death squads carried out mass arrests of the Orthodox Christians in Mostar, the smaller towns and many villages, especially in western Hercegovina, where Croats outnumbered the Serbs. The Ustasha seized, bound and imprisoned thousands of men, women and children, including many of those who had already changed their religion and started to go to Mass on Sundays. The more fortunate Serbs were led to the outskirts of the town or a nearby wood and quickly shot or clubbed to death. However, in many places the Ustasha went to elaborate lengths to dispatch the Serbs with the utmost terror and cruelty, perhaps as a reminder and threat to those who escaped. At the head of a quarry near the Franciscan monastery at the village of Medjugorje, the Ustasha threw 600 women and children, still alive, over the edge of the precipice.

Crimes such as these had until now gone unreported. There were no foreign journalists in the NDH, nor any local newspaper foolhardy enough to defy the Ustasha. The German and Italian occupation forces were nauseated by what they had seen, but had not yet taken action against their NDH ally. Far from protesting against the Ustasha crimes, the Croat episcopate, which had gathered in Zagreb on 26 June, promised slavish support to Ante Pavelić. But one of the bishops who did not attend that meeting, the elderly Dr Mišić of Mostar, now demonstrated his courage and Christian spirit.

After the massacre on St Vitus's Day, the Bishop of Mostar ordered the clergy in his diocese to read out in church a solemn reminder that those who committed the sin of murder could not apply for absolution. Although this may seem to us simply an obvious statement of Christian teaching, priests in the NDH were sentenced to death for saying 'Thou shalt not kill', or even for refusing to say a *Te Deum* on Pavelić's birthday.[32]

Perhaps because of his age and high office, the Ustasha did not persecute Dr Mišić, but neither did they manage to stop him speaking his mind. When Archbishop Stepinac wrote to his bishops in August 1941, asking them to report on the progress of conversion, only the Bishop of Mostar dared to reply with the full truth. His letter, which has been read and tranlated by Hubert Butler and Stella Alexander, shows that the old man did not oppose the principle of converting the Orthodox, only the manner in which it was done:

By the mercy of God there was never such a good occasion as now for us to help Croatia to save the countless souls, people of good will, well-disposed peasants, who live side by side with Catholics . . . Conversion would be appropriate and easy. Unfortunately the authorities in their narrow views are involuntarily hindering the Croatian and Catholic cause. In many parishes in [my] diocese . . . very honest peasants of the Orthodox faith have registered in the Catholic Church . . . But then outsiders take things in hand. While the newly-converted are at Mass they seize them, men and women, and hunt them like slaves. From Mostar and Čaplina the railway carried six waggons of mothers, girls and children under eight to the station of Surmanci, where they were taken out of the waggons, brought into the hill and thrown alive, mothers and children, into deep ravines. In the parish of Klepca seven hundred schismatics from the neighbouring villages were slaughtered. The Sub-Prefect of Mostar, a Moslim, publicly declared (as a state employee he should have held his tongue) that in Ljubina alone 700 schismatics have been thrown into one pit. In the town of Mostar itself they [the Serbs] have been bound by the hundreds, taken in waggons outside the town and then shot down like animals.[33]

The response of Archbishop Stepinac to this astounding letter was, in the words of the Irish historian Hubert Butler, 'curiously narrow and thin-lipped'. He passed on a copy to Ante Pavelić, blaming the Serbs for their own misfortune brought on by 'hatred and Schism'. He excused Pavelić personally from any responsibility in these crimes. Butler compares modern indifference to the massacre of the Serbs with Milton's indignation over the Waldenses:

> Slayn by the bloody Piemontese that roll'd
> Mother and Infant down the rocks.

'There were scarcely ten thousand Waldenses to be persecuted in Piedmont, while the decrees of Pavelić were launched against nearly two million Orthodox.'[34]

The Ustasha persecution of the Serbs in Croatia and Bosnia-Hercegovina would eventually drive them into the ranks of Tito's Partisans and lead to a Communist Yugoslavia. However, during the first three terrible months of the NDH, the Serbs put up little resistance and often allowed themselves to be rounded up and slaughtered. Unlike their fellows in Serbia proper the Orthodox in Croatia had never fought as Chetnik guerrillas against a foreign oppressor; indeed, for hundreds of years they were honoured and loyal *Grenzer* of the Austro-Hungarian Empire. Having never regarded the Catholic Croats as enemies, they did not expect an attack and were taken by surprise. And if the raids were successful, in Ustasha terms, there were never any survivors to spread the alarm to other Orthodox villages.

In Bosnia-Hercegovina, as in Serbia proper and Montenegro, the Orthodox peasants looked on the Muslims as their traditional foe, even calling them 'Turks', although they are Slavs of the same language and blood. To inflame this old enmity, the Ustasha roped in Muslim thugs to participate in the killing of the Serbs, who in May 1941 in turn massacred a thousand Muslims near Banja Luka, and razed many villages in eastern Bosnia and Hercegovina. The Muslim middle classes disapproved of the Ustasha, and signed a petition throughout Bosnia-Hercegovina condemning the massacre of the Serbs.[35]

In July 1941 Milovan Djilas, travelling on a train in eastern Hercegovina, met some of the Serbs who had escaped a Ustasha massacre. One peasant told Djilas: 'They are killing every Serb in sight, like cattle – a blow on the head, then down the ditch. They are mostly Turks. Their time will come. They want to wipe out the poor Serb people.' Djilas remarked that these Serbs were not surprised or horror-stricken: One could not even say they were bitter: a misfortune had come along, terrible because it was human, but perhaps for this reason surmountable.' A girl said calmly that the Ustasha had taken away and killed the priests, officials and merchants of her small town, where the women and children now awaited a similar doom. Djilas turned to the first peasant and asked him why people did not defend themselves. 'Who can defend himself?' came the reply. 'We didn't expect anything. We couldn't believe a government would attack people just like that. We have no weapons. We are left to ourselves like cattle.'[36]

The first people to come to the help of the Serbs in the NDH were not the Chetniks or the Partisans but the German and, still more, the Italian occupation troops. The reports of the SS show that even these hardened killers were horrified by the Ustasha. They dug up some Serbs who had been buried alive in April and filed their documents under the heading 'What the Ustasha did at Bjelovar'.[37] They described with disgust how the Ustasha had made Serb peasants lie on their faces in church, then speared them with pikes.[38] One report by the security police reads:

> The atrocities perpetrated by the Ustasha units against the
> Orthodox in Croatian territory must be regarded as the most
> important reason for the blazing up of guerilla activities. The
> Ustasha units have carried out the atrocities not only against male
> Orthodox of military age, but in particular in the most bestial
> fashion against unarmed men, women and children . . . because
> of the atrocities innumerable Orthodox have fled to rump Serbia
> and their reports have roused the Serbian population to great
> indignation.[39]

The German Plenipotentiary General to the NDH, the historian
Glaise von Horstenau, wrote in June that 'according to reliable
reports from countless German military and civilian observers
during the last few weeks, in country and town, the Ustasha have
gone raging mad'. Early in July von Horstenau reported that the
Croatians had expelled all Serbian intellectuals from Zagreb. When
he went to complain Pavelić promised to give them better treatment; but he did not do so, for on 10 July von Horstenau described
the 'utterly inhuman treatment of the Serbs living in Croatia', and
the embarrassment of the Germans who, 'with six battalions of
foot-soldiers', could do nothing but stand by and watch the 'blind
bloody fury of the Ustasha'.[40] Although von Horstenau was no
doubt right that he and the *Wehrmacht* had a restraining influence
on the Ustasha, the sympathy of the Germans did not extend to the
Jews, and it was they as much as the Serbs who came to look for
salvation from the Italians.

During the first three months of Pavelić's regime, Italian troops
were stationed in the south-western zone of the NDH, as well as
the parts of Croatia ceded to Italy. Whether or not they subscribed
to the Fascist ideology, the Italians were horrified by the behaviour
of their allies. For example, on 21 May 1941 the general commanding the Sassari Division at Knin was approached by three NDH
officials, led by the Franciscan priest Vjekoslav Šimić, who said
they had come to take over the civil government of the region.
When the Italian asked what their policy was to be, the Franciscan
replied: 'To kill all the Serbs in the shortest possible time.'[41] In

due course Friar Šimić not only organised such a slaughter but killed a number of Serbs with his own hands.[42] The Italian general reported this back to Rome where it reached the ears of the French Cardinal Eugene Tisserant.[43]

Although the Italians at Knin were not permitted to interfere in the politics of the NDH, they gave surreptitious support to the Serb guerrillas who took up arms in May. As soon as Father Šimić and his Ustasha colleagues set to work in Knin, a group of local Serb lawyers, merchants and former Yugoslav officers fled to the hills to create the first armed resistance group in the NDH, under the leadership of an Orthodox priest, Momčilo Djujić. Before the war Djujić had been a socialist and a trade union leader, who organised a strike on the Split–Zagreb railway, but he was loyal to king and country and therefore declared himself a Chetnik, after the Serbs who had fought the Turks and Germans. A huge, bearded, commanding figure, whose three great loves in life were said to be 'wine, women and war', Djujić was to lead 12,000 men to asylum in Italy in 1945.

As soon as he took to the hills in May 1941, Djujić got in touch with Italian army officers, who supplied him with food and equipment, and probably with guns. On 25 May 1941 the NDH newspaper *Hrvatski Narod* denounced Djujić and his companions, promising that they would not escape 'Ustasha punishment'. However, the files of the NDH show that even in May the authorities knew of the help given to Serbs by the Italians, and two months later they were complaining: 'The Italian Army in the districts of Bribir and Sidrag does not allow any action against the Chetniks, and anyway this would not lead to success as we lack sufficient force and means.'[45]

The more they saw of the Ustasha, the more the Italians helped the Serbs. In early June, the *carabinieri* in Split reported a stream of Serb and Jewish refugees crossing into Italian territory with stories of Ustasha atrocities. The bodies of Serbs floated in huge numbers down the River Neretva, through Mostar. The Italian Foreign Ministry accumulated a grisly collection of photographs from the NDH, showing the butcher's knives and axes used by the Ustasha to dismember the Serbs, whose corpses are also shown.[46]

On 28 June 1941 the 32nd Infantry Regiment stationed at Bilec were caught in a storm of automatic fire and threw themselves to the ground shouting '*Siamo Italiani!*' ('We're Italian!'). The firing stopped and some Serbs came up to apologise, saying they had thought the Italians were Ustasha. At a nearby village, the Italians discovered 200 Serb corpses.[47] On 1 August a *bersaglieri* officer likened the town of Gračac to the Inferno described by Dante, under the rule of 'arrogant and provocative men with faces like hangmen in Ustasha uniform'. A fortnight later the regiment stopped the massacre of 400 Serbs and protected a column of fleeing Serbs and Jews.[48] As Jonathan Steinberg remarks: 'Italy's allies, the Croats, were turning into enemies, and their enemies, the Serbs . . . were becoming allies.'

Articles hostile to the Independent State of Croatia began to appear in the press of its ally Fascist Italy. The Turin *Gazetto del Popolo* wrote in October 1941:

> It would be ridiculous to deny that the acting powers-that-be in Croatia are former terrorists. These criminals have become generals, ministers, ambassadors, newspaper editors and chiefs of police. In spite of the promotion to higher rank, they have not changed fundamentally. In fact they are exactly what they used to be, including Pavelić and the members of his government.[49]

On 18 September 1941 the Bologna newspaper *Il Resto del Carlino* (*The Change from a Shilling*) contained a report from Corrado Zoli of the Italian Geographical Society describing an interview with a German major in Bosnia:

> There were special bands who performed the massacres and are probably still doing so, actually led and incited by Catholic priests and monks. This is more than confirmed. There was a monk near Travnik with the crucifix in one hand who was inciting a band of

people whom he had organised and was leading. This happened in the first days after my arrival there.

'This therefore means the renewal of medieval times,' remarked the correspondent.

'Yes but made worse by machine-guns, hand grenades, dynamite, barrels of gasoline and other means of terrorism.'

'Was this committed by the local Croat people?' asked Zoli.

'That's it, but by the worst element of the Croat population, just young men of around 20, collected, armed and led by Croats who came from Zagreb. This was all taking place among people who pretend to be civilised and who brag about having accepted the Mediterranean and Roman culture, sometimes even stating that they are the direct descendants of the Goths. It was a terrible massacre! It was a living terror! Entire families, men, women, babies, old men, the sick and children massacred and tormented by the worst imaginable Chinese tortures.'

As an Italian, Zoli was especially enraged by the crimes of the Franciscans:

The first brother of Assisi spoke with the birds and fish, calling them brothers and sisters, but his disciples and spiritual heirs, filled with hate, massacre the people in the Independent State of Croatia, who are before God and the Father, their own brothers, brothers of the same blood, the same language, the same mother earth which has nourished them with the sap from her breasts. They massacre, they kill, and bury people alive. They throw their victims into the rivers, the sea and into crevices. Bands of these killers still exist and they are in a state of frenzied excitement, led on by the priests and the Catholic religious officials.[50]

After a delegation of Serbs had gone to Rome to implore assistance, Mussolini ordered his army back into the NDH to stop the Ustasha persecution. From 9 September onwards, the Italians reoccupied most of Hercegovina, enabling Serbs to go back to their homes and worship at Orthodox churches where there was still a priest alive. In Mostar, a crowd of 10,000 Serb women and children gathered in the main square. A small girl, orphaned by the Ustasha, stepped up to the Italian commander, offered him flowers and begged him, in the name of all present, for the protection of the Italian army.[51]

Virtually all these momentous and frightful events took place before Tito had stirred from his hiding-place in Belgrade.

6

First Clashes with
the Chetniks

Tito remained in Zagreb until early in May 1941 but did not try to mount a resistance to the Ustasha regime. Most Roman Catholics in Zagreb and other towns rejoiced at Croatia's new-found independence, and joined with the Church in acclaiming Ante Pavelić and his backer Adolf Hitler. The Orthodox peasantry in the Military Frontier zone and in Bosnia-Hercegovina had never been proselytised by the Communist Party, and those few who took up arms to protect themselves were either non-political or royalist Chetniks. The Communists in the NDH were for the most part factory workers or sons and daughters of the bourgeoisie who had joined the Party at Zagreb University. In the atmosphere of repression and terror introduced by Artuković, the NDH Minister of the Interior, left-wing Croats feared for their lives as much as the Serbs, Jews and Gypsies. Many Communists joined the NDH's army or its militia, the Domobrans, partly in order to divert suspicion from themselves and partly to get the weapons and military training necessary to serve the Party when the occasion arose. In 1943 these secret Communists helped to bring over whole units of the Croatian forces to fight on the side of the Communist Partisans.

In May 1941 Tito assumed the disguise of a well-to-do engineer and went on a business trip to Belgrade, to live in the wooded, prosperous suburb of Dedinje. He had come to Belgrade because as a revolutionary Communist he wanted to make it his capital and the seat of power. Moreover, having fought the Serbs in the First World War, and come to know their character from his work as a Party official, Tito guessed that the first uprisings were likely to start in Serbia and Montenegro, even if the insurgents there would be unsympathetic to Communism.

Many officers and soldiers of the defeated Yugoslav army had taken their weapons into the hills to continue the fight as the Chetniks had done in the last three years of the First World War. Among them was Colonel Draža Mihailović, a scholarly and intense man stationed in northern Bosnia, who left in May for the Ravna Gora, or 'Flat Mountains', on the Serbian side of the River Drina. Like Charles de Gaulle of France, with whom he came to develop an affinity and friendship – although they were never to meet – Mihailović had been an outspoken and nagging critic of army tactics, especially its lack of defence against armoured and air attack. He had also studied guerrilla warfare. His habit of reading lectures, as well as his mildly left-wing views, made Draža unpopular with the old-fashioned and brandy-swilling senior officers who, had they been English, would have called him 'a bit of a Bolshie'.

The leader of the official Chetniks, a club for veterans of the Turkish and Austrian wars, dismayed most Serbs by calling upon them not to resist the Germans. The aura and name of the Chetniks therefore fell upon officers such as Mihailović, although he always regarded himself as a regular soldier, not a guerrilla. The Yugoslav government in exile in London appointed him first a general and then its Minister of Defence. Mihailović's operations, which began in May 1941, brought greatly needed cheer to the British, then in retreat from the Germans in Greece, Crete and subsequently North Africa. The Chetniks in Serbia were also well placed to attack the railway running from Austria down to Salonika and the eastern Mediterranean.

The German military governed the rump state of Serbia until August 1941, when they installed General Milan Nedić in much the same role as Pétain's in Vichy France. They got further support from the Serbian Fascist leader Dimitrije Ljotić and his followers, for as long as the Axis side was winning the war. The Patriarch of the Serbian Orthodox Church refused to collaborate and spent most of the war in a Nazi concentration camp.

The Gestapo in Belgrade arrested and imprisoned many prominent writers, artists and academics, including Viktor Novak, the author of two volumes on the history of the Croatian Catholic Church and its attitude to Yugoslavia. While in a concentration camp north of Belgrade, Novak met some of the refugees from the NDH, and heard of the crimes committed by the Ustasha and their clerical supporters. On leaving prison in autumn 1941, Novak started to write *Magnum Crimen*, his massive work on the Croatian Catholic Church in the twentieth century.

As well as hearing the refugee stories, the people of Belgrade saw constant evidence of the Ustasha crimes in the thousands of corpses floated towards the city down the Danube and Sava rivers, some of them bearing macabre notes such as: 'To Belgrade, for King Peter.' On one boat was a pile of children's heads beside the corpse of a woman, perhaps the mother, with the inscription: 'Meat for St John's Market, Belgrade.'

In the middle of May 1941, German convoys moved in ever increasing numbers through Yugoslavia on their way to Romania, and Tito heard rumours of the impending invasion of Russia which he passed on to Moscow.[1] When Hitler began 'Operation Barbarossa' on 22 June, the Yugoslav Communist Party issued a formal call to arms, but the entry of Russia into the war had excited millions of Yugoslavs who were not Communist members. Afterwards Tito defended himself against the reproach that he did not enter the war until after Hitler invaded the Soviet Union, explaining that 'so difficult a struggle cannot be prepared in a day'.[2]

According to Djilas, the Central Committee did not spring into action until 4 July, when they met at the villa of Vladislav Ribnikar, the head of *Politika* newspaper and one of the wealthy fellow-travellers of the Communists. Djilas remembers predicting that the Germans would soon be defeated but Tito, an older and wiser man who knew the weaknesses of the Soviet Union, talked of a long and difficult war. At this meeting, Tito ordered Svetozar Vukmanović-

Tempo to Bosnia-Hercegovina, and Djilas himself to his native Montenegro.

When the Italians took over the administration of Montenegro, they behaved with the same easy-going and affable manner that had endeared them to the Croats of the Dalmatian coast, and had led them to be regarded as saviours by the Serbs and Jews. However, in Montenegro the Italians faced a people so proud, warlike and xenophobic that they would fight to the death against all foreign occupation, bad or good, iron-fisted or kid-gloved. Far from being won over by Italian courtesy and friendliness, the Montenegrins saw these things as evidence of effeminacy and weakness.

The Italians hoped to win the hearts of the Montenegrins by restoring the monarchy, which had been overthrown in the First World War and later subsumed into the closely related Karadjeord-jević dynasty of the Serbs. However, the Montenegrin separatists, or Greens, were supported only by older people and some of the clans in the south-west of the country, feuding against the Karad-jeordjević faction, or Whites. Montenegro was also one of the very few parts of Yugoslavia where there were Communists, or Reds, in the countryside, particularly in the northern district where Djilas had his home.

Although for different reasons, the Reds, Whites and Greens all felt an attachment to Russia, going back to the tsarist days when 'We and the Russians together are 200 million strong'. The invasion of Russia on 22 June inspired great drinking of military oaths, cleaning of knives and rifles, and recitation from Bishop Njegoš's gory verses about the massacre of a Muslim village. A Montenegrin girl who flirted with an Italian soldier was stripped naked and crucified as a warning not to fraternise.

Tito did not regard the Montenegrin venture as anything more than a feint to draw Axis troops from the Russian front and simultaneously harden the Communist will to fight: 'Shoot anyone, even a member of the provincial leadership, if he weakens or commits breaches of discipline,' Tito told Djilas. But he added with emphasis: 'Take care not to launch a general uprising! The

Italians are still strong and well organised. They would break you. Just start with minor operations.'[3]

These were hard orders to obey, since the Communist Party in Montenegro did not control even its own supporters, let alone those of the Greens, Whites and Chetniks. Nor had Djilas established ascendancy over his own Party leadership, whose personal feuds and family hatreds reappeared under the guise of disputes on Marxist-Leninist theory or the interpretation of Stalin's speeches. Djilas selected as military leader a Yugoslav army captain, Arso Jovanović, not yet a Party member, but amply endowed with the Montenegrin virtues of courage, loyalty, single-mindedness and tenacity. His matching Montenegrin vices of ambition, vanity, humourlessness and infatuation with Russia would lead to Jonanović's downfall in 1948, when he took Stalin's side in the dispute with Tito. Although Djilas liked and admired Jovanović, he disapproved when the comrades brought him into the Party by acclamation, rather than through the normal stages of candidacy.

It was in Montenegro that two of Tito's favourite lieutenants, Djilas and Moša Pijade, started a quarrel that did not come into the open until twelve years later. As a Jew, a wanted Communist and a painter whose name and appearance were well known in artistic circles, Moša Pijade understandably went in fear for his life in Nazi-occupied Belgrade. He had been in prison earlier in 1941, but after the *coup d'état* of 27 March the new regime released him and he made his way to Montenegro, where rumour had it he was hoping to join the British. Perhaps, like the Jews in the Independent State of Croatia, Pijade knew he was safer under Italian rather than German administration, and it has not been explained how he was hoping to get from Axis-occupied Montenegro to British-occupied Africa or the Middle East. In any case, rumours that Pijade wanted to join the capitalists had spread through Montenegro and reached Belgrade, and Pijade blamed Djilas for spreading the story.

To exacerbate the quarrel, when Djilas summoned a meeting of the Communist Party's Provincial Committee on 8 July, he pointedly did not invite Pijade. In spite of Pijade's experience, prestige and friendship with Tito while in prison, Djilas considered him too old in years and too addicted to habits of factionalism, intrigue and theoretical quibbling. This quarrel with Pijade was set to cost Djilas dear, leading to accusations of arrogance, lack of respect for his elders, and even anti-Semitism. Pijade was often grumpy, pedantic and given to complaining – like Grandpapa in a comedy of the New York Jewish life – but he was popular in the Party for his jokes, his toughness and his devotion to Tito. Although he now wore peasant dress and called himself 'Uncle Janko', the Montenegrins did not regard Pijade as one of themselves but liked him for what he was, a Bohemian Jewish intellectual.

The Montenegrin crisis broke when Italy tried to put its plans to restore the monarchy into action. The only available candidate for the throne of Montenegro did not want to accept such a dangerous honour, and so on 12 July, the Orthodox feast of St Peter, the Italians set up a kingdom under their own High Commissioner. While a few Greens joined in the celebration, on 13 July the majority of the Montenegrins rose in revolt, attacking Italian garrisons throughout the country. Soon the rebels had killed or captured more than 2,000 Italian soldiers and taken over all the towns except Cetinje, the capital. The rapidity and scale of the insurrection shocked and dismayed Djilas, the very man who was supposed to have been its instigator: 'The people overwhelmed their leaders, going beyond our expectations and efforts . . . we had Tito's instructions to begin small actions and made preparations accordingly, but the people had moved ahead of us.'[4]

Loyal to Tito, though acting against his own Montenegrin instinct, Djilas tried to restrain the insurgents but, when they refused to obey him, countermanded the order. Even the Communists were bewildered and angry: 'I've been waiting twenty-five years for this rising,' said Moša Pijade to Djilas, 'and now when it comes, you send out directions that it's not needed, and we should split up instead into small groups.' Djilas tried to explain that these had been Tito's orders and that when he found they did not meet the situation he had countermanded them on his own initiative.

Unmollified, Pijade snapped back: 'A revolutionary should sense that in advance.'[5]

Albanian and Slav Muslim irregulars joined the fighting on the Italian side, and on 5 August the newly arrived Venezia Division put an end to the insurrection. The Communists were now on the run and were widely blamed for the reprisals taken by the Italians and for the free hand given to Muslims to loot and burn. The Chetniks were beating the Communists in the struggle for popularity but the two groups had not yet come into open conflict. In September 1941 a link was formed with the outside world when the Yugoslav government in exile in London sent a mission by submarine to the Montenegrin coast. With it came a British officer, Captain D. T. 'Bill' Hudson, a South African mining engineer who had worked in Yugoslavia and spoke Serbo-Croat. Hudson put the total strength of the 'Montenegrin Freedom Force', of whom the Communists made up the strongest and most aggressive units, at about 5,000 men. However, Hudson and the Yugoslavs did not remain in Montenegro but went on to Serbia to meet Draža Mihailović. Djilas, who at that time suspected all Englishmen of working for the intelligence service, would not allow his men to murder the intruders.

In early November, Djilas received an unpleasant letter from Tito, firing him from the Montenegrin Party leadership because of his 'serious errors'. It was not a mistake to have launched the rebellion, 'but it was wrong to have started it without grass-roots political preparations'. Tito made no allowance for the character of the Montenegrins, who would have launched their revolt without the Communist Party and its indoctrination. Yet many years later, when he had long since broken with Tito, Djilas acknowledged one of his criticisms: 'We in Montenegro were too slow in undertaking the formation of armed units capable of operating outside their own territory.'[6]

Djilas was summoned to Serbia, where the Partisans had joined the Chetniks in fighting the Germans. The final word on the 13 July insurrection in Montenegro comes from Stevan K. Pavlowitch in his book *Yugoslavia*:

So different were the conditions in partitioned Yugoslavia that in one year there had been three different mass risings, in three different regions, for three different reasons, against three different enemies. In the NDH, the Serbs had risen in self-defence against extermination by Croatian pro-Axis extremists. In Serbia, they had risen against the Germans in an upsurge of patriotic, pro-Allied optimism. In Montenegro, they had risen against an Italian formal attempt to put the clock back. Soon divided into Communists and anti-Communists, the insurgents were thereafter to fight a civil war between themselves which, more often than not, took first place over the original aims of their respective risings.[7]

While Djilas was fighting in Montenegro, Tito continued to play a waiting game in Belgrade under the Nazi occupation. Since any attack on German personnel would have invited devastating reprisals, the Partisans chose the easy target of Yugoslav policemen, murdering them in the street. As 'Operation Barbarossa' penetrated deep into the Soviet Union, the Germans covered the walls, hoardings and trams of Belgrade with maps showing the thrust of German panzer columns. Loudspeakers blared the news in Serbo-Croat and special editions of papers announced the German victories. To counteract this propaganda, the Communists seized and burned stacks of the papers that carried the news, and Ranković plotted to dynamite Belgrade radio station. He was betrayed, severely beaten and placed in a prison infirmary, from where he was rescued by Partisans in a raid worthy of Hollywood.

At the end of August, the Germans handed over the government and the preservation of order to General Nedić, the Marshal Pétain of Serbia. As German units were withdrawn to join the assault on Russia, Tito considered the time was ripe to start his rebellion in Serbia. He left Belgrade in early September, travelling south by train in the company of an Orthodox priest and a German-speaking Partisan, until he came to the region of Valjevo. Here Tito continued by horse and cart until he reached the Partisan sentries.[8]

Somewhere on this journey, Tito met up with Alexander Ranković, whom he had chosen to run operations in Serbia, as Djilas was doing in Montenegro, and Kardelj would later do in Slovenia. According to Ranković, Tito amused himself in north-west Serbia by pointing out places where he had fought for the Austrians in 1914, and telling yarns about his war experiences. 'There was a Serb howitzer,' he was fond of relating, 'which hit us every time. And we'd recognise it every time it fired, and we called it "Saint Nicholas".' Ranković warned Tito not to talk about his experiences in the Habsburg army, as this would offend the Serbs.[9]

Yet Tito and his Partisans were already unpopular in every rural part of Serbia. The Communist Party had built up a membership at Belgrade University, in some of the mining camps, and among the artisan class in provincial towns, but made no impression upon the Serb farmers. These tough and freedom-loving peasants were ready to fight for king, country and Church, but they had no wish for a social revolution. They were prepared to take up arms against an invader, when and if the occasion arose, but not to throw their lives away in the Montenegrin fashion. The Serbs saw in Draža Mihailović a leader who understood their beliefs, their loyalties and their interests. The Partisans were outsiders trying to muscle in on a war that did not concern them.

While the Partisans were mostly from Belgrade or distant parts of the country, the Chetniks were local people who worried about their families and their farms. They were vulnerable to the threat from Hitler's decree of 16 September demanding the death of 500 Serbs for every German killed, and 100 for every German wounded.

The attitude of the Partisans to the Chetniks is well expressed by Tito's biographer Vladimir Dedijer, political commissar at Kragujevac in the autumn of 1941:

The Chetnik units were usually made up of older men, married men, peasants of rich families. They remained in the villages, they slept at home, and from time to time they were called to Headquarters where they drilled. I had great difficulty persuading the Chetnick commanders around Kragujevac to take part in the fighting against the Germans. They said they had no orders. On the other hand they criticised our command because we 'wasted'

mercilessly the blood of the Serbian people fighting against the
Germans in an uneven struggle.[10]

In his biography *Tito Speaks*, Dedijer makes no mention of the
horrific massacre at Kragujevac, for which he himself must bear
some of the blame, and which more than anything turned the
Chetniks against the Partisans. In the vicinity of Kragujevac, where
Dedijer was baying for action against the occupiers, a group of
guerrillas (whether Chetnik or Partisan is still not certain) killed
ten Germans and wounded twenty-six. On 20 October the entire
male population of the town was rounded up and, in accordance
with Hitler's decree, about 7,000 were shot, among them hundreds
of schoolboys and one German soldier who had refused to serve in
a firing squad. Another 1,500 civilian Serbs were executed at
Valjevo.

These massacres taught the Chetniks that it was suicidal to fight
the Germans until the balance of war had swung to the side of the
Allies. Until then they should guard their weapons and strength to
preserve the Serbian nation. Tito learned from the same savage
example that local guerrillas are vulnerable to threats against their
loved ones. He was coming to see the need for a mobile army,
willing to fight in any part of the country, without regard for the
consequence. Since the Partisans were now the cause of German
reprisals, the Chetniks came to regard them as enemies. So did
most of the Serbian people.

Tito and Mihailović met three times in the autumn of 1941 but
they could find no common purpose. Mihailović wanted to save the
Serbs, while Tito wanted to use the war to establish a Communist
state, with himself as its President. From what we know of their
meetings, it seems that the two guerrilla commanders did not warm
to each other. Tito remarked on the Chetnik lack of organisation
and discipline, and the 'primitiveness' of Mihailović's staff.[11] In
Tito Speaks the sophisticated Croat recounts his shock when, on
accepting what he at first assumed was a glass of tea from
Mihailović, he found it to be hot plum brandy. In fact this

'Šumadija tea', made only from the weakest slivovitz, is a common drink in the plum-growing district from which it gets its name. In spite of his affected horror, Tito enjoyed strong liquor, although he preferred Scotch whisky and French brandy to Serbian slivovitz.

After the massacres at Kragujevac, the Germans regained control over most of the towns in Serbia, with the exception of Užice, near the borders with Bosnia and the Sandjak, an area populated by many Muslims as well as Orthodox Serbs. It was in Užice, a town of some 12,000 inhabitants, that Tito proclaimed a symbolic 'Red Republic' boasting its own hotel, bank, factories, newspaper and prison. All the future leaders of Yugoslavia held their positions in embryo, with Tito as President, Ranković in charge of the secret police, Kardelj dealing with policy, and Djilas producing the newspaper *Borba*.

Tito worked and slept in the bank, whose coffers provided the Partisan treasury. On top of the bank building Tito erected a Partisan star, which glowed red at night and attracted German bombers. Factories turned out rifles, ammunition, matches and uniforms, in which Tito took a particular interest. He had a Soviet pilot's cap made for himself; this kind of cap, a *pilotka*, was later renamed the *Titovka* and became standard issue to Yugoslav troops. While every other Partisan had a red star of cloth in his cap, Tito wore an enamel Soviet star with a hammer and sickle.[12]

Djilas observed to his wife Mitra, who joined him at Užice, that most of the men in the Central Committee, including Tito, were followed around by pretty secretaries who were clearly more intimate than their duties required. 'It goes with power,' answered Mitra. 'In Serbia, a minister without a mistress is unthinkable.' Djilas grieved that his wife was becoming cynical. In his autobiography Djilas notes that the first Partisan prison was well run and did not differ essentially from the post-war establishments in which he himself was to spend many years. 'Torture was applied selectively, in special cases,' he says, 'and executions were carried out secretly at night.'[13]

An explosion, possibly an act of sabotage, blew up the Red Republic's powder store and armaments factory, and, when

German tanks approached on 29 November, Tito gave the order to leave on the road south to Zlatibor, taking the wounded, the printing-press and several boxes of silver. Having left Užice twenty minutes before the Germans entered, Tito was soon cut off by tanks and came under rifle fire from infantry only 150 yards away. Later that evening, Djilas, Kardelj and Ranković waited anxiously for Tito, who showed up at midnight after a twenty-mile march. Djilas embraced him, and Kardelj was so overcome that for once in his life he could not speak. Tito put down his sub-machine-gun, called for a glass of water and then announced that the flight would have to continue. The walking wounded had left in advance and German tanks could be heard as Tito moved out before dawn on his retreat south.

During his trek through the Sandjak to Bosnia, which lasted from the end of November 1941 to January 1942, Tito endured and overcame the first real crisis in his career as a military and political leader. Driven from Serbia by the enmity of the locals, constantly under attack from the Germans and Italians, and worst of all scorned and rejected by Moscow, Tito was very nearly killed. One morning, at his headquarters in a cottage on Mount Zlatibor, Tito had just completed his daily shave when someone spotted Italians only 250 yards away. Tito grabbed his sub-machine-gun, ran for cover and, after a brief exchange of fire, made his escape. The cottage owner's daughter-in-law, who had given birth to twins the evening before, was left behind and killed in the attack, but the Partisans rescued the babies and called them Slobodan and Slobodanka, the male and female versions of 'Free'. The Italians captured Tito's camera and horse.

As winter came to the mountains, scores of Partisans suffered frostbite and had to undergo amputations of toes and feet without anaesthetic. The Germans took advantage of the deep snow to launch an attack on skis, from which the Partisans had to escape by struggling up the mountainside. Throughout this period of extreme danger and misery for the Partisans, they received no assistance from Stalin. At Užice in November, when the Partisans and Chetniks were already shooting each other, Dedijer was listening to a radio broadcast from Moscow in Serbo-Croat: 'Suddenly I jumped up and told Tito: "Listen. Moscow is speaking of the fighting in Serbia against the Germans. Listen! Listen! They say Draža is leading all the forces of resistance." Tito stood still, aghast. I had never seen him so surprised, either before or after that day. He merely said: "But that's impossible."'[14]

On the retreat into Bosnia, the beleaguered Partisans continued to hear broadcasts from Moscow as well as from London, announcing that Chetnik troops were fighting the Germans, 'although units in the Užice sector have been obliged to retreat before the attack of enemy tanks'. In the United States, *Time* magazine selected Mihailović as the most popular Allied general in 1942, together with MacArthur, Timoshenko and Chiang Kai-shek.[15]

In one of his rare moods of depression, made worse by defeat in a battle against the Italians, Tito offered his resignation as Party secretary, in favour of Kardelj. The Central Committee's response is described by Djilas:

I barely had time to interject 'but that doesn't make sense', when Ribar and Ranković expressed much the same thought. Kardelj took the floor, also rejecting Tito's self-abnegation, less with emotion than reason: in the given situation, Tito's act might be interpreted as an admission of an incorrect policy. We calmed down and discovering within ourselves the inescapable shadow of Moscow, elaborated on our reasons: Moscow would not understand Tito's resignation and would conclude that there was disintegration within the Party and the revolutionary movement. Tito was clearly pleased with our reactions. Yet one should not conclude that he was merely 'testing' us. No, he was guided by a feeling of responsibility for the failure in Serbia . . . [16]

Djilas contrasts this genuine offer of resignation with the one Tito would make in 1948, during the quarrel with Stalin.

Perhaps, in their subconscious minds, Tito and his associates understood how they had gone wrong in Serbia, and why Stalin was backing Draža Mihailović. They were learning the hard way what Mihailović too would come to learn, that in wartime people choose their allies for their fighting power and not for their ideology. Winston Churchill himself declared with reference to the Soviet Union that if Hitler invaded hell he, Churchill, would make a courteous reference to the Devil in the House of Commons. Stalin and Churchill supported Draža Mihailović because he was popular with the Serbs and therefore the man most dangerous to the Germans. They thought that the Partisans, with their Communist slogans and red star caps, were alienating the Serbs and therefore splitting the opposition to Germany. And at that time Stalin and Churchill were right. For the same reasons of *realpolitik*, Churchill and Stalin later switched their support to Tito, betraying the Chetniks.

It was during the painful retreat from Serbia proper, through the Sandjak to Bosnia, that Tito and his associates started to rethink their strategy for success both in war and in Communist revolution. As the most pragmatic and least theoretical of the leadership, Tito himself had the keenest grasp of reality. Thus, when he remarked to Djilas that in war 'the peasant goes with whoever is strongest', this may have been Tito's way of saying that peasants do not like Communism, a lesson he learned in Serbia.[17]

On Stalin's birthday, 21 December 1941, Tito established the 'Proletarian Brigades' which, as Djilas remarked, 'were proletarian not in a literal but in an ideological sense'.[18] Although these brigades later included genuine proletarians such as miners, shipyard workers and almost the whole of Split's 'Hajduk' football team, most of the troops were Party activists from the urban middle class. The Marxist sound of the 'Proletarian Brigades' was to be a disadvantage later, when Tito tried to play down the Communist role in the National Liberation Movement. On the other hand, these brigades formed the nucleus of the mobile, disciplined and fanatical fighting force that became Tito's equivalent of Cromwell's New Model Army.

After the hardships of the retreat through the Sandjak, which came to be known as the First Offensive (i.e. an offensive *against* the Partisans), Tito and his companions enjoyed their stay at the

Bosnian town of Foča which was now in the Independent State of Croatia. They lodged in the town's hotel and were able to take off their clothes at night for the first time in months. The newspaper *Borba* started to reappear, a concert was given, and radio and telephone links were established with other parts of Yugoslavia. The royal Yugoslav stamps, which had already been marked with the NDH's red chequerboard emblem, were superimposed with a red star as well, and used on envelopes that must now be philatelic rarities.

Both Dedijer and Djilas remark on the beauty of Foča, situated at the confluence of two mountain streams and surrounded by orchards. Both men point out that the town had already changed hands several times during the war before they arrived there. Dedijer recalls meeting a canny store owner who, to keep his options open, kept under his counter a German flag, an Italian flag and a Yugoslav flag with the Partisan star.[19] That anecdote, from a book published in 1951, gives an impression of the war as a struggle between the Partisans and two foreign invaders. Milovan Djilas, writing in 1977, tells the true and frightful story of what had really happened at Foča before the Partisans arrived, a story in which the foreign invaders play no part.

In the spring of 1941, soon after the establishment of the NDH, the Ustasha arrived in Foča and, assisted by Muslim thugs, slaughtered the Serbs, beginning with twelve only sons of prominent citizens. In the village of Miljevina, the Ustasha slit the throats of the Serbs over a large vat formerly used to store fruit pulp. Later, Serb Chetniks led by a drunken White Russian officer took their revenge by seizing and binding the Muslims, then throwing them off the bridge to drown. Four hundred Serbs and 3,000 Muslims were reported to have been killed in Foča, but judging by the devastation he witnessed, Djilas believed that the estimated number of Serb casualties was too low.[20]

Although these atrocities do not receive a mention in Dedijer's biography, Tito knew perfectly well what had happened at Foča, and therefore by inference in the rest of the NDH. From then on he understood that the way to win power in Yugoslavia was not by fighting the foreign invaders but by putting an end to internal conflict. Instead of leading a revolution in the way Lenin or Trotsky had done, Tito was to present himself as a Yugoslav patriot, standing above the feuds of religion and history. Many years later, in one of his television reminiscences, Tito let slip that of course he and the Communists had come to power because of the civil war.

Modern Serb historians and the foreign admirers of Mihailović say that he did not approve of the massacre of the Muslims, such as had taken place at Foča in 1941 and later recurred throughout the Sandjak, Montenegro and eastern Bosnia-Hercegovina. However, the documents show that Mihailović approved the establishment of a Greater Serbia and the 'ethnic cleansing' of people of other race or religion. In a typewritten letter to some of his senior officers, dated 20 December 1941, Mihailović listed the aims of his military units. Among them were:

> 2. To create a great Yugoslavia and inside it a great Serbia, ethnically pure inside the boundaries of Serbia, Montenegro, Bosnia-Hercegovina, Srem, Banat and Bačka.
> 3. The struggle to include in our national life all the unliberated Slav territories under the Italians and Germans [Trieste, Gorizia, Istria and Koruška] as well as in Bulgaria and northern Albania, with Shkoder [Scutari].
> 4. The cleansing from state territory of all national minorities and non-national elements.
> 5. To create a direct common border between Serbia and Montenegro . . . and the cleansing of the Sandjak from Muslim inhabitants, and of Bosnia from Muslim and Croat inhabitants.[21]

If this document is authentic, then Mihailović was, by the end of 1941, guilty of just the same 'ethnic', in fact religious, bigotry as his Catholic counterpart Ante Pavelić. However, he did not approve of actually killing people because of their different religion. His use of the word 'cleansing' was not a euphemism for murder, as it was among the Ustasha.

After describing the slaughter at Foča in 1941, Milovan Djilas, the great chronicler of the South Slav tragedy, tries to answer the question: How had it all come about? He thought that in the beginning the Serbs had acted in bitterness and out of a thirst for revenge, but that later the Chetniks had been taken over by officers 'who believed in the higher nationalist aim of exterminating the Muslims'. To the Communists, the Ustasha were 'a totally alien enemy force' and the Chetniks 'a conglomeration of Serbian liberal nationalists, terrified peasant masses, Serb chauvinists and fascists . . . but all had their roots in ancestral traditions, in village life, and in national and religious myths'. Djilas adds that 'not many Chetnik officers, let alone the Chetnik peasant masses, were obsessed with the ideology of extermination'.[22]

Since the Partisans were at that time almost all Serbs or Montenegrins, they sympathised with the Orthodox in the NDH. However, the Serbs in eastern Bosnia were more inclined to look for help from the Chetniks or the Italians than from Communists, who opposed the King, the Church and private property. By April 1942 Tito realised that his Partisans were unwelcome in Foča; ammunition was so short that the Chetniks jeered at them as 'five-bullet men', and the Germans and the Italians were about to launch another offensive.

In May Tito decided to visit Montenegro. His main rival, Draža Mihailović, had also visited Montenegro early in 1942 and found the position favourable. The Chetniks there were loyal to the exiled King and to the Allied cause, but had made an arrangement with the Italians to join in attacking the Partisans. Milovan Djilas, who had travelled widely in Montenegro before Tito arrived in May, found that the suffering of the Partisans at the hands of the Chetniks could 'only be compared with the suffering of the outlawed Chetniks after our victory – in that same region and in that same way'.[23] He noted that when the Chetniks captured a woman named Ružica Rip, a Jewish medical student and a girlfriend of a Partisan officer, they hanged her 'conforming to the Montenegrin prejudice that a woman wasn't worth a bullet'.[24]

In their isolation and hopelessness, some of the Partisans in Montenegro seem to have taken refuge in fantasy. The avant garde painter Moša Pijade, or 'Uncle Janko', started a sovkhoz, or Soviet state farm, on Mount Durmitor, stocked with animals stolen from Chetnik peasants. Uncle Janko busied himself making a detailed inventory of the sheep, cows, bulls, sheds, pens, shepherds, milkmaids, herders and monthly yield.

Soon after Tito's arrival on horseback, the Partisan leaders made their way to the Black Lake (Crno Jezero), stopping to have an impromptu picnic furnished by Djilas:

> Before we reached the lake a plane came upon us and we took cover in a stand of fir trees. I took out of a saddlebag a ham I had brought as a treat for Tito, and Tito, Arso Jovanović and I had a feast, while a plane showered machine-gun fire all around us. The delicious food, the bright sky, and Tito's self-confidence restored my good humour . . .[25]

Tito stayed in a former governor's house that had its own private orchard and apiary, but his worries about the military situation spoilt his enjoyment of rustic life. 'The bees buzzed in the fruit trees as bad news came in from all sides,' Djilas tells us. There was also an ill-natured Eve in this Eden, taking the form of Tito's mistress and secretary:

> Tito's Zdenka was in such a vile temper that she snapped even at Tito. During enemy offensives she always behaved as if the main objective of the Axis powers was to destroy her personally. One day Zdenka really blew her top. Ashamed, Tito asked me in embarrassment, 'What the devil is the matter with her?' 'I think she's in love with you,' I said. 'She's just carrying on.' Tito laughed mischievously. When I mentioned this to Ranković, he said with a guffaw: 'You must be the only one in the army who doesn't know about their relationship.'[26]

Once when Zdenka abused the escorting troops, Tito turned to his elderly Montenegrin bodyguard Djuro Vujović and asked him what he should do with her. 'I would have her shot, Comrade Tito,' came the reply.[27]

A year and a month of the war had gone by, and Tito was past his fiftieth birthday, stuck on a desolate mountainside with a harridan mistress, a weird old Jewish painter fussing over his sheep and cows, and a Montenegrin who thought that a jolly picnic was eating ham under machine-gun fire. Yet it was there in Montenegro that Tito made the decision that took him into the history books. After eight futile months in the border country of Serbia, Bosnia and Montenegro, where most of the population favoured the Chetniks, Tito resolved on a march west to the heart of the Independent State of Croatia, where he believed the Serbs, Muslims and Croats would rally to the Partisans. Like Washington at the Delaware, or Garibaldi landing in Sicily with his thousand men in red shirts, Tito was soon to astonish the world.

7

The Long March

On 23 June 1942, when Tito was setting out on the 'Long March' from Montenegro, King Peter of Yugoslavia met with Churchill and Roosevelt in the United States. News of this meeting further depressed the Partisans, who had recently fared badly in skirmishes with the Chetnik supporters of King Peter. One of the Partisan officers who had been killed was the wife of Alexander Ranković, to whom Djilas was asked by Tito to write a letter of condolence. Djilas himself was on edge, aware that he was widely blamed for the Party's failure in Montenegro. And Tito was fretting over the still hostile attitude of the Russians towards the Partisans. He would snap and shout at his colleagues, then feel ashamed of himself and sulk, like Achilles in his tent. However, as soon as the Partisans left Montenegro and entered Bosnia-Hercegovina, Tito's depression vanished and did not return.[1]

On the 'Long March', as on several subsequent marches and countermarches, the Partisans kept about thirty to fifty miles from the coast, on the ridge of the Balkan mountain range. The journey entailed crossing green, turbulent rivers, then climbing out of gorges up mountains so high that some Partisans suffered from altitude sickness and cold, even in August. On the north-eastern, or Bosnian, side, the mountains are green and constitute some of the largest expanse of primeval forest in Europe, where bears are still found in large numbers, and wolves are heard howling at night. In Hercegovina, near the Dalmatian coast, the mountains are bare, white limestone karst, having been denuded of trees by the Turks, or by the Venetians searching for naval timber. In summer Hercegovina becomes the hottest part of Europe, where imprudent travellers can still die of thirst and exposure, and even motorists in their air-conditioned cars recoil from the menace and glare of the bare hillsides and valleys of scree.

The German and Italian occupying forces seldom ventured far in this mountain wilderness lying between their spheres of influence. The Partisans, on their way through eastern Bosnia and Hercegovina, met only a few scared peasants before they came to the railway line running from Sarajevo down to the coast. One night a column of Partisans stopped at a Serbian village whose inhabitants rather unwillingly gave them shelter; the next day the place was visited by the Ustasha. Djilas saw the results in a heap of women and children's corpses, a larger pile of torsos and severed limbs, and murdered mothers clutching their murdered babies. Tito was visibly moved by the account Djilas gave, and made Dedijer write it down in his diary.

At the beginning of August, the Partisans moved into western Bosnia and Hercegovina, from which the Italian troops had just withdrawn to the coast. At the small town of Livno they encountered 700 Croatian Home Guards, or Domobrans, who quickly surrendered; however, the Ustasha and some German civilians offered resistance before they were overcome. Djilas describes the Ustasha as unpromising store clerks, barbers, waiters, high school drop-outs and village toughs, except for a young woman who proudly refused to recant her principles. She and most of the Ustasha were executed by firing squad. Some of the Partisans wanted to kill the German engineers but Tito thought that they might might be useful as hostages in an exchange of prisoners, having in mind his own former mistress, Herta, and Andrija Hebrang, the Croat Communist leader. One of those who favoured such an exchange was Vlatko Velebit, a suave Zagreb lawyer who spoke German and was later one of the three-man team who participated in talks with the *Wehrmacht*. One of the German

engineers, Hans Ott, was also to play a part in negotiations and
seems to have got on well with Tito. Although Ott was an anti-
Nazi, he almost certainly worked for the *Wehrmacht* intelligence
service.

Moving west to the Krajina district of Hercegovina and Croatia,
the Partisans found many Serbs willing to join their ranks now that
the Italians had gone. 'There were no political groups in the villages
save the Communists,' Djilas reported. 'The local Communists
told us with malicious joy how the Ustasha had first killed off the
bourgeoisie in the towns – priests, merchants, political party
leaders – so that we were left with the people pure and simple. The
Chetniks who showed up there with the Italians were left stranded
and weak when the Italians withdrew to "their" Dalmatia.'[2]

On their way to Bihać in the mainly Muslim north-west of
Bosnia, the Partisans put to the torch the Chetnik villages in the
plain of Grahovo, and almost burnt to the ground the birthplace of
Gavrilo Princip, the Sarajevo assassin of 1914. Three hundred
Chetniks were 'executed', according to Djilas. When the Partisans
took Bihać, the Ustasha defenders killed themselves with their own
hand-grenades rather than asking for quarter, which would have
been refused. Djilas grimly recounts more atrocities:

> Young Ustasha had fun with the girls in this manner: when they
> shook hands with them during walks, they would place human
> ears, fingers or noses in their hands, just like village toughs who
> get a kick out of offering tobacco pouches with snakes in them.[3]

Even many years later, when he no longer had to put forward
the Communist version of events, Djilas dismissed the idea that
the Ustasha massacres caused the Serb revolt in the NDH: 'This
line of thinking never occurred to anyone at the time, and belongs
to a subsequent stereotyped approach to political reality.'[4] However, that line of thinking did occur to the Germans at the time, as
we can see from their military archives. Moreover Tito himself
wrote in *Proleter* in December 1942:

The Serbian people have given the greatest contribution in blood to the struggle against the invader and his traitorous assistants . . . The Serbian people know well why our national tragedy occurred and who the main culprit was, and it is for this reason that they are fighting so heroically.[5]

This article was well received by Communist Serbs in Croatia and western Bosnia-Hercegovina, who understood that the words 'main culprit' referred to the Ustasha, not the foreign invader. In one of his television monologues broadcast in the spring of 1972, Tito himself let slip that the liberation struggle 'was well and truly a civil war, but we did not want to admit it at the time, because it would have been detrimental to our cause'.[6]

In November 1942 Tito set up at Bihać his first tentative form of Communist government, the Anti-Fascist Council for Yugoslavia (AVNOJ). As a classical 'front' organisation, AVNOJ included some of the eminent non-Communist Yugoslavs who were starting to join the Partisans in the autumn of 1942. Among the first of these was Dr Ivan Ribar, who had been president of the Royal Assembly in 1921, and who had banned the Yugoslav Communist Party. His son, Ivo Lola Ribar, a brilliant and brave young man and a favourite of Tito, had brought his father from Belgrade to join in the high adventure. Another arrival at Bihać was the septuagenarian Croat poet Vladimir Nazor, who had at first welcomed the NDH but soon grew horrified by its cruelty. Tito liked to surround himself with artists and writers, and therefore made much of Nazor, though some of the other Communists found him a trial. Nazor suffered from diarrhoea, which had the effect of making him constantly hungry, so that he thought nothing of eating a whole chicken at one meal.[7] Tito was also joined at Bihać by his Croat friend and comrade Andrija Hebrang, who had been released from an Ustasha camp in rather mysterious circumstances.

The arrival of people like Ribar and Nazor meant that Tito now had a miniature court as well as an embryo government in the small town of Bihać. However, in terms of population and territory, Tito had little more power than he had enjoyed the previous year at the

small Serbian town of Užice. In the autumn of 1942 and for almost
a year to come, the Partisans were confined to a small part of the
mountain range running south-east through Yugoslavia. Chetniks
loyal to Draža Mihailović still held much of Serbia proper, the
Sandjak, Montenegro and eastern Bosnia and Hercegovina. The
Serbs round Knin, in the part of Croatia near the Dalmatian coast,
were mostly loyal to the Orthodox priest Pop Djujić, who had now
been given the Chetnik title of Vojvoda (Duke). Some of the men
who fought with him have told me:

> Duke Djujić was a nimble man, as he had to be, fighting so many
> enemies, first the Ustasha and the Germans, then the Partisans.
> His only allies were the Italians, who protected the Serbs against
> both the Ustasha and the Communists. But the Italians dropped
> out of the war in 1943 . . . Duke Djujić was a natural tactician.
> One day someone ran in and asked him to send out some men to
> get back some sheep that the Partisans had stolen, but Djujić told
> them not to worry. Sheep couldn't travel as fast as men. They
> had to stop to graze. The Partisans would leave the sheep behind,
> and they did . . . Duke Djujić enforced absolute obedience. I've
> seen him go into a group of trouble-makers and lay about them
> with a stick . . . There were 300 Croats in his Dinaric Division.
> We even had one Croat commander, he'd been in the Yugoslav
> army in Split. Where Djujić was in command, nobody dared
> harm a Croat.[8]

Although the Partisans captured and briefly held small highland
towns such as Užice, Foča, Bihać and later Drvar and Jajce, they
seldom descended into the cities or the rich lowland plains which
held most of the country's wealth and population. Until the end of
1942, their presence did not much bother the Axis occupation
force. When the Italians moved into the NDH in the summer and
autumn of 1941, this was not to suppress the Partisans but to save
the Serbs from the Ustasha.

The Germans also intervened to restrain and sometimes to hang
the Ustasha in Slavonia and the Srem, but did not at first take the

Partisans seriously. Hitler's vital interests in the former Yugoslavia were first to protect the railway line down the Sava and Morava valleys, and secondly to ensure the supply of strategic ores such as copper and chrome from the mines, which were mostly in Bosnia. Since the Partisans wanted to win power in Yugoslavia rather than damage the Axis war effort, they seldom threatened either of these two German interests.

In November 1942, the Partisans were not even a serious threat to the Ustasha government of the Independent State of Croatia. The Poglavnik, Ante Pavelić, through his Minister of the Interior, Andrija Artuković, exercised absolute rule by terror in Zagreb, Sarajevo, the lowland towns and the populous plain of the River Sava. Whereas in Slovenia most of the Roman Catholic population opposed Italian and German rule, most Croats were pleased by their independence, and many remained supporters of the Ustasha until, and even after, the end of the war. Industry, agriculture and public transport continued with scarcely even a threat of sabotage. Big congregations filled the churches to hear sermons in praise of the NDH, and *Te Deums* in honour of Ante Pavelić. Young men continued to serve in the army, fighting the Partisans at home and the Russians at Stalingrad, where the Germans considered them the best of their allies (*Hilfsvölker*), followed by the Slovaks, 'then the Romanians etc., and last of all the Italians and Hungarians'.[9] The presses of the NDH continued to turn out loyal newspapers and cultural magazines of the highest quality. The Zagreb theatres mounted productions of plays by Croat, German, Italian and Irish writers, but not by Anglo-Saxons such as Shakespeare.

For the Roman Catholics who made up just over half the population, the NDH was a tolerable, even admired, state. For the nearly two million Orthodox Christians, 80,000 Jews and 30,000 Gypsies, the NDH was a slaughterhouse. The Ustasha, like the Khmer Rouge in Cambodia in the 1970s, were dedicated to killing at least one-third of the population.

In the spring and summer of 1941, the Ustasha began their work by making surprise descents on the Serbian villages, killing all the inhabitants on the spot. In the mixed communities they would round up the Serbs and then lead them off to be hacked to death in a forest, or thrown over the side of a precipice. But as the news of the massacres spread, the Serbs grew wary and ran away before they were captured. In the mountainous region of southern Croatia and western Bosnia-Hercegovina, the Ustasha often encountered armed and savage resistance by the Chetnik or Communist bands. In the autumn of 1941, the Ustasha changed to a new method of 'cleansing' the Serbs, Jews and Gypsies, sending them to extermination camps such as Jasenovac, which came to be known as the 'Yugoslav Auschwitz'.

The government of the NDH had built temporary camps in the summer of 1941 to hold the arrested Jews and the Serbs waiting for transportation to Belgrade. When the Italians reoccupied their sphere of influence in the NDH, the Ustasha killed their prisoners rather than let them fall into friendly hands. On the island of Pag the Italians discovered the bodies of 4,500 Serbs and 2,500 Jews, including women and children, all of them murdered.

In September 1941 the Minister of the Interior Andrija Artuković set up a system of concentration camps in the German sphere of influence, to be run by Eugen-Dido Kvaternik, the son of Croatia's Field Marshal. An Ustasha zealot, Maks Luburić, who planned an extermination camp while in exile, was given permission to build it at Jasenovac on the northern bank of the Sava, in the marshes formed by the confluence with the Una. This was the nucleus for a chain, or archipelago, of camps stretching from Sisak, which specialised in the killing of children, to Nova Gradiska, which was mainly for killing women, under the supervision of Maks's sister Nada Tanić-Luburić and her pretty colleague Maja Slomić-Buzdon, both of whom were accomplished stranglers. The Jasenovac complex was linked to the railways bringing in truckloads of Serb and Jewish deportees, who later departed floating along the Sava to Belgrade.

Although the Ustasha tried out poison gas as a way of killing the Jews on special trains, they scorned modern technology at Jasenovac and the other camps. They normally killed with knives, axes and clubs, or by hanging, burning in furnaces or burying alive. One group of Ustasha posed for their photograph as they sawed off the head of a young Serb. The main Jasenovac camp had a regular occupancy of from 3,000 to 6,000 inmates from the autumn of 1941 to the spring of 1945. Few lasted as long as three months, after which time, in accordance with the camp rules, they were murdered.

In the autumn of 1942, just before Tito reached the neighbouring town of Bihać, the Germans and Ustasha swept through the Kozara region south of Jasenovac, killing the Serbs and rounding up 40,000 to go to the death camps. Of the 23,000 Kozara children, 11,000 were murdered and the rest were sent to Zagreb to be brought up by Catholics in orphanages or foster-homes. During the journey by cattle-truck, hundreds of children died of disease and cold, while some grew so hungry that they ate their cardboard identity tags.

One of the first detainees in Jasenovac was Vlatko Maček, the leader of the Croatian Peasant Party, who had declined the German offer to be head of the NDH. Perhaps to be free of a dangerous rival, Pavelić sent him to Jasenovac but then, strangely, let him leave to write his memoirs:

> The camp had previously been a brick-yard and was situated on the embankment of the Sava river. In the middle of the camp stood a two-storey house, originally erected for the offices of the enterprise . . . The screams and wails of despair and extreme suffering, the tortured outcries of the victims, broken by inter-mittent shooting, accompanied all my waking hours and followed me into sleep at night.[10]

Maček noticed that one of the guards who spent his day killing would cross himself on retiring at night: 'I asked him if he were not afraid for the punishment of God. "Don't talk to me about that," he said, "for I am perfectly aware of what is in store for me. For my past, present and future deeds I shall burn in hell but at least I shall burn for Croatia.'"[11]

Another political prisoner in the camps was Andrija Hebrang, the general secretary of the Croatian Communist Party and one of the closest friends of Tito. One NDH document shows that Hebrang, possibly under torture, revealed the names of Tito, Kardelj, Djilas and other prominent Communists, although he probably did not tell the Ustasha anything that they did not know.[12] Soon after making this statement in June 1942, Hebrang was released from prison and in November of that year went to join Tito at Bihać. During the war and after the liberation, Hebrang argued the cause of the Croats in the Party, especially with respect to the frontier with Serbia. In 1948 he sided with Stalin in the dispute with Tito, was sent to prison and died there. Afterwards Ranković said his police had already discovered the statement made by Hebrang to the Ustasha. 'Why didn't you question him then?' asked Tito, to which Ranković answered: 'I thought you'd done that at Bihać.'[13]

Croats did sometimes survive the Jasenovac complex. From the mass of Ustasha documents on the 'cleansing', as well as detailed testimonies of the few inmates who escaped or were released, it seems that at least 70,000 Serbs, Jews and Gypsies were killed at Jasenovac alone. The total number of dead at all the NDH camps is certainly very much higher, though not as high as the million sometimes claimed by the Serbs. It is especially frightful to learn that the killers at Jasenovac included six Franciscan priests, of whom the worst was Father Miroslav Filipović-Majstorović, known to the inmates as 'Fra Sotona' ('Brother Devil'). According to one of the witnesses at the priest's subsequent trial: 'Filipović-Majstorović seemed kind and gentle, except when the massacring was going on. Then he was incomparable. He was leader of all the mass killings . . . He went off to conduct the slaughtering every night and came back in the morning, his shirt covered in blood.'[14]

Another former inmate described how one day Maja Slomić-Buzdon arrived drenched in blood and proudly announced to 'Brother Devil' that she had just 'slaughtered seven of them', at which the delighted Father Majstorović warmly embraced her and said: 'Now I love you, now I know you're a real little Ustasha girl.'[15] Another Franciscan killer, Zvonko Brekalo, was constantly to be found drunk with prostitutes at the local taverns but nevertheless had the letters 'K-R-I-Z' ('Cross') tattooed on the fingers of his left hand. These Franciscans continued to say Mass and preach sermons of loyalty to the Ustasha state.

Apologists for the Croatian Church, and in particular for Archbishop Stepinac, claim that the Ustasha Franciscans acted in disobedience to the Order and the hierarchy. In March 1953 a professor at an American university, Bogdan Radica, wrote in the Catholic magazine *Commonweal* that all the Franciscans directly involved in the forced conversions were excommunicated by the ecclesiastical authorities. However, a few weeks later, the head of the Croat Franciscans in the United States, Dominik Mandić, wrote in the Chicago magazine Danica: 'Not one of the Herzegovinan Franciscans was excommunicated during the war or otherwise punished by church authorities for acts unbecoming a priest.'[16]

Even those Franciscans who did not commit or witness crimes seem to have known what was happening in camps such as Jasenovac. This is made clear by one of the most disgusting documents quoted by Viktor Novak in *Magnum Crimen*. On 31 July 1942 the Franciscan Ivo Brkan wrote from Koraca in Bosnia to the Ustasha prefect at Dervanta, concerning the wives of the Serb men sent to the concentration camps for alleged acts of rebellion:

In the surrounding five villages there are some 500 to 600 widows ready to marry, young and desirable creatures who have quickly forgotten those taken away [i.e. their husbands] . . . Nature takes its course and now these widows would like to marry, naturally with Catholics, for there are [now] no Serbs in the neighbourhood. This is an opportune moment to inculcate them and their children with the Catholic faith and Croatian consciousness in the quickest time and with little difficulty for the government and the Church. The government would have to set up a school to teach Catholicism and Ustasha Croatianism . . . and also authorise the Church to explain the factual truth that the deceas

occurred because of rebellion, so that the widows can now marry
with our people. This materially prosperous community of perhaps 500 houses, and probably more, is ready to change to the
Croat and Catholic faith, so that through marriage, which most
of them want with our people, they can come to our religion . . .
Our people [the Catholics] have already got their eyes on the land
and the beautiful women but are conscious of the difficulty of the
state in admitting to the killing of some 900 to 1,000 people, and
for that reason we are asking for instruction of how we may
legalise their decease while safeguarding the reputation of the
state.[17]

That letter must be one of the vilest documents ever written.

The one man with the authority to put a stop to the Ustasha
terror, the Archbishop of Zagreb, Alojzije Stepinac, continued to
give both public and private support to Pavelić and his regime.
Apologists for Stepinac, who now campaign for his canonisation,
say that he kept quiet in order to stay in office and use his power
on behalf of Ustasha victims. It is certainly true that Stepinac cared
for and helped individual Serbs, Jews and Communists, especially
their children. A Slovene officer in the Royal Yugoslav Army,
Stanislav Rapotec, who went to Zagreb as a British agent in 1942,
said that Serbs and Jews spoke well of Stepinac. In five secret talks,
the Archbishop told Rapotec that he no longer believed in an
independent Croatia and hoped for the resurrection of Yugoslavia
after the war.[18] In view of his later statements in favour of an
independent Croatia, Stepinac was probably telling the Allies what
he then thought they wanted to hear.

Apologists for Stepinac also point out that in 1942 and 1943 he
preached a few sermons mildly rebuking forced conversion and
racial hatred. Yet Stepinac never once denounced in public the
massacre of the Serbs that accompanied forced conversion, nor the
role of the NDH in Hitler's 'Final Solution' to the Jewish question.
In the one strong letter to Pavelić, written on 24 February 1943,
Stepinac denounced the Jasenovac camp as 'a shameful stain on the
honour of the NDH . . . this is a disgrace to Croatia'.[19] Yet he

made this private denunciation only when he discovered that Roman Catholic priests, as well as Serbs, Gypsies and Jews, were among those done to death. The victims were a Croat Father, Franjo Rihar, and seven Slovene priests who had been expelled by the Germans to the NDH, where they failed to respect the shibboleths of the Ustasha. Archbishop Stepinac had written to Artuković, the Minister of the Interior, on behalf of Father Rihar, and received in reply the following letter, loaded with bureaucratic menace:

> Zagreb. 17th November 1942. In connection with your esteemed request of 2nd November 1942, notice is hereby given that Franjo Rihar, by the decree of this office of 20th April 1942, no. 26417/ 1942 was sentenced to forced detention in the concentration camp at Jasenovac for the period of three years . . . because as pastor of Gornja Stubica he did not celebrate a solemn high mass on the anniversary of the founding of the Independent State of Croatia . . . nor did he consent to sing the psalm *Te Deum Laudamus*, saying that it was nowhere prescribed in ecclesiastical usage.[20]

Stepinac appealed but Father Rihar had already spent three months at Jasenovac camp and was therefore dead. As Hubert Butler points out in his essay on Artuković, Archbishop Stepinac could hardly defend Father Rihar when he had himself exhorted his clergy to hold a *Te Deum* to honour the birthday of 'our glorious leader' Ante Pavelić. When the Bishop of Mostar, Alojzije Mišić, the only senior churchman brave enough to defy the Ustasha, died in February 1942, there was not one word of obituary in the clerical papers, nor any expression of sorrow from Stepinac. Indeed Stepinac flew to Mostar in August for the inauguration of Mišić's successor, an Ustasha Serb-hater.[21]

Stepinac's apologists find it hard to explain why he justified the Ustasha regime to its most influential supporter. Pope Pius XII. At least one of the cardinals during the Second World War, the Frenchman Eugene Tisserant, had taken the trouble to learn what was happening in the NDH, and he often rebuked the Ustasha's diplomat in the Vatican, Nikola Rusinović. 'I know for sure that even the Franciscans of Bosnia-Hercegovina have behaved atrociously,' Cardinal Tisserant said in one outburst. 'Father Simić, with a revolver in his hand, led an armed gang and destroyed Orthodox churches. No civilised and cultured man can behave like that.'[22]

Apart from this crusty Alsatian, the cardinals and the Pope himself preferred to listen to lies or cover-ups about the Ustasha regime from its main apologist, Archbishop Stepinac, as can be seen from this letter sent to Zagreb by Rusinović on 9 May 1942:

> As you must know, His Grace Stepinac has now returned to Zagreb after a twelve-day visit to Rome. He was in fine form and took a pugnacious attitude to all the enemies of the State! He submitted to the Holy Father a nine-page type-written report. He showed it to me and I can assure you it stands for our point of view. In attacking the Serbs, Chetniks and Communists, he has found things to say which even I had not thought of. No-one will be allowed to attack the Independent State of Croatia and show the Croatian people in a bad light. This was precisely the reason why he went to Rome, in order to stigmatise the lies that have spread in regard to the Holy See.[23]

On a visit to Rome in May 1943, Archbishop Stepinac told Rusinović's successor, Count Erwin Lobkowicz, that

> he had kept quiet about some things with which he is not at all in agreement in order to be able to show Croatia in the best possible light. He mentioned our laws on abortion, a point very well received in the Vatican. Basing his arguments on these laws, the Archbishop justified in part the measures used against the Jews, who in our country are the greatest defenders of crimes of this kind and the most frequent perpetrators of them.[24]

While the Holy See in Rome supported the NDH government, Italian soldiers and Mussolini's Fascist officials tried to protect its victims. The Italian army began by intervening to stop the slaughter of Serbs and went on to arm the Chetniks in Bosnia-Hercegovina and south-west Croatia. By the end of February 1942, the German Plenipotentiary General Glaise von Horstenau complained to Berlin that the Chetniks 'were parading in every village occupied by the Italians, fully armed . . . In the Herzegovina it has even come to a point where the Italians actually handed over a Croatian military column to the Chetniks. Croatian "independence" is being trodden underfoot.'[25] The Italian General Mario Roatta admitted in his memoirs, written after the war:

> So, in spite of the protests from Berlin and Zagreb and the requests from the government in Rome . . . we continued for our part in the collaboration of the Chetniks. Their units were resupplied with weapons etc. almost regularly until they reached a total force of about 30,000 men.[26]

Like all the Italian generals in Yugoslavia, Roatta would not hand over Jews to the NDH, because 'they would be interned at Jasenovac with the well-known consequences'. On 7 September 1941 his colleague General Vittorio Ambrosia gave his 'word of honour' to protect the Jews. The Italian attitude to the Jews was a constant source of annoyance to their German allies. The German Ambassador to the NDH, Siegfried Kasche, complained that about 500 Jews were living in Karlovac, some of them letting rooms to Italian officers, so that the Croats were unable 'to carry out measures against Jewry'. In December 1941 Oberleutnant Weiss of the German military economic section was shocked to find that in Dubrovnik:

> The relationship between Italian officers, Jews and Serbs is an absolutely undeniable fact. Italian officers are often seen with Jewish women in the Café Gradska . . . In Dubrovnik there are about 500 Jews. Most of them came from Sarajevo and were brought here with Italian help. 10,000 to 50,000 kune is the

normal price for smuggling across the border with false passes
. . . In Mostar things are cruder still. The Italians simply revoke
all Croatian orders and let the city overflow with Jews . . . The
director of the German Academy in Dubrovnik, Herr Arnold,
was invited together with some Croatian officials to a reception
. . . and was outraged by the arrogance of the Italian General
Amico . . . With regard to Croatia he said that the Italians were
there to protect the poor and persecuted – Jews and Serbs – from
brutality and terror.

Some Italians took bribes for helping the Jews but others acted out
of ordinary human decency, as Jonathan Steinberg reveals in a
charming story told to him by one Imre Rochlitz.

He and his family resorted to a trick worthy of the Marx Brothers.
Each member of the family got off the train in Dubrovnik saying
that another member of the family further back had the papers
and the last member said that the first had them. The carabinieri
simply shrugged and let them all off the train.[27]

Perhaps because their hearts were not in the war, the Italian
soldiers were loath to get involved in fighting the Partisans, and in
July 1942 they began to withdraw from the NDH to their territory
on the coast. As the Italians started to leave places like Bihać,
Drvar, Kalinovica, Karlovac and Petrova Gor, the Serbs and Jews
were dismayed to find themselves once more menaced by the
Ustasha. Some fled with the Italians, while those who remained
increasingly looked for protection to the Partisans, who had
reached this area at the end of the 'Long March'.

The Italians continued to help the Jews, who were now under
threat from the implementation of Hitler's 'Final Solution'. On 18
August 1942 Prince Otto von Bismarck, the minister in the German
Embassy in Rome, delivered a written demand that the Italian
government was to 'actuate those measures devised by the Germans
and the Croatians for the transfer in mass of the Jews of Croatia to

territories in the East'. On this document Mussolini scrawled the words 'Nulla osta' ('No objection').

The Italians in Yugoslavia, as in their zones of occupation in Greece and France, quite simply refused to obey this order. On 27 September 1942 General Roatta went to the main camp for Jews at Kraljevica and reaffirmed his word of honour to give them protection, adding that he regretted not having submarines to take them to Italy where they would be even safer. Throughout 1942, and until their country's surrender on 8 September 1943, the Italians did not hand over a single Jew to the Germans, the Croats, or anyone else who intended to kill them.

During the trial of Adolf Eichmann after the war, many survivors of Hitler's 'Final Solution' praised those Italians who had provided false documents, ignored their orders, bent the rules and in hundreds of other ways helped the Jews to escape. The Danes as well had behaved with honour; however, as Hannah Arendt observes in *Eichmann in Jerusalem*: 'What in Denmark was the result of an authentically political sense, an inbred comprehension of the requirements and responsibilities of citizenship and independence . . . was in Italy the outcome of the almost automatic general humanity of an old and cultured people.'

Although the Germans encouraged the persecution of Jews in the Independent State of Croatia, they disapproved of the massacre of the Orthodox Christians and saw that this was driving the Serbs to join the Partisans. German diplomats to the NDH were given a guided tour of Jasenovac camp and later reported back to Berlin that two-thirds of the inmates were Jews or Communists, and were better fed than ordinary workers in Zagreb.[28] However, the German Plenipotentiary General Glaise von Horstenau did not fall for the lies of the Ustasha, and came to regard the regime with detestation. By the autumn of 1942, he was calling Pavelić a man full of deceitfulness, mendacity and malice. He called Dido Kvaternik 'the pathological son of the pathological Marshal', and Dido's mother, 'half Jewish but nevertheless the only worthwhile member of the family'.[29]

Although von Horstenau does not appear to have gone in search of atrocity stories, he used his eyes and ears to record the almost casual barbarity of the Ustasha state. On one occasion, while driving by jeep along the River Sava, he came to what was described by Croatian military as a 'Partisan area':

> We saw no sign of them but there were plenty of ownerless horses and cattle, not to mention innumerable geese. At Crkveni Bok, an unhappy place where, under the leadership of an Ustasha lieutenant-colonel, some 500 yokels (*Lumpen*) of from fifteen to twenty years old met their end, all murdered, the women raped and then tortured to death, the children killed. I saw in the Sava river a woman's corpse with the eyes gouged out and a stick shoved into the sexual parts. This woman was at most twenty years old when she fell into the hands of these monsters. Any-where in a corner, the pigs are gorging themselves on an unburied human being. All the houses were looted. The 'lucky' inhabitants were consigned to one of the fearsome goods trains; many of these involuntary 'passengers' cut their veins on the journey.[30]

On another occasion during the autumn of 1942, von Horstenau witnessed 'more of the unspeakable swinishness of this gang of murderers and criminals'. He went first to Bjelovar where he was told that the Ustasha had apprehended four Communists, but had in fact rounded up and imprisoned 6,500 Serbs of every age and both sexes, before sending them off to the camps. At Sisak main railway station he saw a goods train that had been going back and forth for days, from whose barred windows 'staring women and children looked out, the victims of the magnificent (*herrlich*) Ustasha regime'.

At Sisak, the town where the young Tito had worked as a waiter and bowling-alley attendant and learned the locksmith's trade, the Ustasha had established their principal camp for Serb and Jewish children, which von Horstenau saw and described:

> We now went into the concentration camp in a converted factory. Frightful conditions. Few men, many women and children,

without sufficient clothing, sleeping on stone at night, pining away, wailing and crying. A camp commandant – in spite of the later, favourable judgement of the Poglavnik – a rogue; I ignored him but instead told my Ustasha guide: 'This is enough to make you puke.' And then worst of all: a room along whose walls, lying on straw which had just been laid down because of my inspection, something like fifty naked children, half of them dead, the other half dying. One should not forget that the inventors of the KZ [concentration camp] were the British in the Boer War. However, such places have reached the peak of abomination here in Croatia, under a Poglavnik installed by us. The most wicked of all must be Jasenovac, where no ordinary mortal is allowed to peer in.[31]

Von Horstenau spoke and reached out a helping hand to some of the wretched inmates of Sisak, and hoped that after his visit some would be allowed to go home – or where their homes had been. He also intervened on behalf of the Serbs who had gone to work in Germany and on their return had 'fallen into the claws of these criminals'. His constant intervention on behalf of the Serbs in the NDH was one of the reasons why he quarrelled so much with Pavelić and the Kvaternik family. It cannot be too often emphasised that the Fascist Italians and even the Nazi Germans exercised a humane and restraining influence on the Ustasha Croats.

Apart from any humanitarian feelings, the Germans and the Italians understood that the massacre of the Serbs was forcing survivors into the ranks of the Partisans. Although Tito's forces at the end of 1942 were nothing like as numerous as historians later pretended, he was now the main political force in western Bosnia-Hercegovina, with mounting support from Serbs, Croats, Slovenes and Muslims in other parts of Yugoslavia. Hitler himself was one of the first to spot the Partisan danger. In November 1942 he summoned Pavelić to Vinnitsa in the Ukraine to discuss the situation in Yugoslavia. From 18 to 20 December Hitler, Ribbentrop and Field Marshal Keitel met with the Italians at Görlitz in East Prussia, to make more detailed plans for an operation. There was a further meeting at Rome on 3 January 1943, attended by

General Alexander Löhr, the German commander in south-east Europe, and General Roatta, on the Italian side, as well as Pavelić's generals. Then, on 20 January 1943, four German divisions, including the 7th SS Prinz Eugen Division, four Italian divisions and two Croat divisions came together to start 'Operation Weiss'.

8

The Fourth and Fifth Offensives

From mid-November 1942 to mid-January 1943, Tito presided over his Bihać Republic in north-west Bosnia. The Partisans brought out their newspapers, meted out justice to Ustasha criminals, reopened the schools and permitted freedom of worship to the Muslims and both Christian churches. More was heard of the horrors taking place at Jasenovac camp, which lay downstream from Bihać, on the River Una. Two Jews who had killed their guard and escaped to Bihać recounted their tale to a Partisan newspaper; the newpaper's Jewish typesetter had lost all his family in Jasenovac. A few months earlier the commandant of Jasenovac, Maks Luburić, had arrived in Bihać to teach the local Ustasha some of the tricks of his trade, for instance how one could kill twelve Serbs with a single bullet, and why one must cut open a corpse's belly before it is thrown in the river.

The Muslims, who form the majority in this north-west corner of Bosnia, were beginning to trust the Partisans. Few of the young men wanted to join in the Muslim SS brigades, which Hitler and Ante Pavelić tried to recruit with the help of the violently anti-British Mufti of Jerusalem. A Muslim committee in Sarajevo wrote to Hitler on 1 November 1942, commending his policy in the Middle East but complaining about the Ustasha massacre of the Serbs. In particular the committee accused the government of the NDH of trying to inflame the Serbs against the Muslims:

To achieve two ends with a single stroke, that is to annihilate the Muslims as well as the Orthodox Serbs in Bosnia-Hercegovina, they sent several Ustasha battalions from Zagreb wearing our caps [the fez], with orders to kill the Serbs, at the same time addressing each other with Muslim names. The aim of this devilish plan was to show how Muslims slaughter Serbs.[1]

The journalist turned Partisan Vladimir Dedijer found the Muslims receptive to arguments against the NDH. After a government air raid had destroyed a mosque, Dedijer came across an old Muslim woman weeping beside the ruins. When he pointed out that this was the work of Ante Pavelić, the little old lady exclaimed: 'May a dog f— his mother!' After a speech by Tito to more than a hundred female Partisans, Dedijer was told that in Dalmatia Catholic women were coming to trust the Partisans to protect them from the Chetniks, even shouting the slogan: 'Long live the Virgin Mary and the Communist Party!'[2] A famous Croatian painter arrived in Bihać to join the venerable poet Vladimir Nazor, who now was writing under the Marxist muse:

> With Tito and Stalin
> Two heroic sons
> Not even Hell
> Can bother us . . .

It was during the winter of 1942–3 that Yugoslavia changed from a sideshow into a major theatre of the war in Europe. The German defeat at Stalingrad and the loss of all North Africa convinced first Hitler and then Mussolini that there would soon be an Allied invasion of 'Fortress Europe'. The Anglo-Americans might strike first at France, various Mediterranean islands or the Italian mainland, but Hitler inclined to believe they would opt for the Balkans, the 'soft underbelly of Europe'. At a top-level German-Italian conference in East Prussia from 18 to 20 December 1942 Hitler said that, 'in the event of an Anglo-Saxon landing, assisted by the Balkan nationalists, the situation would be irretrievable', and even the possibility of invasion made it imperative to destroy the guerrillas.[3]

Even before the launching of 'Operation Weiss', the attack on the Partisans, on 20 January 1943, there were signs of a conflict of interest between the Axis allies. The Italian military view presented by General Roatta and justified in his post-war memoirs, was that anti-Communist Chetniks were useful auxiliary troops against the far more dangerous Partisans. The historian F. W. Deakin, who had himself served in the military mission to Tito, wrote in *The Brutal Friendship*, a study of German-Italian relations:

> The real interest of the Italian Command was to execute a gradual withdrawal of all their forces on Yugoslav soil, in order to hold only a central belt against possible Allied landings, to withdraw as many troops as possible for the ultimate defence of the Italian mainland, and to leave Chetnik bands armed with Italian weapons, to foment civil war in the interior against the Partisans.[4]

The Germans, on the other hand, thought that the Chetniks were pro-British and should not be armed by the Axis.

While Draža Mihailović longed for an Anglo-American landing and the return to the throne of King Peter, Tito regarded the prospect with dread and implacable opposition, for just the same reason. He wanted to conquer the Chetniks more than he wanted to drive the foreigners out of the country. This conflict of interests led to the furtive and still mysterious wheeling and dealing by which for a time the Partisans and the Germans made common cause against the Chetniks and the Italians.

Even without the help of an Allied invasion, by early 1943 the Chetniks controlled most of Serbia proper, the Sandjak, Montenegro and eastern Bosnia-Hercegovina, almost down to the coast where the Allies would probably disembark. In many regions, especially the Sandjak, the Chetniks had ruthlessly 'cleansed' the Muslim population, on many occasions slaughtering unarmed men, women and children.[5]

The commandant of Chetnik operations 'somewhere in the free mountains of Hercegovina' sent back this cocky letter to Mihailović on 5 September 1943:

I have been asked to report on the achievements of the Chetnik movement in eastern Bosnia-Hercegovina from Zenica to Dubrovnik . . . In all the towns except Foča, there is about one battalion of the Italian army and a small number of Croat Home Guards. The Chetniks are masters everywhere outside the towns.

Even in the towns we take the decisions and sensibly use the Italians for our purposes. The Croats have no real government. They sit and slumber in their barracks in the towns. They can't move because of the Chetniks. The same goes for the Muslims.

In the villages, the main roads and even in Mostar itself, the air rings with Serbian songs and cheers for the King and his minister Draža Mihailović. They sing:

> Pavelić you're a swine,
> Your army's floating down the Drina.
> Pavelić, you're a pig,
> Your army's pushing up the grass.
> Pavelić, you son of a bitch,
> Where do you think you'll be, come winter?[6]

In spite of German objections, General Roatta determined to use some of his 30,000 Chetnik allies in 'Operation Weiss', which was due to begin on 20 January. They were to be a blocking force to cut the retreat of the Partisans from western Bosnia to Montenegro. In the middle of January, Chetnik units were taken to key points along the route, and Draža Mihailović sent an order to all his commanders telling them to prepare for decisive action.[7]

At this time Tito believed that the British, the Chetniks and the Italians were acting in concert in order to bring back 'imperialism' to Yugoslavia. As early as June 1942, he reported to Moscow that the Yugoslav government in exile had got in touch with the Italians through its representative at the Vatican. Captured Chetniks said that the arms they received from the Italians had been paid for by the British.

When 'Operation Weiss' had begun, Tito reported to Moscow that the Italians had 25,000 Chetniks ranged against him in the Mostar district alone. All this, he believed, was the work of the exiled government in London. His fear of the Chetnik–British–Italian plot sounded at times almost fantastic: 'On Mihailović's staff there are now about twenty-five English officers in Serbian national costume (*u srpskoj nacionalnoj nošnji*) . . . Their senior officer is a colonel who has personally announced that he represents the English government. Moreover Mihailović and the English officers often meet with representatives of the Italian government . . . Not only among our soldiers but among the whole population, hatred is growing against the English for not starting a second front in Europe.'[8] Did Tito really believe that the British were in cahoots with the Italians, or was this a ploy to turn the Russians against Mihailović? I suspect the latter. Whatever he said to Stalin, Tito in fact dreaded an Anglo-American second front – if it should open in Yugoslavia.

Throughout the period of slaughter in Bosnia-Hercegovina starting in January 1943, the four main protagonists – Germans, Italians, Chetniks and Partisans – were all to a certain extent at odds with each other, regardless of any alliance. This led to the strangest episode in the life of Tito, his parley and efforts to make an alliance with Hitler's generals, against the Chetniks, the British and by implication the Soviet Union itself.

'Operation Weiss' began on 20 January 1943 with a huge German bombardment by tanks, artillery and air attacks throughout western Bosnia-Hercegovina, sweeping the Partisans towards the River Neretva where they would face the Chetniks and the Italians. Behind Tito's army there followed a thousand wounded and many more women and children, who saw the Partisans as their only protection. The suffering of this multitude, all of them hungry and some of them barefoot in spite of the snow, was made more hideous by a typhus epidemic.

Although thousands of Partisans were killed, or died of disease

and privations, many more thousands of young men and women
were ready to take their place, in what was at last becoming a mass
revolt. Volunteers poured in from all over the stony land of the
Karst, Dalmatian Croats as well as the Serbs and Muslims from
Hercegovina. This new breed of Partisans from one of the harshest
regions of Europe were fired by a fanaticism that terrified even their
friends. The English writer Stephen Clissold, who always regarded
the Yugoslavs with mixed emotions of admiration and horror, has
told how the young Hercegovinians would, on joining the Communist Party during the war, demonstrate their loyalty by first shooting
their 'bourgeois' parents. Ten years after the war, when I shared a
room in a student hostel in Sarajevo with young Hercegovinians and
Montenegrins, they used to regale each other with stories of what
fun it had been to witness the execution of the Italian prisoners,
especially when the victims wept and called out for their mothers.

These stories came back to me when I read the account by
Milovan Djilas of what happened at Prozor on 17 February, as the
Partisans were fighting their way through a cordon of Chetnik and
Italian troops. During a battle by the River Rama, a tributary of the
main Neretva, the Italians at first refused to surrender, and when
they eventually laid down their arms:

> All the Italian troops – the entire Third Battalion of the 259th
> Regiment of the Murge Division – were put to death. We put into
> effect the conditions they had rejected, and vented our bitterness.
> Only the drivers were spared – to help transport the munitions
> and the wounded. Many corpses were tossed into the Rama River.
> Several got caught among the logs, and I shared with our officers a
> malicious joy at the thought of Italian officers on the bridges and
> embankments of Mostar stricken with horror at the sight of the
> Neretva choked with the corpses of their soldiers.[9]

While the Italians were learning the gruesome nature of war in
Bosnia-Hercegovina, Hitler was trying to make them abandon the
Chetniks. In a letter to Mussolini dated 16 February 1943, he said
that 'Operation Weiss' had started well, with heavy losses to Tito in

men and material. However, Hitler went on to warn: 'If a landing takes place tomorrow, Duce, anywhere in the Balkans, these Communists, followers of Mihailović and all the other irregulars, will be in accord on one thing: launching an immediate attack on the German and Italian armed forces . . . in support of the enemy landings.'[10]

In spite of these admonitions, General Roatta refused to disband the Chetnik troops fighting beside the Italians in a battle where even surrender meant death. When the Italians proved stubborn, the German Foreign Minister Ribbentrop went to Rome on 25 February to reiterate Hitler's annoyance:

The situation which had now arisen in Croatia through Roatta's policy, caused the Fuehrer grave anxiety. The Fuehrer understood that Roatta wanted to spare Italian lives, but also thought that with this policy he was in a sense trying to drive the Devil out with Beelzebub . . . [All] the bands must be destroyed, men, women and children, because their continued existence endangered the lives of German and Italian men, women and children.

Ribbentrop even suggested that the Italians should murder Mihailović.[11]

Perhaps because he had sensed the danger, Draža Mihailović did not command his troops in action along the Neretva valley from February to early April 1943, sitting it out at Lipovo. As Minister of Defence in the government in exile in London, he could not be seen to have direct contact with the Italians. However the Chetniks, the Italians, the Germans and the Croatian legionaries nearly succeeded in trapping and wiping out Tito's army.

Vladimir Dedijer, looking after the sick and wounded at Prozor in central Bosnia, wrote on 6 March of being surrounded, from Gornji Vakuf by Germans, from Konjic by Germans and Chetniks, from Ravno by Germans and NDH legionaries, and from Duvno by Chetniks and Italians: 'In front of us is the Neretva canyon. A fast river, 80 metres wide, on the other side the cliffs of Prenj are 2,200

metres high. And Chetniks all over the surrounding hills. Only the
sky is left to us but even that is full of planes from dawn to dusk.'[12]
Dedijer described in his diary how 25,000 soldiers were struggling
to cross a slippery makeshift bridge on the Neretva. Even the
healthy men felt dizzy when they looked down, and the wounded
crossed on all fours. During the air attacks the horses panicked, and
everyone feared that the Germans might enter the valley at any
moment.

Tito was, as ever, outwardly cool, though Djilas wrote that he
frequently changed his orders. But he was never petty as a commander and did not stifle initiative in his colleagues. Djilas also
remarked that Tito was always more confident when laying down
strategy that was political rather than military. It was now, in the
first days of March, in a mill-house over the River Rama, that Tito
conceived the most daring and controversial stratagem of his long
career. He decided to make a truce, even an alliance, with the
Germans.

In the battle at Gornji Vakuf during the first days of March, the
Partisans captured a number of Germans including one Major
Stoecker. Remembering how the previous year they had used the
German civilian Hans Ott to effect the release of some of their
prisoners, Ranković, Djilas and others suggested to Tito that they
might reopen talks. On the face of it, this was a simple offer to hand
over some of the Germans, including Stoecker, in return for some
of the Communists now in the gaols of the NDH, including Tito's
common-law wife Herta Hass, by whom he had had a child shortly
before the Axis invasion. The Partisans also wished to be recognised
as a 'belligerent force' to ensure the proper treatment of casualties
and prisoners.

In fact Tito wanted very much more than this. His most pressing
need was to break through the Chetnik forces now blocking his way
across the River Neretva and then to press on through eastern
Bosnia-Hercegovina to the comparative safety of Montenegro and
the Sandjak. His long-term need was to come to an understanding
with the Germans by which, in return for ceasing attacks on their
forces and lines of communications, the Partisans would be given

carte blanche to destroy the Chetniks in eastern Yugoslavia. Tito was also willing to talk with the Germans on joint military action against the expected British landing.

Tito authorised Major Stoecker to send a letter through the lines suggesting talks about the exchange of prisoners. A reply came two days later giving the time and place for receiving a Partisan mission. Tito then had to choose the men for what was a risky as well as delicate enterprise, for all of them might be handed over to the Gestapo. One obvious choice was the lawyer Vladimir Velebit, whose father had been an officer in the Austro-Hungarian army and who himself spoke German well enough to pass as a Viennese. While Velebit went as a diplomat, Koča Popović represented the Partisan army, since he had fought in Spain and had proved himself one of Tito's ablest generals. He spoke excellent French as well as some German and he was also violently anti-British, still more so than most of the Partisans. Milovan Djilas represented the Politburo but because of his high position he had to use an assumed name; indeed his identity was kept so secret that his part in the mission was not revealed until thirty years later. Djilas knew only rudimentary German 'but after all we didn't intend to discuss Goethe and Kant'.[13]

Even before the mission departed, Djilas had raised the question that must have been troubling all the members of the Central Committee: 'What will the Russians say?' Tito immediately answered in anger, directed at Stalin rather than Djilas: 'Well, they also think first of their own people and their own army.' That outburst, even more than the truce with the Germans, deeply affected Djilas: 'That was the first time that a Politburo member – and it was Tito – expressed so vehemently any difference with the Soviets: a difference not in ideology but in life.' In one of his regular radio messages to Moscow, Tito mentioned the possibility of an exchange of prisoners but made no reference to any further intentions. The Russians, however, were not deceived and immediately radioed back: 'Is it possible you will cease the struggle against the worst enemy of mankind?'[14]

At the break of day on 11 March, the three Partisan delegates set off for Prozor bearing a little white flag on a stick. When they had made themselves known to a German guard post, the three were blindfolded and taken by car to Gornji Vakuf to meet a German lieutenant-general. After initial coldness, the Germans became more talkative, impressing the Communists by their freedom from Nazi ideology or rigid military discipline. The Germans admired the fighting quality of the Partisans but clearly were horrified by the war in Bosnia-Hercegovina: 'Look what you've done to your own country! A wasteland! Cinders! Women are begging on streets, typhus is raging, children are dying of hunger. And we wish to bring you roads, electricity, hospitals.'

From Gornji Vakuf the three Partisans were taken to Sarajevo, where they encountered Ott, the German engineer they had captured at Livno the previous August. Djilas stayed in a riverside flat that belonged to the wife of a Royal Yugoslav officer who was now a POW: 'Like all Serbian women, she was an excellent cook.' While the other two stayed in Sarajevo, Djilas went back to the Partisans to begin the exchange of prisoners. Tito listened carefully to his experiences and characteristically wanted to hear his impressions about the Germans as human beings. 'Yes,' he said afterwards, 'it seems that the German army has kept something of the spirit of chivalry.'[15]

Although Djilas does not mention this in his memoirs, it is clear that during negotiations the Germans were holding back from hostile action, leaving the Partisans to sort out the Chetniks. Later Djilas returned to Sarajevo, then went on to Zagreb, the capital of the NDH. In Zagreb the talks extended beyond the exchange of prisoners. The Partisans explained that they wanted a free hand to crush the Chetniks, specifically in the Sandjak and more generally in the east of the country. In return they would call off attacks on the Zagreb–Belgrade railway and other German strategic interests such as mining. The Germans did not raise the question of whether the Partisans would continue fighting the Ustasha, thereby implying their approval. Nor did the talks concern the Italians. Both sides talked seriously about joint action against the British in the event of invasion. According to Djilas: 'We didn't shirk from declaring that we would fight the British if they landed . . . and we really believed that we would have to fight them if – as could be concluded from their propaganda and official pronouncements – they subverted our power, that is if they supported the Chetnik establishment.'[16]

Unknown to Tito, the Germans had broken his radio code and knew from his signals to Moscow that he opposed a British invasion. According to William Hoettl, the senior officer of Branch vi South of the *Sicherheits Dienst* in Zagreb: 'All this information was not taken very seriously by the German Secret Service until suddenly the arrival of General Velebit put a very different complexion on the whole affair.'[17] Not knowing the true identity of Djilas, the author thought that Velebit was the leader of the delegation. He and General Glaise von Horstenau now clearly believed that the Partisans expected a British invasion.

Milovan Djilas, who is by far the best source on these 'March Consultations' (as they were coyly described by Yugoslav historians), was called away from the talks in Zagreb to return to the Partisan headquarters. In Sarajevo, while on his way back, he went to the German army intelligence office where they were holding some of the Communist prisoners to be exchanged. A woman washing and scrubbing the floor suddenly called out Djilas's nickname and he recognised one of his close comrades and friends: 'With her wet arms she clasped me about the neck and wailed on my chest. The German officer was moved to tears as I comforted her.'[18]

When Djilas arrived back in Kalinovik, where the Partisans now had their headquarters, Tito seemed much less interested in the progress of the talks: 'The Germans had in fact already called a halt to their drive, while our units had won a hard-fought victory over Pavle Djurišić's Chetniks and were penetrating into Hercegovina towards Montenegro and Sandjak.' From German sources, we know that talks continued after Djilas went back to report to Tito. Glaise von Horstenau seems to have taken a liking to Velebit, especially when he discovered that Velebit's father had served in the Habsburg army, the 'k-u-k' ('kingly-and-kaiserly').[19] They discussed an extension of the truce by which the Germans would refrain from attacking the Partisans in western Bosnia, provided the

Partisans refrained from attacking the Germans in Slavonia, north of the River Sava.

The Yugoslav archives show that Tito wrote to the commandant of the 6th Bosnian Brigade, telling him to continue attacking the Chetniks but to avoid fighting the Germans on the way to the Sandjak. Similar orders, written partly in Spanish, were sent to the 1st Bosnian Corps and the 1st Proletarian Brigade. General Glaise von Horstenau personally made it possible for Velebit to deliver a letter from Tito to the Partisans in Slavonia.[20] It seems that von Horstenau and local German intelligence officers favoured a deal with the Partisans but knew that such an arrangement would not please the German High Command or the Foreign Office. Von Horstenau's approach through the Secret Service and Himmler clearly did not work, for at the end of March Hitler announced that he did not deal with rebels – he shot them.[21]

Djilas believes that the 'March Consultations' could not have led to any significant result: 'This was because we essentially sought a respite, while the Germans were setting a trap for us.'[22] The trap was sprung in May, when the Germans almost succeeded in destroying the Partisans in 'Operation Schwarz', the Fifth Offensive. Meanwhile the 2nd Proletarian Division had scored a crushing victory over the Chetniks; and by early April the Partisans were standing upon the banks of the River Drina, preparing to cross to the Sandjak, Montenegro and, as they imagined, safety.

Tito's escape across the River Neretva, once hailed as a triumph of tactical feint and daring, was really made possible by a deal with the Germans. Nevertheless, Tito was pleased with himself to the point of becoming dangerously overconfident. When a military engineer warned him that the Drina was too swollen to be crossed in safety, Tito brushed him aside and remarked to Djilas: 'You know the experts as a rule don't take into account the human will. Humans who are determined to do something, achieve it, even if it's considered impossible according to calculation.'[23] On this occasion Tito was proved right, though later the gods, or rather the German army, would teach him a lesson about the peril of hubris.

In the six weeks between 'Operation Weiss' and the launching of

'Operation Schwarz', the Partisans rested and even enjoyed themselves at the village of Govža, high in the mountains of the Sandjak.
The local Muslim militia had fled from the villages into the woods,
but even there they did not attack the Communist leaders who
hunted for chamois and roe-deer. Tito was now accompanied by his
common-law wife, Herta Hass. The other Partisan leaders noticed
with satisfaction that Herta's presence had a restraining and calming
effect on Zdenka, Tito's termagant mistress and secretary.

In his 1943 May Day speech, delivered at Govža, up in the
mountains of the Sandjak, Tito predicted, apparently with the
utmost confidence, that next year's speech would be made in Belgrade. One of the reasons for this confidence was Tito's belief that
he was at last starting to win the trust of the Serbs who had been so
hostile eighteen months earlier. The Partisans had won a military
victory over the Chetniks in eastern Bosnia-Hercegovina, and now
believed that their principal foe was morally and politically desperate. In Montenegro, at the end of February, Draža Mihailović had
made an imprudent and possibly drunken speech in which he
declared that his enemies were the Croats, Muslims and Communists, and that only when he had dealt with them would he turn on
the foreign invaders. The senior British liaison officer Colonel
Bailey heard the speech and reported it back to London, where it
served the purpose of those who wanted to abandon the Chetniks.
On 11 May the Yugoslav government in exile, probably under
British coercion, instructed Mihailović to make up his differences
with the Partisans and to join the fight against the Germans.

Those Partisans who knew of the 'March Consultations' heard all
this with private amusement. They still regarded themselves as on
the side of the Germans against the British and the royalist exiles.
Moreover Mihailović and the Chetniks were moving towards a
'Great Serb' chauvinism that made it improbable that they could
ever again rule a united Yugoslavia. And in 1943 Mihailović's
commander in Montenegro issued a circular letter addressed 'To
Chetnik intellectuals', explaining the propaganda they were to
spread in Serbian villages. Among the aims to be announced: 'We
are seeking a pure national state. If we achieve that, there will be

land to spare, because more than 2.5 million minority people will have to leave our country. Everyone will be able to share that land, starting with those who today are striving to build our free state.'[24]

Only gradually did it dawn on the Partisans that the Germans had scrapped the arrangements made during the 'March Consultations' and were now mounting their Fifth Offensive, under the code-name 'Operation Schwarz', to complete the work of 'Weiss'. Although Djilas now seems to believe that the Germans were tricking the Partisans all along, it may be that 'Schwarz' was thought up only after Hitler had said, 'I don't parley with rebels – I shoot them!'

The first warning that 'Schwarz' was under way came from Arso Jovanović, who was proceeding from Slovenia through western Bosnia, and who sent a message ahead to notify the Partisans that they should expect an attack from the force that had carried out 'Operation Weiss'; he promised to come to their aid with the Partisan 2nd Division. Then German units began to appear in the Lim and Tara valleys, two of the gorges and canyons forming the headwater zone of the River Drina. There were soon to be 120,000 German, Italian, Bulgarian and Croatian troops attempting to encircle and then destroy the 20,000 Partisans.

The Battle of Sutjeska (pronounced Soot-yes-ka), as it came to be known, was fought with everything from planes and artillery to knives and rifle butts, and it almost destroyed the Partisan army. It was after the Battle of Sutjeska, in which he was wounded, that Tito began to be seen as a living legend, celebrated in countless songs, kolo dances, histories, novels and even a Hollywood film, in which he was played by Richard Burton. Whatever one thinks of Tito before and after the Battle of Sutjeska, it is hard to deny that during those terrible weeks he was a hero.

As sometimes happened, Tito was nervous before the start of the crisis and took a few days to gather his strength and resolution. When the first report arrived of advancing enemy troops, Tito waved the paper in the air and shouted at Djilas and Ranković: 'The Germans are lying! We have never been in greater danger! We have to go back to western Bosnia. There is no other way out!' 'So much for our negotiations,' Djilas said bitterly; but the ever phlegmatic Ranković told him: 'This is no time to talk about that.'[25]

As the Partisans moved through northern Montenegro towards the head of the Sutjeska gorge, the ever quarrelsome Zdenka chose this time to abuse the guards, the cooks and even Tito himself. Her rival Herta had left, and Zdenka was always able to bully Tito when he was on his own, although he himself had a temper. Djilas thought that Tito was under Zdenka's 'emotional influence . . . she did not have any other influences over him'. On this occasion Djilas himself intervened in his forthright Montenegrin fashion:

> At this point I boiled over and yelled at Zdenka to shut up or I would grab her by the hair and throw her over the cliff, because the Central Committee had other worries than to put up with her hysteria. Tito kept silent; Zdenka got scared and shut up. I then resumed correct relations with her but we were never cordial.[26]

In the first days of June, the 2nd Proletarian Brigade had taken Suha, the entrance to the Sutjeska gorge, but the Partisans were still unaware of the great enemy build-up in the mountains they had to cross to get into Bosnia. The Partisan columns with their pack-horses and wounded came under a storm of machine-gun fire, shells from mountain artillery pieces and, worst of all, incessant bombing by Stukas, Heinkels and even Fieseler-Storch reconnaissance planes.

Tito assigned to Djilas the unenviable task of commanding the rearguard division and trying to bring out the badly wounded. Although Djilas displayed outstanding personal courage in leading his men against a row of machine-gun bunkers – he killed at least two Germans with his knife – he failed in the almost impossible task of saving the wounded. Neither side took prisoners during the Battle of Sutjeska. When one of the Montenegrin women fighting alongside Djilas was hit in the thigh and could not move forward, her own husband shot her and then himself.

Tito commanded the main force in the break-out, supported by

Ranković, Moša Pijade and Tito's biographer Vladimir Dedijer. In the horror and personal tragedy of those days, Dedijer became for a time something more than a journalist. His introduction to *Tito Speaks*, in which he recalls the Battle of Sutjeska, is one of the finest and most affecting accounts of warfare ever written.

At dawn on the day that the battle came to a climax, Tito had reached the summit of Milinklada mountain, towering above the Sutjeska gorge. Dedijer and Moša Pijade were down at the foot of the mountain when the bombing started again. They were waiting for Tito and also for Dedijer's wife, Olga, a doctor who headed the surgical team of the 2nd Division. She too was up near the summit of Milinklada.

About noon a courier came running to us with a letter.

'Tito is wounded. The Germans are advancing. Send the escort battalion urgently.'

We in the valley set off uphill. Suddenly a girl with tangled hair and a flushed face shouted through the woods. 'Comrade Vlado, Olga is calling you to carry her out. She has been seriously wounded.' It was nurse Ruska from Olga's unit. In a few words she told me what had happened. A bomb had hit them and Olga's shoulder had been torn away.

Dedijer hurried up the hill past the wounded coming down in great numbers. The Stukas appeared again, diving almost down to the tops of the beech trees. The stench of powder was suffocating, and day had been turned to night by the smoke. When it cleared, Dedijer saw lying close by a Bosnian youth with large, dark eyes. Both his legs had been blown off: 'He was dying; he waved to me and whispered, "Long live Stalin!"'

Dedijer found his wife, who tried to smile and then said, 'Don't be afraid, but the wound is serious.' Tito came by with his arm in a bandage and asked her, 'How are you Olga? Are you badly hurt?' For more than ten days the Partisans moved as fast as they could, north into Bosnia, under relentless attack. There was no time for surgical operations and Tito was bandaged only once. Dedijer found him one night in a high fever, dictating a radiogram about the battle to Moscow.

Olga kept up with the column, sometimes on horseback, sometimes on foot, until on the ninth day gas gangrene set in, and her arm had to be amputated while German bullets thudded into the wooden walls of the makeshift operating theatre. When she regained consciousness, she said to Dedijer: 'Don't worry, I can't be a surgeon but I'll be a children's doctor.' Just after he left his wife to return to the fighting, Dedijer felt a tremendous blow on the side of the head, and tumbled into a ditch. Shrapnel had lodged in his skull.

The next day, feverish and with the wound still bleeding, Dedijer walked along beside the stretcher bearing his wife. A doctor, a friend of Olga's, wanted to give her a shot of camphor to ease the pain;

> 'Stanokja, don't waste that precious drug,' Olga said. 'Keep it to save some comrades' lives.'
> They put down the stretcher to rest a while. Olga called me:
> 'Take care of Milica. See that she is brought up properly and let her be an army doctor . . .'
> A few minutes later she breathed her last. It was dark, the wind was soughing through the giant spruces. We dug a grave for Olga with knives and our bare hands because we had no spades; the Germans were already in the village down below where we could have borrowed them. Partisan Laza, a miner, threw earth out of the grave with his hands.
> 'Vlado, we're down to the rock,' he said.
> We laid my wife in the shallow grave, covered her with turf and then made a mound of stone. We removed our caps; a salvo of four shots was fired and Partisan Laza exclaimed: 'Long live her memory!' Then we set out through the dark forest to catch up with our units.[27]

The main Partisan army had travelled as far as Kladanj in northeast Bosnia, where they were joined by Djilas and the rearguard on

3 July 1943. Tito no longer wore a bandage and made light of the wound, which he said had been only a graze. Nobody at the time believed the story, later a legend, that Tito's dog had died in an effort to shield his master. However, Tito had lost so much weight that a ring he had bought in Moscow had slipped off his finger and now was lost for ever. Ranković looked like somebody dying of tuberculosis.

Djilas and another officer of the rearguard had to explain their failure to save the wounded. 'Tito listened to our report in despair but without a single word of reproach or criticism,' Djilas records in his memoir *Wartime*, 'nor did he reproach me later, at least not while I was in power. However I was loath to speak of the Sutjeska.' He was obviously loath to write about it more than thirty years later.[28]

The Partisans had lost about 7,000 fighters, more than a third of their army, during the Fifth Offensive. The Germans had also suffered, as their commander, General Alexander Löhr, conceded afterwards:

> The fighting was extraordinarily heavy. All the commanders agreed that their troops were going through the most bitter struggle of the war. A ferocious Partisan attack which struck the Second Battalion of the 369th Division in particular effected a breakthrough on this front near Jelasca and Miljevina. All the enemy forces managed to retreat through this front and to disappear in the mountains to the north. The German troops were too tired and exhausted to be able to do anything about it, and there were no reserves.[29]

From this moment on the Germans considered the Partisans a greater threat in the Balkans than even the possibility of an Anglo-American invasion.

For the first three weeks of July, the Partisans rested and built up their strength in the mountains of north-eastern Bosnia. Tito improved his mind by talking of life and literature with the poet Vladimir Nazor, who had somehow survived the Fifth Offensive.

Although Tito was pleased and flattered by the support of Nazor, who had never been a man of the Left, he was disappointed that he had not been joined by that other distinguished Croatian writer, Miroslav Krleža, who had been a Communist in the 1920s. Nazor himself saw the irony of this. During the Spanish Civil War he had twitted his fellow author: 'You're a Communist, why aren't you in Spain?' Krleža had answered: 'I have a horror of death, corpses and stench. I had enough of it in Galicia in World War One.'[30] In spite of his disappointment, Tito did not hold a grudge against Krleža, and after the war welcomed him back as a friend and member of the Party. This freedom from vindictiveness was one of the pleasantest features of Tito's personality.

A minor incident that occurred during the stay at Kladanj showed not only Tito's readiness to forgive but also his lifelong fondness for animals. After the Fifth Offensive, in which the Partisans had little to eat except grass and bark, they were eager to get some of their weight back. In order to add more meat to the daily rations, the quartermaster-major slaughtered the Partisans' cow, which had stopped giving milk and therefore needed replacement. However, the quartermaster failed to understand that the beast, having gone with the Partisans through several offensives, was now considered a pet or at least an old friend. When Tito heard that the cow was dead, he lost his temper and ordered the quartermaster stripped of his rank.

The wily Ranković, who knew better than anyone how to deal with Tito, told the quartermaster to disappear for a bit, while he worked on the 'Old Man'. A few evenings later, the Partisan leaders were chatting peacefully round the camp-fire, when Ranković let drop in a casual manner: 'You know that cow had a broken leg.' When Tito asked indignantly why no one had told him before, Ranković answered in gentle reproach: 'You blew your top and they were scared.' The quartermaster was reinstated and even promoted, while Tito joined in eating the luckless cow.[31]

Towards the end of July 1943, Tito turned his mind again to fighting. The Allied invasion of Sicily on 10 July, and the fall of Palermo less than a fortnight later, made it probable that the

Italians would soon drop out of the war, giving the Partisans the chance to seize their equipment and much of their territory on the Adriatic littoral.

Tito decided that he, Djilas and Ranković would return to western Bosnia and then go on to Croatia itself, where an increasing number of Roman Catholics were turning against the Ustasha regime. The 2nd Division would go back to Montenegro to stop the Chetniks from getting their hands on Italian equipment, as well as to form a base for a thrust into Serbia proper.

On the march across western Bosnia, Tito heard of the fall of Mussolini on 25 July 1943, an item of news that increased the sense of euphoria in the Partisan ranks. In the villages through which the Partisans passed, the peasants were no longer so frightened of the Ustasha and the Germans, while the Muslims especially seemed to be 'genial, wonderful people'.[32] In this part of the NDH, the Ustasha presence had almost vanished outside the towns, and many of these were falling to the Partisans. Perhaps because he was safest in Partisan country, Tito remained in western Bosnia, sending Djilas and Ranković into Croatia proper, where the Ustasha still exercised power and might have been able to trap the chief of the Communist Party.

Politicians representing the pre-war Croatian Peasant Party had got in touch with Tito, hoping to form some kind of alliance, but few of the Catholic Croats were ready to join the Partisans, with their Marxist, atheist doctrines. In Slavonia, where Djilas went to report on recruitment, the overwhelming majority of the Partisans came from the Orthodox villages. When he enquired of a local commander whether even a third of his men were Croats, the sheepish reply was, 'Well, we're getting there.'[33]

The Ustasha were still a fanatical enemy in the Croatian heart-land and in the Military Frontier region. After a savage battle at Otošac in the Lika, the Partisans yelled at the Ustasha that they had lost the war. 'We know that,' came the answering roar, 'but there's still time to rub out a lot of you.' They had even composed a sardonic song:

Oh Russia, all will belong to you,
But of Serbs there will be few![34]

On 8 September 1943 Tito heard the news of Italy's unconditional surrender, and promptly joined in a race with the Germans
to seize weapons, supplies and territory on the coast and the
islands. Nor did the Partisans forget the thousands of Jews who
had taken refuge with the Italians and were now exposed to the
murderous savagery of the Germans and Ustasha. Several hundred
Jews who had been in a camp on the island of Rab were ferried
across to Crikvenica where they lodged for a time in three empty
boarding-schools. As the Germans advanced down the coast from
Rijeka, the Jews were taken into the hinterland to be lodged in
villages held by the Partisans. Tito decided against forming a
special Jewish fighting unit, which might have attracted Ustasha
attack, so those who were fit to serve were taken into the regular
Partisan army. Many Jews who did not become soldiers went into
shopkeeping or trade, thereby interfering with what was called 'the
Partisan economy'. However, from this point on, all the surviving
Jews were safe in Yugoslavia.

To replace the Italians, the Germans set up a special administration that included the Adriatic littoral, the southern part of
Slovenia and the Julian region around Trieste. This was to be the
area of the fiercest fighting in 1945, when the Partisans almost
came into conflict with the British. In September 1943, the Slovene
Partisans, under the Marxist pedagogue Edvard Kardelj, were
strong in Ljubljana but they had alienated the non-Communist
Catholics and royalists. Kardelj rejoiced in destroying the beautiful
homes of the ancient nobility, under the slogan: 'The castle burns
– the count has fled.' After executing several hundred White Guard
prisoners, Kardelj sneered: 'That ought to demoralise them.'[35] The
vengefulness of the Slovene Communists was to be seen at its worst
in the massacres that took place shortly after the war.

9

The Triumph of
the Partisans

A few days after the Italian surrender, Britain sent two high-powered military missions into Yugoslavia, one to Mihailović under a regular soldier, Brigadier Charles Armstrong, the other to Tito under a wartime soldier, Brigadier Fitzroy Maclean, who plays an important part in the story. A former diplomat to the Soviet Union, where he acquired fluent Russian, a Tory Member of Parliament and a volunteer who had risen from private to brigadier through his gallantry in North Africa, Maclean had caught the attention of Winston Churchill, who shared his love of politics and adventure.

In Maclean's subsequent books *Eastern Approaches* and *Disputed Barricade*, his exploits in Yugoslavia sound like those of his childhood heroes Bonnie Prince Charlie, Lawrence of Arabia and Richard Hannay, the Scottish soldier and secret agent in John Buchan's *Greenmantle*. But happily for the fate of his team, Maclean's Highland romanticism was tempered by Lowland prudence, industry and ambition. His assignment to Tito, although it did not alter the fate of Yugoslavia, succeeded in helping to defeat the Germans in south-eastern Europe.

On the early morning of 18 September 1943, when Maclean 'jumped out and down, into the breath-taking tumult of the slipstream', almost exactly two years had passed since the first British officers had landed in Yugoslavia, bound for the Chetnik headquarters in Serbia. On the way through Montenegro they had encountered a band of Partisans who had to be ordered by Djilas not to murder these capitalist intruders. Tito himself believed that the British attached to the Chetnik forces were working with the Italians for the restoration of the monarchy. In the paranoiac fantasies that he transmitted to Moscow, Tito reported that on Mihailović's staff there were 'about twenty-five Englishmen dressed in Serbian national costume', by which he presumably meant that they were wearing round caps, embroidered waistcoats, knee-breeches and sandals with curled-back toes. In March 1943 Tito was ready to join the Germans in fighting the British.

Between the fourth and fifth German offensives, that is in April or early May 1943, Tito appears to have changed his mind, for he let the British send in an officer from its organisation in Cairo dealing with occupied Europe, the Special Operations Executive (SOE). This was Major William Deakin, an Oxford don who before the war had been a research assistant to Winston Churchill, who was then writing his *History of the English-Speaking Peoples*. Although this had nothing to do with Deakin joining the SOE, the Partisans thought he was Churchill's secretary, in the Balkan sense of a counsellor or *chef de cabinet*. Even those who were most Anglophobic warmed to this friendly and highly intelligent officer. Their liking turned into admiration when Deakin behaved with outstanding courage during the Fifth Offensive, the first occasion in which he had been in battle. Deakin was hit by a chunk of the shell that wounded Tito, and this created a bond of friendship between the two men that lasted until Tito's death.

During the summer of 1943, more British officers parachuted into the territory held by the Partisans, while the RAF started to drop in supplies of clothing and food for the ragged and hungry guerrillas. Tito had not yet lost his fear and suspicion of British political machinations; nor had he cut off his ties with German agents such as the engineer Hans Ott. Even in late November 1943, when Britain was pouring in arms and supplies to the Partisans, Tito's transport department obtained a herd of horses from the Germans, in return for allowing shipments of chrome to enter the Reich.[1]

After the war, with Tito's establishment of a Communist Yugo-slavia, Fitzroy Maclean was often accused of having enabled him to defeat the Mihailović forces. These accusations did not diminish when, after Tito's break with Stalin in 1948, Maclean and his friends could claim that they had recognised Tito's independence of mind from the outset. When, in the 1950s, Maclean started to revisit Yugoslavia and re-establish his friendship with Tito, his critics accused him of hob-nobbing with Communists and even of being a fellow-traveller. In *Eastern Approaches* Maclean recalls his warning to Churchill that Tito intended to set up a Communist state, to which Churchill replied with the cynical question: 'Do you intend to make your home in Yugoslavia after the war?'[2] Critics reminded Maclean of the exchange when during the 1960s he became one of the few foreigners granted permission to own property in Yugoslavia, and bought a villa on the island of Korčula.

One of the most persistent hounders of Fitzroy Maclean was the late Michael Lees, who had served as a British liaison officer with Mihailović's forces in eastern Serbia from 1943 to 1944. In *The Rape of Serbia*, published in 1990, Lees offered fresh evidence to support the accusations that Tito, assisted by Communists in the SOE, had duped Maclean into thinking that the Partisans and not the Chetniks were really resisting the Germans. As Yugoslavia started to fall apart in 1991, Lees's book became a bestseller in Belgrade.

The argument over Britain's role in Yugoslavia had raged for more than thirty years before historians learnt the full truth about why Churchill supported Tito. This came out with the release of the mass of documents known as Ultra, the decodifications of German *Wehrmacht* Enigma cipher, broken in 1940 by cryptana-lysts at Bletchley Park. Thanks to the men and women decoding the Ultra signals, Churchill and the Imperial General Staff enjoyed until the end of the war an invaluable insight into the minds of their opposite numbers in Germany. It was information from Ultra, and not from Deakin or Maclean, that persuaded Churchill to give his support to Tito. Moreover, since knowledge of Ultra was strictly confined to those at the highest level of military planning, and banned to anyone liable to capture, Fitzroy Maclean was himself supposed to be in the dark.[3]

Ultra's first, and isolated, contribution to Balkan intelligence came on 17 January 1943 when three signals gave an advance warning of 'Operation Weiss', correctly stating that it consisted of four German, four Italian and two Croat divisions. More Ultra messages on 'Operation Schwarz' confirmed the reports of Deakin on the battle in which he had fought. Before the Chiefs of Staff Committee discussed the situation in Yugoslavia late in June, Churchill called for a summary of the recent Balkan Ultra, 'as I wanted to have an absolutely factual presentation of the whole scene and balances'.[4] With the benefit of Ultra, the Chiefs of Staff in London, as well as the Middle East Defence Committee in Cairo, were turning against Mihailović.

Ultra revealed that, after the fall of Italy, Tito had managed to acquire enough arms and equipment 'to double the size of his field army and to make it so much more formidable than hitherto, that he was able to enlarge the area of territory he controlled very considerably'. By the end of October, the German General von Weichs told Hitler that 'Tito is our most dangerous enemy', and that defeating the Partisans was more important then repelling an Allied landing.[5]

The ever more voluminous Ultra reports on Yugoslavia in late 1943 and early 1944 revealed both astonishing Partisan progress and von Weichs's terror of losing his 750-mile line of retreat to the Reich.[6] Thanks to Ultra, Churchill knew more about the military situation in Yugoslavia than Tito did himself. By sending missions to both the Partisans and the Chetniks, Churchill was able to give the impression that their reports had caused him to change his mind. It was the kind of subterfuge that the British employed successfully until the end of the war, to prevent the Germans suspecting that their Enigma code had been cracked.

Although Maclean played only a minor part in Tito's rise to power, which was already well assured by September 1943, he remains invaluable as a chronicler of the man and his career. Unlike the other two main sources on Tito – Djilas and Dedijer – Fitzroy

Maclean has an ironic sense of humour and, moreover, remained a friend of Tito's after the other two had fallen from favour. Besides being himself a colourful personality, Maclean introduced into Yugoslavia two grotesques, Randolph Churchill and Evelyn Waugh, who gave to the gory drama a welcome moment or two of farce.

Although it is not true that Maclean and his British colleagues converted Tito from Stalinism and imbued him with his later more liberal views, they certainly made a strong impression. In spite of his Marxism, Tito was always inclined to rate people by their behaviour rather than by their ideas. He was an excellent judge of character both in individuals and in organisations. When Djilas returned from the 'March Consultations' in 1943, Tito was eager to hear what he thought of the German officers, noting with interest that the spirit of chivalry was not dead. And he studied the British officers both as individuals and as representatives of their class and country. As we shall see, he compared the British favourably with the Russians.

By the time Maclean arrived in Bosnia, Tito had made his headquarters at Jajce (pronounced Ya-i-tse), which means literally 'small eggs' and in popular parlance 'testicles'. The town had been important in medieval Bosnia, and Tito made his home there in part of an underground Bogomil church next to the castle on the hillside. On his first evening, Maclean was invited to dinner with Tito, of whom he later wrote:

> He was sturdily built, with iron-grey hair. His rather wide, smooth-skinned face with its high cheek-bones showed clearly enough the stresses and strains he had endured . . . his regular, clearly defined features were haggard and drawn and deeply burned by the sun. His mouth was ruthlessly determined. His alert, light-blue eyes missed nothing. He gave an impression of great strength held in reserve, the impression of a tiger ready to spring. As he spoke, his expression changed frequently and rapidly, in turn illumined by a sudden smile, transfigured with

anger or enlivened by a quick look of understanding. He had an agreeable voice, capable of sudden harshness.[7]

After some formal discussion about how the British could help the Partisans, Maclean and Tito grew more friendly over the slivovitz. Tito talked of his early life, his conversion to Communism and how the Germans had put a price on his head of 100,000 gold marks. He did not mention that the Germans had put an equal amount on the head of Mihailović. They talked about Tito's relationship with the Soviet Union, a country they both knew well, for indeed they were speaking in Russian. Tito complained of Moscow's recognition of the Yugoslav government in exile, and told how he had been reproached for trying to obtain an exchange of prisoners with the Germans. Maclean saw this as Tito's cynical view of Russian motives. Tito was probably watching Maclean to find out whether the British knew what had really taken place in the 'March Consultations' that year.

When Maclean asked outright if the new Yugoslavia would become a Soviet satellite, Tito said haughtily that the Partisans had not fought and suffered to hand over the country to someone else. When Maclean raised the question of King Peter, Tito said the matter would have to wait until after the war. According to Djilas, the Yugoslavs got the impression from Maclean that the British 'would not insist very much on the King'.[8]

After several days of discussion, Maclean arrived at this very favourable view of Tito:

He was unusually ready to discuss any question on its merits and to take a decision there and then, without reference to a higher authority . . . There were other unexpected things about him: his surprising breadth of outlook; his apparent independence of mind; his never-failing sense of humour; his unashamed delight in the minor pleasures of life; a natural diffidence in human relationships, giving way to a natural friendliness and conviviality; a violent temper, flaring up in sudden rages; an occasional tendency to ostentation and display; a considerateness and gen-

erosity which constantly manifested themselves in a dozen small
ways; a surprising readiness to see both sides of a question; and
finally, a strong instinctive national pride.[9]

During this first six-week visit, Maclean travelled back and forth
between Jajce and the Dalmatian coast, which was still almost
entirely controlled by the Partisans. He went to Split where most
of the shipyard workers as well as the 'Hajduk' football club were
now in the Proletarian Brigades. He went to Korčula, his future
home, then on to the outermost island of Vis, and from there to
Bari in Italy, which later became the Allied base for operations in
Yugoslavia. In early November Maclean flew back to Cairo.

Maclean's official report on 6 November 1943 caused great
excitement in Cairo and London. Dealing first with military
matters, he said that the Partisans controlled large parts of Yugoslavia and that Tito's forces comprised twenty-six divisions, totalling 220,000 men, of which 50,000 were in Bosnia, 15,000 in the
Sandjak, 50,000 in Croatia, 10,000 in Slavonia, 50,000 in Slovenia
and Istria, 25,000 in Dalmatia, 10,000 in Vojvodina, and 30,000 in
Serbia and Macedonia. He estimated that Tito's forces pinned
down fourteen *Reichswehr* divisions.

Turning to political questions, Maclean reported that in the
areas run by the Partisans there was freedom of religion, no
interference with private property, no class warfare and no mass
execution. He said Tito wanted a federalist system to solve what he
called the 'nationalities problem'. Dismissing the Chetniks,
Maclean said that the Partisans were between ten and twenty times
as numerous, infinitely better organised, better equipped and better
disciplined. Moreover they fought the Germans, while the Chetniks
'either help the Germans or do nothing'.[10]

The Maclean report caused consternation among those in Britain
who wanted to see King Peter back on the throne of Yugoslavia.
To the present day it is blamed by Serb nationalists for helping
Tito to power. The report was indeed grossly unfair to the
Chetniks. Mihailović had begun the anti-German insurrection in

May 1941, while Tito was still inactive because of the Hitler–Stalin pact. Savage reprisals, such as the massacre at Kragujevac in October that year, had convinced the Chetniks that further attacks on the Germans would lead to the wiping out of the Serbian people. However, there were in Serbia probably 200,000 men able and willing to take up arms for the Allies when the occasion arose, and it is doubtful if there were even 30,000 Partisans, as Maclean alleged.

Outside Serbia, the Partisans were probably almost as strong as Maclean suggested, and growing stronger all the time. This was confirmed by Ultra. While Maclean had guessed that Tito was holding down fourteen *Reichswehr* divisions, Ultra disclosed there were thirty divisions of German, Croatian and Bulgarian troops, most of whom were deployed against the Partisans. The Joint Intelligence Committee took particular note of an Ultra interception of a German claim to have killed 6,000 Partisans and only fifteen Chetniks, during a period when there were twice as many Chetniks taken prisoner. While the Foreign Office argued the case for King Peter and Mihailović, the military wanted to back the Communist Tito. The Commander-in-Chief Middle East Command, General Maitland 'Jumbo' Wilson, was so impressed by Maclean's report coming on top of Ultra that he proposed that Mihailović should be left 'to rot and fall off the branch, rather than be pushed'.[11]

Maclean's diplomatic skill and his good connections certainly helped in putting the case for Tito. His arch-enemy Michael Lees believes that Maclean would have made an equally brilliant case for Mihailović, had he been sent to Serbia. The historian Mark Wheeler makes the point that men such as Bill Bailey on the Mihailović staff did not have a golden background: 'These people didn't have access, hadn't been to the right schools, were not part of the Establishment. A class interpretation is possible. Bill Bailey was Emmanuel School, Wandsworth; Deakin and Maclean were Winchester and Eton products.'[12]

However, it has to be pointed out that many of Churchill's protégés in the two world wars, from Lawrence of Arabia to the peculiar Zionist Orde Wingate, did not come from the top drawer. Moreover it was Bill Bailey who more than anyone helped to wreck the career of Mihailović. He reported back to the British the outburst of 28 February 1943, when Mihailović said that he wanted to liquidate all his enemies, Partisans, Croats, Muslims and Ustasha – in that order – before he dealt with the Axis forces.[13]

While Maclean was in Cairo promoting the cause of the Partisans, Tito convened a second meeting of AVNOJ in order to set up a new Yugoslav government with himself as President. Delegates came from all over the country by car, on horseback or on foot, but all of them armed in case they should encounter the Germans, Ustasha or Chetniks. When Djilas arrived at Jajce after a tour of Croatia and Slovenia he noticed a spirit of triumph and animation. There were military bands and parades including Muslim girls in baggy pantaloons; there was a ballet and a production of Gogol's play *The Inspector General*. The Serb littérateur Radovan Zogović had arrived in town and, according to Ranković, he was writing an ode to Tito. The Croat sculptor Antun Augustinović was making a bust of Tito in clay in front of the Bogomil church. Djilas noticed a change in the object of all this adulation. 'Tito had suddenly become heavy, never again to regain that look of bone and sinew which made him look so distinguished-looking and attractive during the war.'[14]

Djilas suggests in his memoir *Wartime*, published in 1977 when Tito was still alive, that in 1943 the Communist leader changed his headquarters because it was vulnerable to air attack. In his later biography, Djilas suggests that, in Jajce and later on, Tito was much concerned with his personal safety and spent much of the time in a cave. Certainly Tito moved from the fragile Bogomil church to a headquarters close to an air-raid shelter. Perhaps having come so far and achieved so much, Tito was more than ever aware of his responsibilities, and felt that he should not take the risks of a junior, front-line soldier. But he certainly did not lead a sheltered life, even at Jajce. On the eve of the AVNOJ convention, German bombers raided the town, and afterwards Tito assisted at an operation on one of the wounded, a Partisan whose stomach had been partly blown away:

> I was holding the head of the boy. He was sweating. The operation was done without anaesthetics. The wounded Partisan did not want to show how much he suffered. I told him: 'Never mind, you'll get through all right.' A few seconds later his head dropped and so he died in my hands.[15]

A few days before the AVNOJ convention, the Party leaders met to discuss the various plans for a federal Yugoslavia after the war. This involved the delicate 'nationalities problem' dividing the Serbs and Croats in Croatia itself and in Bosnia-Hercegovina. It was the very question that fifty years later would plunge Yugoslavia back into civil war. Although most of the Communists refused to admit the fact, the 'nationalities problem' was the cause of their rise to power. The Ustasha massacre of the Serbs in Croatia and Bosnia-Hercegovina, followed by Serb reprisals and 'ethnic cleansing' of Croats and, still more, Muslims, had caused a horrendous three-way civil war and then a revulsion in favour of Yugoslavia. This was the strength of the Partisans. However, they could not admit this even to themselves, for the 'nationalities problem' did not fit their Marxist theory. They thought of themselves instead as 'anti-Fascists' battling against the Axis occupation.

Although the Communists talked of a 'nationalities problem', they knew that the only real difference between the Serbs and the Croats lay in religion. But religion also did not fit into the Marxist scheme of things, which divided people according to class. The account of their meeting given by Milovan Djilas shows the embarrassment caused to the Communists, even Tito, by this delicate 'nationalities problem'.

The debate was opened by Moša Pijade who, according to Djilas, 'had the reputation of being the most zealous Serb among us'. Since Pijade was a Jew he was obviously not a Serbian nationalist of the kind who would celebrate the Battle of Kosovo and eat his portion of wheat on the name-day of his saint. He was a zealous Serb in that he feared the bigotry of the Croatian Catholic Church, as shown by the recent Ustasha pogroms. Pijade had gathered a mass of statistics on population to back up his plan for a series of semi-autonomous Serbian enclaves in Croatia. According to Djilas, Pijade's plan was received with embarrassment:

> Everyone was silent, perplexed. I think I saw dejection even in Tito's face; perhaps as a Croat he found it awkward to oppose the idea . . . I was the first to come out against Pijade's proposal; the segregated territory was unnatural, lacking a centre of viability, and moreover provided fuel for Croatian nationalism. Kardelj immediately agreed . . . Ranković squelched [Pijade] by remarking that the Serbs and Croats were not so different that the Serbs and Croats had to be divided.[16]

The Party leaders then turned to the question of Bosnia-Hercegovina. It had been assumed in the past that this central region should not become a republic like Serbia or Croatia but should have autonomous status. However, now it was felt that this would imply autonomy under Serbia. As most of the people present knew, the behaviour of the Chetniks in eastern Bosnia-Hercegovina had made the very name of the Serbs unpopular with the Muslim population. As Djilas says: 'Autonomy under either Serbia or Croatia would have encouraged further strife and deprived the Muslims of their own individuality. The Bosnian leadership, too, like every authority that grows up out of an uprising, insisted on their own state, and later even on their own historical outlet to the sea. But the republican status of Bosnia-Hercegovina was not decided at the time.'[17]

At the second session of AVNOJ, the delegates became a legislative assembly under the Presidency of Tito, who was proclaimed Marshal. The birthday of the new Yugoslavia, 29 November 1943, remained a national holiday until the death of the federation almost fifty years later. But, as if to remind the Partisans that their infant state was born in a world of mortal danger, disaster and tragedy struck on the eve of the celebrations. A deserter from the Croatian air force had recently brought to the Partisans a German light bomber, a Dornier 17, which now was waiting at Jajce's makeshift airfield. Tito decided to use the plane to transport to Cairo the Yugoslav military mission that Fitzroy Maclean had asked him to send. The man chosen to head the mission was Ivo Lola Ribar, the youngest man in the leadership and the dearest to Tito personally. Just as the mission were boarding, a German bomber appeared and scored a direct hit on the plane, killing most of the people inside, including Ivo Lola Ribar.

On the very day of this tragedy, Lola's father, who had left the safety of his retirement to join the Partisans the previous year, returned to Jajce from a stay in Slovenia. He knew neither of Lola's death nor of that of his only other son, Jurica, who had been killed one month earlier. The Partisan leaders decided that Tito himself must break the terrible news. When Dr Ribar called to pay his respects, Tito told him of Lola's death. The old man held back his tears but asked only: 'Is Jurica far away and has he been told of Lola's death? It will be a heavy blow for him.' Tito was silent for a moment, wondering what to do. Then he approached Ribar, took him by the arm and said gently: 'Jurica was killed too, fighting the Chetniks in Montenegro a month ago.' Old Ribar embraced Tito, saying: 'This fight of ours is hard.'[18]

At the memorial service, during which even hardened fighters like Milovan Djilas wept uncontrollably, the oldest Party leader Moša Pijade was called on to give an oration about the youngest. For once the garrulous Moša fumbled for words, so great was his own emotion. Then he fetched from the mental storehouse of all he had read the words of a French political combatant: 'Revolutionaries are dead men on leave.'[19]

The sufferings of the Ribar family were not at an end. Ivan's wife, the mother of Lola and Jurica, was arrested and executed by the Gestapo for helping her husband to join the Partisans. Before Lola was killed he had written to his fiancée, Sloboda Trajković, who was a Belgrade student, a letter to be shown to her only if he was dead. 'I love you very, very much, my own!' it concluded. 'And I hope you will never receive this letter, but that we shall greet the hour of victory together.' The letter was never delivered. Sloboda Trajković, together with her father, mother, sister and brother, was taken by the Gestapo and killed in one of their gas-chamber lorries. Soon after the war Dedijer took Lola's letter to show to Tito but found him in a mood of despondency over the human tragedy of the war, so 'after his words about the one million, seven hundred thousand dead, I refrained. Tito had dearly loved Lola Ribar ever since the first day they had met in the autumn of 1937.'[20]

The death of Ivo Lola Ribar gave added solemnity to the acclamation of Tito as Marshal the following day. The title had been proposed by the Slovene delegates, and their leader Kardelj broke the news to the Politburo beforehand. When he heard of the honour, Tito blushed, whether from pride or modesty we cannot know, although Djilas suggests he may have been wondering what the Russians would think. The delegates to the second AVNOJ conference gave tumultuous, overwhelming approval to Tito's new status. This loyalty was absolute in the highest rank of the leadership. Djilas says that among the triumvirate of his immediate entourage, Kardelj had been bonded to Tito during their stay in Moscow in the 1930s while Ranković was 'unconditionally devoted to Tito, sentimentally and ideologically'. And what about Djilas himself? He may have begun to suspect in his deep subconscious that Tito had weaknesses but he seems to have been unaware of them on a conscious level. Not once during the forty years since his own disgrace and rejection, has Djilas ever denied Tito's power as a leader of men.[21]

During the winter of 1943–4 the Germans carried out 'Operation Kugelblitz' ('Thunderbolt'), which the Partisans called the Sixth Offensive. Its aims were to retake the former Italian zone of southern Slovenia, the Adriatic coast and the islands, and also to smash the three Partisan divisions in north-east Bosnia. By the end of the year the Germans commanded the towns on the coast and all the islands except Vis, where the Royal Navy and RAF offered protection. After the war Maclean expressed his regret that the British had not established a base on the coast, for example at Split, during the autumn of 1943, but Tito would not have welcomed them. In north-east Bosnia, the Germans recaptured the town of Tuzla but failed to destroy the Partisans north of Sarajevo.[22]

During 'Operation Kugelblitz' Tito thought it prudent to move his heaquarters south from Jajce to the small town of Drvar, also in western Bosnia. He established his base in a cave on the mountainside, lending support to Djilas's view that Tito was anxious about his safety, but events were to prove that Drvar too was vulnerable to German attack. In January 1944 Fitzroy Maclean came back to Bosnia with two remarkable proofs of Winston Churchill's regard for Tito. One was a personal letter expressing warm admiration and support. The other was Winston's son Randolph Churchill, who was now an officer in the British military mission. The fact that one of the 'Big Three' Allied leaders had sent his only son to fight on the side of the Partisans was a staggering propaganda triumph for Tito. It enormously strengthened both Tito's and Maclean's position when, in February 1944, the Russians finally sent a military mission to join the Partisans they had so long slighted.

The head of the Soviet Mission was the Red Army's General Korneyev who had lost a foot at Stalingrad and therefore could not parachute into Yugoslavia, coming instead with the rest of his staff in a pair of American gliders. On their arrival the aircraft were found to contain not only General Korneyev and numerous colonels, but case upon case of caviare and vodka. With his habitual cynicism, Stalin had sent the Partisans a man he despised. 'The poor man is not stupid,' Stalin later told Djilas, 'but he is a drunkard and an incurable drunkard.'[23]

General Korneyev and his team were resplendent in gaudy uniforms with gold epaulettes and tight, shiny boots. The Partisans were amazed to be asked the whereabouts of the General's lavatory. 'But the British don't have a lavatory,' came the reply; 'the British general [Maclean] goes behind the nearest tree.' The Russians insisted, so the Partisans dug a deep hole, erected a wooden hutch, whitewashed it and left the excavated earth in a mound outside. Not surprisingly, the first German plane to spot this gleaming object flew in low, strafed and then bombed it.[24]

Tito took a dislike to Korneyev, as did his wolfhound Tigger, which was always trying to bite him. Tito would watch this, chuckle and say: 'Anti-Russian dog'. In a dispatch to Churchill, Maclean suggested that Tito was playing off the British against the Russians: 'Marshal Tito has, in his reception of the newly arrived Soviet Mission, gone out of his way to emphasise that their status here is to be exactly the same as that of my mission. There can be no doubt that they have seen the advantage of maintaining good relations with other Great Powers beside the Soviet Union.' Because Maclean spoke Russian, Korneyev would call on him and pour out his woes. He confided that he had hoped for a comfortable job as defence attaché in Washington but instead had been sent to Yugoslavia. 'I don't know what I've done to deserve to be posted to this awful country with all these horrible Balkan peasants,' he would complain. 'Who are these Partisans anyway? Do I command them or do you?' Maclean replied that he certainly did not, but Korneyev could try if he liked and see how he got on.[25]

Tito now had the backing of two of the 'Big Three' powers but not, as yet, that of the United States. An American engineer, Major Linn 'Slim' Farish, had joined Maclean's mission in late 1943 and helped in building the airstrips. His initial support for the Partisans was turned to disgust by their lies and boasting, by their routine killing of prisoners, and most of all by the way that they hounded the Chetniks.[26] American policy towards the warring factions in Yugoslavia was influenced by professional rivalry between the Office of Strategic Services (OSS – the forerunner of the CIA) and the British SOE. The director of the OSS, General William Joseph 'Wild Bill' Donovan, had tried to establish his own mission to Tito, independent of Maclean's. In January 1944 he turned down a British proposal that all American officers should be based at Drvar, and therefore under Maclean's control. Instead, Donovan sent a series of high-level missions to Mihailović, inspiring him with the hope that the United States would rescue him from the Communists.

Although Donovan's interference was mostly to do with the empire-building common to all intelligence services, politics also played a part. In 1944 President Roosevelt was seeking re-election for a fourth term in office and did not want to offend any substantial body of voters, such as for instance the Jews, Italians, Irish and Poles. Although neither the Serbs nor the Croats formed an important vote on their own, they both stood for Roosevelt's principle of national self-determination. Roosevelt appeared to believe that Yugoslavia was an unreal state, formed by committee, and that Serbs and Croats should be allowed to go their separate ways. He did not share Churchill's enthusiasm for Tito, and in December 1943 he announced his continued support for King Peter. To emphasise this commitment, he made a gift of four US planes to the Royal Yugoslav Air Force.

President Roosevelt wanted to rid the world of empires, whether that of the British in India or of the French in Indo-China, and this attitude may have coloured his outlook on Yugoslavia. Fitzroy Maclean's biographer Frank McLynn suggests that Donovan and his State Department backer Robert Murphy were Irish-American enemies of the British Empire who thought the British wanted control over Greece and Yugoslavia in order to safeguard the route to Suez and India. McLynn goes still further:

The problem was that at bottom American decision-makers of the time were not interested in whether the Russians overran Eastern Europe. Their main target was the British Empire, which they were determined to prevent from emerging stronger than ever after the war. There was always in American plans for the post-war world a concealed economic agenda, and it was no accident that the important figures of the US corporate structure were also the important foreign policy decision-makers. It is not an exaggeration to say that corporate America was running the war – in the shape of the 'six wise men' and figures like Donovan and the financier John J. McCloy.[27]

These are the views of Maclean's biographer and not necessarily those of Maclean himself. However, his record in politics after the war shows Maclean to have been a strong advocate of Britain's continued imperial role, and one of the most gung-ho supporters of Eden during the Suez crisis of 1956.

As the Communists were on the verge of taking power in Yugoslavia, millions of Christians looked to their churches as a way of preserving their freedom of mind and sense of nationhood. The Croatian Catholic Church boasted of 1,300 years of connection with Rome and thus with hundreds of millions of fellow believers throughout the world. The Serbian Orthodox Church, created by Sava during the thirteenth century, embodied his slogan that 'Only Unity Saves Serbs'. After the Battle of Kosovo in 1389 and throughout the centuries of Ottoman rule, the Church was the voice and leadership of the Serbian people. Although the Church created by Sava was formally independent of Constantinople, it maintained liturgical and doctrinal unity with the parent Church as well as with those of Russia, Ukraine, Romania and Bulgaria. For both the Serbs and the Croats the Church was at once an expression of nationhood and a bond with an international Christian community. However, in 1944 the Serbian Orthodox Church faced hardship and peril far greater than those confronting the rival Croatian Catholic Church.

The suffering of the Serbian Orthodox Church in the Independent State of Croatia has already been told in earlier chapters. In Serbia itself the Patriarch Gavrilo Dožić was put on trial by the Germans for having supported the *coup d'état* of 27 March 1941. He was kept in prison in Yugoslavia until August 1944 when he was taken in an exhausted and sick condition to Dachau and other concentration camps in Germany. Throughout his imprisonment, Patriarch Gavrilo sternly refused to collaborate with the enemy occupation. A few Serbian priests joined the Chetniks or the Partisans but the great majority stuck to their pastoral duties, which now included looking after the refugees from the NDH.

Unlike the Catholic Croats, the Orthodox Serbs had virtually no support from the outside world. The Bolshevik revolution had tried to abolish religion in Russia and the Ukraine, killing most of the clergy and sending millions of Christian believers to the Gulag Archipelago. Although Stalin had eased the persecution during the war, the Church had little power to protect its flock in Russia and the Ukraine, and none whatsoever to help the Serbs. After the war, when Romania and Bulgaria also fell to Communism, the Serbian Orthodox Church had no sympathetic hearers outside the country. The story of its suffering under the Ustasha in the NDH, from 1941 to 1945, was to remain unknown for the next fifty years.

At the Orthodox Easter in 1944, the Serbian Synod sent out a message that spoke of the sacrifice made at Golgotha and prayed 'that every Serb home and family be morally and spiritually renewed and born again, be in itself a small Church of God in which our fatherland and government have always rested . . .'[28] Over that Orthodox Easter the Anglo-American Balkan Air Force carried out carpet-bombing attacks on Belgrade for three days running. On St George's Day, a very important feast of the Orthodox Church, the Balkan Air Force bombed the Montenegrin towns of Nikšić, Danilovgrad and Podgorica.

In his book *The Rape of Serbia* Michael Lees suggests that British officers sympathetic to Tito may have chosen the targets for the Balkan Air Force: 'It is claimed today in some Serbian circles that the Allied air support was exploited by Tito to turn the people against Britain. The theory is that strikes by Western Allied aircraft of the Balkan Air Force were called down specifically against Serbian towns and villages, cynically choosing Serbian Orthodox religious holidays for the bombing.' Lees offers no proof to support this suggestion but points out that 'the files of the Balkan Air Force are permanently closed . . . one wonders why'. Lees is probably right when he says: 'I feel certain that the Allies would never have contemplated a blanket bombing of Paris, for example, on Easter Sunday – or any other day – however many German tanks were passing through.'[29]

The pro-British, anti-German demonstration on 27 March 1941 had brought down on the Serbs and their capital city the terrible Palm Sunday bombing. Three years later the British themselves

bombed Belgrade over Easter. In 1941 the Croats had welcomed
the Germans into Zagreb and then declared war against Britain.
But when the Balkan Air Force bombed Zagreb on 22 April 1944,
killing seven Dominican priests and harming two churches, Archbishop Stepinac denounced the raid as a blow 'to the living
organism of the Croatian people, who have been called by the Pope
the outer bulwark of Christianity'. While Stepinac proclaimed that
there were no military targets in the area of the cathedral, other
witnesses spoke of a lorry depot and fuel dump next to the
theological faculty.[30] The closer the NDH came to defeat, the
fiercer Stepinac grew in his denunciation of Communism. Back in
1942 he had told the British agent Rapotec that he wanted a
reunited Yugoslavia after the war, but in 1944 he had gone back to
praising Croatia's 'struggle for freedom over the centuries'.[31]

Archbishop Stepinac had come to believe that America favoured
the Independent State of Croatia. Although the Pope had always
been well disposed to the Ustasha regime, the Italians and even
some of the Germans condemned its brutality. The Americans who
were now installed in Rome were better disposed to Stepinac and
Croatia. By far the best friend of Croatia's cause was Cardinal
Francis Spellman, the Archbishop of New York, a strong anti-
Communist and an influential voice in Washington. Throughout
the war, Spellman served as a trouble-shooter and close adviser to
President Roosevelt, whom he had known as a New York
politician.

In March 1943, when Italy was still at war with the United
States, Spellman visited Rome to talk with the Pope and other
functionaries in the Vatican. There he met Count Erwin Lobkowicz, the NDH emissary to the Holy See. After their meeting on 6
March 1943, Count Lobkowicz sent back to Zagreb a resumé of
Spellman's remarks. While reading it, one should remember that
at this time the NDH was an ally of Hitler's, at war with the
United States, and engaged in the mass murder of hundreds of
thousands of Serbs, Gypsies and Jews. The report from Lobkowicz
was certainly read by Archbishop Stepinac as well as the Ustasha
leaders:

Accompanied by the office secretary, Wurster, I was able to visit the Archbishop of New York, Spellman. As is known Archbishop Spellman has been in Rome for about a fortnight . . . At present he is completely in President Roosevelt's confidence . . . Spellman received us very politely and said straightway: 'There's not much you can tell me about your affairs that I don't know. I'm well informed on everything and know the Croatian question well. A few years ago I travelled through your country, and even then the difference between Belgrade and Zemun [on the other side of the Danube], not to mention Zagreb, told me enough. There are two worlds. They cannot co-exist.' We pointed out that the present State is now in a very special position in the context of its Catholicism and especially through its position between East and West, that the frontier of the Drina guarantees the maintenance of the Catholic position in that sector; and that the rebuilding of Yugoslavia would mean not only the annihilation of the Croat people but also of Catholicism and western culture in those regions. Instead of a western frontier on the Drina, we would have a Byzantine frontier on the Karavanke. Spellman agreed with these observations and added that President Roosevelt wants freedom for all peoples and that obviously includes the Croats.[32]

From this astonishing interview, Archbishop Stepinac and the Ustasha leaders learned that President Roosevelt wanted an independent Croatia stretching as far as the River Drina, that is, including all Bosnia-Hercegovina. The interview also helps to explain why Stepinac later refused to accept the new Yugoslavia, and why the Ustasha leaders escaped all punishment for their crimes.

In May 1944, when the Allies were preparing for the invasion of France, the Germans unleashed their seventh and final offensive in Yugoslavia, this time directed at Tito personally. The first inkling of danger came on 22 May, when a German reconnaissance plane made a long and careful surveillance of the Drvar valley, keeping well out of range of ground fire. The acting head of the Anglo-American mission thought that this was the prelude to a bombing attack, and he therefore moved equipment and staff to a nearby hillside. The reconnaissance was in fact a preparation for 'Operation Rosselsprung', which was to involve the killing or capturing of Tito by a paratroop attack, followed by a drag-net through the Dinaric Alps, from Bihać to Šibenik on the coast. 'Operation Rosselsprung' was planned as a nasty surprise for Tito's official birthday on 25 May, when at 6.30 a.m. two Focke-Wulfs came in low over Drvar. Then fifty bombers flattened the town, followed by six Junker transport planes dropping paratroopers, then thirty gliders bringing in more soldiers with heavy equipment, making a total of 1,000 crack troops. A second parachute drop made the capture of Drvar complete.

The attackers made straight for Tito's cave, spraying the entrance with machine-gun fire, so that no one could leave. However, Tito and his companions, with the wolfhound Tigger, managed to climb up the watercourse of the falls at the back of the cave, then up through a tunnel to the top of the cliff. There Ranković and his squad held off the attackers while Tito went to the nearest Partisan unit at Potoci. He linked up with the British and Russian missions, then marched for a week through the forest to Kupresko Polje. Although Tito had escaped from 'Rosselsprung', his wireless communication system was no longer working so that he could not control operations throughout the country. Reluctantly he took the advice of the Russians and left on one of their planes for Bari, in Italy, and from there to the island of Vis. The near catastrophe of the Seventh Offensive led to recriminations between the British and Tito, who now became cooler towards Maclean.[33]

The Seventh Offensive showed that the Germans regarded Tito as a serious, even potentially deadly, foe. Himmler said in a speech later in 1944: 'He is our enemy, but I wish we had a dozen Titos in Germany, men who were leaders and had such great resolution and good nerves that though they were constantly encircled they would never give in.'[34] For everyone besides the German and British military leadership, Tito remained an enigmatic figure, as can be seen from an article in the Spanish paper *Madrid* reporting on 'Rosselsprung' on 15 June:

> Tito escaped on a horse he had stolen that morning from a farm near the town. Passing through villages and settlements, Tito is committing every possible crime. A captive gave an account of the incredible crimes committed by Tito, who kills for the sake of killing . . . Tito wears a long, utterly unkempt beard, his features are hard.[35]

Even among the Allies in Cairo and Bari there was mystery surrounding the identity of Tito. Rumour described him variously as a Russian officer, a Ukrainian, a Polish count or a Polish Jew, while many believed that he did not exist at all and that TITO was an acronym for Third International Terrorist Organisation. The *New York Times* correspondent Cyrus Sulzberger first put into print the story that Tito was really a woman, an idea that appealed to the novelist Evelyn Waugh, who arrived at Vis in July 1944. Randolph Churchill had pleaded for Waugh to join the mission because he was bored and wanted someone to talk to from White's, his London club. Maclean agreed but later came to regret the decision as Waugh became insubordinate. From his diaries we know that Waugh took an instant dislike to Maclean: 'dour, unprincipled, ambitious, probably very wicked; shaved head and devil's ears.'[36] Having decided at once that Tito was really a secret lesbian, Waugh hammered the joke with constant references to 'her'. When the novelist and the Communist leader were first introduced, Tito had just emerged from a dip in the sea and was wearing exiguous bathing trunks. After shaking hands, Tito asked point blank: 'Captain Waugh, why do you think I am a woman?' For once, Waugh was abashed and silent.[37]

When he reached mainland Croatia, Waugh was put in charge of helping the displaced Jews who had joined the Partisans after Italy's surrender. Later he served as a kind of British consul in Dubrovnik, the once independent city that never gladly accepted

rule by Venice, Austria and the first Yugoslavia, and certainly did
not like the Communists. Waugh's experiences in Yugoslavia are
brought into his pessimistic but grimly amusing novel *Unconditional Surrender*, the third part of the *Sword of Honour trilogy*. As a
Catholic and reactionary, Waugh hated the Partisans and accused
them of persecuting the Church in Croatia. He wrote a report on
this for Maclean and, when it was not taken seriously, he circulated
extracts in England, risking a court martial for breach of the
Official Secrets Act. Although Waugh suppressed or never discovered the truth about the Church's behaviour under the NDH,
he was one of the first outsiders to sense the character of the
Croatian Franciscans:

> For some time the Croat Franciscans had caused misgivings in
> Rome for their independence and narrow patriotism. They were
> mainly recruited from the least cultured part of the population
> and there is abundant evidence that several wholly unworthy men
> were attracted to the Franciscan Order by the security and
> comparative ease which it offered. Many of these youths were
> sent to Italy for training. Their novitiate was in the neighbourhood of Pavelić's HQ at Siena where Ustasha agents made contact
> with them and imbued them with Pavelić's ideas. They in turn,
> on returning to their country, passed on his ideas to the pupils in
> their schools. Sarajevo is credibly described as having been a
> centre of Franciscan Ustashism.[38]

In July 1944, when Evelyn Waugh encountered a near-naked
Tito, the island of Vis was a busy military base, its road jammed
with lorries and jeeps, its new airstrip filled with traffic, its shores
surrounded by Royal Navy vessels. British, American and Russian
officers vied for the attention of Tito at his headquarters, once
again in a cave. The Hollywood actor Douglas Fairbanks, one of
the US 'beachjumpers' on Vis for joint operations with British
commandos, recalls how Tito came to inspect them and afterwards
promised some token of his esteem. The commandos and
'beachjumpers', hoping to get a ribbon or even a Partisan star,

were disappointed when Tito gave them each two tins of anchovies.[39]

Churchill and Foreign Secretary Anthony Eden persisted in putting pressure on Tito to compromise with the government in exile. Tito persisted in his refusal to meet King Peter or let him return to Yugoslav soil. He at one time refused to meet the British in Italy because the young king was there at the time. It was not until the end of July that Tito agreed to visit General 'Jumbo' Wilson at his villa in Caserta. He took with him five staff officers, including his son Žarko, his interpreter Olga, the dog Tigger and two of his most frightening bodyguards, Boško and Prlja. These last took up positions during the formal lunch, the one behind Tito, the other pointing his sub-machine-gun at General Wilson, much to the terror of the Italian waiters.

> The strain of passing the vegetables, under the baleful eye of a heavily armed and extremely grim-looking guerilla warrior, who clearly did not like Italians, was too much for the Italian mess waiter. With an exclamation of despair he let a large dish of French beans crash on the table, and at once pandemonium reigned. The trigger-finger of the bodyguard twitched menacingly; Tigger, roused from his uneasy slumbers beneath the table, let out a long wolf-like howl and started to snap at everyone's ankles . . . It was then that General Wilson started to laugh. Gently, almost silently at first, and then more and more heartily, until his whole frame quaked and rocked . . . In a flash Tito was guffawing too, and soon the whole table was convulsed with merriment. Even the Italians sniggered nervously . . . while a grim smile spread over the stern features of the bodyguard.[40]

Churchill cabled to say he was coming to Naples the following week and wanted to meet Tito. For security reasons, Tito could not be told of this, so Maclean had the task of keeping him occupied with visits to military installations and then a sightseeing tour of Rome. Here Boško and Prlja once more created a problem. Since Tito insisted on wearing his dazzling Marshal's uniform, drawing attention to himself in a country swarming with Germans, Chetniks, Ustasha and other potential assassins, the presence of a bodyguard was perhaps a wise precaution, but when Boško and Prlja, toting their sub-machine-guns, insisted on following Tito into St Peter's Basilica, Maclean protested that this would offend the worshippers. Tito ordered the gunmen to leave but they would not budge from his side: 'Comrade Tito, for more than three years we have protected you from Nazi attacks and we're not going to fail you now.' Tito shouted at them, a curious crowd appeared and, as Maclean says, 'the situation could scarcely have been more embarrassing'.[41]

Tito's first meeting with Churchill, at Jumbo Wilson's villa, is seen by Maclean as a great occasion unfolding beside the Bay of Naples:

> Tito, resplendent in gold braid, red tabs and tight-fitting grey serge, arrived first and was looking out across the glittering waters of the bay to where a plume of smoke rose lazily from the summit of Vesuvius, when suddenly he became aware of the Prime Minister of Great Britain advancing on him with out-stretched hand.[42]

A haughty man from the Foreign Office, Pierson Dixon, observed that 'Tito was cautious, nervous and sweating a good deal in his absurd Marshal's uniform of thick cloth and gold lace'. It was, as they all agreed, a scorchingly hot day.[43]

The first topic of discussion was Tito's claim to Istria, Trieste, Venezia-Giulia and southern Carinthia. Churchill warned Tito that Allied forces might liberate these places before the Partisans could. They discussed means of cutting the German retreat through the Balkans. They debated how to reconcile *de jure* recognition of King Peter and his government in exile with *de facto* recognition of Partisan power. Tito avoided committing himself on any of these matters.

Churchill read Tito a lesson on the collectivisation of agriculture: 'My friend Marshal Stalin told me the other day that his battle with the peasants had been a more perilous and formidable undertaking than the battle for Stalingrad. I hope that you, Marshal, will think twice before you join such a battle with your sturdy Serbian peasantry.' He said the Allies would lose interest in the Partisans if they turned their guns on the Chetniks instead of the Germans. When Tito showed signs of anger, his interpreter Olga toned down some of Churchill's remarks.

Just before lunch the notorious bodyguards Boško and Prlja nearly caused a disaster. The two delegations had gone off to wash at bathrooms in different parts of the villa and five minutes later converged from different directions at the same corner. Suddenly the Prime Minister found himself looking into the barrels of two sub-machine-guns, and so, being a fan of Hollywood movies, Churchill drew out his gold cigar case, about the size of a Colt revolver and pointed it at Tito's stomach. Maclean continues:

> What he did not know (but I did) was that Boško and Prlja, after three years as guerillas, were men of lightning reflexes, who took no chances and who, if they thought their Marshal's life was in danger, would gladly have wiped out all three of the Big Three with a single burst. For the space of a single second I saw their trigger-fingers twitch, and only had time to hope that I for one would not survive what came next. But then, Tito began to laugh. Winston, seeing that his little joke had been a success, laughed too.[44]

There were two more meetings, at which the leaders produced some vaguely worded statements about the future of Yugoslavia; but Tito had no intention of sharing power with the King. Churchill had nothing to offer Tito in return for concessions. The historian Mark Wheeler thinks that Tito 'wasn't as romantic and impressive as Churchill had expected and was proving reluctant to fit in with Churchill's pet schemes – beating the Russians to Vienna by going through the Ljubljana Gap, or the landings in Dalmatia'.[45] Naturally Tito opposed both schemes, which would have frustrated his territorial claims on Italy and Austria, and impeded his rise to power in Yugoslavia. Tito and Churchill had quite different and sometimes contradictory war aims. By the end of the summer of 1944, Tito was preparing to abandon his British allies and turn his mind to gaining two of the objects against which Churchill had warned him: crushing the Serbian peasants and winning the race for Trieste.

By September 1944 the Red Army was crossing Romania and approaching the Danube and the frontiers of Yugoslavia. Fitzroy Maclean drew up the plan code-named 'Ratweek', by which the British would join with the Partisans in a land, sea and air operation to disrupt the German withdrawal through Yugoslavia. Ultra signals showed that the Germans were in confusion. Hitler was still obsessed by his fear that the British would land on the 'soft underbelly of Europe', and therefore kept many divisions idle along the Dalmatian coast. The generals of Germany's South-East Europe Command believed, correctly, that the main attack would come from the Russians and Partisans on Belgrade and then up the Danube and Sava valleys. In either event, the German retreat from Greece and Serbia would have to battle across the mountains of Bosnia-Hercegovina. Ultra also revealed that Draža Mihailović, in his rage at the British for having 'handed the country over to Bolshevism', was offering help to the German Army Group E's retreat through Sarajevo.[46]

'Operation Ratweek' consisted largely of Flying Fortress raids on German lines of communication along the Sava and Morava valleys. Maclean himself watched the obliteration bombing of Leskovac where the Germans had a concentration of armour. For the remaining British officers with the Chetniks, such as the then Captain Michael Lees, this bombing of Serbian towns with a largely civilian population was wicked and unnecessary. He thought the Allies were trying to do from the air what the Chetniks could have achieved on the ground by sabotage and guerrilla raids. Indeed Lees himself had frequently blown up the Belgrade-Salonica railway. In *The Rape of Serbia*, Lees contradicts Maclean's assertion that during the autumn of 1944 the Serbs were deserting the Chetniks to join the Partisans. Allied airmen forced down over

Serbia found that the Chetniks controlled the countryside. Lees himself moved freely around south Serbia and even as far as the Ravna Gora without ever meeting or hearing about the presence of Partisans. The abandonment, or as some would say the betrayal, of the Serbs in the interest of *realpolitik* was especially repugnant to those who remembered their heroism during the First World War. The French, who had fought beside the Serbs on the Salonica Front from 1916 to 1918 were most unhappy. General Charles de Gaulle always honoured Mihailović.

Late in September, the British on Vis suddenly woke up to the fact that Tito had disappeared from the island. In Churchill's phrase, he had 'levanted' to Moscow. At 11 p.m. on 21 September, Tito boarded a Russian plane in the greatest secrecy: 'As he was leaving, his dog Tigger refused to keep still. He was kept close to his master and Tito had to take him on the plane. In case the dog barked when they were boarding the plane, a sack was pulled over his head.'[47]

After four years, Josip Broz was back in Moscow, not as a secret agent, a man in hiding from the police, who travelled on false passports and went by the code-name 'Walter', but as Marshal Tito, the President of the National Council. Yet when Tito asked for a tank division to help in the final assault on Belgrade, Stalin answered: 'Walter, I shall give you not one division but a whole tank corps.' Stalin agreed that, after taking Belgrade, the Red Army would move into Hungary, leaving the Partisans, or the People's Army as they were now called, to drive the Germans out of Yugoslavia, as well as supporting the Russian left flank. Tito pointed out that the Red Army had only a limited role in Yugoslavia: 'Otherwise, the first meeting was very cool. The basic cause, I think, was the telegram I had sent them during the war, especially the one I began with the words, "If you cannot send us assistance, then at least do not hamper us."' The Bulgarian Georgy Dimitrov, always a trusted friend, told Tito that when Stalin saw that message he stamped with rage.[48]

In another conversation, Stalin told Tito that he should reinstate King Peter:

The blood rushed to my head that he could advise us to do such a thing. I composed myself and told him it was impossible, that the people would rebel, that in Yugoslavia the king personified treason, that he had fled and left his people in the midst of their struggle, that the Karageorgević dynasty was hated among the people for corruption and terror.

  Stalin was silent, and then said briefly:

'You need not restore him forever. Take him back temporarily, and then you can slip a knife into his back at a suitable moment.'[49]

On his way back from Moscow, Tito crossed from Romania into north-east Serbia, from where he directed the Yugoslav troops in the joint attack on Belgrade. The Kalemegdan fortress at the confluence of the Danube and Sava rivers, the key to command of south-east Europe under the Roman, Austrian and Turkish empires, fell to the Russians and Partisans on 20 October 1944.

The capture of Belgrade occasioned the first open quarrel between the Yugoslav and the Soviet Communists. During and after the battle, the Red Army went on the rampage against the supposedly allied Serb population, raping more than 200 women, half of whom were afterwards murdered. One Soviet officer raped a woman Partisan as she brought him a message during a battle. When Tito made a complaint, General Korneyev, the head of the Soviet military mission, at first refused to listen and then grew angry, at which point Milovan Djilas intervened to say that enemies of the revolution were making propaganda out of the rapes: 'They are comparing the attacks by the Red Army soldiers with the behaviour of the English officers who do not indulge in such excesses.' Korneyev exploded with fury: 'I protest most sharply against the insult to the Red Army in comparing it with the armies of capitalist countries.'[50] The exchange was reported back to Moscow and rankled in Stalin's mind.

By November 1944 Tito was also on a collision course with the British. The immediate point at issue was Churchill's intervention in Greece on the side of the right-wing against the left-wing guerrillas. This reawakened Tito's fear that Churchill would step in to save the Chetniks, or even the Croat separatists. Having earlier given permission for British troops to move inland from Dubrovnik to harass the German retreat, Tito ordered them back to the coast in November. Tito's distrust of Churchill grew when he heard of plans for a large-scale British landing on the Dalmatian coast.

In spite of discord between the British and the Partisans, the German retreat through Bosnia-Hercegovina cost them about 100,000 dead and twice as many prisoners. In the wake of the Germans came thousands of Chetniks, harried on all sides by vengeful Partisans, Muslims and what remained of the Ustasha. In the flatlands of Slavonia, north of the River Sava, the Germans used tank and artillery fire to cover their slow retreat towards Zagreb, and the Reich itself. In the mountains of Bosnia and Hercegovina, they fought at close quarters, even in hand-to-hand combat. The SS and Ustasha Franciscans fought side by side and literally to the last man to defend the monastery at Široki Brijeg.

The Independent State of Croatia remained in existence into the spring of 1945. The Jasenovac concentration camp went on with its deadly work, and as late as March the Ustasha succeeded in murdering a hundred wounded Serbs at Knin. On 24 March 1945, only six weeks before the end of the war, Stepinac and four other bishops, including Archbishop Šarić of Sarajevo, met in Zagreb to draw up a pastoral letter. Rejecting any suggestion that the Church had itself been guilty of misdeeds, the letter protested against the 'systematic torture and murder of innocent Catholic priests and people', suggesting that accusations of war crimes now being made by the Partisans were 'simply a means of destroying those people whom the Communists considered to be an obstacle to the creation of their party program'. The letter, published also in English and French, concluded with a reaffirmation of faith in an independent Croatia: 'History is the witness that the Croatian people through its 1,300 years has never ceased to proclaim through plebiscites that it will not renounce the right to freedom and independence which every other nation desires.'[51]

On 10 April 1945, the fourth anniversary of the NDH, Stepinac celebrated Mass in Zagreb Cathedral and *Te Deums* were sung in praise of what remained of the Ustasha state. On Sunday, 15 April, as Pavelić, Artuković, Budak, Archbishop Šarić of Sarajevo and Luburić, the commandant of Jasenovac, were preparing to go into exile in Argentina, Spain or the United States, Archbishop Stepinac devoted his sermon to what he believed was Croatia's worst sin, not mass murder but swearing. His lack of any sense of proportion amounted almost to madness. Stepinac could see no distinction in the degree of evil between cursing a neighbour and hurling that neighbour over the side of a precipice.

Archbishop Stepinac may well have continued to believe until the last weeks of the war that the Western powers would somehow step in to save Croatia from Communism. Because Tito feared the same thing, he refused to allow the British to land their troops on the Dalmatian coast. When HMS *Delhi* put into Split without any previous warning, the landing party was met by machine-gun fire.[52] On the other side of the Adriatic, the Allied advance up the Italian peninsula met with stubborn German resistance. The British did not achieve their breakthrough at Bologna until April 1945, less than a month before victory in Europe.

When the breakthrough came, the New Zealand Division advanced at almost reckless speed up the coastal plain, turning east to take Padua, Venice and part of Trieste, where it confronted the Partisans. Within hours of their meeting, the two Allied armies faced each other at gunpoint. An intelligence officer with the New Zealand Army, Geoffrey Cox, describes in his book *The Race for Trieste* how he spent VE Day drawing up urgent plans for a war against Yugoslavia. In the subsequent forty days until 12 June 1945, the Partisans in their part of the city carried out a massacre of the defeated Germans, Italian police and officials and many anti-Fascists who thought that Trieste should be Italian. At the end of the 'Forty Days', as they are still recalled with horror by older Triestini, the Allied military government estimated that 2,000 people had disappeared, but locals put the figure at ten times as many. The gorge at Bassovizza, where the arrested were stripped, shot and toppled into a mass grave, was said to contain 500 cubic metres of corpses.

At the end of the 'Forty Days', Tito backed down from the confrontation and withdrew his troops to the hinterland, afterwards known as 'Zone B'. The historian Cox deduces that Stalin abandoned Tito because he had learned of America's atom bomb, and also because there were US troops in the part of Germany earmarked for Soviet occupation. This betrayal, as Tito saw it, played a part in the breach with the Soviet Union three years later.

10

Power

The British *Official History of the Second World War* reminds us how threatening Tito's aggression was in May 1945: 'The Trieste crisis blew up with an intensity which at the time suggested that it might lead to the last battle of the Second World War or the first of the Third World War.'[1] For the next three years Trieste was one of the places where the Cold War could ignite. As Winston Churchill declared in a famous speech in 1946: 'From Stettin in the Baltic to Trieste in the Adriatic, an iron curtain has descended across the continent.'

During those tense three years, which also witnessed the Berlin airlift, the start of the Greek Civil War and the Communist takeover of Czechoslovakia, Tito appeared to the West as an ogre second only to Stalin, and Yugoslavia was known to the press as 'Soviet Satellite Number One'. Not only did Tito's army menace the borders of Italy, Greece and Austria, but his air force shot down two US military planes that had flown over Yugoslavian airspace. On the second of these occasions the New York *Daily News* called for an atom bomb to be dropped on Belgrade; the US Embassy warned of an air and sea invasion, and during the funeral of the American pilots a US officer yelled out 'Tito – Heil Hitler'.[2]

The Yugoslav Communists brought in a one-party state with a fraudulent parliament; they imprisoned some of the 'bourgeois' politicians, and closed independent newspapers by thuggery, arson or printing strikes. The Croat Andrija Hebrang introduced a five-year plan of rapid industrialisation based on the megalomaniac schemes of Stalin during the 1920s and 1930s. Like the Russians, the Yugoslavs made up their workforce from hundreds of thousands of German POWs, native political prisoners, and almost as unwilling 'volunteers' recruited from peasants who wished neither to join collective farms nor to sell their produce at uneconomic prices.

Milovan Djilas recalls writing an article in 1948 in which he boasted that in ten years' time Yugoslavia would catch up with Britain in economic production. Reflecting on this almost forty years later, Djilas says 'Of course the country had to industrialise, had to renew itself. But our helter-skelter scramble and distorted economic development can be explained only by a doctrinaire, Stalinist, mythological obsession with heavy industry and by the yearning of a new, revolutionary social power to build a happy, "perfect" society at once.'[3]

In their craze for industrialisation, as in everything else, the Yugoslav Communists were devoted to Stalin and all his works. The fact that they too had come to power through successful war and revolution gave them a deeper sense of comradeship with Lenin and his revered successor. The Serbs and still more the Montenegrins also identified with the Russians as Slavs, although they no longer acknowledged the tie of the Orthodox Church. Yugoslav children after the war were taught to chant:

> Zdravo Stalin, Stalin zdravo!
> U svakom slučaju imaš pravo!

which, roughly translated, means:

> Hail Stalin, Stalin hail!
> In every case your views prevail!

A whole generation of young people grew up believing this nonsense. When I first got to know Yugoslavia, several years after

Tito's break with Stalin, many young Communists told me of how they had suffered because, they said, 'Stalin was like a father to us'. Even the growing adulation of Tito was partly a way of aping the cult of Stalin. There was no comparable cult in the other countries of eastern Europe because there were no available heroes of revolution and war; the leaders were Party bureaucrats who had sat out the war in Moscow. But cults would arise around military heroes like Mao Zedong in China, Ho Chi Minh in Vietnam and Fidel Castro in Cuba. Many years later the most fanatical cults of all would surround Kim il-Sung in North Korea, Enver Hoxha in Albania and the unspeakable Nicolae Ceauşescu in Romania. Perhaps such cults were the logical outcome of Marxist-Leninist theory.

Unlike these other dictators, who glorified their own egos, Tito preferred to enjoy the pomp and luxury of his life at the top. It was not his idea that the youth of the country hold a relay race on his birthday (or putative birthday), although he permitted the practice when it was introduced. Although his speeches were published in many unreadable volumes, Tito never regarded himself as a serious thinker, but jokingly left the ideas to people like Kardelj and Djilas. Although he was understandably proud of his wartime career, Tito never tried to take credit away from his lieutenants, even from those with whom he later quarrelled. Unlike most dictators and most democratic politicians, Tito never held personal grudges and never exacted revenge. Some heads of state react to assaults from even the smallest foreign newspapers, but as Tito said in one of his very rare interviews, to a fringe American journalist in 1948: 'Of course I am aware of the campaign in the hostile press. I am not interested. I do not think press campaigns of great importance. I do not think the press of great importance.'[4]

The acquisition of power gave Tito the chance to indulge his passion for finery, stately living and luxury transport. Even before the end of the war, Tito had moved into some of the royal palaces in the Dedinje suburb, south of Belgrade. He also took over the other royal properties in the country, many estates belonging to private landowners, and all the best game reserves for the shooting of bears, boars, stags and wildfowl. He also took possession of the royal military stud-farm, turning it into a racing stable. When race meetings resumed after the war, the newspaper sports sections started to write of horses 'from Marshal Tito's stable'.[5]

Tito took over the former royal train, installed more luxurious furnishings and added two armoured carriages for his entourage and security guard. Wherever his train went, Tito was met by cheering crowds, brass band music and children with posies of flowers. Djilas recalls how shortly after the war Tito and his colleagues watched the Chaplin film *The Great Dictator*:

> Along came the scene when the train engineer keeps trying to align the doors of the car from which the dictator is about to emerge, with the carpet spread out in his honour. We all felt ill at ease and grew sober and subdued. The scene was identical with what happened whenever Tito got out at a station, except that his engineer was more adroit. Tito noticed the similarity and turned around to us, left and right, laughing with mischievous irony, as if to say: 'That's the way it goes – now he's got no way out!'[6]

Tito saw the joke of his own kingly splendour, and used to speak with half-ironic approval both of the Austro-Hungarian Empire and of the Montenegrin King Nikola who went into exile in 1916. He did not approve of the Karadjeordjević kings, although he had taken over some of their customs as well as all their property. It was an old tradition, in Serbia at least, for kings to act as godfathers for any ninth son. Tito resumed the custom, not because he desired it personally but in response to appeals from simple people, who understandably looked on him as another king. Tito came to enjoy dispensing this favour, along with a gift in cash from the public purse, and since there was no discrimination of sex in socialist Yugoslavia, he sponsored ninth daughters as well, and later tenth and eleventh children. There were mutterings in the Party at Tito playing not only a kingly but clearly a religious role. Could he be ambivalent in his attitude to God?

In spite of his power and wealth and devoted friends, Tito was missing the thing he needed most in life, a young and beautiful woman in his bed. His first and legal wife, Pelagija, had vanished into the Gulag Archipelago. His second or common-law wife, Herta Hass, has sadly accepted in 1943 that Tito no longer wanted her, and was now in Belgrade with a legal husband. The termagant Davorjanka Paunović, commonly known as Zdenka, had passed through many German offensives only to catch tuberculosis and, after an unsuccessful cure in the Soviet Union, came back to Belgrade to die. Milovan Djilas, who once had threatened to pick Zdenka up by the hair and throw her over the side of a cliff, was touched to see that her smile was now sickly, as though she were asking forgiveness for her unpleasant behaviour. He reflected more kindly now that 'her smouldering disease may have accounted at least in part for her fits of fury, her frenzy, her idiosyncrasies'.[8] It is not even known when Zdenka died, though Tito buried her in the White Palace garden. Tito's official biographers do not mention her, and she does not appear in the photographs from the war. Yet according to Ranković, who understood Tito's emotions better than anyone else, the 'Old Man' was very upset by Zdenka's death.

In spite of his power, wealth and legendary sex appeal, Tito was not in a good position to find a new female companion. During the underground years and the wartime battles, the high-minded Communists were prepared to allow a Herta or a Zdenka, but now they demanded that Tito adhere to their own stern morality. Belgrade was not like Stalin's Moscow, where Party bosses could take their pick from the terrified girls of the Bolshoi Ballet, by threatening them and their families with the Gulag. Tito was free to flirt, as he did, with one of the stars of the Belgrade Opera, but she in turn was free to refuse him, as she did. Since Tito was always accompanied by his trigger-happy security guards, he could neither slip away to a secret rendezvous, nor bring a woman unnoticed into his bedroom.

Tito's main hope of finding a female companion lay in his entourage, and so it was that he met Jovanka Budisavljević, thirty-two years his junior. She was a Serb from the Lika district of

Croatia, a wartime Partisan and a member of Tito's security guard as well as the head of his household. The gallant Milovan Djilas, a champion of Jovanka during her later years of rejection and ostracism, describes her in 1946 as

> a striking beauty, a healthy Serbian beauty, with black hair, fair complexion. She was without coquetry, yet feminine. Her femininity was subdued. She was like a nun or a peasant woman who has vowed to give her life to her husband and children. Always dressed in the uniform of an army officer, because she was always on duty, she looked tall though in fact she was of medium height. Under her slightly tilted Partisan cap was the silkiest and most luxuriant hair I have ever seen. She had large eyes, set off by the delicate flush of her cheeks, eyes full of patience, care and devotion.[9]

By 1946, some of Tito's friends had come to suspect his attraction to Jovanka, although she was not admitted into his social life and had to wait for hours on guard in the hall. Some of the other security staff were jealous and even obliged her to taste the first spoonful of all the meals she cooked for Tito with such loving care. Djilas suggested to Ranković that he had planted Jovanka as a suitable mate for Tito, but the policeman denied this 'with a glint in his eye'.[10] Jovanka would have to wait six years before she achieved that closeness to Tito that led him to make her his wife.

The biographer of Tito is tempted to pass quickly over the three grim Stalinist years after 1945, to the more dramatic confrontation with Russia, the liberalisation of Communism, the downfall of Djilas and Tito's emergence on to the international stage. Such events, which appeared important and often exciting in Tito's lifetime, divert attention away from the deeper nationalities problem, especially the quarrel between Serbs and Croats, that led to the posthumous collapse of Tito's Yugoslavia. Tito himself was always very aware of the nationalities problem because he had seen its ghastly results in the war.

At the end of the Second World War and in its immediate

aftermath, hundreds of thousands of anti-Communist Yugoslavs attempted to flee the country, took to the hills to continue fighting, or went into civil opposition. Tito's effort to solve, or at least patch up, the nationalities problem went almost unnoticed abroad because he could not admit in public that such a problem existed. The Serb and Croat nationalists were depicted either as Nazi or Fascist quislings, bourgeois reactionaries or agents of Anglo-American imperialism. Even the names Chetnik and Ustasha seldom appeared in the press, and those they had killed were vaguely described as 'victims of Fascism'.

The nationalities problem resulted in the campaign for 'Brotherhood and Unity' ('Bratstvo i Jedinstvo'), the slogan used for the Zagreb–Belgrade motorway built by the Yugoslav youth and foreign zealots. Every summer until 1948, thousands of young Western Communists came to wield their picks on the highway, to chant slogans in honour of Stalin and Tito, to flirt with the Partisan girls, and in the evening to dance the kolo and drink plum brandy under the warm, socialist sky. Few of them understood the nationalities problem.

Settling Scores

By the end of 1945, about a half a million Yugoslavs had become refugees, or 'displaced persons' as they were called at the time. This figure includes forced labourers in the German Reich who did not want to return home after the war, but does not include 360,000 ethnic Germans (*Volksdeutsche*) driven from Yugoslavia. Nor does it include the unknown number of Ustasha, whose names never appeared in the books of the refugee organisations.[1] The 'displaced persons' eventually merged with the long-standing communities of the South Slavs in western Europe, North and South America, and Australia and New Zealand. From the 1950s, when the restrictions on travel were lifted, hundreds of thousands of South Slavs, and proportionally still more Albanians from Kosovo, emigrated to join the existing diasporas. The very large number of overseas Yugoslavs, many harbouring grudges from the Second World War, contributed to the nationalities problem inside the country.

Most of the Yugoslav 'displaced persons' were anti-Communist soldiers who had escaped to Italy or Austria and there been accepted as political refugees. Long after the war there came to light two strange and sinister features of Allied policy towards the escaping Yugoslavs. The British in Austria sent back by force or deception probably 30,000 Serbs, Croats and Slovenes who had not been found guilty or even accused of any crime other than opposition to Communism. Many, if not most, of these people were promptly killed. Having sent back thousands of possibly innocent people to death or imprisonment, the Allies refused to hand over and even protected Ante Pavelić and most of the leading Ustasha.

The first anti-Communists to escape the country were between 10,000 and 12,000 Chetniks from Croatia under their leader, the Orthodox priest Duke Momčilo Djujič. He and his men from the region round Knin had been the first to take up arms against the Ustasha in May 1941 and had later made an alliance with the Italians. When Italy dropped out of the war, Duke Djujić continued to fight the Ustasha but made an arrangement with the Germans against the Partisans. In the spring of 1945, Djujić led his Dinaric Division to Italy, where he was sheltered by the Catholic Church, ironically, since the Croatian Catholic Church had tried to wipe out his religion. In 1946 the British appointed a special commission under Fitzroy Maclean, to screen the remaining Yugoslav and Ukrainian 'displaced persons' in Italy, to determine who were refugees and who if any were war criminals trying to escape from justice. In spite of his pro-Tito reputation, Maclean was sympathetic towards the Chetniks, and all the surviving members of the Dinaric Division eventually settled in Britain in 1947, though Djujić himself went to California.[2]

The great majority of the anti-Communist Yugoslavs, including the Chetniks from Serbia, Montenegro and Bosnia-Hercegovina, were heading for Austria in May and early June 1945. Just as Tito was claiming for Yugoslavia the largely Italian-speaking province of Venezia-Giulia, so he demanded the largely German-speaking southern part of Carinthia, because of its Slovene minority. When troops of the British 5th Corps entered Klagenfurt on 8 May, they reported it swarming with Partisans: 'The Yugoslavs were attempting to seize public buildings and key installations.'[3]

The Partisans on either side of the Karavanka mountain range were also hoping to intercept the hundreds of thousands of German and anti-Communist Yugoslav troops who wanted to give themselves up to the British. Winston Churchill had made it clear in a message delivered on 29 April that all surrendering Yugoslavs should be disarmed and held in refugee camps awaiting a further decision about their future. The Partisans were meanwhile using the threat of their military presence to back the demand that all Yugoslavs should be repatriated.

Tito's main object was to prevent the escape of the former political leaders of the Independent State of Croatia. On 13 May he instructed his First Army: 'A group of Ustasha and some Chetniks, a total of 50,000 men, is reported by Third Army in the area towards Dravograd. It includes Pavelić, Maček, the Croatian Government and a huge number of criminals. They are attempting to cross at Dravograd and give themselves up to the British. You must move your forces most urgently from the Celje area . . . in order to concentrate for an attack aimed at the annihilation of this column.'[4]

As we shall see, the Ustasha leaders and 'a huge number of criminals' succeeded in getting to Austria and then vanished. A large number of less important Croats gave themselves up to the Partisans on the promise of fair treatment. The Partisans drove these men and their families back into Yugoslavia on a long, cruel forced march that ended for many with execution. However, the report by Cowgill, Brimelow and Booker discounts the allegations of mass executions at Bleiburg in Austria.[5]

On 13 May Tito warned the British that he had the support of the Soviet Union for Yugoslavia's 'claim to Austrian territory', meaning presumably southern Carinthia. Perhaps because of Tito's threat and the ever more menacing attitude of the Partisans in Austria, the British 5th Corps changed their policy on repatriation. On 17 May Brigadier Toby Low (the future Lord Aldington) directed that: 'All Yugoslav nationals at present in the Corps will be handed over to Tito forces as soon as possible.' The following day a supplementary order explained that this was to include 'all non-Tito soldiers of Yugoslav nationality and such civilians of Yugoslav nationality as can be claimed as their camp followers'. The authors of the report on repatriations comment: 'In other

words the groups comprised precisely those categories of dissident
Yugoslavs whom Churchill had in mind when on 29 April he had
ruled that they should not be handed over to Tito . . .'[6]

From 18 May to 2 June, the British in Austria carried out the
forced repatriation, mostly by train, of about 26,000 anti-Communist Yugoslavs. Sometimes the victims were tricked into going
quietly by being told that the train was travelling to Italy; sometimes they were forced on board. In either case, this business
shamed and revolted most of the British troops involved. According
to Djilas, even the Yugoslavs were surprised that the British had
fallen for their bluff of a threat to annex Carinthia. On the very
day after the start of repatriation, Tito ordered the Partisans out of
Austria, and on 9 June he signed a treaty formalising the troop
withdrawals from both Carinthia and Venezia-Giulia. In an angry
speech delivered at Ljubljana on 27 May, Tito made a veiled attack
on the Soviet Union, then called for the punishment of Yugoslav
'traitors'. This apparently led to the massacre of some or all of the
people who had been repatriated.[7]

On 13 May, the head of the Independent State of Croatia, Ante
Pavelić, accompanied by such eminent Ustasha as the Minister of
the Interior, Andrija Artuković, the Minister of Religious Affairs,
Mile Budak, the Archbishop of Sarajevo, Ivan Šarić, and probably
by the commandant of Jasenovac concentration camp, Maks
Luburić, travelled towards the Austrian frontier in what Tito
described as a column of 50,000 men. If Tito knew this, the British
almost certainly knew as well, from aerial reconnaissance, radio
interception and ground observation.

Since most of the Ustasha leaders were very high on the list of
enemy war criminals wanted to stand trial, one can assume that
their names, appearance and records were well known to all units
in Austria of the US Counter-Intelligence Corps and the British
Intelligence Corps, whose Field Security Police were supposed to
keep watch on all refugees. Yet somehow, in May 1945, almost all
the leading Ustasha vanished in Austria and did not reappear until
several years later in Argentina, Spain and the United States. The
only prominent Ustasha to be returned to Yugoslavia after the war

were the Kvaternik father and son, who were in disgrace for plotting against their leader, Ante Pavelić.

Many years later, various authors in and outside Yugoslavia attempted to piece together the few known facts about the escape of the Ustasha leaders, but the only first-hand account was given by Pavelić's daughter Marija, when she returned to Croatia to rebuild her father's Ustasha organisation, now called the Croatian Liberation Movement (Hrvatski Oslobodilački Pokret), or HOP. In an interview with a Zagreb magazine, Marija Pšeničnik, as she is called by her married name, explained that she was sent to Austria in advance of her father's escape from Yugoslavia.

> We were lucky. We landed on an Austrian who saved father. For money. He put him up on a peasant estate in the Alps, with false Austrian papers . . . The only person who lived with father in that house was a maid, an Italian woman. We (the family) lived elsewhere in San Egilgen. We reported to the Americans, as this zone was under American control . . . We met up with our father one to three times a week, in the woods. He spent his time in the woods, picking mushrooms and catching fish. He even sent us some of these and we in turn sent him some of the bread rations we had received. One day at the end of summer 1945, it was raining and mother wasn't feeling well and she asked me to go out and meet father. I found him alone in the woods, with a backpack, preparing to escape. When he had gone home the maid had waved as a signal that the police were there.

At this point in the interview Marija's husband, Dr Srečko Pšeničnik, the President of HOP, interrupted to clarify who the policemen were:

> It was the Austrian police who were acting on behalf of the American secret service as well as the English. Had he been arrested he would certainly have been handed over to Yugoslavia. He had already once been in the hands of the Americans and English but they hadn't recognised him.[8]

It is hard to believe that the British and American counter-intelligence failed to recognise a man whose face was as well known in Yugoslavia as Hitler's was in Germany. It is even harder to believe that if they had wanted to find Ante Pavelić they would not have kept an eye on his wife and family, rather than leaving the search to the Austrian police, who were themselves under suspicion of war crimes and did not handle political matters.[9]

Marija Pšeničnik went on to explain how her father then lived for four years in Rome before going to Argentina: 'We had spent our childhood in Italy [when the Ustasha were in exile in the 1930s] . . . There was no similar "witch-hunt" going on there . . . Both father and mother managed to cross into Italy . . . Who helped us most? The Jesuit Order. They sheltered father because he had gone to a Jesuit school in Travnik. According to their tradition, every pupil of theirs had an everlasting right to be sheltered. That's how they saved father.'[10]

The Jesuits may have helped another distinguished old boy, Archbishop Šarić of Sarajevo, but most of the Ustasha leaders came from the rival Franciscan schools such as Široki Brijeg in Hercegovina. The 'Scarlet Pimpernel' who organised the escape of Artuković and many other Ustasha was the Franciscan Father Krunoslav Draganović, a former professor of theology at Zagreb, the mastermind of the punitive laws against Serbs and Jews, a temporary military chaplain at Jasenovac concentration camp, and from 1942 an emissary in Rome. From there in May 1945 on, he helped to run the 'Ratlines' organisation providing false papers, travel documents, bribes and hide-out addresses for Nazi and Ustasha members on their way to havens abroad.[11]

The 'Yugoslav Himmler' Andrija Artuković spent some time in a British camp before he was freed by what Hubert Butler described as a 'mysterious intervention'. The former Ustasha head of the diplomatic service, the Muslim Mehmed Alajbegović, met him in Austria: 'Artuković showed me how the British had stamped his pass to say that he did not constitute a danger to public order and security, and said they did this when they released him and other members of the government from the camp at Spittal.'[12] The authors of *Ratlines* suggested that Artuković was a British Intelligence agent even before the Second World War. Through Father Draganović, whom he met at an Austrian monastery in November 1946, Artuković got to Switzerland and then to the Republic of Ireland, where he spent a year with Franciscans in Dublin and Galway before joining his brother in California.[13]

Except for the Kvaternik father and son, all the prominent Ustasha made good their escape. The novelist Mile Budak, who had first made public the Ustasha policy towards the Serbs of 'convert a third, expel a third and kill a third', became an adviser on security to Juan Perón, the dictator of Argentina. The Archbishop of Sarajevo, Dr Šarić, retired to Spain to continue writing his poems in praise of Archbishop Stepinac and Ante Pavelić. The commandant of Jasenovac concentration camp, Maks Luburić, took a villa in Spain. He later broke with Pavelić to form a more extreme terrorist organisation in Europe and Australia.[14]

Although half a million opponents of Tito had left Yugoslavia after the Second World War, a far greater number remained in the country, most of them Serb or Croat nationalists. Many anti-Communist Serbs and Croats were not at the same time separatists, but Yugoslav feeling was stronger among the smaller groups, such as the Slovenes and Bosnian Muslims. The only armed resistance to Tito came from a handful of Ustasha in Croatia and western Bosnia-Hercegovina, and from much larger bands of Chetniks in eastern Bosnia, Montenegro and western Serbia, especially the Ravna Gora retreat of Draža Mihailović.

Many anti-Communists clung to the hope that the Western Allies and in particular the United States would step in to save them from Communism. We know that as early as 1943 Roosevelt's adviser Cardinal Spellman assured a representative of the NDH that the United States wanted an independent Roman Catholic Croatia. Until the very end of the war the US government continued to back and encourage the Chetniks in Serbia. Milovan Djilas says that as late as August 1946 the American Embassy fostered hopes of intervention: 'Its employees were arrogant and provocative, even going so far as to promise certain individuals – our enemies and some leaders of former parties – that parachute troops would take over Belgrade and the navy would seize the Adriatic coast.'[15]

The Ustasha resistance soon crumbled because it had little or no support among the Croatian peasantry. The Chetniks, however, were still generally popular in Serbia proper. Most of them shaved their beards off after the war and acted as part-time guerrillas only. The OZNA secret police, the forerunners of UDBA, carried on a relentless search for the Chetniks, treating the Serbian peasants rather like citizens of an occupied country. Even Ranković was appalled when he heard that his agents in eastern Bosnia had put on display in the centre of Tuzla the severed head of a Chetnik warrior.[16]

The capture of Draža Mihailović came in March 1946. One of his senior commanders was lured to Belgrade, arrested, recruited by OZNA and sent back to Ravna Gora to lead Mihailović into a trap, fulfilling the Serbian dread of betrayal, as at the Battle of Kosovo. Ranković was away in Moscow when preparations began for the trial, so Djilas took over the job of formulating the prosecution case. To counter accusations of national bias, the judges and prosecution lawyer were Serbs from Serbia proper. To counter hostile critics abroad, the prosecution concentrated on Draža Mihailović's alleged collaboration with the Germans, rather than on his opposition to Communism. At this time, only a handful of people knew that Tito too had collaborated with Germany in the 'March Consultations' of 1943.

Mihailović was not tortured, drugged or made drunk, although he was given brandy. He gave his evidence honestly, for his conscience was clean, and he made a moving speech from the dock in which he quoted the poet Njegoš on how he had been caught up in the 'whirlwind of the world'. Tito was in two minds over the death sentence for what he admitted to be a 'political' trial, but the 'leading triumvirate' of Kardelj, Djilas and Ranković told him that any other verdict would dismay the Partisans and outrage the relatives of the Chetniks' victims: 'Tito bowed silently to the arguments, more readily because he himself was not opposed.'[17]

Although he had planned the prosecution and argued in favour of execution, Djilas speaks with respect of Draža Mihailović:

> a brave man, but extraordinarily unstable in his views and in his decision-making. A traditionalist, he was incapable of grasping stormy times, let alone navigating through them. For him the common people, especially Serbs, were deeply religious, patriotic and in their good-natured way devoted to king and country . . . Although his units – sometimes at his direct orders – carried out mass crimes against the non-Serbian population, wantonly executing Communists and their sympathisers, Draža himself was not considered harsh or fanatic.[18]

The trial of Draža Mihailović, and his execution by firing squad on 17 July 1946, brought condemnation of Tito from Western statesmen, especially Churchill and de Gaulle. But condemnation of Tito was not the same as sympathy and support for Mihailović's long-suffering people. The majority of the Serbs in Serbia, as distinct from the Orthodox in Croatia and Bosnia-Hercegovina, were, as Djilas put it, 'deeply religious, patriotic and in their good-natured way devoted to king and country', in other words anti-Communist.

However, it is the fate of the Serbs that although their vices are known abroad – their stubbornness, their recklessness and their habit of starting wars – their virtues have gone unnoticed. They come to the attention of the Western world only when causing trouble, as in 1875, 1908, 1912, 1914, 1941 and 1991. This is largely because they belong to a Church which, though in theory universal, is really confined to eastern Europe. Although, in the nineteenth century, Serbia enjoyed the support of its fellow Orthodox Christians in mighty Russia as well as the neighbouring states of Romania, Bulgaria and Greece, all but the last of these countries were ruled by atheists after the Second World War. There was nobody in the outside world to speak for the Serbs, except Serbs in exile.

While the anti-Communist Serbs had few friends outside their country, the Croats had the support of the worldwide Roman Catholic Church. The Partisans who entered a silent Zagreb on 8 May 1945 were not encouraged to take revenge on the capital of the Ustasha. As a Croat who understood, if he did not share, the pride and touchiness of his fellow-countrymen, Tito was anxious to win over the followers of the previous regime. From about 1943, when morale had started to crumble among the troops of the NDH, the Partisans had encouraged and welcomed deserters without too many questions being asked. As the Partisans advanced, they arrested and almost immediately executed Ustasha guilty of crimes, including scores of priests and at least two nuns. However, their propaganda tended to play down Ustasha crimes and play up those of the foreign invaders. The hundreds of thousands of Orthodox Serbs who had perished during the early years of the war were lumped together with the rest as 'victims of Fascism'.

Tito's motives were no doubt mixed. He feared that a full-scale war crimes trial, with all the horrific publicity that would follow, might cause an explosion of anti-Croat hatred among the Serbs, and burden the whole Croat nation with an undeserved and unbearable guilt. We can also assume a less honourable motive. As Tito knew perfectly well, the Partisan army had come to power not as agents of revolution, not even as patriots fighting the foreign invader, but as the defenders of Serbs in the NDH. Without the Ustasha government and its murderous policy towards the Serbs, the Partisans would have had few recruits, and the Communist Party would never have come to power. This was the principal reason why Tito did not want to rake up the Ustasha crimes.

Almost everyone who had stayed in Zagreb during the war was to some extent compromised, as Hubert Butler explains in his essay 'Nazor, Oroschatz and the Von Berks'. Soon after the liberation, a magazine published in Zagreb reprinted various odes, declamations and pictures which had appeared under well-known names in praise of the Ustasha and the Germans. According to Butler, who came across the magazine in 1946: 'The editor pointed out that these people were now ardent Partisans and supporters of the

government. It was, I believe, the last freely critical paper published since the liberation and it was very quickly suppressed.'[19]

Soon after the liberation, Tito made courteous approaches to
Archbishop Stepinac, asking for help in reconciling the Serbs and
Croats after the horror of the Ustasha years. He also suggested that
the Croatian Catholic Church should become more 'national', that
is to say less dependent on the Vatican. In one of his talks with
Church officials, Tito went so far as to speak of himself 'as a Croat
and a Catholic', although this comment was cut out of the press
reports on the orders of Kardelj.[20] The government gave permission
for a march on 8 July 1945 to the shrine at Marija Bistrica, which
was attended by 50,000 faithful.

While Tito was trying to be conciliatory, the authorities went
ahead with the trials of priests who were said to have 'blood on
their hands'. The monstrous Filipović-Majstorović, the Jasenovac
killer known to the inmates as 'Brother Devil', was hanged in his
friar's robe. The new authorities closed the religious schools and
stopped religious teaching in state education. Civil marriage was
introduced, and with it the prospect of easy divorce. As part of its
programme for the collectivisation of land, the government confis-
cated most of the Church's property.

In his resistance to all these measures, Stepinac was from the
start 'completely uncompromising', as his biographer Stella Alexander says.[21] Throughout the summer of 1945 he issued a torrent
of circulars, pastoral letters and scarcely veiled threats to disrupt
Yugoslavia's relationship with the Vatican. In a circular to the
clergy and in a letter to Tito, Stepinac rejected the separation of
Church and State and claimed for the former the right to religious
education, an uncensored press and the receipts of revenue from
its land.

Through a series of articles in the diocesan press, Stepinac
defended the role of the bishops under the NDH and blamed any
'errors' that had occurred on 'people who often behaved as if there
was no church authority'. Even Stella Alexander, who is sympathetic to Stepinac, says that writing about the massacres as a series of
errors gave a 'deplorable impression of self-righteousness and self-

justification'.[22] It is difficult not to agree with the angry statement by Tito, printed on 25 October 1945, in which he asked a number of pertinent questions: 'Why had the bishops not issued a pastoral letter against the terrible killing of the Serbs in Croatia [i.e. the NDH]? Why were they spreading racial hatred at a time when everyone ought to be helping to heal the wounds of the war? If the bishops said now that they were ready to sacrifice themselves, they must have kept silent under the Ustasha not from terror but because they agreed with them.'[23]

Although Stepinac had in effect invited arrest and trial in September 1945, the Communists waited a year before taking the action which, as they knew, would outrage world opinion. And the longer they waited, the harder it was to answer the obvious question: if Archbishop Stepinac committed crimes during the war, why was he not arrested and brought to trial as soon as the war was over?

A few years later, Tito explained to a sympathetic American journalist how he had tried to avoid a trial, in spite of Stepinac's clear-cut guilt: 'I asked Cardinal Stepinac to leave the country – go anywhere, go to Rome. But he refused. I appealed to the Pope [Pius XII] to intervene but did not get a reply from the Vatican. There was at that time a papal nuncio in Belgrade, Bishop [Joseph Patrick] Hurley [of St Augustine, Florida], so I asked him to intervene with the Vatican and get Stepinac out of the country. Bishop Hurley was sympathetic. He took the documentation of treason and sent it to Rome. But he also got no reply. It was only then that the authorities arrested Stepinac.'[24]

As Tito had foreseen, the trial, which began in September 1946, was a propaganda disaster for himself, and an undeserved triumph for the Archbishop. For reasons already mentioned, the government dared not say that Stepinac, the hierarchy and much of the Croat nation had backed the Ustasha regime, and either approved or ignored the murder of 350,000 Serbs as well as the Jews and Gypsies. The principal charges levelled against Stepinac were that he welcomed the Ustasha government while Yugoslavia was still at war; that he persecuted the Serbs in the interests of 'the Vatican and Italian imperialism'; that since the war he had entertained Ustasha representatives from abroad. The second charge was especially disingenuous, since the Italians had protected the Serbs from Croat persecution.

In the course of a long and fair trial, Stepinac often refused to answer questions, confining himself to saying that his conscience was clear. In a statement from the dock, he expressed his detestation of Communism, especially its atheistic teaching in schools, and he once more declared his faith in an independent Croatia: 'The Croat nation unanimously declared itself for the Croatian state and I would have been remiss had I not recognised and acknowledged the desire of the Croatian people enslaved in the former Yugoslavia.'[25]

Stepinac was sentenced to sixteen years' hard labour but served only five years at Lepoglava, under conditions more comfortable than those Tito had experienced in the 1930s. He was released in 1951 and once more offered the chance to go into exile, but he chose instead to stay under house arrest in a village south-west of Zagreb. When Stepinac died in 1960, Tito allowed a funeral service in Zagreb Cathedral, which did not appease the Catholic Croats but much enraged the Orthodox Serbs who continued to look on Stepinac as the man chiefly responsible for their suffering during the Second World War.

His trial and imprisonment made Stepinac a hero and martyr to Croats in exile, to Roman Catholics throughout the world and to most anti-Communists outside Serbia. For many years I was among those who thought that Stepinac's crime 'was not that he fraternised with the fascists but that he refused to fraternise with the Communists.'[26] Having since examined the history of the Croatian Catholic Church, especially Viktor Novak's monumental indictment *Magnum Crimen*, I now believe that Stepinac was guilty of complicity in the Ustasha crimes.

Stepinac welcomed the Independent State of Croatia, knowing full well the character of its leader Ante Pavelić, a terrorist murderer even before the war. For at least a year, Stepinac uttered no word of public or even private complaint about the Ustasha murders, of which he was fully informed by his bishops. From 1942 he began to make mild public criticism of the Ustasha regime and even made contact with enemies of the regime such as the British agent Rapotec, to whom he said that he hoped for the restitution of Yugoslavia after the war. In retrospect it appears that Stepinac was simply hedging his earlier bet on an Axis victory. Even before the end of the war, when the Western Allies were growing hostile to Tito, Stepinac returned to his earlier faith in an independent Croatia.

Stepinac betrayed his Christian duty during the war but his greatest crime was committed afterwards. Not only did he refuse to accept any blame for the forced conversion and massacre of the Serbs but he never expressed so much as a word of contrition, regret or ordinary human sympathy for the bereaved. By insisting as head of the Church that his conscience was clear, he exculpated the rest of the Church, including the Ustasha priests and pious laymen such as Pavelić, Budak and Artuković. By reaffirming support for the Independent State of Croatia, Stepinac gave retrospective approval to what it accomplished. By disclaiming any responsibility for the massacre of the Serbs, he helped to encourage the legend that this massacre never took place.

At the end of her biography *The Triple Myth*, Stella Alexander quotes with approval the judgement on Stepinac made by the sculptor Ivan Mestrović: 'He was a just man condemned as it has often happened in history that just men are condemned by political necessity.'[27] The Irish historian Hubert Butler, who attended the trial and spoke to Stepinac in prison, described the archives of the Croatian Catholic Church as 'the Rosetta Stone of Christian corruption'. In writing of priests such as Stepinac who welcomed and worked with murderers and terrorists, Butler asked rhetorically: 'Is it not clear that in times like these, the church doors should be shut, the Church newspapers closed down and Christians who believe that we should love our neighbours should go underground and try to build up a new faith in the catacombs?'[28]

After his visit to Zagreb in 1946, Butler gave an Irish radio talk on Yugoslavia but did not mention the Communist treatment of the Church, nor the gaoling of Archbishop Stepinac: 'I could not refer to the Communist persecution of religion without mentioning the far more terrible Catholic persecution which had preceded it, so I thought silence was best.' Nevertheless, Ireland's leading Catholic weekly *The Standard* published a harsh attack on Butler for which he demanded but did not receive an apology.

The foreign editor of *The Standard*, an Austro-Irishman named Count O'Brien of Thomond, went on to publish a book called *Archbishop Stepinac: The Man and his Case*, which carried commendations from leading churchmen such as Cardinal Spellman of New York. Yet Butler says that 'there was a major error of fact, or interpretation, or a significant omission, on almost every page'. The climax of Butler's annoyance came when the Irish Minister of Agriculture advised a meeting of law students to model themselves on Archbishop Stepinac and on Ante Pavelić, the Ustasha leader. Butler could stand it no longer: 'I felt that the honour of the small Protestant community in Southern Ireland would be compromised if those of us who had investigated the facts remained silent about what we had discovered.' He wrote letters to the Kilkenny and Dublin newpapers giving his version of Pavelić.

A few years later it was announced that Tito was going to visit England, sparking off anti-Communist demonstrations there and in Ireland. Butler attended a meeting in Dublin in which the editor of *The Standard* spoke on 'Yugoslavia: The Pattern of Persecution'. Afterwards Butler started to make a reply when a stately figure rose from among the audience and then stalked from the hall. It was the Papal Nuncio to Ireland. The subsequent newspaper scandal – 'Pope's envoy walks out; Government to discuss insult to Nuncio' – led to Butler's expulsion from several local government posts as well as the loss of his honorary secretaryship of the Kilkenny Archaeological Society.

Before he resigned, Butler decided to tell the society's two or three hundred members why he had challenged the Church's version of the events in wartime Croatia. In particular he wished to refute the allegation by Count O'Brien that all the Catholic bishops had opposed the 'evil plan' of Pavelić for the forced conversion of

Orthodox Serbs. According to O'Brien's book, Archbishop Stepinac had swept into Pavelić's office: '"It is God's command," he said, "Thou shalt not kill," and without another word he left the Quisling's palace.'

In his letter to the members, Butler quoted at length from Archbishop Stepinac's letter to Pavelić, and gave the Bishop of Mostar's account of the massacre of the Serbs in Hercegovina. The Bishop of Mostar's account was published several times in the Dublin and Kilkenny press, yet as Butler ruefully said: 'It struck me as odd that nobody in the British Isles, at a time when so much was written and published about the imprisoned Archbishop, ever commented on it, quoted from it, or wrote to me to enquire how I had secured it.'

The memory of the Ustasha crimes continued to be confused or effaced. Articles in the Irish press compared Pavelić with Roger Casement and Patrick Pearse, as a simple-hearted patriot. He was photographed in the Argentine sun with his wife and family and their pet dog. Butler was bewildered. Three centuries earlier, Milton had given lasting notoriety to the massacre and forced conversion of the Waldenses in the Alps, yet no one now bothered about the recent and far greater forced conversion and massacre of the Serbs. Butler worked off some of his anger in a sonnet:

> Milton, if you were living at this hour
> they'd make you trim your sonnet to appease
> the triple tyrant and the Piedmontese.
> 'Why for some peasants vex a friendly power?
> We'd like to print it, but Sir Tottenham Bauer
> and half the Board would blame us. Colleen Cheese
> would stop its front-page ad. They're strong RCs.
> It's old stuff now, and truth, deferred goes sour . . .'[29]

12

The Quarrel
with Stalin

The execution of Mihailović and the imprisonment of Stepinac made Tito an object of loathing throughout the West. Cartoonists depicted him as a Hermann Goering figure, with corpulent body bursting out of a uniform covered with medals. The editorial writers called Tito a slavish puppet of Stalin, and Yugoslavia the 'Satellite Number One'. Not a single Western observer foresaw that Tito and Yugoslavia were about to leave the Soviet bloc.

The quarrel with Stalin is rightly seen as the greatest crisis of Tito's career and a turning-point in Yugoslav history. Perhaps we shall come to see it as well as a turning-point for the Soviet Union, and even as the start of the slow collapse of international Communism. The emergence of 'Titoism' meant more than a crack in Soviet power; it challenged belief in the infallibility of the Marxist-Leninist theory. Until 1948, the strength and attraction of Communism lay in its absolute certainty, based on the supposedly scientific laws of dialectical materialism. To become a Communist was to join a movement backed by 'history', a word and a concept that greatly appealed to Marxist theoreticians. Because it was on the side of 'history', the Communist movement was indivisible and monolithic. All this changed with the emergence and the reluctant acceptance of 'Titoism' as an alternative form of Communism. Whereas 'Trotskyism' during the 1930s was only a heresy to be

sniffed out and destroyed, 'Titoism' was now a separate, established church, with a geographical base from which to send out
missionaries.

Thanks to a piece of rare good fortune, one of the main
protagonists in the quarrel with Russia was the writer and daring
political thinker Milovan Djilas. His account of what happened,
Conversations with Stalin, remains one of the most important books
of the century. Having played a key role in the break with Stalin,
and therefore in the creation of 'Titoism', Djilas went on to break
with Tito, becoming the first opponent of Communism from inside
the ranks of the hierarchy.

When the Partisans were first invited to Moscow in March 1944,
Tito chose Djilas, the youngest of the triumvirate, to lead the
delegation. After stopping off along the way in Cairo and Teheran,
Djilas finally arrived in the Soviet Union and, after a few weeks
spent touring the front and fretting in Moscow, was summoned to
the Kremlin. To Djilas at this time, 'Stalin was something more
than a leader in battle. He was the incarnation of an idea,
transfigured in Communist minds into pure idea, and thereby into
something infallible and sinless.'[1] Stalin the man came as rather a
disappointment: 'He had quite a large paunch, and his hair was
sparse, though the scalp was not entirely bald. His face was white,
with ruddy cheeks. Later I learned that this coloration, so characteristic of those who sit long in offices, was known as the "Kremlin
complexion" in high Soviet circles. His teeth were black and
irregular, turned inward. Not even his moustache was thick or
firm.'[2] In a later article for *Borba*, Djilas did not mention these
unprepossessing traits but said that Stalin had caring yellowish
brown eyes and an expression, though stern, of beautiful, simple
serenity.[3]

At this and a subsequent meeting, Stalin said that the Partisans
should try to conceal the fact that they planned a Communist
revolution. 'What do you want with red stars on your caps?' he
asked, and would not accept Djilas's explanation that these were
already a popular symbol. Having warned that the British must not
be frightened off by displays of Communism, Stalin said:

Perhaps you think just because we are the allies of the English, we have forgotten who they are and who Churchill is. There's nothing they like better than to trick their allies . . . And Churchill? Churchill is the kind of man who will pick your pocket of a kopeck, if you don't watch him. Yes, pick your pocket of a kopeck. Roosevelt's not like that. He digs in his hand only for bigger coins. But Churchill will do it for a kopeck.[4]

Djilas noticed that Stalin always used the term 'Russia', not even 'Soviet Russia', rather than 'Soviet Union'. Yet Djilas came away from his first visit to Moscow more convinced than ever of Stalin's greatness, humanity and uniqueness.

Stalin was pleased by what Djilas wrote about him in *Borba* but not by what he later said of the Red Army soldiers raping and looting in Belgrade. In particular he resented the statement made to General Korneyev, that enemies of the Partisans compared the Russian soldiers unfavourably with the British. A few months after the liberation of Belgrade, during the winter of 1944–5, Stalin received a Yugoslav delegation including Djilas's then wife Mitra Mitrović. He criticised the Yugoslav army, then made an attack on Djilas personally:

He spoke emotionally about the sufferings of the Red Army and about the horror it was forced to undergo fighting for thousands of kilometres through devastated country. He wept, crying out: 'And such an army was insulted by no one else but Djilas! Djilas, of whom I could least have expected such a thing, a man whom I received so well! And an army which did not spare its blood for you! Does Djilas, who is himself a writer, not know what human suffering and the human heart are? Can't he understand it if a soldier who has crossed thousands of kilometres through blood and fire and death has fun with a woman or takes some trifle?'[5]

Stalin proposed more toasts, wept more tears, then finally kissed Djilas's wife, protesting his love for the Serbian people, and hoping aloud that this loving gesture would not get him accused of rape.

When Djilas himself returned to Moscow with Tito in March 1945, he had to endure much needling from Stalin. At a banquet marking a Soviet-Yugoslav Treaty of Friendship, Stalin taunted Djilas for not drinking spirits: 'He drinks beer like the Germans! He is a German, by God, a German!' Stalin then handed Djilas a glass of vodka, insisting that he drink a toast. Although he does not like spirits, Djilas accepted, thinking that this was a toast to Stalin. 'No, no!' said Stalin, 'just for the Red Army! What, you won't drink to the Red Army?' Stalin's rude references to the Partisans even succeeded in riling Tito.[6]

Early in 1945 the Russians sent a film crew to Belgrade to make a film about the Partisans called *In the Mountains of Yugoslavia*. Although the actor playing Tito was given the major role, the script included a Russian acting as a guardian angel to the Partisans. After seeing the completed film, Tito 'raged with shame when he realised how subordinate his role had turned out to be, both in the plot and in history'.[7]

Later it was discovered that the Russians had used the filming of *In the Mountains of Yugoslavia* to set up a network of Soviet intelligence agents. The film crew spent several months travelling round the country and holding banquets that afterwards turned into orgies. Many Yugoslav Communists who had entered too freely into the party spirit were afterwards blackmailed or bribed by intelligence officers posing as members of the film crew. One of the principal roles in *In the Mountains of Yugoslavia* was given to Tito's dog Tigger, not the original one, which was killed in the Fifth Offensive, but a similar German shepherd that had been captured from the enemy. To keep Tigger happy, the Soviet film crew brought along Tito's personal bodyguard, who knew the beast better than Tito did himself. This vain and stupid soldier was lured into a sexual orgy, blackmailed and then enrolled by the Russians, who therefore had as one of their agents the man supposed to be guarding Tito's life.[8]

By early 1945 reports were coming into the Central Committee from Yugoslav Communists who had been asked to spy for the Soviet Union. A Russian major had tried to seduce and then recruit a young woman cryptographer from the Central Committee itself. Although she may have succumbed to the major's sexual advances, the young comrade balked at the other proposition and took her story to Ranković, who told the leadership of the Party. Tito was furious: 'A spy network is something we will not tolerate! We've got to let them know right away.' Djilas agreed, but at that time could not understand why the Russians were trying to suborn their devoted fellow Communists.[9]

The Russians learned to play on Serb–Croat rivalry in order to cause dissent among the Yugoslav Communists. The Croat Andrija Hebrang had been unhappy about the borders given to his republic, and came to oppose the Zagreb–Belgrade motorway of 'Brotherhood and Unity'. He said there was insufficient traffic to make the project viable, but most of the leadership thought he was merely 'anti-Yugoslav'. As head of the project for rapid industrialisation, Hebrang relied on plant and economic expertise from the Soviet Union, and came to be seen as Moscow's man in the leadership. In 1945 he wrote a report for the Kremlin on differences in the Yugoslav Party.[10] When he was dropped from the Politburo in April 1946, Hebrang looked to the Soviet Union for sympathy and support.

Tito's differences with the Soviet Union were first made public, and then only in a veiled and guarded form, when he was forced to withdraw his troops from Austria and Trieste. In a speech at Ljubljana on 27 May 1945, Tito said that the Yugoslavs would not allow themselves to become entangled in political spheres of influence: 'We will not be dependent on anyone ever again, regardless of what has been written and talked about – and a lot is being written, and what is written is ugly and unjust, insulting and unworthy of our allies. Today's Yugoslavia is no object for bartering and bargaining.'[11]

When Tito complained of what had been written he was clearly referring to the Western press, but the remarks about 'bargaining' and political spheres of influence could be seen as a reference to the Soviet Union, which had sacrificed Trieste to acquire a bigger portion of Germany. Stalin obviously thought that the speech was a criticism of him, for early in June a diplomatic letter was sent to the Soviet ambassador in Belgrade, to be passed on to Kardelj and the other Yugoslav leaders: 'We regard Comrade Tito's speech as unfriendly to the Soviet Union . . . Tell Comrade Tito that if he should once again mount such an attack on the Soviet Union, we would be compelled to respond openly in the press and disavow him.'[12]

There were other differences with the Soviet Union in the years leading up to the final breach in 1948. The joint-stock companies that were the basis of Soviet economic aid proved cumbersome and disadvantageous to Yugoslavia, but did not become an issue until the quarrel had started. As the head of the news and propaganda department, Djilas resisted the Soviet efforts to feed information into the Yugoslav press, but he certainly did not regard this as a hostile or sinister trend. Although Stalin appeared to take a special interest in the neighbouring Communist states of Albania and Bulgaria, he did not at first press Tito to form a Balkan alliance or merge with them in a federation. Yet it was on this question that Stalin decided to pick a quarrel.

Soon after a leading Albanian Communist, Naku Spiru, killed himself in a dispute over relations with Yugoslavia, a dispatch came from Stalin in late December 1947 asking the Yugoslav Central Committee to send a small delegation to Moscow to talk of the matter. The invitation specifically mentioned the name of Milovan Djilas, perhaps because he had been to Albania and knew the problems involved, or perhaps because Stalin wanted to set him up as a rival and even successor to Tito. Later, Djilas came round to this second interpretation.

The relationship between Yugoslavia and Albania resembled that between the Soviet Union and Yugoslavia. The Yugoslavs were providing economic experts and even food to help the Albanians, and had recently set up some joint-stock companies. They were now proposing to send in two divisions to reinforce Albanian defence, as a civil war raged in Greece to the south. Both governments agreed in principle that their countries should unite, which incidentally would help to solve the lingering problem of Kosovo. However, one faction of the Albanian Communist Party, including the late Naku Spiru and the future dictator Enver Hoxha, was fearful of coming under the power of Yugoslavia. Moreover, Communists were not immune to the ancient bad blood between the Albanians and Slavs.

On the journey to Moscow by train, Djilas stopped off at Bucharest and Iaşi, and was shocked by the arrogance of the Russians towards these 'Rumanian maize-eaters'; the Russians even repeated the joke about the supposed dishonesty of Romanians: 'They are not a nation but a profession!' Djilas and the other Yugoslav delegates were in turn amused by the Soviet railway carriage: 'We thought it comical with its huge brass handles, old-fashioned decor and a toilet so lofty that one's legs dangled in mid-air. Was all this necessary?... And what was most grotesque of all in that car, with its pomp of tsarist days, was the fact that the attendant kept, in a coop is his compartment, a chicken which laid eggs.'[3]

Djilas arrived in Moscow expecting the usual wait, but was summoned almost immediately to the Kremlin, where Stalin came right to the point:

> 'So, members of the Central Committee in Albania are killing themselves over you! This is very inconvenient, very inconvenient.'
>
> I began to explain: Naku Spiru was against linking Albania with Yugoslavia; he isolated himself in his own Central Committee. I had not even finished when to my surprise, Stalin said: 'We have no special interest in Albania. We agree to Yugoslavia swallowing Albania!' At this he gathered together the fingers of his right hand and, bringing them to his mouth, he made as if to swallow them.

Djilas was thunderstruck and could only say it was not a question of swallowing but of unification. 'But that is swallowing!' Molotov interjected, and Stalin repeated his brutal gesture: 'Yes, yes.

Swallowing! But we agree with you: you ought to swallow Albania
– the sooner the better.'[14]

After a short business meeting, the Yugoslavs were taken to
Stalin's villa for one of his late-night suppers. Everyone was obliged
to guess the temperature outside, and to drink a glass of vodka for
every degree they were out. Stalin asked Djilas how many Jews
there were in the Yugoslav Central Committee, then interrupted
his explanation: 'In our Central Committee there are no Jews. You
are an anti-Semite Djilas, you too, Djilas, you too are an anti-
Semite.' Also present at table were Molotov and the cultural
overseer Andrey Zhdanov, who aired his views on dealing with
smaller nations: 'We made a mistake in not occupying Finland.
Everything would have been fine if we had.' Molotov disagreed:
'Ach Finland – that is a peanut!'[15]

At one point in the dinner, Zhdanov asked Djilas: 'Do you have
any opera in Yugoslavia?' Djilas said there were nine theatres
putting on opera, and thought to himself how little these people
knew or cared about Yugoslavia. It was simply a place on the map,
or a peanut, like Finland. The talk about opera inspired Stalin to
go to the gramophone and put on a record of a coloratura soprano
warbling against a background of the yowling and barking of dogs.
'He laughed with an exaggerated, immoderate mirth,' Djilas
recalls, 'but when he saw how puzzled and unhappy I looked, he
explained, almost as though to excuse himself, "Well it's still
clever, devilishly clever."'[16]

On 8 February 1948, after almost a month in Moscow, Djilas
was joined by Edvard Kardelj, since Tito himself had declined to
come for health reasons. Perhaps he remembered the fate of the
previous general secretary of the Yugoslav Communist Party,
Gorkić, who went to Moscow in 1937 and never came back. Now,
in 1948, the Yugoslavs were under persistent and obvious surveillance, so that Djilas had to resort to stealth to talk to his colleague
in their dacha: 'That same night, while Kardelj's wife was sleeping,
and Kardelj was lying next to her, I sat down on the bed by him,
and, as softly as I could, informed him of my impressions from my
stay in Moscow.' Kardelj whispered back that the direct cause of

dispute with the Soviet Union was the agreement between the Yugoslav and Albanian governments to send two Yugoslav divisions into Albania. Moscow did not accept that the troops were there to defend Albania from Greek 'monarcho-fascists', and, in his wire, Molotov threatened a public breach. Here it would seem that Djilas's whisper took on an indignant tone: '"Whatever possessed you to send two divisions now?" I asked Kardelj. "And why all this feverish involvement in Albania?" With resignation in his voice, Kardelj replied. "Well, the Old Man is doing the pushing. You know yourself . . ." Indeed I did!' This suggestion that Tito himself was risking a confrontation with Stalin was left out of *Conversations with Stalin*, 'to avoid feeding Albanian-Soviet propaganda with ammunition at a time when this was still a living issue'.[17]

The Russians had also invited a delegation from Bulgaria, led by the veteran Dimitrov, who was a friend and patron of Tito's from before the war. The Soviet newspaper *Pravda* had recently criticised Dimitrov and disassociated itself from his 'problematic and fantastic federations and confederations'. This was a reference to the Bulgarian plan for a customs union with Romania and also perhaps to the recent Bulgarian-Yugoslav Treaty of Friendship, signed at Bled in Slovenia. The time had come for the Russians to curb these impudent underlings.

At the fateful meeting on 10 February 1948 Molotov started off with an angry, humiliating attack on Dimitrov, for trying to establish relations with the other 'people's democracies'. Djilas comments:

> It became evident that to the Soviet leaders, with their great power mentality . . . and especially as they were always conscious that the Red Army had liberated Rumania and Bulgaria, Dimitrov's statements and Yugoslavia's obstinacy and lack of discipline were not only heresy but a denial of the Soviet Union's 'sacred' rights. Dimitrov tried to explain, to justify himself, but Stalin kept interrupting without letting him finish. Here at last was the real Stalin. His wit now turned into crude malice and his

aloofness into intolerance . . . he upbraided the Bulgars and
bitterly reproached them, for he knew they would submit to him,
but in fact he had his sights fixed on the Yugoslavs – as in the
peasant proverb, 'She scolds her daughter in order to reproach
her daughter-in-law.'[18]

Stalin then called for a federation of Yugoslavia, Bulgaria and
Albania: 'This is the federation that should be created, and the
sooner the better – right away, if possible tomorrow. Yes,
tomorrow, if possible! Agree on it immediately.' One of the
Yugoslavs said that they were already preparing a federation with
Albania, but Stalin shouted him down: 'No, first a federation
between Bulgaria and Yugoslavia, and then both with Albania.'
And he added: 'We think that a federation ought to be formed
between Rumania and Hungary, and also Poland and Czechoslovakia.' From this and other allusions, Djilas got the idea that Stalin
was planning to join the Soviet Union with the 'people's democracies' – the Ukraine with Hungary and Romania, Belorussia with
Poland and Czechoslovakia, and Russia itself with the Balkan
countries.

After humiliating Dimitrov, Stalin turned his sarcasm and fury
on Kardelj: 'What do you say about Albania? You did not consult
us at all about the entry of your army into Albania.' Stalin returned
again to the worthlessness of customs unions but Kardelj, who was
not a man to be bullied, said that some were successful, 'for
instance Benelux, where Belgium, Holland and Luxembourg
joined together'.

'No, Holland didn't,' Stalin interrupted him, 'only Belgium and
Luxembourg.' 'No, Holland is included, too,' Kardelj persisted.
'No, Holland is not!' roared Stalin, and nobody dared to point out
that the 'ne' in 'Benelux' stood for the Netherlands.[19]

After this meeting, Djilas felt empty and bitter. The normally
calm and precise Kardelj was so upset that he signed in the wrong
space on a treaty. Djilas says that they did not fear for their
physical safety – they were representatives of a foreign state – but
he longed to get back to the forests of Bosnia. On the plane back

to Belgrade a few days later, Djilas felt 'more and more like a happy child but felt also a stern, serious joy'.[20]

Soon after Kardelj and Djilas got back from Moscow, Tito convened a meeting of the Politburo and a few other senior Communists such as Moša Pijade. Among those present was Sreten Žujović, an economics expert known to be sympathetic to the now dismissed Andrija Hebrang. He took lengthy notes of all that was said and certainly passed this information back to the Soviet Embassy. Tito outlined the history of the disagreement with the Soviet Union, stressing the Soviet refusal to sign a trade agreement, and the Albanian question. After declaring that the relations between the two countries had reached an impasse, Tito unexpectedly added: 'If they continue such a policy towards us, I will resign.' Milovan Djilas comments:

Probably no-one there was naive enough to take this threat seriously, certainly not I. He threw it out to test us, to see if anyone would approve of his resignation as the most sensible way out. But everyone – except for Žujović who was noticeably silent – cried out against any such idea. Tito did not mention it again.[21]

This was the second time Djilas had heard Tito offer his resignation. The first was in December 1941, when the Partisans had been driven out of Serbia, and Moscow was still supporting the Chetniks. Then Tito really had come close to despair. Now, in February 1948, Tito felt strong enough to stand up to the Russians.

Although Žujović reported back to the Soviet Embassy, the others present at Tito's villa kept quiet about the quarrel with the Soviet Union. The only hint of it in the outside world appeared in the French newspaper *Le Figaro* on 12 February, in an article from Bucharest. A sharp-eyed reporter had noticed workmen taking down the picture of Tito. Otherwise Yugoslavia went on with its militant pro-Soviet policy, threatening war on the frontiers of Greece and Italy.

Tito's friend and future biographer Vladimir Dedijer was not in the highest leadership of the Party, having joined it only during the war, and therefore did not attend the first crisis meeting. One evening in February, while he was preparing to accompany a delegation to India, Dedijer received an invitation to Tito's residence at 15 Rumunska Street. As in his account of the Battle of Sutjeska, Dedijer conveys the greatness of Tito in times of danger:

I walked slowly to 15 Rumunska Street. The officer at the gate admitted me and I trod the familiar winding lane towards Tito's villa . . . As I entered Tito was working at his desk; he raised his eyes from the report he was reading, and motioned me towards the farther end of the study. He seemed to me to be tired. That surprised me for he does not usually look tired.

I expected we should begin our talk about my journey when Tito lit a cigarette and sticking it, as is his habit, into his silver-studded, pipe-shaped holder, inhaled and crossed his legs. He appeared to be a man who wanted to talk to someone about something complex and to hear his reaction. I was quite familiar with his gesture.

All happened in a matter of moments. Although I had known Tito then for fully ten years and been in frequent contact with him, I could still never have guessed what he was going to tell me. I was taken aback when, instead of the expected question about my journey, he said: 'Have you seen what has happened in Rumania? They have ordered all my photographs to be removed! Surely you have read it in the reports of the foreign news agencies?'

I was astonished by the seriousness of his voice. I had read these reports, but I was convinced that there was no truth in them. I have always thought myself awkward when talking to Tito, because I have hardly ever voiced the thoughts I have prepared in answer to his question, but simply what first comes off my tongue. So from my lips fell the words: 'How is that? Isn't it all the usual falsehood?'

Anguish suddenly overspread his face. Only at that moment did I look at him better and see clearly that his appearance had altered. His face had darkened, and deep worries had lined it. Pouches under his eyes were evidence that he had not slept . . .

1a Josip Broz (centre, back row in cap) at the metal goods factory
at Kamnik, Slovenia in 1912.

1b Josip Broz (with hat and long tie) and the owners and staff
of the mill at Veliko Trojstvo, Croatia in 1924.

2a Josip Broz at Maribor, Slovenia in 1933 after five years in prison.

2b Stalin, the former idol whom Tito came to despise.

3a The founders of the Communist state at Jajce in 1943.
From left to right: Ranković, Djilas, Tito, Žujevic, Hebrang, Pijade, Kardelj.

3b Tito and Churchill meet in the Bay of Naples, 1944.

4 Tito in 1952 with his second wife Jovanka
and his son Misa by Hertha Hass.

5 Tito in 1950
posing with one of a line of dogs called 'Tiger'.

6a Tito welcomes Nikita Khrushchev at Belgrade airport in 1963.

6b Tito and his biographer Vladimir Dedijer.
On the right is Koča Popović.

7a Tito receives Richard Burton and his wife Elizabeth Taylor on Brioni island in August 1971. Burton is to play Tito in the Hollywood film *The Battle of Sutjeska*.

7b Tito in hospital shortly after the amputation of his right leg in January 1980.

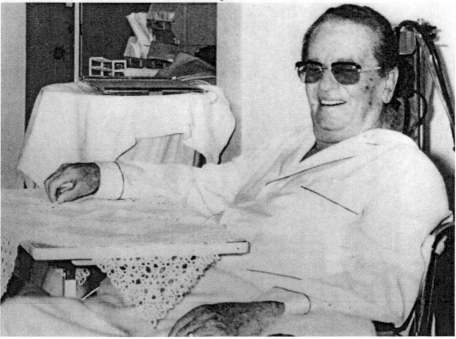

8 Tito's funeral was attended by Britain's Prime Minister Margaret
Thatcher, who, ten years later, advocated the break-up of Yugoslavia.

Crossing his legs again nervously, Tito took a long pull at his cigarette and, as if he had not heard my confused question, continued: 'You are a lucky man. You don't know anything yet. Those were wonderful times during the war, during the Fifth Offensive, when we were surrounded by the Germans on all sides. We knew then we had been left to fend for ourselves, and we fought our way out as best we could. But now . . . when all the conditions are there to help us, the Russians are hindering us.

I was tongue-tied. Thoughts swarmed like lightning and clashed in my brain, causing almost physical pain. I recalled a conversation I had had a few days back with Kalinin, the new VOKS [the Soviet organisation for cultural relations with foreign countries] representative in Belgrade. He told me that the Yugoslavs did not love the Soviet Union, that Russian was studied little, that there were more courses in English and French, that things were quite different in Bulgaria, where the Society for Friendship for the Soviet Union had almost a million members. I had not taken Kalinin's words seriously, because it did not enter my head that this little Soviet clerk could lecture Yugoslavia . . .

But what Tito had just told me meant that this zealous clerk, recently come from Moscow, was speaking according to instructions recently received from above. I recalled his boast that Zhdanov personally had sent him to Yugoslavia. I connected all this with what Tito was telling me at this moment, so it was not by chance. This meant a conflict with the Soviet Union, a conflict with Stalin. But surely that was impossible?. . . Tito noticed the impression his words had made on me. I was gradually realising the import of the lines on his face and that tired expression. A fateful decision was pending, perhaps the most fateful decision in our latter-day history . . .

Today I realise that Tito, that day, was making his decision. Before him lay two roads, and on only one of them could he travel. He had fought with Stalin, he had looked to Stalin for support, the Soviet Union had been his beacon. The lines on his face were the outward sign of a soul in torment.[22]

Dedijer was a journalist and sometimes arranged or doctored his stories to make them more interesting. However, one can be certain that such a meeting took place, and on Tito's initiative. Although Dedijer gives the impression that Tito had called him over to unburden his heart to him and hear his friend's reaction, there was probably another motive. Tito wanted to test people, face to face, to see if they would be loyal in the coming conflict. Although Tito probably had few doubts about Dedijer, a personal friend, he wanted to warn him about the crisis, rather than let him learn about it first in the Indian newspapers. While Tito was in Belgrade warning people like Dedijer about the approaching conflicts, his closest lieutenants, Ranković, Kardelj and Djilas, were sounding out the loyalty of the leadership in the various republics.

On 20 March Tito told the triumvirate that Moscow was recalling its military instructors. As the meeting was still in progress, news came through that the Soviet economic experts were also leaving. Tito wrote back a mild and unprovocative letter in which he denied that the Yugoslavs had been unfriendly towards the Soviet experts, that they 'distrusted' them or kept them under surveillance. Very soon Tito would come to wish he had distrusted and watched the Russians a good deal more.

The Soviet reply addressed to 'Comrade Tito and the other members of the Central Committee' was signed by Molotov and Stalin, in that order. Accusing the Yugoslav Communist Party of lack of democracy, the letter insisted that 'such an organisation could not be regarded as Marxist-Leninist or Bolshevik'. It mentioned by name four 'questionable Marxists' in the leadership, including Djilas and Ranković, and warned that 'the political career of Trotsky is quite instructive'. When the four named people offered their resignations, Tito said bitterly: 'Oh no! I know what they want – to smash our Central Committee. First you, then me.'[23]

Even the date of the Molotov–Stalin letter, 27 March 1948, was seen as a provocation and insult. It was the seventh anniversary of the *coup d'état* in protest against the alliance with Hitler, the day when the Belgrade crowd attacked the German tourist office and tore up the swastika flag. Belgrade's defiance of Hitler, which led to invasion, the breakup of Yugoslavia and one and a half million deaths, was widely regarded, especially by Croats, as rash and self-destructive. Were Stalin and Molotov trying to convey a message? If so, they might have considered that past attempts to threaten or bully the Yugoslavs, and especially the Serbs, had been counter-productive.

Tito decided to call a plenary session of the Central Committee – the first such meeting since 1940, when he had taken over the leadership of the Party. Although the mood of the meeting was overwhelmingly loyal to Tito, a dissident voice was heard from Sreten Žujović. The leadership was aware of his frequent meetings with Hebrang, now openly on the Soviet side, and with the Russian ambassador. Žujović made an appeal to the Central Committee's 'revolutionary conscience' and asked its members not to make statements offensive to Stalin. Milovan Djilas describes the reaction:

> No sooner had Žujović begun his appeals than Tito jumped up and began pacing to and fro. 'Treason!' he hissed, 'treason to the people, the state, the Party!' Tito repeated the word 'treason' many times over, then just as quickly sat down, kicking aside his briefcase. But I jumped up in turn, tears of pain and anger filling my eyes. 'Crni,' I shouted ['Crni', literally 'black' or 'swarthy', was Žujović's nickname], 'you've known me for ten years – do you really think of me as a Trotskyist?' Žujović answered evasively. 'I don't think that, but you know some of your recent statements about the Soviet Union . . .'[24]

Amid the fury and bitterness of the plenary session, Moša Pijade as usual provided some comic relief, saying that what had surprised him most in the Molotov–Stalin letter was its ignorance. When Tito spoke for the second time at the meeting, he called for loyalty to a leadership that had remained united for eleven years, through the harshest trials, and now was bonded in blood with the people. Rising from his seat, he called out: 'Our revolution does not devour its children! We honour the children of our revolution.'[25]

On May Day that year, 'Black' Žujović was not invited to the reviewing stand and ostentatiously marched in the crowd in his general's uniform with its array of medals. Soon afterwards, he and Hebrang were arrested and kept in solitary confinement. Later in May, Stalin himself intervened on behalf of Hebrang and Žujović, accusing the Central Committee of planning to murder them, as he would have done himself. He further demanded the presence of Soviet officials in the inquiry into their conduct. As Moša Pijade pointed out, in 1914 the Austro-Hungarian government had demanded that its detectives should go to Belgrade to investigate the murder of the Archduke Franz Ferdinand, and Serbia's refusal had sparked off the First World War. The Soviet Union also repeated its invitation, in fact a demand, to the Yugoslavs to attend the forthcoming meeting in Bucharest of the Cominform, the Communist Information Bureau. Whether or not to attend this meeting became the key issue dividing those loyal to Tito from those loyal to Stalin, who later were known as the Cominformists (*informburovci*).

The Yugoslavs refused to travel to Bucharest where the storm was about to break. Djilas recalls from that anxious June a conversation with Blagoje Nešković, who was soon to become a Cominformist:

> Would Moscow attack us? Neither of us could believe that would happen but for different reasons, both ideological. He asserted that it was impossible for one socialist state to attack another, whereas I held that it would mean the disintegration of ideology and Communism as a world movement. We carried our dispute a step further. 'We'll fight them,' I said categorically. Nešković backed away. 'The Red Army? No, I wouldn't fight the Red Army.'[26]

After lunch that day, Djilas discussed the same matter with Tito: 'At one point, when we were on the subject of Soviet intervention, he exclaimed in bitter exaltation, "To die on one's own soil! At least a memory remains."'[27]

At last the Cominform, meeting in Bucharest, announced to a startled world the expulsion of Yugoslavia's Communist Party, for crimes ranging from 'grandeeism' to wanting the restoration of capitalism. As with the Molotov–Stalin letter, the most provocative feature of this Cominform resolution, at any rate in the eyes of the Serbs, was its date, 28 June, St Vitus's Day. Even Communists like Djilas, who pretended not to bother about medieval history, were taken aback by the Cominform's timing:

> The resolution did not contain anything new or surprising. But its promulgation on the anniversary of the tragic battle in 1389 at Kosovo, which had inaugurated five centuries of Turkish rule over the Serbian people, cut into the minds and hearts of all Serbs. Though neither religious nor mystical, we noted, with a certain relish almost, this coincidence in dates between ancient calamities and living threats and onslaughts.[28]

Djilas stayed up most of the night preparing the Party's reply to the Cominform resolution.

More than thirty years after the breach with Stalin, when Tito himself was near to death, a Zagreb studio turned the events of 1948 into a tragicomic film called *Visoki Napor* (*The Big Effort*). It starts on an ancient steam train bringing volunteers to build the 'Brotherhood and Unity' motorway, except that these are not real volunteers but employees of the Rade Končar engineering works in Zagreb, forced to give up part of their holidays. However, the heroine and her handsome but earnest boyfriend are happy in love and in building the new Yugoslavia. The other employees at Rade Končar include a spectacled boffin and a priggish but highly sexed Communist Party organiser, who gets the firm to adopt her slogan: 'We build generators! The generators build us!' At a works outing, up in the mountains, the hero and everyone in trousers are chased by the Communist girl until she finds a man to take her into the bushes. The farce continues back at the Rade Končar plant, where, as part of the workers' cultural improvement, a fat soprano bellows out Verdi. Up to this point *The Big Effort* is farce, a kind of *Carry on Communism*.

We then see the Rade Končar workers march in the May Day procession of 1948, bearing portraits of Stalin and Tito. Then, at the end of June, comes the news of the Cominform resolution and Yugoslavia's reply, both printed in *Vjesnik*, the organ of the Croatian Party. At a meeting in Rade Končar, the workers are at first silent and baffled until the heroine rises to speak: 'We don't have to believe that Stalin is right in every respect. We don't have to go to church to pray to the God Stalin . . .' A picture of Stalin drops from the wall and the glass is shattered. However, the hero, the priggish Communist girl and a few other Rade Končar workers take the Cominform side and hold a separate meeting. 'What do they want, that tomorrow we turn our guns on the Russians?' the hero asks, and they stand up to sing The Internationale. It is a strangely moving incident in a film that began as farce.

Fear and suspicion take over at Rade Končar. Old comrades quarrel during a game of billiards. The hero goes to the heroine's village and abuses her over the anti-Stalinist speech reported in *Vjesnik*, then whacks her over the head with a rolled-up copy of the paper. The Cominformists are visited at night by OZNA and taken away to prison or to a camp. The hero tries to escape to the East and is shot by the frontier guards. The heroine swallows her grief and goes back to building generators. The appearance of a film that treated the crisis of 1948 with humour, and even some sympathy for the Cominformists, was proof in itself of how much the country had changed in Tito's lifetime, especially since most of eastern Europe was still part of the Soviet empire. However, for most Yugoslavs, especially perhaps the Communists, there was nothing amusing about those years of crisis.

When Tito said that the Yugoslav revolution did not devour its children, he meant that it did not kill them off, but it did beat and torture them to within an inch of their lives. The only man who may have been murdered was Andrija Hebrang, the Croat who was arrested in May and died in prison by what was called suicide. Several Yugoslav Communists were killed when trying to escape to one of the Cominform countries. By far the most important of these was Arso Jovanović, the Montenegrin soldier who rose to be Chief of the General Staff in the war and during the confrontation over Trieste, where his first-name lent itself to a coarse adaptation among the British troops. On the pretext of going on a hunting trip, Jovanović had tried to cross the Romanian border but met and opened fire on a Yugoslav border patrol, who fired back and killed him. There was no truth in the later rumour that he was murdered and his body dumped on the border.

Only a handful of Cominformists, such as Hebrang, Žujović and Jovanović, came from the highest ranks of the Party, but about ten thousand were found in the broader membership, which stood at about half a million. The overwhelming majority were Serbs, with the highest proportion of all from Montenegro, the ancient ally of Tsar and Stalin alike.

Most of the Cominformists in Croatia came from Dalmatia or from the Serb minority in the Military Frontier, the strongholds of the Partisans during the war. Many Yugoslavs who had studied or worked in the Soviet Union turned out to be Cominformists, as did the wives of those who had married there. Another suspect group were those like Arso Jovanović who had previously served in the Royal Yugoslav Army before they became Partisans. Many of those who were hounded as Cominformists were probably guilty of little more than indiscretion, or were the victims of envious colleagues. Wives were obliged to denounce their husbands and some took advantage of this to get a new man. The fear and suspicion among the lower ranks of the Party is well portrayed in a film made in Bosnia during the 1980s, told through the eyes of a small boy, and ironically titled *Daddy Has Gone Away on a Business Trip*.

Although these were frightening times for the rank and file of the Party, the persecution of Cominformists never became a witch-hunt, similar to the smelling out of 'Trotskyists' and 'saboteurs' in the Soviet Union during the 1930s. The great majority of the people arrested in Yugoslavia really were Cominformists, sticking fast to their Leninist principles. Although Tito was ruthless to those he perceived as traitors, he did not have a suspicious nature,

and tended to give people the benefit of the doubt. On one occasion
Ranković and Djilas interrogated a Montenegrin air force pilot
suspected of planning an escape to Albania. The accused man wept
as he proclaimed his loyalty: 'Comrades, give me a bomber and I'll
show Sofia and Budapest and Tirana who is a revisionist, who is a
traitor. Let me serve my country and my Party! Let me die
honourably as a soldier and a revolutionary!' Djilas was less
prepared than Ranković to accept this appeal, 'especially since it
came from a Montenegrin – and Montenegrins are prone to
pathetics and hysteria', but the man had been brave in the war, so
they let him go free. When Tito was told of this a few days later,
he was delighted, and preached the virtues of toleration and
leniency:

> We must not be sectarian. We mustn't allow petty suspicions to
> lead us, like the Russians, into destroying our comrades. We
> have to give our comrades a chance to correct their mistaken
> views. Take the pilot, now – he's ready to fly to his death
> tomorrow, if need be. And yet we play the narrow sectarians.[29]

A few days later, the pilot tried to escape to Albania, using hand-
grenades and an automatic rifle against the frontier guards before
he was shot.

The most important surviving Cominformist, Sreten Žujović,
remained in prison without a trial until 1950, when Djilas and
Ranković set out to win him back to the fold. They first sent him
the transcript of one of the trials in eastern Europe, in which
Communists were accused of plotting with Tito to bring back
capitalism, and then, at his own request, a complete run of *Borba*
since his imprisonment. This course of reading made Žujović
realise that he had misjudged Tito, and when Djilas and Ranković
came to visit him in prison he greeted them warmly and volunteered to write a retraction in *Borba*. He was released from prison,
allowed back into the Party, and finally buried with full military
honours in 1976.[30]

Tito was lenient to Žujović, yet he sent thousands of Cominformists to slave in the camp on Goli Otok (Naked Island), opposite Senj in the north Adriatic. From autumn 1948 until well into the 1950s, about 12,000 men and some women as well were shipped to this inhospitable rock to quarry for marble. The camp was run on the principle of making the prisoners earn their release by breaking the will of those who had not yet made a confession and recantation. All new arrivals were made to run a gauntlet of beating, followed by constant physical and verbal abuse. The prisoners were not allowed visitors, and relatives were not even informed as to the whereabouts of their loved ones; they were merely told that 'Daddy has gone away on a business trip'. All those released from Naked Island were sworn not to talk about it, under pain of returning there. Even after the end of Communism in Yugoslavia, veterans of Naked Island were loath to speak of their hellish experience.

Tito set up the Naked Island camp through Ranković, although even Ranković did not know, or want to know, exactly what went on there. According to Djilas, Tito was more than once heard to exclaim in 1948: 'Off to jail with him! Off to the camp! What else can he expect if he works against his own Party?' The horror of Naked Island did not become known even to senior Communists until 1953, when the Partisan general and novelist Dobrica Ćosić visited there and came back aghast. Conditions were then improved. Even the very existence of the camp did not become generally known in Yugoslavia until the 1960s, and the disgrace of Ranković. Although the Naked Island camp was not an extermination camp, like Jasenovac in the Independent State of Croatia, it nevertheless remains a blot on Tito's record, comparable with the massacre of the Serbs and Slovenes handed back by the British in 1945.

The period after the break with Russia was frightening for the Yugoslav Communists, and grim for the rest of the population, especially the peasants. Tito was stung by the Cominform's accusations of 'revisionism' and wanting to introduce capitalism, so he resolved to outdo Stalin at Stalinism, to prove himself more Catholic than the Pope. The five-year plan was to go forward.

Indeed Boris Kidrić, the head of the Federal Planning Commission, indicted Hebrang and Djujović, the previous economic bosses, for sabotaging and holding back 'the construction of socialism'. They were accused of attempting to check overambitious planning, and of insisting on the profitability of individual enterprises.[31] The Second Plenum of the Central Committee in February 1949 prescribed 'greater boldness and a faster pace in setting up collective farms'.[32] Although collectivisation in Yugoslavia was not as murderous as it had been in the Soviet Union, it caused immeasurable suffering, anger and waste. In Macedonia there were only two collective farms in 1945; by the end of March 1949 there were 400. In Croatia the number doubled during the first quarter of that year. Collectivisation provoked violent resistance in north-west Bosnia, the Muslim region round Bihać, where Tito had established his headquarters in 1943. The failure of the collective farms caused food shortages in the towns.

The Soviet block's economic embargo or sanctions against Yugoslavia made life even harsher but did not succeed in breaking the will of the people or causing revolt. The Communists remained loyal to Tito, while the anti-Communists liked the Russian version even less than the local brand. In Belgrade, in 1953, there were many self-styled reactionaries who professed to believe that the quarrel with the Soviet Union was just a pretence to deceive the West.

Stalin knew better. Although he personally did not mention Tito by name, he directed the propaganda campaign, the show trials of 'Titoists' in eastern Europe, perhaps even the plans to have Tito murdered. From June 1948 onwards, the Cominform printing-press sent out a torrent of articles, pamphlets and books unmasking Tito as a Trotskyist, an American spy and even, in one memorable phrase, 'the paid troubadour of the worst Wall Street hangmen'. The Russians did not reveal, or perhaps did not know, that Tito had dealt with the Germans during the 'March Consultations' of 1943. The British Communist James Klugmann, who had been with the SOE in Cairo during the war, and was afterwards blamed by Michael Lees for helping to put Tito in power, wrote a book called *From Trotsky to Tito*.

Such Western apologists also attempted to justify the trials in which east European Communists stood accused as agents of Tito and Western imperialism. Among those executed for 'Titoism' were Laszlo Rajk in Hungary, Trajko Kostov in Bulgaria and Kochi Xoxe in Albania. The Polish Communist Wladislaw Gomulka, who actually had tried to intercede on Tito's behalf, was given only a gaol sentence and later returned to power to introduce reforms of a 'Titoist' nature. These east European 'Titoist' trials, even more than the Treason Trials in the Soviet Union during the 1930s, show the diseased suspicion of Stalin's mind. In one trial, in Romania, the prosecution claimed that Tito had plotted together with Noel Coward, the English playwright and nightclub entertainer, who had worked for naval intelligence during the war.

In *Tito Speaks* Vladimir Dedijer accused the Soviet Union of sending assassins to Yugoslavia to kill its opponents. After the fall of Communism in Russia, reports appeared in the press that SMERSH, the murder organisation popularised by the James Bond thrillers, had tried to get into Yugoslavia from Italy. Whether or not these stories are true, the best account of Stalin's desire for revenge against the Yugoslavs appears in Solzhenitsyn's novel *The First Circle*. In the small hours of a January morning in 1950, the secret police chief Abakumov approached his master:

> He announced that a delayed-action bomb would be put on board Tito's yacht before it sailed for the island of Brioni.
> 'And Ranković?' asked Stalin.
> 'Oh, yes! The moment will be chosen so that Ranković and Kardelj and Mosha Pijade – the whole clique – will be blown into the air together!'

The imaginary Stalin in Solzhenitsyn's magnificent novel is almost as sinister as the real-life Stalin described by Djilas.

Until his death on 5 March 1953, Stalin enforced the isolation of Yugoslavia throughout the Communist world. The Chinese leader Mao Zedong was a lifelong Stalinist and quarrelled with the Soviet

Union only when the reformists took over. American liberal
opponents of the Vietnam War used to suggest that Ho Chi Minh
might have become an Asian Tito, but for the stupidity of the US
State Department.[33] In fact Ho Chi Minh was a fierce opponent of
Tito and at first would not establish relations with Yugoslavia.
Pictures of Stalin were on display in Hanoi as late as 1982. In
Europe, the Greeks were the only Communists who at first
maintained a connection with Yugoslavia, their main supplier of
arms; but they too broke off relations. In 1949 Stalin ditched the
Greek Communists, ending their insurrection.

The quarrel with Stalin effectively ended all Tito's chances of
acquiring Trieste, or anywhere else in Venezia-Giulia. Even before
the dispute, he had offered to cede Trieste in exchange for the
smaller town of Gorizia, which has a larger proportion of Slovenes
in its population. After the Cominform resolution, Tito returned
to his earlier hard-line demand for the city and port of Trieste
itself. The army was now in a state of alert on all Yugoslavia's
frontiers, preparing to meet an attack from the East, and preparing
to launch an attack on the West. Tito's adamant and aggressive
stance against the Anglo-American presence in Trieste continued
even into the period when he was receiving arms and aid from the
West.

The Cominform resolution came as a blessing to the Italian
Communist Party, which had lost an election in 1947, largely
because it supported Yugoslavia's claim to Trieste. The Italian
Communists now became the most fervent anti-Titoists, while in
Trieste itself the Party split along ethnic lines. Street battles took
place in which the Italian Communists killed and even castrated
their Slovene comrades. Stalin established an anti-Tito propaganda
organisation, 'Vidali', named after the boss of Trieste's Communist
Party, Vittorio Vidali, a thug who had made a name for himself by
murdering Trotskyists in Mexico. The Vidali Communists in
Trieste continued to fight the Anglo-American troops, the Christian
Democrats and the Fascists (MSI), but now concurred in keeping
Trieste Italian.

The Italian Communists as well as the right-wing Triestini

crowded the cinema showing a film *La Città dolente* (*The Sorrowing City*), the title being taken from a line in Dante's *Inferno*; however, the city referred to was Fiume (Rijeka) rather than Hell. The film's action takes place in 1945, when the Italians are living in terror of Tito's Communists. The young Italian hero wants to escape with his fiancée, but he has caught the lustful eye of a female Serbian Partisan officer, dressed in a cap with a red star, breeches, knee-length boots and a revolver on her hip. She gives him a choice between her bed and a concentration camp. He tries to escape and, as far as I can remember, pays for his virtue with his life. The story was unconvincing, since Italian men are not renowned for their chastity, while some, I suspect, might have enjoyed the idea of a dominant Serb woman in jackboots. However, the Italian women of Trieste loved *La Città dolente*, and wept throughout the film.

In spite of the tension on the border running through the bare mountains overlooking Trieste, a large number of refugees continued to arrive. Although many were Yugoslavs who had crossed illegally, a growing number came from the Cominform countries such as Hungary, Romania and Bulgaria. They had read the attacks on Tito in their press and had escaped to Yugoslavia, hoping to find that it was in fact on the side of the West. The Yugoslav authorities did not welcome these anti-Communists but did not turn them back, and after making them toil for a few months on one of their economic projects, pushed them over the frontier into Trieste. By the abysmal standards of Communists in 1949, the Yugoslavs were humanitarian. They treated the foreign victims of Stalin better than Stalin treated his own people. Some of the refugees, especially the Hungarians, bore the scars of the torture endured in their own countries, but none that I met complained of similar treatment in Yugoslavia.

The Yugoslav refugees told of the poverty, the forced collectivisation, the futile toil in factories and the overall harshness of life, but they did not complain of living in terror. It was clear that even in 1949–50 Yugoslavia was changing into a different sort of Communist country under a system that came to be known as 'Titoism'.

13

Titoism

There was no precise month or even year when Yugoslavia changed from a Stalinist police state into a virtually open society. When I visited Zagreb in August 1951 I was horrified by the wretchedness of the shops, the cafés, the clothes people wore, and above all by the atmosphere of suspicion and menace. Just over two years later, when I began an eight-month stay in Belgrade and Sarajevo, I found the country far better off materially, and the people no longer frightened of talking to a foreigner. Even in 1953, Yugoslavia was far more liberal than the Soviet Union or any other country in eastern Europe until the collapse of the Communist system. Although there were countries such as Poland, and to a lesser extent Hungary, where people were able to voice their opposition to Communism, they looked on their governments as foreign occupations, as indeed they were. In Yugoslavia a great many people, if not the majority, came to accept and even admire Tito, and many now look back on his rule as a golden age.

It used to be said that Yugoslavia's break with the Soviet Union represented the triumph of nationalism over a universal ideal, in much the same way that the French Revolution changed into Napoleonic imperialism. Yugoslavia was seen as the first in a line of national Communist states such as Mao Zedong's China, Hoxha's Albania and Ceauşescu's Romania, all of them more or less hostile to the Soviet Union. Quite recently we have seen the rival

Communist states of Vietnam, China and Cambodia actually making war on each other, in unashamedly racial hatred. Yet as we know, Yugoslavia under Tito was not the single, united nation it seemed to foreigners at the time, but a federation trying to heal the wounds of a terrible civil war. The breach with the Soviet Union had the effect, for a time, of uniting Serbs and Croats against an outside danger; but there was never a real Yugoslav nationalism or patriotism.

Moreover, nationalism cannot explain why Yugoslavia developed its liberal and tolerant form of Communism. There was no such thing in the other national Communist states such as China, Romania, Albania or North Korea, all of which were at times as ghastly as Stalin's Soviet Union. A few other Communist governments tried to make their regimes more acceptable to the populace, notably Poland and Hungary, Czechoslovakia in 1968, and more recently Vietnam; but none came near to achieving the freedom enjoyed by Yugoslavs.

It is sometimes said that economic necessity forced Tito to make his regime more tolerant, that he introduced reforms in return for help from the West. But Ceauşescu got arms and financial aid from the West without relaxing his tyranny. Fidel Castro is still, at the time of writing, letting his people starve in defence of his principle 'Socialism or Death'. Historians under the Marxist influence believe that because something happened, then it was bound to happen, that Yugoslavia was bound to develop as it did. But why did the same thing not happen in other Communist countries? The answer to that lies partly at least in Tito's will and leadership.

At about the time when the Cominform crisis started to come off the boil, Tito decided to marry the faithful Jovanka. In 1951 he had suffered a gall-bladder attack and was nursed by her before and after the operation. When Djilas arrived to see Tito in hospital, a tearful Jovanka asked him: 'What will happen, Comrade Djido?' Djilas adds that this was the first time Jovanka had ever addressed a member of the Politburo. After Tito recovered, he married Jovanka privately at the beginning of 1952. According to Djilas, Tito's illness had also strengthened his friendship with the triumvirate. 'Not since the war had we felt our bond with him to be so close and warm, and I for one felt it to be permanent and unbreakable,' he later wrote. As for Jovanka, 'We leaders accepted her warmly and trustfully.'[1]

In the lower ranks of the Communist hierarchy, women especially were envious of Jovanka. She was at first nervous and shy, then veered in the other direction, and was accused of overdressing, loudness and vulgarity. Djilas says that Tito's sons resented their stepmother. The eldest, Žarko, who had lost an arm during the war, had turned out wild. The younger boy, Miša, was growing into a sullen adolescent. Again according to Djilas, Jovanka wanted a child of her own but Tito would not oblige her. Instead Jovanka started a busy social life among artists, movie people and journalists. The gossips accused her of plotting with pro-Soviet generals, and liked to say that 'the Serb blood came out in her'.[2] In spite of his marriage, Tito maintained and surely enjoyed his fame as a lady's man.

Tito's domestic happiness may have contributed to the genial mood in which he presided over the liberalisation of the economy, the law, the press and foreign relations. The collectivisation of land, which had begun in earnest in 1949, was put in reverse, so that decollectivisation was almost complete by 1953. The peasants were not allowed to own large farms, or to employ labour outside their families, but they started to get reasonable prices for their goods, so that food became plentiful in the cities.

The economic overlord Boris Kidrič started to unravel his own plan for centralisation and state control, allowing the introduction of small private businesses. In the Belgrade street where I lived in 1953–4, there were rows of private restaurants, cafés and shops, selling everything from cakes to clocks, from cloche hats to religious medallions. As early as 1950, Kardelj and Djilas argued for the creation of workers' self-management in the state-run companies. At first Tito opposed this, saying the workers were immature, but later agreed to the concept, saying: 'But this is Marxist – factories to the workers.' Having accepted it, Tito himself advanced the Workers' Council plan that same year.[3]

Although Western economists sneered at the Workers' Councils, calling them window-dressing, some proved very effective. Since wages depended on high production, the councils would not accept inefficient management staff, especially Communist Party hacks. The ex-Partisans and the Party stalwarts moved out of industry into the civil service, the army and the police. Once I spent a whole day talking to management staff and workers at a Sarajevo clothing factory, and thought it was much better run than those I had visited in Lancashire.

The reform of the legal system and the police was begun by Ranković in 1951 with a startling paper entitled 'Towards the Further Strengthening of the Judiciary and the Rule of Law'. Ranković showed that the whole system was shot through with abuse and lawlessness. Different courts meted out utterly different punishments for the same offence. He gave instances of 'rash deprivation of civil rights by certain agencies'. Criminal charges unjustly pursued amounted to 40 per cent in Serbia, 47 per cent in Montenegro. In Bosnia-Hercegovina, no out of 184 judges had no legal training, while three district-court judges had only elementary education. As Djilas so rightly says: 'The weight and credibility of this shattering criticism were greatly enhanced by the fact that they came from the chief of the entire police force, who was simultaneously organisation secretary of the Party.'[4] In what other country would the Minister of the Interior try to diminish rather than add to his power?

Milovan Djilas, as propaganda chief, led the way in the liberalisation of literature and the press, in particular in providing a fair and extensive coverage of events in the West. As early as 1951, Yugoslavia started to publish books and articles on the Soviet Gulag Archipelago, without of course mentioning Naked Island. Oddly enough the Russians, in their attacks on Yugoslavia, also failed to mention the cruel punishment of Cominformists.

Prominent Yugoslavs, especially journalists like Djilas and Dedijer, were sent on missions abroad to meet non-Communist politicians and write about their experiences. When in London, Djilas went to see Churchill who asked after 'my old friend Tito'; and

Djilas came to know and admire the Labour politician Aneurin Bevan. He made a long tour of the East, getting on especially well with the Indian Socialists, not forgetting to stop at Damascus on his way back, to buy Tito the fabric for a camel-hair coat. Another old comrade, Moša Pijade, when asked by Tito to bring him some gift from a foreign visit, is said to have answered grumpily that he did not fight through the Second World World in order to end his days as an errand boy.

In March 1953 Tito himself went on a state visit to Britain, much to the rage of his old antagonist Evelyn Waugh, who wrote to Nancy Mitford:

> I am becoming a Russian imperialist, a reaction to the politicians. What is wrong is not Russia but Communism. Our policy is to bribe all the small states to remain Communist but quarrel with Russia. If they're going to be Communist, it's much better that Russia should rule them. Great Empires never seek war; all their energies are taken up by administration. Our troubles now come from Clemenceau destroying the Austro-Hungarian Empire. The one certain way to start a Third World War is to establish half a dozen atheist police states, full of fatuous nationalism and power hunger.[5]

Tito was not put out by Tory attacks, nor by the Roman Catholic protests against the continued house arrest of Stepinac, who was now a cardinal. The year 1953 had begun with Tito's appointment as Yugoslav President over the three Vice-Presidents Kardelj, Ranković and Djilas. On 6 March 1953, a few days before he began his visit to London, Tito heard of the death of Stalin, the former idol whom he had come to despise. Seven or eight months later, Tito remarked about Stalin: 'It is incredible how quickly a man like that was forgotten.'[6]

That same year saw the worldwide publication and triumph of Vladimir Dedijer's *Tito Speaks*, his sympathetic but not hagiographic biography, much of it told in the first person singular. Although Dedijer's book glosses over, omits and sometimes distorts many aspects of Tito's career, it is now astonishing more for what it reveals than for what it hides. In particular one is astonished by Tito's denunciation of Stalin, more than three years before Khrushchev's revelations, and twenty years before Solzhenitsyn's *Gulag Archipelago*. In 1953 there was still enormous credulity in the West about the nature of 'Uncle Joe' and the 'Socialist Sixth of the Earth'. Those like the British journalist Malcolm Muggeridge who knew the Soviet Union and told some of the truth about it were still generally written off as at best 'cold warriors' and at worst 'McCarthyites', after the US Senator Joseph McCarthy who led an anti-Communist witch-hunt.

Towards the end of *Tito Speaks*, Dedijer gives an account of the great man's daily life at his home in 15 Rumunska Street – not in the former royal palace as sometimes alleged in the foreign press. He awoke at 5.30 a.m. in summer and 7 a.m. in winter, did Swedish exercises and took walks in the park, regardless of the weather. He breakfasted on coffee, rolls and occasionally an omelet, followed at lunch and dinner by ordinary Central European food, sometimes varied by Zagorje dishes, such as his mother once cooked. Of these his favourites were chicken *čorba*, a thick broth laced with sour cream, and *štruklje*, a home-made pastry with cottage cheese. He drank little at meals except for a glass of beer or Yugoslav wine.

Each morning Tito studied the Yugoslav papers, especially the correspondence columns, 'which often show the feelings of the people', then scanned the bulletins of the international news agencies, British, American, French, German and Russian. He also received the London *Times, Economist, New Statesman and Nation*, Aneurin Bevan's *Tribune*, the European edition of the *New York Times* and the *New York Herald Tribune, Foreign Affairs, Neue Zürcher Zeitung* and Moscow *Pravda*. He smoked while going through the papers – some of his twenty cigarettes a day – and had to use reading glasses ever since an accident years before when a pin had got into his eye.

After the newspapers, Tito would study his correspondence and his official papers, then receive visitors: 'A special category of

visitors consists of Tito's old friends and kinsmen. Usually once a
year Tito's schoolmates and acquaintances from villages round
Bjelovar, where Tito lived after the First World War [at Veliko
Trojstvo, the Holy Trinity, which rather surprisingly kept its name
under the Communists], and from factories in Zagreb, come to
visit Tito, stay a day or so, receive gifts and then take their leave.'

He travelled widely around the country, visiting farms and
factories, joining in celebrations and anniversaries. Dedijer
described going to Užice in western Serbia late in 1951, for the
tenth anniversary of the short-lived 'Red Republic': 'We arrived by
car and we were met near Užice by a group of more than 500
Partisans . . . Fires had been built on a hill outside the town and
lamb roasted whole on the spit. The old Partisans took Tito there,
sat around the fire, ate and then sang old Partisan songs.'

Dedijer discussed security measures taken for Tito's protection:

The Kremlin would like above all to see Tito assassinated . . . In
summer 1952, they sent a terrorist group into Yugoslavia from
Bulgaria. This group killed a lieutenant-colonel who had the
medal of National Hero. The Russians have many means of
smuggling terrorists over the Yugoslav border, which is more
than 1,250 miles long on the satellite side. The Danube, too,
flows through Yugoslavia and Russian, Hungarian and Rumanian
vessels can easily bring in groups of terrorists. In spite of the
constant danger, no extraordinary security measures are taken for
the protection of Tito when he goes to meetings. The measures
are about the same as those taken to protect an American
President when he goes to New York to address the United
Nations.

Tito received many foreign visitors. He usually had an interpreter present when meeting with the Americans and British, for
although he understood almost every word of English, he always
had difficulties in speaking the language. Besides Russian, Czech
and Slovene, Tito spoke German well with a Viennese accent, and

Kirghiz, which he learned in Siberia, and he could also read French and Italian.

After lunch, he would go to his library to read books recently published in Yugoslavia, among which he enjoyed Milovan Djilas's study of Petar Njegoš, the Montenegrin poet.[7] Tito's favourite foreign authors were Balzac and Stendhal, Goethe, Dreiser, Mark Twain, Jack London, Upton Sinclair, Sinclair Lewis and Kipling. It is worth pointing out that five of the nine are Americans, none are Slavs. Tito's literary tastes were formed in his youth, when he dreamed of emigration to the United States.

After lunch, Tito occasionally played chess but not very well, since Dedijer once beat him six games to two: 'Tito is usually very jovial when he plays chess. He always comments on the move of his opponent, but when he is in difficulties, he cogitates a long time before he makes his move.' Sometimes he would ride or play tennis during the afternoon. Sometimes he would shut himself in his room and play the accordion sent to him for his sixtieth birthday. He preferred light Viennese music and, among the classics, Beethoven and Tchaikovsky. Jazz he regarded as pande-monium, and when it was pointed out that the young people loved it, he answered: 'True, but I belong to the old generation.' He liked Renaissance art and, among the later painters, Delacroix and the early impressionists. He despised the Russian socialist realist school: 'You have the impression that the paintings are done by people without a soul, as if they were wielding spades instead of brushes.'

In the evenings, Tito often watched films, preferring above all Laurel and Hardy. He would play billiards and talk with his friends, especially Kardelj, Djilas and Ranković: 'These are fair discussions, in which of course everyone reacts according to his temperament, but there is one thing which is particularly charac-teristic, and that is that all four of them endeavour to understand one another, see eye to eye with one another, although they need not necessarily reach the same conclusion.'[8] A few months after the publication of *Tito Speaks*, this friendly quartet was broken up by the fall from grace of Milovan Djilas.

The year 1953, which had opened for Tito so hopefully, was to end with two unexpected and bitter disputes. One was the decision by the United States and Britain to hand 'Zone A' of Trieste to the Italians. The other was the publication of articles by Djilas that were to lead to his fall from office and later imprisonment. Although both these crises were seen at the time as setbacks to liberalisation, I now believe that they furthered this process, while the Djilas affair was a major event in the slow decline of international Communism, comparable to Khrushchev's speech to the Twentieth Party Congress, or Solzhenitsyn's *Gulag Archipelago*. Both the Trieste crisis and the Djilas affair took place while I was living in Yugoslavia, and greatly excited the people around me. Although I have here attempted to put these events within the context of Tito's career and Yugoslav history, I have also included some personal recollection and observation.

The Anglo-American statement on Trieste came on the afternoon of 8 October 1953. Early that morning I had arrived in Belgrade after standing all night on the train from Slovenia, so I was tired when I arrived at the Student House Ivo Lola Ribar on Boulevard Revolution (formerly Boulevard King Alexander, later Boulevard Red Army). Having exchanged friendly greetings with the Yugoslav students who shared the room, I got into bed and went to sleep. A few hours later I was woken up by shouting both inside and outside the student house. The students who had been so friendly a few hours earlier now told me grimly about the Trieste decision and argued among themselves whether to give me a *batina*, or beating as I discovered from my dictionary.

That day a crowd went on the rampage through Belgrade, roughing up British and American citizens, and smashing the offices of the respective reading rooms, as a mob on 27 March 1941 had attacked the German tourist office and torn up the swastika flag. Although the government at first approved the demonstrations, they got out of hand, so that Ranković had to send a troop of cavalry into Knez Mihailova Street. Banners appeared repeating the chanted slogans '*Trst je naš*' ('Trieste is ours') and

'*Život damo, Trst ne damo*!' ('We will give up our lives but not Trieste!').

On Sunday 11 October, a meeting began at the Slavija Hotel, then moved to Republic Square for a mass demonstration, the leaders carrying Djilas on their shoulders. With friends from the Student House Ivo Lola Ribar, I went to Republic Square to hear Moša Pijade, Belgrade's favourite orator. As we waited in the enormous crowd, the students told me some of the many stories and legends concerning Pijade, for instance his answer to Stalin in 1948: 'Moscow has asked us for a reply to the Cominform resolution. This is our answer to Moscow: "Up your mother's ****!"' On this occasion Pijade concentrated his witty, obscene attacks on Clare Boothe Luce, the US ambassadress in Rome whom the Yugoslavs blamed for the loss of Trieste.

Although the Belgrade mob talked of marching on Rome, it did not occur to me at the time that this was a real possibility. Even when Tito said in a speech at Leskovac that if the Italian army entered 'Zone A' his troops would follow, I thought this was bluff. Many years later Djilas revealed that Tito was ready for action: 'I asked him, "How are we going to fire at the Italians, when they are protected by the Americans and the English? Are we going to fire on them as well?" He answered, "We'll go in if the Italians go in . . . Then we'll see."'[9] In another account of this meeting, Djilas says:

Tito's demeanour on this occasion was that of a general at his command post. From the 'front' outside Trieste they were transmitting reports and requesting instructions. I think it was to General Kosta Nadj that Tito gave orders to send in Soviet, not American, tanks, 'otherwise it will be awkward'. I asked questions, unable to picture the entry of our troops into Zone A with British and American troops present. 'We will go in!' Tito declared. 'But what if they open fire?' 'They won't. And if the Italians start firing, we'll fire back.' I approved of our troops entering Zone A, though I thought then and still think that the whole campaign was too abrupt, too violent. Once the British

and Americans backed down from their position and the atmosphere had relaxed, I had the impression that Tito saw how
sudden and drastic our action had been.[10]

Tito said he was taking a hard position on 'Zone A', to stop the
Italians making a bid for 'Zone B'. Djilas believes his decision was
'also part of a carefully devised plan to stress Yugoslavia's independence of the West at the very moment when there were indications
of change in the Soviet Union in the wake of Stalin's death'.[11] This
probably credits Tito with too much foresight. He was not a good
chess player, as Dedijer reveals, leaping rashly into attack without
having considered alternative moves, then cogitating on how to get
out of trouble. In May 1945 Tito had risked a Third World War
by laying claim to Trieste, only to find that the Soviet Union would
not support him. Now, eight years later, he once more threatened
and ranted from a position of weakness. Nobody outside Yugoslavia backed Tito's claim to the overwhelmingly pro-Italian, anti-
Communist city. At the London talks that followed in 1954, Tito
quietly agreed to Italy taking Trieste. However, to Tito's credit,
once he had lost Trieste he took his defeat with grace and even
nonchalance. He was not the man to brood over disappointment,
let alone yearn for revenge. Queen Mary of England, after the loss
of her last Continental possession, claimed that when she was dead
they would find the word 'Calais' written upon her heart. The
French, in the late nineteenth century, could not forget the loss of
Alsace-Lorraine. But Tito forgot the city to which he had no proper
claim.

The excitement over Trieste at first distracted attention from the
development of the Djilas affair. On the very day that Djilas was
carried shoulder-high by the crowd in Republic Square, the first of
his controversial essays appeared in the Party newspaper *Borba*.
The gist of it was as follows:

Revolution cannot be saved by its past. Revolution has to find
new ideas, new forms, new challenges, different from its everyday

self; a new style and language. The bourgeoisie and the bureaucracy have already found new forms and slogans. Democracy
seeks them, too, and it will find them – in order for Yugoslavia
and that spark of opposition in today's world to move ahead.[12]

Such phrases, in *Borba* and in the turgid ideological journal
Nova Misao (*New Thought*), would not have attracted attention
anywhere in the West, but were studied excitedly in the Student
House Ivo Lola Ribar. Although Djilas was forty-two, Vice-
President of the country and leader of the National Assembly, he
still affected the air and trappings of student bohemianism. He
went about in an open-necked shirt and a cloth cap; he occasionally
rode the Belgrade trams; he sometimes took his coffee at the
Moskva Hotel, and he was known to despise the wealth and
privilege of his office. His following of the simple, socialist life
added weight to the *Borba* and *Nova Misao* articles. Perceptive
readers noticed that some of the strictures aimed at the Soviet
Union could just as well be applied to the Yugoslav Communist
Party, with its 'intrigues, mutual scheming and trap-laying, pursuit
of power, careerism, favouritism, the advancement of one's own
followers, relatives, "old fighters" (*stari borci* – ex-Partisans) – all
of it under the mask of high morality and ideology'.[13]

We know from Djilas's later memoirs that he was growing
uneasy during the summer of 1953, suspecting that Tito was using
the death of Stalin as an excuse for putting the brakes on
democratisation, or, in Marxist jargon, for the 'return to Leninist
norms and dictatorship of the proletariat'. Such things were on the
agenda of the Second Plenum held at the end of June at Tito's
residence on the island of Brioni, a former holiday home of the
Archduke Franz Ferdinand. As Djilas recalls in his memoirs:

The very fact that we were meeting on Brioni provoked my
disapproval – something I neither could nor would conceal. It
had always been our custom to hold plenums of the Central
Committee in Belgrade, seat of that committee and of the
government. I felt that to convene the plenum on Brioni, Tito's

best known residence, was to subordinate the Central Committee to Tito, instead of subordinating Tito to the leading body.[14]

Djilas expressed these feelings to Kardelj and Ranković, and also complained of the armed security in the hotel and even in Tito's villa, although the island was guarded both by the army and the navy. Djilas was clearly in an obstreperous mood. During a break on the terrace of Tito's villa, a senior comrade asked Djilas's opinion of an Augustinčić sculpture of a swimming maiden. 'Charming,' said Djilas, 'and there are five thousand others in the world just like it.' 'Tito likes it,' the colleague replied. 'That's his taste,' Djilas retorted. On the way back to Belgrade by car, Djilas told Kardelj he could not support the new 'Brioni' line. They stopped to go trout fishing, and once more Djilas became aware of his privileged status: 'Kardelj loved the fishing. Our luck was superb, perhaps because we were in a reserved stretch of the river, not the open stream.'[15]

Djilas's opposition to the 'Brioni' line expressed itself in the autumn series of articles in *Borba* and *Nova Misao*. While these were appearing, Djilas had to take part in the National Assembly elections in which he stood as a candidate in Montenegro. Although for the first time electors were given voting papers, separate booths in which to record their mark, and a choice of candidates from the Party's front organisation, the Socialist Alliance, the results were as usual a foregone conclusion. Djilas describes an impulse that many of us have known in a church or solemn assembly:

> In Titograd I felt the malicious, childish urge to shout out that, being the only candidate, I would be elected no matter what. Out of respect for my listeners I squelched that urge – were they to blame for participating in such 'elections'? I did insist that there be no official dinner in Pozaravac, and so we dined in the apartment of a local Party official, without fanfare or state expense.[16]

Although, as usual, official candidates all got 95 per cent of the vote, Djilas won 98.8 per cent, even exceeding Tito's majority.

Djilas recalls his last frank conversation with Kardelj and Ranković, which took place as they were walking down Užička Street, where both they and Tito had villas:

> In recent years thick walls had gone up around Tito's residence, and as we passed them I remarked that these walls symbolised the bureaucratic way of looking at things, or words to that effect. Kardelj said: 'Everything has changed or is changing, except for the Old Man and all that relates to him.' I then observed that Tito should somehow be brought to realise the impropriety of his style and all this pomp. But Ranković interrupted: 'Let's not talk about it here.' Kardelj and I took that to mean that even the street was bugged.[17]

On 29 November 1953 the leaders gathered at Jajce for the tenth anniversary of the AVNOJ assembly and Tito's appointment as Marshal. On the eve of the celebration Djilas and Koča Popović looked at some photographs taken ten years earlier. When Djilas made the somewhat banal comment that all of them had put on weight, Popović pointed out a photo of Djilas, shrewdly remarking of his appearance: 'A religious fanatic' At Jajce fortress the following day, Tito, Kardelj, Ranković and Djilas were photographed together for the last time.[18]

On 29 November, the day of the celebrations in Užice, *Borba* started to publish a second and far more sensational series of articles by Djilas. After the second of these, entitled 'Is there a Goal?' – to which the reply was 'Yes! A continuing struggle for democracy' – Djilas went through a psychological crisis, strangely similar to a religious experience:

> It was the night of 7–8 December 1953. Although I had as usual, fallen asleep about midnight, I woke up suddenly smitten within by some unfaltering, fateful realisation that I would not be able to abandon my views . . . I tried to thrust away my forebodings, obstinate in their insistence that something final had come to pass, something within me, or something affecting me, which

meant that I would have to subordinate my way of life, my hopes
– and, what is worse, subordinate my family or even sacrifice it
altogether. I knew that I had no prospect of winning. I recalled
Trotsky's fate and said to myself: better Trotsky's fate than
Stalin's, better to be defeated and destroyed than to betray one's
ideal, one's conscience.[19]

After this night of resolution, the *Borba* articles grew more
intense: 'No one party, not even a single class, can be the exclusive
expression of the objective imperatives of contemporary society.'[20]
'Every limitation of thought, even in the name of the most beautiful
ideal, only degrades those who perpetuate it.' The greatest crimes
and horrors in history – the fires of the Inquisition, Hitler's
concentration camps, Stalin's labour camps – stemmed ultimately
from a denial of free thought, from the exclusive claims of
'reactionary fanatics who have a political monopoly'.[21]

The articles were becoming a national and international sen-
sation, attracting more interest in the foreign press than any event
in Yugoslavia since the quarrel with the Cominform, as Tito later
sourly remarked. In the Student House Ivo Lola Ribar, each new
Borba article was read aloud in a hubbub of excitement. Although
Tito at this stage made no comment, Ranković told Djilas flatly: 'I
hope I'll never have to bother with philosophical ruminations, but
let me tell you that what you've written is hurting the Party.' While
Ranković was concerned with power, Kardelj was more concerned
with theory, and told Djilas: 'I don't agree with you at all. You
want to destroy the whole system!'[22]

In his next *Borba* article, Djilas replied to those unnamed critics
who called him a 'philosopher divorced from reality' and accused
him of writing for a foreign audience, bringing grist to the mill of
the reactionaries, and departing from Marxism-Leninism. It was
the leadership of the Party that had divorced itself from the masses.
If foreigners and reactionaries took comfort from his words, he was
sorry but not to be blamed; it was the fault of the bureaucrats in
power. He believed that truth emerged from the cumulative
thought and initiative of the common people.[23]

In his next article, Djilas passed from defence to attack. The Communists, he declared, had divorced themselves from the masses, claimed privileged positions and turned themselves into 'priests and policemen of socialism' who 'centralised and regularised everything from ethics to stamp-collecting'. Most Party meetings, he wrote, were a waste of time and 'in my opinion should convene very rarely'. Most political workers had no real function any more: 'Once men gave up everything, even life itself, to become professional revolutionaries. They were indispensable to progress. But today they are obstacles to it.'[24]

These *Borba* articles, which continued to appear until 7 January 1954, delighted the rank and file of the Party but worried and angered the leadership. In the end, however, it was not his theories that brought about Djilas's downfall, but a *Nova Misao* article called 'Anatomy of a Moral', criticising and mocking the private lives of the Party élite. In the previous summer, Djilas had been best man when his close friend and wartime comrade Peko Dapčević married Milena Versajković, a young and beautiful actress with no Partisan or Party background. She had been cold-shouldered and virtually ostracised by dowdier wives of the Party leaders, notably Milica, wife of Svetozar Vukmanović-Tempo, who like Djilas and Dapčević was a Montenegrin. The article in *Nova Misao* mentioned no names but described in detail how Milica had snubbed and humbled Milena in the VIP stand at a football match.

From there, Djilas went on to lash out at 'all those exalted women [who] came from semi-peasant backgrounds and were semi-educated', and seemed to think that their wartime services entitled them to 'grab and hoard de luxe furniture and works of art, tasteless of course, but by means of which they satisfied their primitive instincts of greed and imagined and puffed-up notions of their social class'.[25] The general public, the Ivo Lola Ribar students and even the lower echelons of the Party, loved all this, but the wives of the leadership wanted Djilas's head on a platter.

On 10 January 1954 *Borba* formally disavowed the views expressed by Djilas in his recent articles, adding that the affair would be taken up at the Central Committee's forthcoming

Plenum. Meanwhile Djilas wrote to Tito, requesting a personal interview. He still hoped that if he withdrew from the Executive Committee (the former Politburo and in effect the Cabinet) he might remain on the Central Committee and put forward his views in an unofficial and moderate way. He still clung to belief in Tito himself: 'I attributed to Tito democratic traits and initiatives which, in my heart of hearts, it was my hope, rather than my conviction, that he possessed.'

In the seventeen years of their comradeship, Djilas had never challenged Tito's authority and regarded him with almost filial devotion: 'If someone had asked me five or six months before the rift opened between us, whether I could conceive of any force that could separate me from Tito, Kardelj and Ranković, I would have said "No – not even death could separate us."'[26] Djilas seems to have been unaware of the anger caused in the Party by his *Nova Misao* article 'Anatomy of a Moral'. Nor did he seem to appreciate that his fiercely anti-Soviet *Borba* articles were embarrassing Tito in his attempts to improve relations with Stalin's successors.

This last meeting of Djilas with Tito, Kardelj and Ranković took place in the White Palace a few days before the Plenum. Tito began by saying that Djilas was a 'changed man', though he himself was obviously out of sorts. When Djilas asked for coffee because he had not been able to sleep at night, Tito said pointedly: 'Others are not sleeping either.' Tito repeated more harshly what he had told Djilas two months before, that one could not bring in democracy while the 'bourgeoisie' was so strong. Kardelj chipped in with an accusation of 'Bernsteinism', while Ranković, who was closest of all to Djilas, sat glumly silent. Tito asked for Djilas's resignation as President of the National Assembly, adding, 'What must be, must be.' 'As we said good-bye,' Djilas recalls, Tito 'held out his hand but with a look of hatred and vindictiveness'.[27]

The proceedings of the Plenum, which started on 16 January 1954, were broadcast live, and I heard them among an anxious gathering of students at Sarajevo University. Most of the 105 Central Committee members came by car but Djilas arrived on foot with his friend Dedijer. Tito spoke first, more in sorrow than in anger, referring to Djilas as 'Djido' (his nickname in the Party). Tito said that he himself was partly to blame for not having acted earlier to curb the tone of the articles. Only towards the end of December, when he had been able to read them more closely, had Tito realised just what poison they were spreading. The *Nova Misao* article proved that Djilas wanted a showdown. Tito said that Djilas's trips abroad had 'counteracted the influence of our reality, our revolutionary past and of all revolutionary experience'. He himself, Tito proclaimed, had been the first to speak of the withering away of the Party, 'but I did not say it should happen within six months or one or two years'. It could not happen 'before the last class enemy had been neutralised'. Tito accused Djilas of 'advocating democracy at any price, which is exactly the position of Bernstein'.[28]

In Sarajevo, where we were listening, one of the students turned to me almost in tears and said: 'I can't believe it. I was sure the Old Man, at least, would stand by him.' Djilas's feelings were angrier: 'Tito's speech was a piece of bitingly intolerant demagoguery . . . As Tito was speaking, the respect and fondness I had once felt for him turned to alienation and repulsion. That corpulent, carefully uniformed body with its shaven, pudgy neck filled me with disgust . . . But I hated no-one . . .'[29]

After Kardelj had found fault with his Marxist theory, Djilas rose to reply in a manner that was conciliatory but not apologetic. He admitted to being 'revisionist' about Leninist theory, but claimed to be loyal to Tito and to the League of Communists, as the Party was now called: 'On questions of foreign policy and on the fundamental issue of the brotherhood and unity of our people, I have always been completely at one with the Party leadership.' This was a coded way of saying that Djilas was neither a Cominformist nor a Serbian nationalist. As Stephen Clissold comments: 'Djilas had wanted to be conciliatory; but it was not through conciliation that the Partisans had fought their way to power and were now resolved to keep the fruits of victory. He wanted to reconcile the irreconcilable; to be a free man, as he put it, whilst remaining a Communist.'[30]

When the debate was thrown open, Moša Pijade grabbed at the chance to revenge the real or imagined wrongs that Djilas had done to him in Montenegro in 1941. He dismissed the *Nova Misao* article as 'political pornography'. What else could one expect from such a hypocrite?

> Now he has a villa and two cars and so forth; he has far more than those he describes as a repulsive caste. He has retained all his posts and privileges while renouncing only the hard work connected with them. While his closest comrades are sweating under the heavy burden of administrative work for state and society, he sits in comfort and writes and writes, and then, as a recreation, shows himself as a good democrat and drinks in cafés . . . His articles in *Borba* alone netted him 220,000 dinars . . . At forty a man should mature and enter middle age, but Comrade Djilas evidently has not made this progress, he has rather reverted to the preceeding stage of adolescence – to the early days before the war when he wrote his poem: 'I wander whistling through the streets . . .'[31]

Only Djilas's first wife, Mitra, and Vladimir Dedijer spoke up for him. In fact Dedijer made two telling points. At the end of December, when most of the *Borba* articles had already appeared, Djilas was unanimously elected President of the National Assembly. The charge of 'revisionism' now levelled at Djilas was just the one that the Cominform had levelled against the Yugoslav Party in general.

After the first session, Djilas felt crushed and during the night decided to make a recantation. The next day he said he had been wrong and his ideas were mistaken. The Central Committee had not neglected the struggle against bureaucracy. After taking part in the propaganda campaign against the Cominform, he had wrongly come to imagine that these criticisms of Soviet Russia also applied to Yugoslavia. He had indulged in abstract theory, which meant the 'mobilisation of the petty bourgeoisie, of social democracy, of the West'.

After this recantation, Djilas was expelled from the Central Committee but allowed to remain in the Party after a 'final warning'. In a conference with foreign journalists, Tito said that the affair was over and that Djilas was now politically dead. 'When I heard and read about this,' Djilas wrote later, 'something strong and instinctive came over me – something which had nothing to do with Communism but welled up from the ancient springs of my Montenegrin blood. "No it won't be quite like that!" I said to myself, "I will never give in; never – as long as I live!"'[32]

Very soon Djilas started to write the books and articles in the foreign press that would lead at the end of 1956 to the first of two stretches in prison, totalling seven years in all. He at one time feared that he might be sent to a camp resembling Naked Island. In one book he claims to know that elements in the secret police had recommended a 'physical resolution' to the Djilas case, in other words murdering him, but thinks that Ranković had protected him, 'probably because of our long-standing friendship'.[33] Ranković also knew that the death of Djilas would catastrophically damage Yugoslavia's foreign relations. Tito was clearly reluctant even to put him in prison because of the adverse publicity.

Inside the country, Djilas had few political friends and supporters. The young Communists, such as the students I knew in Belgrade and Sarajevo, were thunderstruck by the fall of their hero, but their response was disillusion rather than rage. To them, Djilas had been the incarnation of pride in the revolution and hope of building socialism. After the Djilas affair, they started to lose their ideals. From that time on, I cannot remember meeting a Communist true believer. Most of my friends in the 1950s and 1960s were Party members, but only so as to hold their jobs as doctors, lawyers, journalists, teachers or policemen. In private, none was a Marxist or even left wing. None of these people supported Milovan Djilas.

The Belgrade 'reactionaries', as the royalists liked to call themselves, were amused by Djilas's article 'Anatomy of a Moral', but they did not like the man. Often they called him the 'worst of the bunch', and recalled how, after some black marketeers were sentenced to prison, Djilas had written in *Borba* demanding that they should be executed.[34] The fact that Djilas was Montenegrin endeared him neither to other Yugoslavs nor to his fellow-country-men. What Dr Johnson said of another nation could well be applied to the Montenegrins: 'The Irish are a fair people – they never speak well of one another.'

Even Djilas's closest friends in the Communist Party turned against him. For example Peko Dapčević, whose wife was the subject of 'Anatomy of a Moral', denounced the article as without foundation. Even more painful was the behaviour of Vladimir Dedijer, Tito's biographer and a journalist on the staff of *Borba*. Dedijer was a passionate and rather unstable man, a champion boxer and a heroic soldier during the war. He had joined the Communist Party late, and was never a serious Marxist. During the Plenum he stood by Djilas, and afterwards went to see Tito, shouted at him and seemed to be on the point of using physical violence, for all of a sudden the bodyguard leapt into the room. Dedijer stood trial with Djilas in 1955 and like him was given a suspended sentence.

For a long time afterwards, Dedijer and his family were sub-jected to psychological persecution by the police, which led to a suicide. It seems that Dedijer had never recovered physically and emotionally from the Battle of Sutjeska, when he received a head wound and witnessed the death of his first wife. In the 1960s, Dedijer went into semi-exile in England, becoming involved with the Bertrand Russell campaign against the American action in Vietnam.

In the 1970s Dedijer returned to Yugoslavia and seems to have made his peace with Tito, but by now he had developed a strange and obsessive dislike of Djilas, perhaps motivated by envy. In a series of ever more wild and rambling studies of recent Yugoslav history, including a new version of *Tito Speaks*, Dedijer attacked the reputation of Milovan Djilas and even that of his son Aleksa, who now was also a writer. Like so many Yugoslavs, Dedijer was riled by Djilas's puritanism, especially his strictures on sexual morals among the comrades before the war:

In several of his memoirs Milovan Djilas, carried away by his own vanity, tries to insinuate that he was the main subjective factor influencing Yugoslav Communists to take up revolutionary asceticism . . . I should like to add too, in the interests of historic truth, that, lacking the courage to be straight with himself, Djilas is applying a double standard. It is true that on more than one occasion he preached a ban on free love; he even hounded to his death the young Bosnian militant Paternoster, who had loved two girls at once. But as his closest friend of that period, who never left his side, I must tell the truth: that was the time when Djilas himself was having several so-called 'healthy' love affairs.[35]

Djilas has patiently answered these and other attacks on himself and his family in his own memoirs, such as *Rise and Fall*. At one point Djilas wearily asks: 'What is the matter with Dedijer? Slovenly research? Malice? Madness? Or all three at once?'[36]

Djilas had realised all along that there would be no Djilasites. The friends who stood by him were people outside politics, above all his devoted second wife, Stefica, a Croat who, after her husband's long imprisonment and ostracism, had to endure the further anguish of exile by civil war. Their son Aleksa, who went on to write an excellent book on the Yugoslav nationalities problem, has always been firmly loyal. Milovan Djilas came to see that his quarrel with Tito was not simply a matter of politics. He was trying to find his identity as a human being, to find peace in his conscience and freedom of mind.

Although an atheist, Djilas has a profoundly religious view of life. His biographer Stephen Clissold offers the brilliant perception that Djilas sees the world as a Manichaean struggle in which the Devil rather than God appears to be gaining the upper hand:

The Bogomils of Bosnia had held this doctrine, which won many converts among the medieval Slavs and gave their land its national religion. Djilas felt the appeal of the Manichaean concept . . . It accounted for the legacy of rival fanaticisms disputing possession

of that troubled borderland, the militancy of the normally meek
Franciscans striving there as missionaries, the avidity with which
the heretics embraced Islam rather than submit. The Bogomils
. . . held that the Devil had been given dominion over all material
things; only a tiny elite, the 'Perfect', denied him earthly
allegiance by embracing a life of extreme abstinence and austerity
. . . a hyper-puritanism which appealed to a spiritual minority as
strongly as did the sect's uninhibited sensuality to the majority.
The idealistic revolutionaries of his youth seemed to Djilas the
heirs of the Bogomil 'Perfect'.[37]

Throughout the Second World War, Djilas had carried with him a
copy of Bishop Njegoš's epic poem *The Mountain Wreath*. During
his second term of imprisonment under Tito, Djilas set himself the
task of translating into Serbo-Croat Milton's *Paradise Lost*, a work
that is often accused of exalting Satan over God. Perhaps Djilas, as
he sat in his prison cell recalling the days of power with Tito,
consoled himself with the words of Lucifer: 'Better to reign in hell,
than serve in heaven.'

There were some outsiders, myself included, who, although they
admired and honoured Djilas, unhappily found themselves on the
side of Tito. When Tito said that Yugoslavia was not ready for
democracy, he justified this by the strength of the 'bourgeoisie' and
the 'class enemy'. He was in fact referring to the Serb and Croat
nationalists, the followers of the Chetniks and the Ustasha. This is
also what Djilas meant when he spoke at the Plenum, avowing
support for 'brotherhood and unity'. In 1954, when Djilas quarrelled with Tito, the wartime hatreds were still uncomfortably
fresh in everyone's mind, although little was said about it openly.
In my first published article, written from Sarajevo in 1954, I
argued that only Tito could hold Yugoslavia together. This conviction coloured my view of the Djilas affair.

Djilas regarded democracy and freedom of speech as absolute
principles, to which he adhered with the same fanatical devotion
he had once given to Communism. Perhaps he was right. Perhaps
if the Yugoslavs in 1954 had been given the chance to vote in fair

elections, they would have chosen national leaders willing to hold the federation together. Supporters of Tito felt that it needed many more years of his strong and paternal rule to heal the wounds of the war. Such people valued the concept of Yugoslavia more than abstract isms and ocracies. The choice between Djilas and Tito was like that described by Bertolt Brecht in his play *Galileo*: Is it worth killing the oyster to get a pearl? Humankind will always be divided on Brecht's answer: 'To hell with the pearl! Give me the healthy oyster!'

14

Yugoslavia's Place
in the World

The downfall of Djilas in January 1954 helped to patch up the dispute with the Soviet Union; however, the first response of the Soviets had not been conciliatory. At the end of January, the Cominform journal *For a Lasting Peace, For a People's Democracy* carried an article denouncing both the 'revisionists' and the 'Tito clique', which had been forced to move against Djilas only because of the pressure from 'the great masses of toilers'. In the Soviet Union, the Yugoslav issue figured in the power struggle between the three main contenders for the succession to Stalin – the foreign affairs expert Molotov, the Prime Minister Georgi Malenkov and the former Ukrainian Party boss Nikita Khrushchev.

Both Tito and Djilas had met Khrushchev in March 1945, when they stopped off at Kiev on their return from Moscow. Although they had been surprised that a Russian should be the Party boss of a foreign country, Tito and Djilas had both taken a liking to Khrushchev because of his frankness, good humour and interest in the lives of the ordinary people: 'None of the Soviet leaders went to collective farms, except occasionally to attend some feast or parade,' wrote Djilas in *Conversations with Stalin*.

Khrushchev accompanied us to a collective farm and, without harbouring in any little corner of his mind the slightest doubt of the justice of the system itself, he not only clinked huge glasses of vodka with the collective farmers, but he also inspected the garden hotbeds, peeped into the pigsty, and began discussing practical problems. During the ride back to Kiev he kept coming back to the question of the collective farms and openly talked about their shortcomings.[1]

Khrushchev in turn took a liking to Tito, whom he called lively and sympathetic, and also to Djilas: 'When I first met him he impressed me with his quick and subtle wit. He struck me as a good man. I won't deny that I now have a quite different opinion of him, but that's beside the point.'[2] Nine years later, Khrushchev exploited his old acquaintanceship with the Yugoslav leader to boost his own position. At the end of the summer of 1954, Khrushchev suggested in confidence to the Belgrade government that, since the Soviet Party had got rid of the secret police chief Lavrentia Beria, and the Yugoslav Party had sacked the 'revisionist' Djilas, the obstacles to *rapprochement* had now been removed.

In 1955, when Khrushchev had made his position safe in Moscow, he started a foreign tour with a state visit to Yugoslavia, during which he was seldom sober, ending up by signing a 'Belgrade Declaration', formally ending the quarrel between the two states. In the following year, Khrushchev made a sensational speech to the Twentieth Communist Party Congress, denouncing the crimes and follies of Stalin. In the course of these revelations, Khrushchev recalled that during the quarrel with Yugoslavia in 1948 Stalin had boasted: 'I will wag my little finger and there will be no more Tito.' The secret speech, which was soon to be leaked to the Western press, prepared the way for Tito to visit the Soviet Union in June 1956 and sign a 'Moscow Declaration', leading towards a *rapprochement* between the Communist Parties as well as the two states. The Yugoslav ambassador in Moscow, Veljko Mičunović, has described Khrushchev's new style of conducting business. Their motorcade had stopped in a Moscow suburb:

In order to avoid the crush in the streets, Tito and Khrushchev went into a shop selling cakes and ice cream . . . The customers we found inside the shop started to move away, but Khrushchev asked everyone to stay where they were. Khrushchev and Tito ordered ice cream. But when it came to paying for this, it turned out that neither Khrushchev nor Tito had a kopek in his pocket.[3]

Khrushchev's denunciations of Stalin, his friendship with Tito and his boisterous, clowning manner led the West to believe that he was a 'liberal', new-style Communist of the Yugoslav kind. However, in some respects, Khrushchev was even more despotic and cruel than Stalin, particularly in his persecution of Christian believers. In a major offensive against the Russian Orthodox Church, Khrushchev imprisoned scores of bishops, priests and nuns on trumped-up 'criminal' charges. He reduced the number of churches to 7,000, representing a loss of two-thirds. The seminaries were reduced from eight to three, and the number of functioning monasteries from sixty-seven to twenty-one. Especially drastic punishment was imposed on anyone teaching religion to the young.[4] The persecution of Christians in Russia, which lasted into the age of glasnost and perestroika, went virtually unreported in the Western press.

Although Khrushchev gave his tacit approval to the developments in Yugoslavia, he tried to stamp out the spread of 'Titoism' in other countries of eastern Europe. The first challenge to Khrushchev came from the Poles in 1956 when, after a riot at Poznan, the Stalinist leader was replaced by Gomulka, who had served three years in prison as a 'Titoist'. In October 1956 Khrushchev was so alarmed by the liberalisation of Poland that he dispatched Red Army tanks to Warsaw, only to find that their way was blocked by tanks of the Polish Army. The Warsaw crowd chanted 'Katyn! Katyn!', referring to the massacre of 12,000 Polish officers by the Russians during the Second World War. Khrushchev had to back down from a confrontation with Poland, but meanwhile Hungary too had revolted against the Soviets and the local Communists.

Faced by this new crisis, Khrushchev flew to Yugoslavia for

three days of urgent secret talks with Tito on the island of Brioni. Khrushchev said that in Hungary Communists were now being butchered, and that in Moscow people were saying that such things could not have happened in Stalin's time.[5] Tito agreed to give Khrushchev his qualified support, but he allowed the rebel leader Imre Nagy to shelter in the Yugoslav Embassy in Budapest. When Nagy left this sanctuary under a promise of safe conduct, he was arrested and shot by the Russians. This led to a serious rift between Tito and Khrushchev.

Another casualty of events in Budapest was Milovan Djilas, who chose this moment to break his political silence. After a number of statements to Western reporters, Djilas published an article in the American magazine *The New Leader* (19 November 1956) that began: 'With the victory of national Communism in Poland a new chapter began in the history of Communism and of the subjugated countries of Eastern Europe. With the Hungarian people's revolution, a new chapter began in the history of humanity.' He went on to criticise the ambiguous attitude to Hungary of the Yugoslav government, which had shown itself 'unable to depart from its narrow ideological and bureaucratic class interests' and had betrayed 'those principles of equality and non-interference in internal affairs on which all its successes in the struggle with Moscow had been based'.[6]

Having at first ignored various statements by Djilas, Tito took action over *The New Leader* article. Failure to silence Djilas would have been seen as sympathy with his views. Claiming that Djilas had violated his undertaking to refrain from 'hostile propaganda', the authorities revoked the suspension of the prison sentence handed out the previous year. On 12 December 1956, after a seven-hour trial held in camera, Djilas was sentenced to three years' strict confinement, and was taken to the prison at Sremska Mitrovica, where he had served a similar term in the 1930s.

It was said that in 1956 the Hungarians had behaved like Poles, the Poles had behaved like Czechs, and the Czechs had behaved like pigs, because they had made no effort to win their freedom. From this time onwards, only Poland of all the countries of eastern

Europe enjoyed anything like the freedom of Yugoslavia, and even in Poland this freedom did not entail any real support for the Communist Party. The Roman Catholic Church had become in effect the political voice of the Polish people, rendering unto Caesar only a sullen obedience. In return for this, the Poles were allowed to speak their minds, to pack the churches on Sunday, and to honour their dead on All Souls' Day.

On my first visit to Poland, in November 1959, I witnessed a strange manifestation that I would later come to understand as of great importance also to Yugoslavia. An old woman, walking through what had once been the Warsaw Ghetto, had seen what she thought was the Virgin Mary appearing above a nineteenth-century church. She told her friends, who came to join her in front of the church, and after a few days vast crowds started to gather each evening. I saw an immense crowd of tens of thousands waiting patiently in the November rain; soldiers had to be called in to help keep order.

The Warsaw apparitions did not recur and were soon forgotten. However, in 1966 I was lucky enough to get permission to see the Polish millennial celebrations at Częstochowa, where half a million Catholics knelt in a field before the statuette of the Black Madonna, chanting 'Hail Mary, Queen of Poland!' It was then that I realised that Communism was doomed in all eastern Europe. In 1978 I was again in Poland to see the reaction to the enthronement of a Polish Pope, John Paul II. I noticed two army officers beside the road listening to the ceremony in Rome on transistor radios, while tears of pride and devotion streamed down their faces. Poland also produced one of the most amazing photographs of the twentieth century: the strikers kneeling at prayer in front of the Lenin Shipyard at Gdansk.

Although in Poland I felt only joy at sights like this, in Yugoslavia I had misgivings. In Poland the Roman Catholic Church represents almost the whole nation. In many respects it actually is the nation, having survived when there was no Polish state. Moreover the Polish Catholic Church has not tried to exterminate the Jews, Gypsies or Orthodox Christians. In Yugoslavia, however, the Croatian Catholic Church identifies with only a third of the nation, and it has blood on its hands.

Although Tito paid lip-service to friendship with the Soviet Union and membership of the 'Socialist camp', virtually all Yugoslavs, whether or not they were Party members, regarded themselves as closer to the West. Perhaps I can best explain this by two anecdotes. While staying in Warsaw in 1959, I happened to meet a Montenegrin journalist who was writing a series of articles on eastern Europe for *Borba*. He was contemptuous of all the east European countries, regarding even Poland as a colony of the Soviet Union. He was especially scornful of Czechoslovakia, once the most Western and prosperous of all the Slav nations. The Czechoslovaks had provided him with a female interpreter who, he assumed, reported on his activities. She had gone to bed with him, and gave the appearance at least of being in love. At the end of his stay, so the Montenegrin told me: 'She came to the station to see me off. She said she was really sad and wanted to see me again, and suggested we meet for our next summer holiday – the Czechs can go on holiday to our Yugoslav coast. So I told her she was the most beautiful secret policewoman I'd ever screwed. And you know, she was such a good actress that when I said that, she actually burst into tears.'

In Communist Cuba I happened to meet a diplomat from the Yugoslav Embassy. Apparently Fidel Castro's bodyguards had recently shot up the embassy car and wounded one of their personnel, so he was not feeling well disposed to Cuba. But even this could not explain the flow of invective to which he subjected the country, making no effort to keep his voice down. He said that Fidel was just a tin-pot Latin American fascist, similar to Juan Perón, the Argentine dictator. He said that the Cubans lived in terror and hoped only to reach the United States. He added that when the revolutionary leader Che Guevara disappeared to try and start a revolt in Bolivia, Fidel Castro had an affair with Guevara's wife. All this was told to me by the diplomat of a country supposed to be on the best of terms with Communist Cuba.

The clearest proof I had of where Yugoslavia stood between East

and West came in 1962, during a long assignment to follow the
Iron Curtain from Kirkenes, on the Barents Sea in Arctic Norway,
down to the Turkish frontier with Bulgaria. During my autumn
journey, the Cuban Missile Crisis heightened the tension along the
frontier. Once, when I focused a pair of field-glasses to get a better
look at an East German watch-tower on the other side of the
minefield and the electrified barbed wire, I found myself staring
into the barrel of a gun. The photographer I was with was arrested
in Greece, and we both were detained for the night in a Turkish
frontier police station. In Yugoslavia we wanted to see the Romanian frontier, north-east of Belgrade, where Arso Jovanović and his
friends had been shot attempting to escape in 1948. We drove to a
muddy village near to the frontier in the Banat, and were stopped
by two gendarmes who asked to see our permits. We explained
that we did not have any permits, whereupon they said we were
under arrest. At this point a small crowd of villagers came up and
started to remonstrate with the two policemen. We were English,
they said, and the English had been on their side in two world
wars, and were on their side today. Soon the policemen bowed to
public opinion, smiled, shook hands, and allowed us to talk to and
photograph local people. In Yugoslavia, quite as much as in
Norway, Finland, West Germany, Austria, Greece and Turkey, we
knew we were on the right side of the Iron Curtain during the
Cuban crisis.

The Cuban crisis passed and in 1963 Khrushchev showed signs
of wanting to patch up his relations with the West. In the summer
of that year he accepted Tito's invitation to holiday in Yugoslavia.
Since I was in the country at the time, I sought permission to join
the party of journalists, most of them correspondents stationed in
Moscow, who were covering the story. Although I did not report
on the whole visit, and missed the reception at which Khrushchev
was said to have danced with Tito, I did gain some insight into the
way that the Yugoslav Communists dealt with their troublesome
Soviet counterparts.

On his previous visit, in 1955, Khrushchev had arrived in
Belgrade wearing a white suit, only to find Tito dressed in black.

Khrushchev was wearing a black suit when he stepped off the plane in 1963, to be met by a Tito dressed in white. The following day they had both switched colour again to visit the tractor works at Rakovica, near Belgrade. True to his reputation, Khrushchev was really interested in the factory, questioning all those he met on the Workers' Council system. At first he appeared determined to prove that the system was no good: 'Each worker wants to receive more. He says give me more money. The director says he needs more money for investment, or their production will be unprofitable.' The Rakovica management told Khrushchev that this was an outdated point of view. Many Workers' Councils invested too much in the hope of getting a bigger return on capital, even accepting wages lower than the minimum level. The main problem facing the Workers' Council was the demand by local politicians to put all their money into the district, whether or not this was economic. After his tour of Rakovica, Khrushchev made the ambiguous comment that Yugoslav Workers' Councils were 'not what they were ten years earlier'.

Khrushchev and Tito went to the Macedonian city of Skoplje, largely destroyed by an earthquake a few days before. In the wreck of a high-rise hotel, the only survivors had been some revellers trapped in the cellar nightclub who, when they were dug out, asked: 'Who won the war, America or Russia?' Or so the story went. The sight of Tito and Khrushchev among the ruins did not greatly excite the homeless people camped in the park. Instead they asked me about the two big news stories from England that summer: the Profumo Affair and the Great Train Robbery.

A few days later, I caught up with the party again at Koper, or Capodistria, in the old 'Zone B' of Trieste. They had spent the weekend at Tito's island home on Brioni, where Khrushchev had got very drunk and was now in a foul temper. A reporter who asked Khrushchev an awkward question that morning was told: 'You are the kind of man who sees a beautiful woman and wants to sniff around her anus.' The next day, during a tour of a pig farm in Slovenia, Khrushchev compared these beasts with the reporter. The trip through Slovenia included a visit to a handsome mining village, where colliers in black and brown uniforms, faced in green, sang in a fine male-voice choir. Afterwards we were taken to watch a roller-skate ballet by girls of the local school, where all went well until one of the dancers slipped and fell very heavily on her bottom. Turning towards the guests of honour, I noticed Khrushchev scowling, Tito puffing impassively on his cigarette, and Ranković grinning broadly. Afterwards Khrushchev put on a miner's black jacket and forage cap, then delivered one of his cryptic speeches, this time on the subject of Mao Zedong and China: 'If the Chinese want to reach heaven so quickly, we'll gladly fire them into outer space in one of our rockets.'

On the following day, the group moved on to Zagreb, where there were hundreds of troops as well as policemen thronging the streets, no doubt from fear of a Ustasha terrorist attack. After a tour of the new OKI petrochemical works, the party went to the Workers' University, whose female principal gathered the guests in a small private room to tell them about the curriculum. One of the Moscow correspondents and I were able to slip in as well and hear an illuminating discussion.

As Khrushchev listened through an interpreter to the principal's explanation of what courses were open to part-time students, he grew visibly angry and impatient, until he interrupted her: 'The workers should stay at the factory bench. We had this adult education after the Civil War, when lots of people had never even finished middle school. Now everyone goes to school until they're fifteen. If they're good they can go on to night school or university. But we want people with a deep knowledge of technology and science and Marxism, not Latin or playing the piano.'

At this point Ranković interrupted Khrushchev to shout back that the Yugoslavs respected the workers and wanted them to develop their talents and interests. Then Khrushchev shouted back louder still: 'We criticised Stalin because he destroyed Lenin's principles of the school system and went back to the classical gymnasiums. There they prepared girls for marriage and boys for taking a stroll. They twirled their moustaches but still hadn't learned anything.' By this time both Khrushchev and Ranković, not to mention the principal of the Workers' University, were seething with rage, while Tito, taking his cigarette-holder out of his mouth, calmly asked 'our dear comrades' to cool down. After hearing such an exchange over adult education, I wondered how these people conducted their serious affairs.

Khrushchev fell from power in October 1964 but his successor, Leonid Brezhnev, continued friendly relations with Yugoslavia. Tito's only remaining clash with the Soviet Union occurred in 1968 over events in Czechoslovakia. Tito himself had been one of the tens of thousands of Serbs and Croats before the First World War who had gone to the Czech and Slovak lands to share with these fellow Slavs the dream of unity and independence from Austria. Although Tito, as a manual worker, had not gone to study in 'Golden Prague' and sit at the feet of Professor Thomas Masaryk, he had learned the language and felt at one with the people.

After the Second World War, but before the Communist *coup d'état* of February 1948, Tito visited Prague and was given a warm welcome. Djilas, who accompanied him, wrote a rapturous account of Prague during its last years of bourgeois democracy:

> The Czechs were just as we had imagined them to be: happy, kindly, well-dressed, in ecstasy over their democracy and their Slavism, and fond of the South Slavs. Their squares had been transformed into flower gardens, their streets into fields of human grain and blossoming meadows. There were people of all ages festively dressed, and swelling tides of young girls and boys in folk costumes. Sitting there next to Tito – and concerned for his security, because in this country there were fugitive Ustasha – I was nevertheless carried away by the enthusiasm, fervour and colourful crowds. And Tito even more: he smiled, waved his hand, jumped up from his seat, and all but lost his dignity.[7]

In spite of his Communist principles, Tito liked and admired the 'bourgeois' President Edvard Beneš, and still more the witty and charming Foreign Minister Jan Masaryk, son of the famous professor and first Czechoslovak President. After the Communist seizure of power in 1948, Beneš resigned in despair, and Jan Masaryk fell to his death from a window in Prague, whether as a suicide or as a murder victim was never established. Although Tito had welcomed the brutal new regime, Czechoslovakia joined in denouncing the Yugoslav Party later in 1948. In the dungeons of 'Golden Prague', Communist men and women were tortured into confessing that they were 'Titoists', and then either hanged or sent to work in the salt-mines.

Czechoslovakia became the most docile and spineless of all Soviet satellites. The 'happy, kindly' people who greeted Tito before the *coup d'état* were now suspicious and miserable. When the Communist Party put on a rally, tens of thousands of people turned out for fear of being reported by their neighbours. In the tragic Jewish Museum in Prague, specially preserved by Hitler, the woman guide trotted out a Party-line attack on the state of Israel to the West German tourists. Even if these were her genuine views, it was certainly not the place to express them.

Tito had served on the Galicia front in 1915 near to the Czech unit of Jaroslav Hašek, the future author of *The Good Soldier Švejk*. Whereas Tito had been unwillingly taken prisoner, and stayed loyal to the Habsburgs in captivity, Hašek deserted to the Russians, betrayed the Austro-Hungarian Empire as well as the Czechs, and joined the Russian Communist Party, becoming a commissar. In Communist Czechoslovakia, Hašek was idolised, and Švejk, the sly, passive resister to Habsburg rule, was elevated into a national hero. However, the Czechs were now faced by a very much nastier government. Hašek's novel begins at a real-life pub, U Kalicha, shortly after the 1914 assassination in Sarajevo, as a secret policeman tries to draw Švejk into making subversive comments. Finally he arrests Švejk for saying that the flies had left their trade mark on the Emperor Franz Joseph's portrait. Fifty years later, the Emperor's portrait still hung at U Kalicha, now a tourist attraction. However, the customers drinking the still delicious beer were far too frightened to enter into a talk with a foreigner. The one man ready to make some banal conversation about the weather or sport actually fled in terror as soon as I mentioned *The Good Soldier*

Švejk. A university lecturer who was an authority on Hašek inadvertently let slip a trace of Švejkian humour. When I asked if the book was not considered subversive and whether it was freely allowed to be read, he replied: 'Yes, everywhere – except in the army.'

During the late 1950s and the 1960s the Czechoslovaks were permitted to go on holiday to Yugoslavia, but only in groups under surveillance. Once I travelled by train with such a group through Austria and Slovenia, and heard the leader inculcating the rest with anti-Tito propaganda. He made feeble jokes about the Yugoslav policy of decentralisation, asking if anyone had 'the decentralised time'. He made jokes about Djilas, then sang in a sarcastic fashion the Partisan song about Tito, 'Little White Violet'. This was in 1958, after the Czechoslovaks had already endured ten years of cruel dictatorship.

It was not until January 1968 that an honest and decent man, Alexander Dubček, ousted Anton Novotný as Communist Party leader, introducing what came to be known as the 'Prague Spring'. The excitement was greatest among the students and middle-class intellectuals, for many working-class Czechoslovaks clung to their feather-bedded jobs. But now in U Kalicha, the talk flowed free, and I stayed at another of Hašek's favourite inns, the Golden Goose. By June, the streets of Prague were starting to fill with impromptu clusters of ten or twenty people discussing the progress of reform and the threat of Soviet intervention. Once I was watching a foreign TV crew film a street debate, when the reporter asked the young woman orator if the Czechs were afraid of a Russian invasion. '*Ne bojemy!*' ('We're not afraid!') she answered, whereupon she was shouted down by the rest of the group with the plaintive cry of '*Bojemy!*' ('We're afraid!'). The east European observer Neal Ascherson, who was also present, remarked that we would not have heard that response in Budapest, Warsaw and above all Belgrade. The spirit of Švejk may have brought down the Habsburg Empire but could not get rid of the Russians.

A few days before the invasion of Czechoslovakia, Tito himself visited Prague and was given a joyful reception. He endorsed the

Dubček reforms but warned against a revival of German aggression against the country. A hostile author, Nora Beloff, has seen this as an example of Tito's equivocal attitude to the cause of freedom. Or perhaps Tito suspected even then that the old German dislike of Czechs and Serbs might one day help to break up Czechoslovakia and Yugoslavia, as indeed happened twelve years after Tito's death.

At the start of 1968, Tito did not envisage a year of crisis and even the threat of war, for in deference to the tourist trade he closed the important army and naval bases in and around Dubrovnik. The news of the Warsaw Pact invasion of Czechoslavakia on 22 August came as a shock in Belgrade, where I saw the old city once more gird itself for battle. Rumours spread of a mass mobilisation along the northern and eastern frontiers. The many Czechoslovaks on holiday in Yugoslavia flocked to their embassy on Boulevard Revolution, where they were joined by a huge crowd of Yugoslavs shouting support. From that typical Belgrade demonstration, awash with patriotism and plum brandy, I even heard calls for the invasion of Russia: 'To Moscow! To Moscow!'

Tito condemned the intervention and stated his country's resolve to resist aggression. In this he had the support of the new Romanian Communist leader, Nicolae Ceauşescu, who also denounced the Soviet action in public. Tito and Ceauşescu met on their common border on 24 August and again on 4 September, when they repeated their joint resolve to resist aggression. Tension rose in late September and early October. Articles in the Soviet and east European press once more denounced Yugoslavia's political and economic system, and accused Tito himself of supporting the counter-revolution in Czechoslovakia.

The Metropol Hotel in Belgrade became a gathering place for Tito's old friends and comrades-in-arms. Sir Fitzroy Maclean was staying there, and Milovan Djilas frequently came to the foyer to hear the gossip and give his own support to Tito's stand on the Czechoslovak crisis. He told me not only that he still admired Tito and wished to be friends with him again, but that in some respects he, Djilas, had been in the wrong: 'At the time of the Hungary crisis [in 1956] I criticised Tito in public for not taking a firmer stand against Russia. For this I was afterwards punished . . . I think that Tito was right and I was wrong.'[8]

In October 1968 Djilas was given a passport to visit the United States and Britain, where he repeated his backing for Tito's policy and asked the West for support against Soviet threats to Yugoslavia. Over a lunch at Simpson's-in-the-Strand and at a subsequent television interview, I found Djilas to be in excellent spirits and optimistic about the future. However, he did not achieve the hoped-for reconciliation with Tito, for reasons well explained by his biographer Stephen Clissold:

> The first move would have to come from Tito, and Tito felt absolutely no inclination for any reconciliation. It was not that he was by nature vindictive or vengeful, or even lacking in magnanimity, but the break with 'Djido' had caused him real pain. He looked upon it not only as a defection from the cause but a personal betrayal. It aroused in him anger and a deep, persistent resentment . . . The mere mention of Djilas's name was apt to enrage him.[9]

The fact that Tito's views were now close to those of Djilas could only mean that the former had shifted his ground, and that was humiliating. Besides, Djilas was anathema to the Russians, with whom Tito would sooner or later have to come to terms again.

Although Tito made common cause wth Ceauşescu during the Czechoslovakia crisis, he was too good a judge of character not to see through this vain and shabby man. However, he admired the way in which Ceauşescu, by posing as a maverick Communist, had persuaded the United States to give him the technological know-how to build military planes for sale to Third World countries. Yugoslavia joined Romania in making the ROM-YU fighter (or YU-ROM fighter, as it became known when Tito suggested this sounded better). The former head of Romania's secret service Ion Pacepa has given a racy account of the Ceauşescus' visits to Brioni and Tito's yacht: 'At that time their relations were excellent. It was

only later when the two men started to know each other better, and
when Elena was put down by Jovanka's festive elegance, that the
personal relations started to deteriorate.'[10]

Soon after the quarrel with the Soviet Union in 1948, Tito had
hoped to ally himself with the Chinese Communists who, like the
Partisans, had come to power through battle. However, Mao
Zedong was loyal to Stalin during his lifetime and even after
Khrushchev's posthumous attack. During the 1960s, some Western writers began to make an analogy between Yugoslavia and
North Vietnam, between Tito and Ho Chi Minh. Both were
guerrilla fighters, great leaders of men who held the respect of
many outside the Communist Party, without demanding a slavish
adulation. As Tito had told the British during the Second World
War that he was fighting to free his country from German
occupation, so Ho Chi Minh had told the Americans that he was a
patriot trying to free his country from Japan and the French
colonialists. Like Tito, the Vietnamese Communist played down
Marxist dogma, and, when he addressed a crowd in Hanoi in 1946,
he took care to quote the American Declaration of Independence.

The analogy between Tito and Ho Chi Minh became popular
with liberal American opponents of the Vietnam War. The historian Barbara Tuchman advanced the idea that in 1945-6 the US
State Department could have turned Ho Chi Minh into a Tito for
Indo-China:

> In Indo-China, choice of the alternative would have required
> imagination, which is never a long suit with governments, and
> willingness to take the risk of supporting a Communist, when
> Communism was still seen as a solid block. Tito was then its only
> splinter, and the possibility of another deviation was not
> envisaged.[11]

Such a policy would indeed have required imagination, since in
1945-6 Tito had not yet emerged as a deviationist. At that time the
State Department believed him to be the most loyal of Stalin's

creatures, and an implacable enemy of the United States. From 1948 onwards, Ho Chi Minh slavishly followed the Cominform line of denouncing Tito. Like Mao, he venerated Stalin and he gave the latter's portrait a place of honour in Hanoi, where it remained until long after Ho Chi Minh's own death.

Barbara Tuchman suggests that Ho Chi Minh could have been a Tito for Indo-China; but Indo-China was even less of a nation state than Yugoslavia. The two other peoples of Indo-China, the Laotians and the Cambodians, have always detested the Vietnamese, who are different in language, race and even skin colour. The North Vietnamese have been fighting the South Vietnamese since the early sixteenth century, except during the French colonial rule. In Indo-China, as in Yugoslavia, Communism tried to impose its rule on deeply divided peoples. In both countries it failed.

From the break with Stalin in 1948 until the Czechoslovakia crisis twenty years later, Tito succeeded in keeping his country independent of both the capitalist and the Communist blocs. From about 1953, Tito became increasingly keen to establish links with former colonial countries in Africa, Asia and Latin America. Thanks to his journeying in these hot parts of the earth, and his acting as host to Third World leaders in Yugoslavia, Tito became the informal head of an organisation of 'non-aligned' states that flourished during the 1960s and early 1970s. This hectic and sometimes ludicrous international hob-nobbing gratified Tito's passion for tourism. To a certain extent it was also useful to Yugoslavia. It opened markets for Yugoslav exports, especially in engineering. It provided employment for Yugoslav graduates whose qualifications might not be acceptable in the West. It boosted the country's prestige. And most important of all for Tito, it made him the head of a third, if feeble, bloc between East and West. Tito was in a position to say, in a paraphrase of the claim by Lord Canning: 'I called the Third World into existence to redress the balance of the First and Second.'

Tito's interest in the Third World first became evident during the winter of 1953-4, when Yugoslavia had still not made peace with the Soviet Union, and was quarrelling with the West about the future of Trieste. Tito's first overtures were made to another remarkable ruler, Emperor Haile Selassie of Ethiopia. The latest Emperor in a line that traces its origins to the Queen of Sheba, he had exercised power since 1916, but had not been crowned until 1930. In 1936 Ethiopia was conquered and Haile Selassie deposed by the Italian dictator Mussolini. In 1941 Haile Selassie came back to power with the assistance of the British army, and since then had ruled his exotic country by taking aid and advice from various foreign powers, without becoming beholden to anyone. In 1953 he invited Yugoslavia to send out experts, especially medical doctors, to work in Ethiopia. One frequently met people in Belgrade who, when they were quarrelling with their wives, or doing badly at work, or simply drunk, talked of starting a new life in Addis Ababa. The alliance between these two eccentric countries was made apparent when Tito became the first foreign head of state to visit Ethiopia, and in 1954 Communist Yugoslavia was visited by the Emperor Haile Selassie, the Conquering Lion of Judah, Elect of God and King of the Kings of Ethiopia.

The Yugoslavs also wanted to make money from Ethiopia. Besides sending doctors, they also sent a construction team to build a hospital in Addis Ababa, but when the Ethiopian government fell behind on payment, work was stopped on the site. In the 1960s a Yugoslav company won a contract to build a barrage on the Tisisat Falls, near where the Blue Nile leaves Lake Tana to start its 2,750-mile journey to the sea. The water diverted by this barrage would flow into a hydroelectric turbine made by the Rade Konćar company in Zagreb. The chief engineer at the small town of Bahir Dar had a comfortable bungalow, a garden of dazzling flowers, a portrait of Tito and several brands of Scotch in his cupboard. He spoke of his Ethiopian staff with tact but disdain: 'They are, how shall I find the right word, unlearned. They are so-so.' Some of his colleagues were less restrained when I met them in the Gondar Bar, one of the town's three mud taverns, where girls with names like Lemlem danced with the customers for the price of a bottle of beer. One of the three Yugoslavs took a revolver out of his pocket and told me to leave, then changed his mind and started muttering to himself. His two colleagues poured out their troubles to me, a fresh pair of ears: 'You think the Ethiopians are good people? They're one hundred per cent bad. A man goes to study for one year and he thinks he can be an engineer . . . They're worse than the Montenegrins!' His colleague, also a Croat, disagreed: 'The Montenegrins are more advanced but in some ways they're even worse than the Ethiopians. But that's politics.'[12]

After Haile Selassie's visit to Yugoslavia, Tito took off on a long trip through Asia, ending up at Bandung in Indonesia, for a conference bringing together twenty-nine Asian and African states. This was in 1955, before the 'wind of change' had brought independence to dozens of African countries. During the winter of 1958–9, when Yugoslavia was once more quarrelling with the Soviet Union, Tito went on a three-month trip that took him to Indonesia, India, Sri Lanka, Ethiopia, Sudan and Egypt. In the last of these countries he made a special ally of Colonel Nasser.

To please the Egyptian leader, Tito jeopardised Yugoslavia's relationship with France by helping Algerian nationalists. At a press conference in 1959, President de Gaulle included Yugoslavia among the countries of eastern Europe whose regimes, imposed by the Soviet Union, would disappear in a free election.[13] In return for Tito's support, Colonel Nasser backed the first conference of non-aligned states, held in Belgrade in 1961. Tito used his position as host to give a pro-Soviet, anti-Western slant to the conference. This suited his purposes at the time.

At the second non-aligned conference, held in Cairo in 1964, the number of participants had risen to forty-seven, all Afro-Asians except for Cuba and Yugoslavia. Most of the delegations talked of their own particular problems, such as India's quarrel with China. Although Tito strutted upon the stage of Third World conferences, he much preferred to do business with individual leaders he knew and respected. Among these was Prince Norodom Sihanouk of Cambodia, head of the Royal Buddhist Socialist Party. A past master at playing off the Soviet Union against America, Thailand against China, and North against South Vietnam, the Prince followed Buddha's own teaching that the truth, the 'Middle Way', is sometimes arrived at through paradox and confusion. Unlike his enemy Ho Chi Minh, the Prince was indeed an Asian Tito, determined to maintain his independence.

Tito encountered but did not encourage brutal and crackpot Third World leaders such as Idi Amin of Uganda. Nor did he lend support to terrorist organisations such as the African National Congress, which was subsidised by the Soviet Union. Both Haile Selassie and Sihanouk were threatened by Communist terrorists of the Soviet or Chinese brand. In spite of the cost of Tito's junkets, Yugoslavia profited from some of the non-aligned ventures. The Rade Končar company sold transformers and generators throughout the Third World. The shipyards of Solit and Rijeka furnished much of the Indian merchant navy. The Yugoslavs became the jobbing builders of Africa, constructing the conference hall of the Organisation of African States in Gabon, as well as a 'palace complex' in the Central African Empire.

During the Czechoslovakia crisis of 1968, Tito found to his chagrin that most of the non-aligned countries either made no comment about, or even approved of, the Soviet invasion. In order to rally support for his point of view, in late 1969 Tito began a long African journey from Algiers to Dar es Salaam, then up through East Africa to Cairo, to meet Colonel Nasser for the twenty-third time in fifteen years. At the third non-aligned conference, held in Lusaka in 1970, Yugoslavia was still the only European member of a body that was now almost wholly devoted to driving the whites out of Africa. Moreover, at the age of seventy-eight, even Tito was starting to lose his wanderlust. However, he still had many young Third World admirers, including the Panamanian leader Omar Torrijos, the friend of the novelist Graham Greene, who wrote about him in *Getting to Know the General*. In fact Torrijos said that Greene reminded him of Tito.

Tito's rivalry with the Soviet bloc and his leadership of the non-aligned states kept him constantly in the headlines but diverted attention away from his greatest achievement in foreign affairs, the *rapprochement* with western Europe. This was especially apparent in Yugoslavia's relationship with its two old enemies Austria and

Italy. In May 1945, when Tito was claiming southern Carinthia and most of Venezia-Giulia, the Yugoslav armies confronted the Allies in Klagenfurt and Trieste, threatening a Third World War. The massacre of Italians during the 'Forty Days', and of Serbs and Slovenes forced back from Austria, gave Tito the reputation of a fanatic and monster. For another three years Trieste was, after Berlin, the most dangerous place on the long Iron Curtain. The shooting down of American planes on the Austro-Yugoslav frontier prompted demands in the New York press for an atom bomb to be dropped on Belgrade. Even after the quarrel with Stalin, Tito declared that Yugoslavia's claim to southern Carinthia would never be taken off the daily agenda. As late as October 1953, he talked of sending tanks into Trieste. Yet only a few years later, Austria and Italy were Yugoslavia's warmest friends.

In May 1955, the month in which Khrushchev made his first visit to Yugoslavia, acknowledging that there were 'different roads to socialism', the Soviet Union signed a treaty ending the military occupation of Austria. After the ceremony in the Belvedere Palace, the government pledged that Austria would maintain and defend its 'perpetual neutrality', and would neither join any military alliance nor allow a foreign military base on its soil. As a neutral country outside the Warsaw Pact and NATO, Austria naturally wanted to be on good terms with its neutral neighbour, Yugoslavia. The Austrian Socialist Party, which still retained some of its Marxist trappings, was ideologically close to the now revisionist Yugoslav Communist Party. Their differences over Carinthia faded away as Austria became involved in a far worse quarrel with Italy over Tyrol.

First Austrians and then Germans started to pour into Yugoslavia as tourists, to the ski resorts in the winter and to the coast in the summer. Staying at Bled in northern Slovenia during the late 1950s, I met a Yugoslav army captain who spent his holidays serving the German and Austrian women who went there for sexual adventures. Yet during the war, the Slovenes had been the most fiercely anti-German and anti-Italian of all the Yugoslavs, as well as the most fanatically Communist. From the late 1950s, hundreds of thousands of Yugoslavs went by train into Austria to their jobs as *Gastarbeiter* in Germany, Sweden or Belgium, to come back a few years later driving the cars they had bought with their earnings. Slovenia itself was becoming almost as well-to-do as Carinthia over the border.

Yugoslavia's quarrel with Italy came to an end soon after the London treaty of 1954 disposed of the Trieste problem. One of the first manifestations of friendship came in an increase of trade and investment. One initiative that delighted the Yugoslav public was the setting up of a car factory at Kragujevac, run by a Yugoslav enterprise in conjunction with Fiat. The *rapprochement* also produced a craze for Italian culture and style, in everything from art and films to clothes, popular music and football.

Gradually the Yugoslavs made peace with their former arch-enemies, the Vatican and the Italian Communist Party (PCI). The imprisonment of Archbishop Stepinac eventually led to the breaking off of diplomatic relations with the Vatican in October 1953, the time of the Trieste crisis. Relations improved after Stepinac's death in 1960, and still more after the Second Vatican Council of 1962. A protocol restoring diplomatic relations was signed in 1966.

Yugoslavia's relations with the Italian Communist Party improved in 1955 after Khrushchev's visit to Yugoslavia. The PCI was sympathetic to 'Titoism' in Poland, and wholeheartedly took the side of Tito during the Czechoslovak crisis of 1968. During the 1960s, even before the talk about 'Eurocommunism', the PCI had become remarkably open, pragmatic and sensible. It provided efficient and honest local government in the cities that it controlled, such as Bologna, as well as in cities where it performed a campaigning role, such as Venice and Palermo. In all these cities during the 1960s, the Communists spoke admiringly of the 'Yugoslav road to socialism'.

Trieste itself gave fullest expression to the *rapprochement*. In 1963, at the dockland offices of the PCI, once the citadel of the Stalinist bully-boys, an affable journalist for the paper *l'Unità* spoke with irony of those distant days of battle against the Titoists. During the 1970s, when Italy was in the throes of strikes and financial crisis, Trieste bore the brunt of the economic difficulties. Rome had refused it a free-trade zone to compensate for the loss of the Austro-Hungarian hinterland. The shipyards could not compete with those of Split and Rijeka. Since most of Trieste's food was now imported from Yugoslavia, the price of meat was higher there than it was anywhere else in Italy, and rose with every fall in the lira. The streets were jammed with Yugoslav cars, and the café waiters had learned to take orders in Serbo-Croat or Slovene.

The Slovenes in the mountains outside Trieste now moved freely across the border that had once been the grimmest stretch of the Iron Curtain. At a wine festival I attended at San Antonio in Bosca, only a hundred yards inside Italy, Yugoslav policemen joined in the drinking, the choir came from Ljubljana, and everyone knew the Yugoslav songs. This was the frontier where, during my army days, escapers crossed in terror of the machine-guns. Now there were Yugoslav soldiers in uniform, riding on the funicular tram from Trieste up to the village of Opcina. The Yugoslav visitors in Trieste were smug, even triumphalist: 'We used to come here to buy better quality,' a woman shopper told me, 'now we come because it's cheaper.' On the other hand the Italian Triestini bewailed the change in the relationship of the countries. These were some of the comments I noted in visits during the 1970s:

We depend on the Yugoslavs now . . . Fifteen years ago I had a car and the Yugoslavs had nothing to eat. Now they have a car and I don't have two. The fact is that they are advancing and we are going backwards . . . They don't have our wages but they don't have our worries about paying for health and their children's education. The money they make they can spend and have a good time here in Trieste . . . It's terrible here, strikes, inflation, and an old lady like me doesn't dare go for a walk at night. But over in Yugoslavia it's fine. If we could vote again, I'd vote for Trieste to go to the Yugoslavs . . .

Sixty years earlier, the young Josip Broz had walked to Trieste from Ljubljana, hoping to find a job and gazing in awe at the ocean-going liners. Thirty years earlier, Tito's troops had stormed into Trieste and carried out the atrocities of the 'Forty Days'. Now Tito's Yugoslavs came to Trieste to shop and enjoy the cafés.

15

The Return of the
Nationalities Problem

The opening up of the frontiers with Italy and Austria contributed
to the worsening of the nationalities problem inside Yugoslavia.
Geographical proximity meant that the Slovenes and Croats gained
disproportionate benefits from the connection with the West. More
than 90 per cent of the tourist money was spent in Slovenia and
Croatia, with only a fraction going to Bosnia-Hercegovina and the
Montenegrin coast. Although some tourist income reached the
federal exchequer through taxes paid by hotels, most of it benefited
the local communities. Proximity to the economic centres of
western Europe gave an edge to Slovene and Croatian enterprises
in manufacture, mining, transport, electrocommunications and not
least agriculture. As we have seen, the Yugoslav farmers provided
most of the food for Trieste. Slovenian Rieslings, but not the
excellent red wines of Serbia, were commonplace in the supermar-
kets of Britain. Slovene and Croat exports to western Europe were
simply nearer the market than those from south-east Yugoslavia.
In 1961 the average per capita income in Slovenia was six times
that in Kosovo; another estimate says that Slovenia was economi-
cally on the level of Italy, and Kosovo on the level of Thailand.[1]

A high proportion of *Gastarbeiter* came from those parts of the
country that suffered most from the nationalities problem and
memories of the civil war. These regions were the old Military
Frontier of Croatia, the hinterland of Dalmatia, Bosnia-Hercego-

vina, the Sandjak, Macedonia and above all Kosovo. The Albanians of Kosovo, with their families averaging eight or nine children, sent emigrants not only to Switzerland, Belgium and the United States, but increasingly to the richer, north-western parts of Yugoslavia. Traditional dealers in sweet Turkish cakes and filigree jewellery, the Albanians spread into all forms of commerce, becoming a large minority even in cities as distant as Zagreb.

The proximity of the Slovenes and Croats to Austria and Italy contributed to a sense of being more 'Western' and cultivated than fellow Yugoslavs to the south and east, whom they came to regard as 'Byzantine', 'Balkan' and 'primitive'. They tended to look on the Bosnian and Macedonian peasants, hanging around the railway stations in Zagreb and Ljubljana, in much the same way as the French regarded Algerians, or the Germans regarded Turks. The Slovenes and Croats also complained of having to subsidise the poorer, backward and 'lazy' parts of the country, rather as northern Italians complain of the cost of the Mezzogiorno. The grumblers forgot that they themselves enjoyed the reward of the tourist trade that provided half of the country's foreign earnings. Moreover the factories of the north bought raw materials cheap from the south and east of the country, while selling their goods to a guaranteed market.

Slovenes and Croats visiting Graz, Klagenfurt and Trieste could see in the very buildings evidence of their common heritage from the Austro-Hungarian Empire, in which Ljubljana and Zagreb (or Leibach and Agram, as they were then called) had been two of the finest cities. The fact that the Communists disapproved of nostalgia for the Habsburgs served only to make it more enticing. Besides, anyone reading between the lines of Tito's own printed memoirs could see that he looked back lovingly to the dancehalls of old Vienna, the taverns of 'Golden Prague', and Trieste's age of glory as the gateway to central Europe.

Some Slovenes and Croats may have dreamed of once more joining a multinational state, while others considered independence. For Slovenes this was a new idea, since historically they had never enjoyed or even aspired to anything more than provincial status. To Croats, the prospect of independence was real and disturbing. A few may have hankered after the Austro-Hungarian Empire; many, especially the young, believed in Yugoslavia; others wanted to resurrect the Independent State of Croatia. Among those who desired an independent state, the most famous was Archbishop Stepinac, who had proclaimed his loyalty to the NDH in his speech from the dock in 1946.

Outside Yugoslavia, the great majority of the Croats were loyal to the principle of the NDH and to Ante Pavelić personally. When he moved from Rome to Buenos Aires in 1950, the former Poglavnik changed the name of his organisation from Ustasha to Croatian Liberation Movement (HOP), setting up branches and putting out publications in North America, Australasia and western Europe. Pavelić also received support from non-Croatians, such as the young right-wing French deputy Jean-Marie Le Pen, who published a book, *La Croatie martyre*, sporting the red-and-white chequerboard flag.

After surviving a murder attempt in 1957, Pavelić moved from Argentina to Spain, where he died in his bed three years later. During their exile, the Ustasha split into two rivals camps. Ante Pavelić and his HOP had mellowed to the extent of seeking to make an arrangement with some of the right-wing Serbs, to carve up Yugoslavia. This would entail the division of Bosnia-Hercegovina into a Serb and a Croat region, similar to the *Sporazum* of 1939. Some of the hard-line Ustasha balked at the prospect of any compromise with the hated Serbs, and wanted an independent Croatia comprising all Bosnia-Hercegovina. This faction was led by Maks Luburić, the former commandant of Jasenovac concentration camp, now also living in Spain. He set up a radical terrorist group based first in West Germany and then in Australia. On 20 April 1969 Luburić was found dead near his villa in the Valencia region, murdered by blows to the head from an iron bar, as well as five stab wounds.[2]

Argentina and Spain were right-wing dictatorships, ready and eager to give asylum to former Ustasha. However, Andrija Artuković, the former NDH Minister of the Interior, chose to stay with his brother in California, after a quiet year in Ireland. When the news of his real identity broke in 1950, the Serbs in exile in the United States sent a memorandum to the Fifth Assembly of the United Nations, asking it to implement the resolution of 1946, branding genocide as a crime under international law. They requested the UN member states to take into custody, pending trial, some 120 Croats including Pavelić, Artuković, Archbishop Šarić and Father Draganović, the 'Scarlet Pimpernel' who had helped many other Ustasha escape. The memorandum made little impression on the UN, since it did not come from a member nation and indeed accused a member nation, Yugoslavia, of sheltering Ustasha criminals and employing them to break down the resistance of Serbs.

It was not until 1952 that Yugoslavia asked for the extradition of Artuković, and he was not arrested until six years after that. In the mean time, he had become a member of the Knights of Columbus and a much-respected figure who gave lectures to institutions and interviews on TV. When he was arrested, 50,000 Knights sent petitions on his behalf to Congress, and the West Pennsylvania lodges of the Croatian Catholic Union forwarded a resolution that 'his only crime is his ceaseless fight against Communism'. Franciscan journals in Chicago not only supported Artuković but urged readers to send subscriptions for Ustasha refugees to his home in Surf side, California. Another ally was Father Marinko Lacković, the former private secretary to Archbishop Stepinac, now living in Youngstown, Ohio. Father Lacković told the Los Angeles *Mirror News* (24 January 1958) that Artuković had seen Stepinac almost daily and had been 'the leading Catholic layman of Croatia and the lay spokesman of Cardinal Stepinac and had consulted him on the moral aspect of every action he took'. As Hubert Butler drily comments: 'The murderers of the Old World had become the martyrs of the New.' Although the Jews living in California came out against Artuković (and were eventually to have him sent back to Zagreb for trial in 1986), most Americans felt what Butler calls 'the easy charity of indifference' for this refugee and his five children.

The Yugoslav government did not press for Artuković's extradition and dropped the demand in the 1960s. They had made good business deals with the United States and did not want to offend public opinion. For similar financial reasons, the Belgrade government took the line that Artuković had been a helpless tool of the Nazis, and that therefore West Germany should pay compensation for damage done by him and his colleagues. Tito knew that a public trial of Artuković in Yugoslavia would show the public support enjoyed by the Ustasha during the war, and would cause deep hatred between the Serbs and Croats. Yugoslavia not only did not press for the extradition of Ustasha criminals but let back into the country Father Draganović, who had helped frame the laws for the forced conversion of Orthodox Christians, and later planned the escape of men like Artuković. The 'Scarlet Pimpernel' of the Ustasha gave a press conference praising Tito's 'democratic' Yugoslavia, then went to live in a monastery near Sarajevo.[3]

The refusal of the Croatian Catholic Church to apologise for, or even acknowledge, the crimes committed during the war disturbed and angered the Orthodox Christians, especially those in Croatia and Bosnia-Hercegovina. There were anti-Communist Serbs in the 1950s who criticised Tito for not having hanged Archbishop Stepinac; I heard this view from an otherwise gentle woman whose mother's family came from the Military Frontier. Many Serbs were enraged when Tito permitted Stepinac's funeral and burial in Zagreb Cathedral. Although the Orthodox Serbs in exile tried to compile the facts about the Ustasha murders, their scholars inside the country were not given access to records of the NDH and the Catholic Church. The Orthodox Serbs came to rely on *Magnum Crimen*, the monumental history of the modern Croatian Church by the Croat historian Viktor Novak. This book was placed on the Papal Index of Prohibited Books and, paradoxically, it was also withdrawn by the Yugoslav Communist government soon after its publication in 1948. Nobody who read the book could ever again believe that the Ustasha were German puppets, or that Stepinac was innocent of the Ustasha crimes.

The Orthodox Church, although patriotically Yugoslav, was

never closely associated with Great Serb nationalism, or with the Chetniks during the war, since 'Duke' Djujić at Knin was a rare exception. Most priests and nuns devoted themselves to prayer or to looking after the wounded and refugees. However, just as the Serbian Patriarch went on the air in March 1941 to denounce the pact with Hitler, so his successor, during the Orthodox Christmas in January 1954, paid a call on Tito to pledge his support during the crisis over Trieste. In his turn, Tito often went to the beautiful Serb medieval churches and monasteries. The abbess of one establishment, much in need of repairs, wrote a letter addressed to 'Tito and Jovanka', just as she might have done to a Karadjeordjević monarch, and promptly received the requested help. When Tito visited Decani with Jovanka, the monks gave her one of the silver filigree cradles brought by the local women in thanksgiving for safe childbirth. To Jovanka, who had no baby, it may have been a distressing gift.[4]

In contrast to Stepinac, the Patriarch of the Serbian Church had refused to collaborate with the invaders during the Second World War, and nearly died in a German concentration camp. Most Orthodox priests were shocked by the trial and execution of Draža Mihailović in 1946, but, in the tradition of their church, they made no overt protest. By 1953 the Communist Party's hostile attitude to the Church had changed to indifference. Although in Belgrade there were only small congregations at Sunday worship, most non-Communist families kept their *slava*, or name-day feast, as well as Easter and Christmas celebrations. The government at first expropriated most church property, but later permitted and even encouraged some of the well-run farms attached to monasteries. In her fascinating travel book *The Mountains of Serbia*, Anne Kindersley has described the work of Abbess Barbara at Ljubostinja, near the River Morava:

Her energy and enterprise are remarkable. Ljubostinja was always a good wine-growing area; she has completely re-planted the neglected vineyards with Black Hamburg and Hercegovina vines, and now produces 10,000 kilograms of wine a year. Under the old guesthouse on one side of the courtyard, with its black beams and brown-tiled roof, stood a large pile of crates labelled EXPORT. She also supplies one of the best hotels in Belgrade with her wine. She has created a small industry of wicker-work chairs and embroidery; most of this, too, goes to the capital. She fattens calves for the local Co-operative; they were shown at the biggest Agricultural Fair in Yugoslavia, in Novi Sad, while the Co-operative Director told the newspapers: 'A calf reared by Mother Barbara is as good as a calf from the best stock-breeder in Serbia.'[5]

During the 1960s the Serb–Croat discord began to appear in the public life of the country, that is to say in the Communist Party and the press. There had been hints of stresses within the Party even before and during the war, when the Croat Andrija Hebrang accused the Serbs of unfairly fixing the boundaries of the republics. His wounded Croatian feelings may have led Hebrang to take the side of the Russians in 1948. However, Serb–Croat differences affected neither the argument over the Cominform resolution nor the Djilas affair.

The argument in the 1960s began over the economy. Liberalisation and opening up to the West had led to rapid and often rash industrial growth that called for retrenchment, by closing down uneconomic enterprises and sacking superfluous workers. Such an application of market principles was bound to affect more the poorer southern and eastern parts of the country, previously subsidised by the north-west. It followed that the 'reformers', or economic liberals, tended to come from Slovenia and Croatia, while the 'conservatives' came from the poorer parts of the country. Typically the latter were Serbs from Croatia or Bosnia-Hercegovina rather than from Serbia itself. Of the two remaining members of the triumvirate under Tito, Kardelj was seen as a reformer and Ranković as a conservative. As head of the secret police, Ranković also feared the liberal reforms might weaken the state's defence against hostile elements such as the Albanian nationalists and the Ustasha.

Although Tito was always inclined to resist reform or any weakening of the central power, he seems to have concluded in 1966 that Ranković was divisive to the Party. He may also have heeded the whispers in Zagreb that Ranković was a Great Serb who was planning to use the UDBA to establish his personal power. Some of his rivals discovered that Ranković had planted electronic bugging devices in Tito's residence. At the Central Committee Plenum held on Brioni in July 1966, Ranković was obliged to resign his Party offices and his post as Vice-President. Since it was not suggested that Ranković was guilty of any crime, he retreated quietly into private life and retirement. At about the same time, his old friend Djilas was let out of prison and also went into private life, though he was now very famous outside Yugoslavia. Oddly enough it was Ranković, rather than Djilas, who was popular with the Belgrade public. When Djilas entered a café, no heads were turned; when Ranković entered a restaurant soon after retirement, the whole room stood to applaud. This incident, described to me by an eyewitness, was no doubt a manifestation of growing Serb nationalism, but also another example of that puzzling phenomenon, the likeability of Ranković.

The sacking of Ranković did not appease Croatian resentment, for the following year brought a crisis over the language issue. This had been settled the first time as long ago as 1850, when an agreement was reached in Vienna by Serb and Croat men of letters, under the influence of the lexicographer Vuk Karadjić. His solution had been that Serbs and Croats should speak and write the 'pure' language of Hercegovina, the former using Cyrillic, the latter Latin script. More than a century later, at Novi Sad in 1954, a group of scholars refined the Vienna agreement, allowing for different spellings of the variations in speech. The word 'speech' would appear as 'riječ' when spoken by Tito, a Croat, but 'reč' when spoken by a Serb. To foreigners it all seemed very trivial; but not to the Croats.

Then, on 17 March 1967, Zagreb's main literary weekly published a declaration by various cultural groups, such as the nineteenth-century Matica Hrvatska (Croat Queen Bee), and by thirteen intellectuals, most of them Party members and among them Miroslav Krleža, which damned the Novi Sad agreement and called for the recognition of Croat as a distinctive language. Immediately, forty-five Serbian writers, most of them Party members, came back with counter-demands including the use of Serb alone for teaching the children of 700,000 Serbs in Croatia. This would have meant separate schools for Orthodox and Roman Catholic children throughout the old Military Frontier region. The government came down hard on the signatories of both these ridiculous documents. Some were expelled from the Communist Party, while others resigned, Krleža for the second time in forty years. This was another blow to Tito, who had been disappointed during the war that Krleža did not join the Partisans. Now people remembered that Krleža had spent the war peacefully in Zagreb, apparently with the protection of the Ustasha cultural minister Mile Budak.

In the following year, 1968, there were demonstrations in Belgrade of a radical rather than nationalist kind. This was the year of the Vietnamese 'Tet Offensive', the anti-war protests in the United States, the 'Prague Spring' in Czechoslovakia, riots in West Berlin and the Paris '*événements*' that almost brought down General de Gaulle. The Belgrade University students staged strikes and demonstrations against the growing inequality of what they denounced as 'a consumer society'. Among their slogans were, 'Bureaucrats, hands off the Workers!', 'Down with the princes of Socialism!' and 'More schools, fewer automobiles!'[6] Although the students echoed some of the criticisms made by Djilas fifteen years earlier, they did not look to him as a leader; however, they greeted him courteously when he came to chat.

Like their Paris confrères the Belgrade students tried to make common cause with the factory workers but found to their chagrin that these people actually wanted the cars and TV sets of the 'consumer society'. Nor did the Belgrade students represent Serbian nationalism, since they enjoyed support in Zagreb and Sarajevo universities. However, Tito took these manifestations seriously enough to make a speech in Belgrade on 'Guidelines for Further Measures of Economic and Social Reforms'. The demonstrations fizzled out with the start of the summer vacation and then the Soviet intervention in Czechoslovakia. The outside threat to Yugoslavia also stilled for a time the discontent of the Croats.

The return to better East–West relations in 1970 encouraged Yugoslavs to resume their mutual bickering. There was more debate on investment in different republics, the Croats wanting a bigger share of the tourist earnings, the Slovenes wanting better motorways, and the other four opposing both these demands. The Matica Hrvatska, true to its name, produced a swarm of branches throughout Croatia, the other republics where Croats lived, and among the *Gastarbeiter* in Germany. At this time 27 per cent of the Croats lived in other republics of Yugoslavia, while Croats amounted to 80 per cent of their own republic; 27 per cent of Serbs lived outside Serbia, while in the republic 25 per cent were non-Serb, most of them non-Slav Albanians in Kosovo and Magyars in Vojvodina. Only 56.5 per cent of the Serbs lived in inner Serbia.[7]

In 1970 Tito set himself the task of 'confederating' his own state office. He was seventy-eight years old and had to consider the prospect that his retirement and death would lead to a scramble for power between the different republics. He therefore proposed that he be replaced by a Collegiate Presidency, with a devolution of power from the federal capital. This confederalising process alarmed the Serbs in Croatia and only inflamed the nationalism of bodies like Matica Hrvatska.

Throughout Croatia in 1971 there were incidents of smashing signs written in Cyrillic, waving the red-and-white chequerboard flag and brawling with the Serb minority. In the old Military Frontier, Orthodox villagers armed themselves against a Catholic attack. In April the students at Zagreb University carried out a kind of nationalist *coup d'état*, installing a rector who called himself a 'Catholic Titoist'. Soon, leading politicians had joined Matica Hrvatska in calling for an autonomous, virtually independent state. Tito arrived in Zagreb in July to give the Central Committee a furious harangue: 'Under the cover of "national interest", all hell is collecting . . . even to counter-revolution . . . In some villages the Serbs out of nervousness are drilling and arming themselves . . .

Do we want to have 1941 again?' Tito went on to warn the Croat Central Committee that chaos in Yugoslavia could lead to foreign intervention, reminding them, apparently for the second time, that Brezhnev had offered 'fraternal assistance'. Tito went on:

> Are you aware that others would immediately be present if there were disorder? . . . I'd sooner restore order with our own army than allow others to do it. We've lost prestige abroad, and it will be hard to get back. They are speculating that 'when Tito goes, the whole thing will collapse' and some are seriously waiting for that. The internal enemy has plenty of support from outside. The great powers will use any devil that will work for them, whether he's a Communist or not . . . All kinds of things are being said. Now it is being said among you that I invented my conversation with Brezhnev in order to frighten you and force you into unity.[8]

Although Tito did not mention the Ustasha or their friends in the West, it must have been clear to his listeners what he had in mind. On his visit to Prague in August 1968, Tito had warned the Czechoslovaks against the aggressive intentions of West Germany. He may also have wanted to scotch the rumour current in 1971 that Brezhnev would intervene on the side of the Croats, in order to get rid of Tito.

Tito's warning may have impressed some of Croatia's Central Committee but did not deter the ever more strident Matica Hrvatska. In November 1971 the society published proposals for a revised Constitution for 'the sovereign national state of Croatia', including the right to secede. This new Croatia would have the control of all the revenue it collected in its territory, with only voluntary contributions to federal Yugoslavia. Croatia would have its own territorial army, and Croat recruits to the Yugoslav army would do their service only in their republic. At meetings of Matica Hrvatska, speakers discussed the revision of frontiers and even separate membership of the United Nations.

In November 1971 the Croat Student Federation called a strike at Zagreb University over the issue of the Republic's right to retain foreign currency, in effect to take all the profits from tourism. At this point Tito lost patience. In a nationwide broadcast on 2 December, he accused the Croatian leadership of having pandered to nationalism and separatism, deploring their 'rather liberal attitude' to what was effectively counter-revolution. Ten days later, three top Party officials were made to resign, the police arrested the student strike leaders, and troops were deployed in Zagreb to deter demonstrations. By mid-January 1972, 400 nationalists had been arrested, and Matica Hrvatska banned. Later that year, in order to show fair play, Tito ordered a purge of 'liberals' in the Serbian Communist Party, and put into motion the constitutional changes by which Vojvodina and Kosovo were to become autonomous regions within a depleted Republic of Serbia. So ended the last great crisis in Tito's career.

One of the Croat politicians who changed during this period from a Communist to a nationalist was Franjo Tudjman, the future President of an independent Croatia. Tudjman was born in 1922 in the Zagorje region near Tito's birthplace at Kumrovec, though unlike Tito he managed to lose his regional accent. Unusually for a Catholic Croat, Tudjman joined the Partisans as early as 1941 and ended the war as a major and also as political commissar in the 32nd Division. Later he went to the Yugoslav High Military Academy. While pursuing his career as a staff officer, Tudjman wrote the first of a long series of books on military and political history, *War Against War*, which met with opposition from what he later called 'centralist-dogmatic positions'. In a history of his own unit, *The Warpath of the 32nd Division*, as well as in other books and articles, Tudjman advanced the dubious claim that the Croats had played an equal role with the Serbs in the Partisan army. This irritated the Serbs in the veterans' associations but gratified Tito, who made Tudjman a general in 1960, the youngest ever in peacetime Yugoslavia.

In 1961 Tudjman gave up his army career, and moved to Zagreb to become the director of the Institute for the History of the Working-Class Movement in Croatia, commanding a team of more than 200 researchers. In 1963 he was also appointed professor of history at the Zagreb University Faculty of Political Sciences, the only applicant without the usual prerequisite of a Ph.D. In 1964, when the institute of which he was director revised the official history of the Croatian Communist Party, Tudjman was accused by the Serbs of a 'bourgeois-nationalist deviation' in treating the 'national question'. To this was added the stronger charge of 'chauvinism'.

In 1965 Zagreb University refused to accept Tudjman's doctoral thesis, 'The Causes of the Crisis of the Monarchist Yugoslavia from its Inception in 1918', refuting the imputation of Croat treachery in April 1941. 'Already during the same year,' Tudjman later boasted, 'I was the first to re-open the issue of wartime victims of fascism' and its related 'myth of Jasenovac'. Tudjman stopped the setting up of a cenotaph at the camp because, he said, the inscription exaggerated the number of victims.

During the mid-1960s, Tudjman became involved in Matica Hrvatska, especially in its relations with the Croats of the diaspora, and in 1967 he signed the declaration about the language. For this he was thrown out of the Party and stripped of his two official positions. During the crackdown on nationalists in the winter of 1971–2, Tudjman was arrested and charged with espionage, presumably because of his contacts with Croats abroad. However, Tito intervened to drop the more serious charges, and Tudjman spent only ten months in gaol. During the rest of the decade that ended with Tito's death in 1980, Tudjman was unable to publish his views in Yugoslavia, although he was ready to talk to foreign journalists.[9]

The revival of Croatian nationalism inside Yugoslavia coincided with a revival of Ustasha terrorist outrages carried out by Croats abroad. Although Ante Pavelić and most of the prominent Ustasha settled in Argentina and Spain, the right-wing dictatorships in those countries did not encourage their guests to engage in acts of violence, even against a Communist state. The Ustasha, now called the HOP, and the other Croatian terrorist groups found a more tolerant home in such democratic countries as Canada, Sweden, West Germany and above all Australia. The Liberal Party governments in the 1960s not only welcomed but gave support to these anti-Communist militants. Ustasha soldiers trained with the Australian army near Woodonga, Victoria. The editor of the HOP newspaper *Spremnost*, Fabian Lovoković, who was also a prominent Liberal Party politician, was able to boast in 1963 that the ASIO, the Australian intelligence service, 'does not view the Croatian Liberation Movement in an unfavourable light'. Thanks to the tolerance shown them by the authorities throughout the 1960s and early 1970s, the various Ustasha groups in Australia were able to carry out bomb attacks on Yugoslav consulates, a bank with a display of Yugoslav dolls, the Adriatic Tourist Agency in Sydney, and a cinema showing a Yugoslav film, and to make three separate attempts on the life of a prominent anti-Ustasha Croat. Due to the favourable political climate, the most violent of the Ustasha groups, the Croatian Revolutionary Brotherhood, established its world headquarters in Australia in 1968, when it was banned by West Germany.

The front page of *Spremnost* in January 1963 carried a story on Ustasha military training under the banner headline: 'Today on the Murray River – Tomorrow on the Drina' ('*Danas na Rieci Murray – Sjutra na Drini*'). To prove that this was no idle boast, an Ustasha group from Australia attempted to start an uprising in eastern Bosnia, not far from the River Drina. This first of several Ustasha gangs to be sent from Australia to Yugoslavia was rounded up and its members imprisoned. In 1970 Vladimir Rolović, the Yugoslav Assistant Secretary for Foreign Affairs, visited Canberra to hand over an *aide-mémoire* giving specific details of Ustasha personnel, organisations and involvement in terrorist actions. The Australian authorities, who had not only tolerated but even trained the Ustasha, took no action except to inform them of Rolović's information about them. The following year, when Rolović had become his country's ambassador in Sweden, he was murdered by two young Ustasha who claimed they were taking revenge for his mission to Canberra. The murderers of Rolović were released when the Ustasha hijacked and threatened to blow up a plane.

The Ustasha were the first terrorist group to threaten to plant bombs on aircraft, and the Yugoslav national airline, JAT, was the first to institute baggage and body searches. Despite these precautions, in Stockholm in January 1972 Ustasha agents succeeded in planting a bomb on a JAT DC9, which blew up over Czechoslovakia. The sole survivor, a Montenegrin air hostess, fell 33,330 feet without a parachute, to enter the *Guinness Book of Records* Hall of Fame.10 In 1976 the Ustasha hijacked an aircraft flying from Chicago to Paris, forcing a detour to London to scatter leaflets over the city. A number of Ustasha bomb attacks inside Yugoslavia, in cinemas and at Belgrade railway station, caused people to grumble that the UDBA had become less efficient since Ranković's sacking. Moreover those countries in western Europe that had abolished capital punishment refused to extradite terrorists to be executed in Yugoslavia. The UDBA therefore sent death squads to gun down Ustasha in Munich and other centres abroad, leading to diplomatic incidents with the governments concerned.

The revival of the Ustasha came at the same time as renewed troubles in Ireland. The Ustasha and the IRA had friendly relations even before the Second World War, and Ante Pavelić stated that Ireland, Slovakia and Croatia were to be friendly states in Hitler's 'New Europe'. Zagreb theatres in the Independent State of Croatia staged Irish but not English plays. Once again in the 1970s, Croatian nationalists sympathised with the IRA in its struggle against what they called British hegemony. Significantly the Belgrade newspapers were almost alone in Europe in taking the side of the British army in Northern Ireland.

During the nationalities crisis of 1971–2, the main antagonists were on the one hand Matica Hrvatska and the Zagreb students, and on the other the Orthodox Serbs in Croatia, most of them in the old Military Frontier, but with large minorities in cities such as Zagreb and Rijeka. Foreign observers tended to see the dispute as a struggle for power between the republics of Serbia and Croatia, not, as was in fact the case, as a return of ancient religious rivalry going back almost a thousand years. The quarrel also involved in the most dangerous fashion the intermediate republic of Bosnia-Hercegovina, where there were Orthodox, Roman Catholics and also a third religious group, the former Bogomil heretics who had converted to Islam.

Although Matica Hrvatska took up the cause of the 'Croats' in Bosnia-Hercegovina, it did not dare to advance the claim once made by Starčević and Pavelić to include the province into a Greater Croatia. Croats abroad had no such inhibitions. The Croat claim to all territory west of the River Drina was doubly alarming to Bosnian Muslims, reminding them of the threat from the Serbs as well. For centuries during the Middle Ages, the Bogomils had endured persecution both from the west, in the form of papal crusades and the Franciscan Inquisition, and from the east, in the form of oppression by Serb Orthodox kings. For another five centuries of the Ottoman Empire, the Serbs had dreamed of revenging themselves against the 'Turks', as they called the South Slav converts to Islam. In 1806 Serb insurgents crossed the Drina to attack the Bosnians. Serbian soldiers went into battle during the First World War to the sound of the stirring 'March on the Drina'. In 1941, when Bosnia-Hercegovina became part of the Independent State of Croatia, Serbian Chetniks physically and symbolically crossed the Drina to slaughter Muslims in towns such as Foča and Goražde. The very name of the Drina sounds like a battle-cry to South Slav ears. The nationalities crisis of 1971–2 was followed with apprehension by many in Bosnia-Hercegovina who dreaded the reappearance of the Ustasha and the Chetniks.

When Tito talked of the Serbs in Croatia arming themselves against attack, he did not explain that they were under threat because of their religion. To explain away the religious factor, Communist history books tried to suggest that the Serbs and Croats were separate nations even before they left their original home beyond the Carpathians, and then settled in Serbia and Croatia. Those history books could not explain how a third people, vaguely described as 'Slavs', had come to settle in Bosnia-Hercegovina. Because the Communists would not acknowledge religious differences, they fostered belief in 'racial' or 'ethnic' differences, reinforcing the bigotry of the Ustasha and Chetniks. In Bosnia-

Hercegovina, Tito compounded this folly by calling the Muslims a separate 'nation', which they are not.

Just after the Second World War, the historian Husein Ćišić, from one of the oldest Muslim families in Mostar, wrote a superb book that the authorities would not publish.[11] His study of Bosnian history, based on extensive research in the Turkish archives as well as medieval Christian records, destroys the fantasies of the Serb and Croat nationalists, especially their bogus racial theories. He dismisses the Croat claim that they and the Muslims are ethnically and linguistically identical, but completely different from the Serbs. He pours scorn on the Serb belief that the Bosnian Muslims are ethnic Turks who somehow learned to speak Serbo-Croat.

Although Tito respected Husein Ćišić and tried to get him to join the government, even though he was not a Communist, he did not take his advice on the nationalities question. This advice was to call not just the Muslims but all the people of Bosnia-Hercegovina one nation. For so they undoubtedly are in the eyes of other Yugoslavs. Since Sarajevo and all the towns are predominantly Muslim, while the countryside is more Christian, it is in the towns that one gets the sense of a distinctive Bosnian culture influenced by Turkish taste in food, music and architecture, but characterised as well by humour, sensuality and a love of conversation. Sarajevo under the Ottoman Empire was famous for the toleration it showed not only to Christians but to the Sephardic Jews who fled there from Spain at the end of the fifteenth century. A Bosnian Serb who had been in Sarajevo as a child under the Independent State of Croatia, told me that not one of his family's Muslim and Catholic friends or neighbours would ever have thought of handing him over to the Ustasha.

Perhaps from the best of motives, Tito and his historians tried to disguise the fact that the carnage in Bosnia-Hercegovina during the Second World War was caused by religious intolerance, involving first a gigantic Catholic massacre of the Orthodox, and then a smaller Orthodox massacre of the Muslims. Because religion of any kind was frowned on after the war, the churches were not encouraged to make amends or show repentance for crimes committed by Christians. Just as Stepinac disavowed any responsibility for the Ustasha massacres, so in Bosnia most of the Catholic Church remained impenitent. In the Catholic Cathedral in Sarajevo, where during the war Archbishop Šarić preached hatred against the Serbs and Jews, I heard a priest in his sermon boldly denouncing those 'like Napoleon' who set themselves above God's law – a not very subtle reference to Tito.

Although most of the Catholic hierarchy was unrepentant, the Franciscans of Bosnia-Hercegovina accepted the Communist invitation to form a state-sponsored priests' association called Dobri Pastir (The Good Shepherd). The Slovene clergy had also established a priests' association based on Christian socialism, but the Church in Croatia condemned the idea. Dobri Pastir was formed by the Franciscans at a meeting in Sarajevo on 25 January 1950, attended by leading representatives of the Association of Orthodox Priests in Serbia. The head of the Muslim community sent his greetings. The Good Shepherd organisation helped the Franciscans in their long-standing battle with the diocesan clergy over the tenure of parishes. At that time, the strongly Ustasha Bishop of Mostar, who had been appointed in 1942, was still in prison, but on his release in 1956 the number of the diocesan clergy in Hercegovina started to rise. In 1968 the Holy See ordered the Franciscans to give back five parishes; they grudgingly gave back two. In 1975 the Franciscans in Hercegovina publicly and collectively denounced a new papal decree on parishes, even though at that time they administered Mass to 80 per cent of the faithful in the region. As a punishment for this disobedience, the Province and the Provincial lost their authority, and the Hercegovinian Franciscans lost their votes to elect a new General of the Order. The new General, as soon as elected, called on the friars in Hercegovina to show obedience to their bishop.[12] Hostility between the Franciscans and the diocesan clergy was soon to develop into another momentous episode in the history of the Order in Bosnia-Hercegovina.

The only part of Bosnia-Hercegovina where the three faiths worked together for reconciliation was Banja Luka, south of the

River Sava, and scene of some of the most terrible massacres in the war. In Banja Luka, according to Stevan Pavlowitch, writing in 1971,

> there is now a solid tradition, not only of toleration but also of mutual co-operation, between Orthodox and Catholic, and between Christians and Muslims as well. Mgr [Alfred] Pichler and his Orthodox colleague Bishop Andrej, continuing the work initiated by their respective predecessors after the war, had by the end of the sixties, set up – discreetly and modestly – a model church fellowship about which not enough is known elsewhere in Yugoslavia, let alone abroad. Churches are open to the faithful of both confessions, and the two bishops in many ways act as joint pastors of a common flock.[13]

Bishop Pichler was well aware that in 1941 the Orthodox Bishop of Banja Luka, Platon, was tortured to death by the Ustasha, and he wanted to make amends. In his Christmas message in 1963, Bishop Pichler admitted that during the last war their brothers of the Orthodox Church had been killed simply because they were Orthodox and not Catholic and Croat, by men who called themselves Catholics and carried Catholic baptismal certificates. 'We acknowledge with anguish the terrible crimes of these misguided men,' the Christmas message continued, 'and we beg our Orthodox brothers to forgive us as Christ on the Cross forgave all men. We in our turn forgive all those who have wronged or hated us. Today, gathered around Christ's cradle, let all debts be cancelled and may love reign.' According to Stella Alexander, the Bishop's Christmas message 'provoked deep anger among Catholic Croats, and in his own diocese some priests refused to read it from the pulpit, or read only extracts'. The only Catholic paper aside from the diocesan gazette in which the message appeared was *Danica*, published by the government-sponsored Association of Catholic Priests in Croatia.[14]

In Bosnia-Hercegovina, more than anywhere else in Yugoslavia, one becomes oppressed by a sense of ancient religious passion and hatred of which the massacres during the Second World War were only the latest manifestation. A Bogomil tomb standing alone in the mountains, a thirteenth-century Franciscan monastery in a village, and everywhere the elegant minarets are physical testament to the old crusades, inquisitions and slaughter. Reading the books on Bosnia-Hercegovina written by Arthur Evans during the 1870s, one feels he is talking about the country's future as well as its past and present. He predicts the catastrophes of the First and Second World Wars.

In Sarajevo I came to regard with ever increasing revulsion the plaque erected in honour of Princip's crime, for which his fellow Orthodox were to pay a penalty in blood. After the Second World War, the authorities compounded the insult shown to the Roman Catholics by adding a Princip Museum to the plaque and the footprints carved in the pavement. In the Museum's visitors' book an English tourist wrote: 'Good shot, mate!' In 1954, the fortieth anniversary of the murder, I went to see one of the two surviving assassins, Cvetko Popović, then head of the Ethnographic Department of Sarajevo Museum. He showed me his prize exhibits, among them some Jewish pictures of Old Testament stories such as Moses and the Burning Bush, and Abraham and the sacrifice of Isaac. Since Popović did not appear to have heard of either of these biblical stories, I assumed that he held his job for being a would-be assassin, not for being a scholar. Although he did not want to talk about that fatal day, he demonstrated his lack of repentance by turning up at the fortieth-anniversary celebrations.

A few years later Bosna Film was planning a drama about the assassination but could not find a foreign company suitable for a joint production. The director Voja Kravić told me that some of the foreigners wanted to show the assassins as 'bandits'. Another company wanted to show Princip lusting after a big-bosomed girl in the Turkish quarter of town. Kravić called these things 'lemonade' but added that he did not want too much blood either. 'I could have made the film already,' Kravić told me, 'but I wanted it to be a world film, the greatest since *War and Peace*.' The problem was that Princip, although 'he had a fine heart', was far from handsome.

Kravić wanted to concentrate on another assassin, Čabrinović, the one who first threw a bomb at the Archduke, missed him, then swallowed poison to no effect, then finally tried to drown himself in the Miljačka stream, which is about three inches deep. The director said that Čabrinović was 'nonchalant, gay and pursued by women', even comparing him to Errol Flynn. He also wanted to bring in a further assassin, Mehmedbašić, to show that the Muslims supported the Serbs against the Austrians.

In fact the Muslims had not supported the Serbs against the Austrians, and after the murder they joined with the Croats in sacking Serbian premises such as the Evropa Hotel. Moreover, after the First World War the government of the new Yugoslavia expropriated the big Muslim landlords and distributed their property to the largely Serbian peasants. Even after the Second World War, the glorification of Princip did not go down well with the Muslims.

However, in most respects the Communists treated the Muslims more tactfully and respectfully than they did the Christians, so that even in 1954, when there were few private cars in Yugoslavia, I often noticed a mullah in a chauffeur-driven limousine. When foreign journalists wanted to write about Islam in Yugoslavia, they were taken to see a famously drunken mullah, who gave them good copy in return for a bottle or two of whisky.

In the 1950s one still heard gruesome stories about the war, above all about the Ustasha murders. There were still occasional trials of wartime criminals who had only just been recognised and arrested. One Ustasha described to a Mostar court how he had killed Serb children by picking them up by the heels and dashing their brains out against a wall. The *Oslobodenje* reporter said that he spoke of this work like a baker explaining how he made bread.[15] Occasionally I met people, usually drunks, who boasted of what they had done in the war. One man held a knife at my throat and asked if I would have been on the side of Tito or Mihailović, to which I gave a prudent rather than truthful answer. From my diary, I quote an entry dated 8 August 1958 describing an occasion on which I showed a Dane around Sarajevo:

We stopped at the Dva Ribara [Two Fishermen], stared at the sheep being roasted on the spits, and were hailed by three shabby men at a table. They turned out to be Ustasha. I had never before met an avowed supporter of this loathsome group. The most intelligent and sober of them began by complaining that, of his 12,000 dinar salary, 3,000 went on lodging and 7,000 on food. Then he reminisced fondly of how it was during the war, 'when the rivers of Bosnia ran red'. He had fought with the SS. 'What are your politics?' the Dane asked. 'A Fascist. That's a man who is against Communism. Fifty per cent of the country are Fascists. You can tell the real ones by the "U" tattooed on the chest.' The Dane asked if the Fascists were organised. 'No, but they'll be ready when the time comes.'

Occasionally I became aware of tension between the Muslims and Christians, especially out in the countryside. Early in June 1957, I went with two Yugoslav journalists on a trip to Hercegovina to see the annual herding of sheep from the coastal plains to the cool mountain pastures of Bosnia. Already more than a million head of livestock, or 'throats' as the Yugoslavs say, were starting to leave the region of Stolac, south-east of Mostar, the capital of the province. Perhaps because I had heard so much of its terrible history, I always found Mostar a sinister as well as a beautiful town. It lies in a valley picked clean of its vegetation by goats, or by Turks, and in the summer becomes the hottest place in Europe. We sat at a restaurant near the Turkish bridge on the green River Neretva, down which so many corpses had floated during the Second World War. We sat among elderly, dignified men in fezzes, taking a meal of liver, bread, wine and cool water. When Hercegovinians arrive at a strange place, they always begin by asking, 'How is the water?'

From Mostar we went east to Stolac where the sheep were already starting to bleat, as instinct told them to make for the hills. A few years earlier, a co-operative farm with modern ideas had taken its livestock to Bosnia by lorry, but many died because of the too sudden change in temperature and altitude. The flocks were led by shepherdesses, most of them Muslims in Turkish-style pantaloons, but even the Christian women wrapped their faces in scarves against the dust. Most of the women spun from a distaff as they walked. We learned that it was especially hard for the Muslims when Ramadan fell in early June, for not only must they refrain from food and drink from dawn till dusk, in the month with the longest days in the year, but they were not even permitted to swallow their spittle. Yet in spite of their mournful songs – 'Oh mother, why must I go to the mountains when the blossom is starting in the valley?' – most of the shepherdesses enjoyed the trip into Bosnia and did not envy the women who stayed behind to tend the vines and tobacco.

The wolves, whose howling we heard at night, seized some of the sheep, while others fell off the path and broke their legs and had to be left to the crows and ravens. Most of the sheep were hobbling after the first few days, and strayed so little that the shepherdesses no longer had to keep them in line by throwing stones. After a time we crossed into the cool, green uplands of Bosnia, where for miles there were no roads or signs of habitation except for a Muslim cemetery and a Bogomil tomb. The elements had smoothed the carving but I could make out the cattle and sheep by which this man wanted to be remembered. That same morning I saw a shepherd boy playing his pan-pipes on a mountainside.

Trouble broke out between the shepherds from Stolac, most of them Muslim, and Bosnian Serbs in the district of Ulog. Beside a small thatched hut, a Muslim called Mehan, with a yellow beard and piercing blue eyes, gave us bread with clotted cream before reciting his troubles. The previous night a bear had killed eight of his lambs. Although for as long as anyone could remember, the people of Stolac had brought their flocks to pasture here, the Ulog co-operative would not allow their sheep to graze. Last night, seven peasants and two policemen had threatened him with knives and guns. We arrived at Ulog, which stands on either side of the upper Neretva, close to the place where in 1943 the Partisans shot their Italian prisoners and threw the corpses into the river to frighten their fellow-countrymen at Mostar. The inhabitants of Stolac, especially the village policemen and the teacher, were almost as hostile to us as to the shepherds from Stolac. The youths of the town took turns with an air-rifle to shoot at the women crossing the bridge.

Twenty years later, I went back to Stolac in early June but found that the sheep, which once could be counted in thousands, were now reduced to a few small flocks. Where once our jeep had travelled on open ground, there were now metalled roads and even police radar traps. The exodus to the cities or to work in western Europe had meant the decline of agriculture and of the rural population. A shepherdess with one of the few flocks we met in Hercegovina said that it was not so much fun now taking the sheep into Bosnia, but that the wolves were still a danger. Unfortunately this depopulation in eastern Bosnia-Hercegovina and over the River Drina in Serbia had not diminished the tension between the Orthodox Christians and the Muslims.

The Yugoslav journalist who had come with me in the hope of photographing thousands of sheep noticed an article in one of the Belgrade magazines, on a village in Serbia said to be overrun by bears. The people of Jagostica, on Tara Mountain overlooking the River Drina, were reported to be at their wits' end as the bears stole their fruit, killed their sheep and chickens, and even attacked human beings. The secretary of the village Communist Party, Ljubomir Spasojević, was quoted as saying: 'Here it is not a question of liberalism or nationalism. But worse than that – bears. It's a real invasion, and that's why we talk about them at our Party meetings. We're seriously thinking of leaving.'

We drove first to the town of Višegrad, the inspiration of Ivo Andrić's epic novel of Bosnian history, *Na Drini Ćuprija* (*The Bridge on the Drina*). The hotel was full, so we drove over the river to the little Serbian town of Kremna, to find that people were indeed talking of bears. 'A few years ago a lot of them came across the river from Bosnia,' the landlord told us; 'they love to swim, plunging up and down in the water. They formed themselves into a kind of brigade and took over the district. Then the farmers got permission to shoot some and they lay low for a while.'

At Perušac, an old-timer told us the way to Jagostica: 'You drive as far as Rastišta and then you go up a little dirt road to the forestry camp, and from then on you have to walk up at least five hours . . . As you get near Jagostica, you'll see bears, wild boars and wolves. Are the villagers frightened of the animals? Yes of course they are, especially of the wild boars. They're the most dangerous.' The dirt road began at a crack in the cliff face at the side of the main highway. We came to the forestry camp, where one of the loggers grinned at our question: 'So you've read *Ilustrovana Politika*. I can tell you, eighty per cent of that was lies.' He hinted that the authorities were using the bears as a pretext to move the villagers down from the mountain, to avoid the cost of installing a road and electricity.

A woman of sixty-nine, Tijana Djukić, led the way up the mountain, of which the inhabitants used to sing:

> Planina Tara,
> Puška sara
> Ovaca gara
> Ne bojim se ni Cara.

> With Tara Mountain,
> An ornamented gun
> And a black ewe,
> I fear not even the Tsar.

Tijana had been on a shopping expedition and held her purchases in a bundle slung from a pole on her shoulder, but in spite of this extra burden she set the pace in the two-hour climb up Tara Mountain, leaping nimbly over the streams and never slipping on pine-needles or mud. Far from needing to save her breath, she treated us to her life story, bellowed forth with all the strength of her mountaineer's lungs:

I died when my son died but after seven days I lived again. That was eighteen years ago, and now God wants to give me death again . . . In the last war, one of my brothers went to Užice to join the Proletarian Brigade. The other went to form his party of warriors [Chetniks] to fight the Turks at Višegrad . . . The sons of the Serbs will die again, and the Turks will come back again, because we have no more heroes – I f— your mother! The children won't eat bread now, they won't eat *kajmak* [a sort of cream cheese], they won't drink milk – I f— your mother and sister! They want chocolate and biscuits. And a girl will go into a man's room alone. Why don't they keep their virginity till they're twenty? – I f— your bloody God!

By the end of Tijana's story, of which I noted only a fragment, we had left the dark forest and come to the rolling pasture under the summit of Tara Mountain. It is fertile land, especially good for fruit trees, and although we passed several deer we saw no sign of a dangerous animal. In Jagostica, we stayed with the brother and sister-in-law of the Party secretary, eating delicious meals of home-made bread, potatoes, cheese and *kajmak*, washed down even at breakfast by plum brandy, distilled in the backyard, next to the shed for making jam and drying fruit. The tiny Orthodox church and the village school stood close to the edge of the cliff overlooking the Drina. When I asked if the strip of white cloth fluttering from a pole was intended to keep birds away from the fruit trees, I was told that it kept the eagles out of the chicken run. However, the bears were less of a problem.

The Party secretary Ljubomir Spasojević said that some of the young were leaving the village and going to Užice because there was no electricity, roads, shops, cinemas or television, but nobody blamed this exodus on the bears:

That story about the Party is old, it happened years ago. We get on all right with the bears, in fact we're glad of them because bears and wild boars don't get on together, and now the boars have gone back to Bosnia, which is fine for us because the boars are more dangerous and we don't get any compensation for the damage they do . . . You never see the bear that steals your

animals or fruit. A bear can make a raid and then he'll wait three
nights until you think he's gone.

He had a characteristically Serbian explanation of why the normally
vegetarian bears had taken to eating meat:

> They're Bosnian bears. Across the river there's no corn or fruit
> for them to eat, so they start stealing sheep and chickens. And
> when the peasants start shooting them, they swim over the Drina
> and start killing our livestock . . . There's a Muslim village over
> there, across the Drina, where a bear broke into the mullah's
> house and smashed his television set.

However, some forest rangers in Užice told me that Bosnian
bears are no more carnivorous than their fellows in Serbia. Moreover they cross the Drina not so much to eat as to mate. The
animals on either side of the river belong to the same species, *Ursus
Arctos Bosniensis*, just as the human beings on both sides are South
Slavs.

In the last year of Tito's life, there were rumours that the
religious troubles of Bosnia-Hercegovina might be made worse by
a wave of Islamic fundamentalism and even by demands for a jihad
or a holy war. Early in 1979, the Shah of Iran had been deposed by
the Ayatollah Khomeini, and later that year the Soviet Union went
into Afghanistan, causing unrest in its Muslim population. Early
in 1980, as Tito lay dying, I went to Sarajevo to find out if there
existed a Bosnian ayatollah. One of the first Muslims I met on this
visit, an old man of eighty, described himself as an ayatollah, but
since he was drinking plum brandy, smoking and telling dubious
jokes in a bar, he clearly felt little respect for Khomeini. Most
people laughed at the very idea of Islamic fundamentalism in
Bosnia, and a mullah in the sixteenth-century mosque behind the
Evropa Hotel said it was not even a possibility. The Muslims in
Europe have always belonged to the Sunni rather than Shiite
branch of Islam, and have always behaved with tolerance towards
the people of other faiths. Since the Bosnian Muslims are Slavs,

they feel no racial tie with the Turks, who in turn tend to look down on the Arabs.

The Bosnian followers of Islam have always intermarried with Christians, so that in most old families in Sarajevo and Mostar there is a mixture of Muslims, 'Serbs' and 'Croats'. The Bosnian Muslims are just as keen on adultery as on alcohol. 'All they think about is chasing women,' I was told by a laughing Serbian woman who lived in a Muslim quarter. The pornography on display in Sarajevo, as everywhere else in Yugoslavia, would shock many Western readers, let alone Muslim fundamentalists. Even serious magazines felt obliged to have a nude on the cover and several pages of lurid erotica at the back. One such magazine, showing a two-page sketch of a black man servicing two women at once, also contained a good and informative article on whether the Muslim community in the Soviet Union would imitate the Islamic puritan-ism of Afghanistan and Iran. The writer assumed that this was a problem facing the Soviet Union, not Yugoslavia.

In February 1980 Sarajevo struck me as cheerful and confident. For one thing, its football team stood at the top of the First Division and looked set to remain there. 'It's all to do with politics,' an enthusiast told me. 'When you were here there were three teams, weren't there – Partisan, Red Star and Hajduk from Split? All the teams were given financial support for political reasons. Partisan was the army team, Red Star was the Party team and Hajduk was the Croat team, and they wanted to please the poor old Croats. Now there's a free market in players, and Sarajevo has come out on top.'

Yugoslavia's debts to the international banks had not caused any real suffering in Sarajevo. One evening I went twenty miles into the mountains to eat at an inn called the Scots House, run by a man from Stirling and his Yugoslav wife. She had just received a letter from her father-in-law, saying how lucky she was not to be living in Britain, where there were strikes and a recession.

The only cloud on the future was Tito's illness and approaching death. 'If Tito goes, do you think we'll all start killing each other again?' I heard a man asking his friends in a café. I went to a jolly

Muslim wedding breakfast, held in a new Chinese restaurant on the quay, only a few yards away from the place where Čabrinović threw his bomb at the Archduke Franz Ferdinand. Singing began soon after the meal, and although the selection began with such Bosnian favourites as 'Little Red Slippers' and 'My Heart is Aching', the loudest, most heartfelt singing went into the hymns of praise for Tito, made up by the Partisans in the mountains of Bosnia nearly forty years earlier. Almost everyone I met in Sarajevo was fond of Tito and sad about his approaching death. They even said a mass for his health in the Roman Catholic cathedral.

On this last visit to Sarajevo in Tito's lifetime, I went to look again at the fatal plaque in honour of Gavrilo Princip. Once more it gave me a sense of foreboding, so that I ended my article with these words: 'Since terror always produces a counter-terror, so the assassination by Princip led not only to World War One but to the cycle of violence between the Serbs, Croats and Muslims, to the chronic hatred that still slumbers beneath the surface in Sarajevo and could break out once more. Then more shots might be heard that would echo around the world.'[16]

16

The Final Years

The nationalities problem and consequent threat to the very existence of Yugoslavia overshadowed the last twelve years of Tito's life. In a moment of desperation in 1971 he admitted that enemies of the country were saying, 'When Tito goes the whole thing will collapse.' In his struggle to keep the Yugoslavs in 'Brotherhood and Unity', and to leave the country a legacy of peace, Tito suffered his only defeat. In the 1930s he won the leadership of the Yugoslav Communist Party when most of the other contenders were murdered by Stalin. During the Second World War he fought and survived battles against the Germans, Italians, Chetniks and Ustasha, to end up as head of a Communist Yugoslavia. In 1948 Tito successfully challenged the Soviet Union to make Yugoslavia an independent country, enjoying considerable freedom and prosperity. He had taken on and bested the royalist Yugoslav government, the Axis invaders and their Yugoslav allies, and then the rest of the Communist world, but he could not conquer religious intolerance. He could shoot Mihailović but he could not stop the Serbs from wanting to drive out the 'Turks'. He could jail Stepinac but could not stop the Croats from wanting to 'cleanse' their land of 'Slav-Serbs' and 'schismatics'.

Tito's failure to settle the nationalities problem made it hard for him to conduct a graceful retirement, or groom a successor. Of his old friends and comrades from before the war, Moša Pijade was dead, Djilas and Ranković were in disgrace, while only the dour Kardelj was left. Young and ambitious politicians looked for careers in the local rather than federal Party machines. Although Tito, a Croat, was still widely popular with the Serbs and still more with the Muslims, few other Yugoslavs were equally honoured outside their own republic.

From the end of the 1960s, Tito spent less of his time on the day-to-day business of government, saving his energy for the major problems such as Czechoslovakia and Croatian nationalism. He had never been interested in the running of the economy, and as he grew older he tended to be imprudent, running up debts to the international banks. This failing cannot be attributed to the Communist system, since certain east European countries, notably Czechoslovakia and the German Democratic Republic, were cautious with money, while many capitalist countries, such as the Philippines, Brazil and sometimes Britain, were profligate in the spending of borrowed cash. Tito's imprudence was a personal weakness, perhaps inherited from his father.

During the last years of his life, Tito still travelled occasionally, returning once more to the Soviet Union, which he had known since its inception, more than sixty years earlier. In Yugoslavia he spent as much time as possible at his favourite home on Brioni, receiving his relatives, old friends and comrades as well as officials and foreign visitors. Although he talked of writing his memoirs, and even employed a team of researchers to go through the documents from the war, Tito never got down to this task. Instead he gave a series of television interviews, virtually monologues, in which he recalled his early life and wartime experiences. These were really a televised version of *Tito Speaks*, and as in the book he came across as likeable and humorous. The 'Old Man', as he really was by now, had not been impaired by age.

Because of the tragedy that befell Yugoslavia twelve years after Tito's death, we tend to forget his mighty achievements in rebuilding a country devastated by war. Starting in 1968 and continuing into the 1970s, I visited some of the places that featured in Tito's early life, to see how they fared in Tito's Yugoslavia. His birthplace

of Kumrovec was a favourite destination for coachloads of school-
children, factory workers, veterans' groups and even a few foreign
tourists. It was served by an excellent road, and was signposted
prominently from the outskirts of Zagreb. At Tito's old house,
now of course a museum, a bossy woman curator told us stories
about his childhood: how he went hungry but never begged for
food; how he was banned from the choir for being cheeky to the
bullying priest; how he was the ringleader in fights and raids on
the local orchards; how he worked from his early years to help
keep the family. One of the Yugoslav visitors pressed the pillow on
Tito's wooden bed, exclaiming in wonder, 'Straw!' 'Yes, of course
it's straw,' said the schoolmarmish curator, 'Tito came from a
working-class background.'

Tito had gone to work as a waiter at Sisak, and it was there he
served his apprenticeship as a locksmith and general mechanic. In
this he was similar to the kind of people who flourished in modern
Sisak, people who would go to work for a few years in Germany,
then come home to invest their savings in land or a private business.
These 'independents' in Yugoslavia were frequently better off than
their counterparts in Britain, the self-employed who faced the
hostility of the trade unions, the chain stores and monopoly
brewers, as well as feeling the burden of heavy income tax, rates,
VAT and employee liability. The Yugoslav 'independents' used
their extended families as a workforce.

The many Serbs in the old Military Frontier had suffered terribly
in the Second World War. Within days of coming to power in
April 1941, the Ustasha in Sisak arrested a Serb merchant and
flayed him alive. The German Plenipotentiary General Glaise von
Horstenau gives a harrowing account of the Ustasha camp at Sisak
for the extermination of Serb women and children. The Jew's
Hotel, where Tito worked for a time as a waiter, had disappeared,
but the bowling alley where he put up the skittles survived as part
of the local apprentices' club. A portrait of Tito hung on the wall,
but the patrons were blasé about him. The manager told me: 'It's
a very old alley, nothing like those automatic ones they have in
Zagreb. But here at Sisak we produced one really great man, who

bowled year after year for Yugoslavia. A few years ago he had a heart attack during the match and died, as he had lived, in the alley.'

In Zagreb flats were expensive and hard to find. The Party bosses after the war had taken over the mansions of the bourgeoisie in the old town and the leafy suburbs up on the hill. The hundreds of thousands of country people who came to the city to participate in the process of industrialisation lived in the tower blocks of New Zagreb, on the other side of the River Sava. Some of the flats were provided by employers, but they could also be bought through a housing co-operative. There was no equivalent of a council flat provided by the municipality, and no question of giving flats to the unemployed, unmarried couples or single mothers. The great majority of the flat-dwellers had homes in the country where their parents lived and where they could go for weekends, holidays and perhaps their retirement. Old people living alone in New Zagreb were encouraged to take on a student lodger, in return for domestic help.

Although the concrete cliffs of New Zagreb looked grim and depressing when seen from the highway, they were surprisingly pleasant places to live. Because people valued their homes, they were house-proud with respect both to the individual flats and to the buildings. There was no vandalism of either the properties or the trees and the lawns that served as playgrounds. The administration by block committees was one of the chores that went with the privileges of Party membership.

In Zagreb, as in the rest of Yugoslavia, there was no local bureaucracy such as is found, for example, in British cities. The functions of the professional social worker were carried out by priests, doctors and the extended family. Although divorce was legal and not infrequent, the family moved in to help the children of broken homes. For those who did not have motor cars there was an excellent public transport service, in which children invariably offered their seats to the old. Parents heaped praise on the State education system. The police were popular and would come round in five minutes on the report of a crime or even a noisy neighbour.

The old part of Zagreb had changed from the glum, impover-
ished place I remembered from 1951 into one of the pleasantest
and most handsome cities of what was once the Austro-Hungarian
Empire. The seventeenth- and eighteenth-century charm of the
Capitol, from the cathedral uphill, remained intact. The late-
Habsburg pomp of nineteenth-century Zagreb, north and west
from the magnificent railway station, was undefiled by ring-roads,
skyscraper office-blocks, shopping complexes, and all the horrors
that now afflicted my own country. My admiration and liking for
Zagreb grew with every visit.

When Tito became a political activist in 1925, the Party sent him
to Kraljevica to organise the shipyard workers. Milan Modrić, the
manager of what was now called the Tito Shipyard, told me that
Tito had earned the then excellent wage of six and a half dinars an
hour. One of Tito's elderly former colleagues, Filko Pavesić, added
that the future Party leader had been an industrious worker who
never skived and took a pride in his craftsmanship. Another old
workmate, Fabio Polić, told me of Tito's political activities:

> We used to go to the forest, a group of workers, and we always
> kept a look-out man who'd start to play the violin if someone was
> coming. Comrade Broz – I never can get used to calling him Tito
> – would talk about politics in this country and in the world
> outside. It wasn't just the working classes that liked him but
> everyone in the town – old, young, men and women, even
> enemies of his political ideas. In the evening he'd read and study
> and carry on his political agitation, but sometimes he and his first
> wife would come to my house. Last year he invited me to Brioni,
> and I spent the day with him and his present wife, Comrade
> Jovanka. What was his first wife like? Well, what would Jovanka
> say if I answered 'Attractive'?

In his hostile memoir, Milovan Djilas suggests that Tito felt
ashamed of his humble origin as a metalworker. In fact he was
proud of his time at Kraljevica, and kept a lathe at Brioni to
practise his craft.

From 1928–33, Tito spent most of his time at Lepoglava prison, studying Marxism under the tutelage of Moša Pijade. Forty years later, the present governor of the prison told me:

> The Communists in that time managed to get special treatment. They made it clear that they were different from ordinary prisoners . . . After the war we took over the building again because we thought it was a necessary way of dealing with some of our enemies. Now we haven't got a single political prisoner. In fact there are very few in all Yugoslavia and they are mostly *émigrés* who have been sent from abroad to cause trouble. Lepoglava today is a very advanced prison. All the prisoners learn a trade. We have two psychiatrists on the staff and twenty-seven penological experts, including technical workers and lawyers. Many penologists come here from abroad, and some of them from West Germany say we're too lenient, too humane.

One of the Lepoglava psychiatrists, Franj Bartolović, said it was virtually an open prison, but they had no attempts at escape: 'You see they haven't got anywhere to escape to. There's no criminal underworld in this country.' After he had showed me Tito's cell, with its absurd statue, I asked Bartolović about Archbishop Stepinac. 'He had a very comfortable apartment,' came the reply, 'and he was free to perform religious duties.' And was there a chaplain now for the prisoners? 'No,' the psychiatrist said, 'they're allowed to say their prayers, but they're not allowed to see a priest. But then, in seven years, I've never heard of a prisoner asking to see a confessor.' However, Milovan Djilas says that many of his fellow prisoners in the 1960s complained of not being allowed to see a priest.

From the time he left prison until the invasion of Yugoslavia in April 1941, Tito was often abroad or hiding out in a suburb of Zagreb. It was not until May 1941 that he went to live for the first time in Belgrade. Tito's first visit to Serbia had been as a soldier in the invading Austro-Hungarian army in 1914, and in 1926 he had worked for a few months in a factory at Smedereovska Palanka. He

moved to Belgrade in 1941, partly to get away from the vigilant
Ustasha and also to prepare for the insurrection in Serbia. However, since he was virtually in hiding in the suburb of Dedinje,
Tito never became familiar with the café life of the city centre.
When he returned to Belgrade in 1944 as the ruler of Yugoslavia,
he once more lived in isolation in Dedinje. So, although Belgrade
was the official capital, Tito was never regarded as a local man.
Even Communist Serbs always thought of him as a Croat, while
the reactionaries said that Tito was really a Russian, and often
referred to him as 'the parachutist'. Even late in the 1960s, some
of them still refused to believe that Tito had ever quarrelled with
Stalin, and thought it was all a trick to get money out of the West.

Some blamed Tito for the impoverishment and dilapidation of
Belgrade, especially in comparison with Zagreb, the capital of his
native Croatia. Little of architectural merit survived the various
poundings in two world wars, and even what did remain looked
shabby and woebegone. The New Belgrade that arose on the other
side of the River Sava was built on a grander scale than New
Zagreb and also included the university halls of residence, vast
hotels and an international conference centre. However, it never
endeared itself to the people of old Belgrade, who thought it remote
and inhuman.

The trouble with Belgrade was not of Tito's making, but was the
result of it being the centre of government. Whereas Zagreb, like
Sarajevo or Ljubljana, lived off manufacture and commerce, Belgrade was a city of bureaucrats. Besides being the capital of the
country and of the Serbian Republic, it was the seat of power for
the country's three most powerful institutions; the Communist
Party, the UDBA and the Yugoslav People's Army. Just as Tito
and senior officials lived in pleasant suburbs like Dedinje, the rank
and file of the Civil Service, the Party, the UDBA and the army
lived in the tower blocks of New Belgrade. This concentration of
government gave the whole city a dull and dispiriting air to match
its appearance.

Although Djilas and others have castigated Tito for his extravagant taste in palaces, castles and villas, it should be pointed out

that he built neither those residences nor any other monuments to his own importance. Among Tito's contemporaries, Stalin erected grotesque, wedding-cake skyscrapers such as the Palace of Culture in Warsaw. Mao Zedong flattened the medieval centre of Beijing to create the expanse of Tiananmen Square. Ceauşescu destroyed a third of Bucharest to make his own Champs-Élysées and Versailles Palace. Even in democratic Britain and France, successive political leaders have built grandiose cultural centres and airports, unwanted national libraries and even a Channel Tunnel as monuments to their vanity. Tito was free of the building mania characteristic of most politicians. He was quite content with the houses he took from their previous occupants.

Rather than building expensive monuments, Tito attained glory for free by lending his name to selected towns throughout Yugoslavia. One of the towns thus honoured was Užice in the west of Serbia, where Tito established his brief 'Red Republic' during the autumn of 1941. In Titovo Užice, as it had now become, I went to the little museum and saw the display of rifles produced at the local arsenal, uniforms made by the local tailors, packets of 'Red Star' cigarettes and copies of the locally printed *Borba*.

Although Tito attended a feast on the tenth anniversary of the 'Red Republic', he was not altogether popular, both as a Croat and as a Communist, in what was a Chetnik area during the war. When I had been at the nearby village of Lepoglava, investigating the bears on Tara Mountain, the locals had told me that after the war some of the Communist leaders went there to hunt, mentioning specifically Djilas and Ranković, both of them Serbs and both now in disgrace. Tito, they added pointedly, had never been to Tara Mountain. Since then, permission to shoot bears was never given to Yugoslavs but sold instead to rich foreign hunters, causing annoyance in Titovo Užice.

When the secretary of the Titovo Užice Party heard that I was around and interested in bears, he asked me to come at nine next morning to meet some of his colleagues and two of the Tara gamewardens. When we had taken our seats, the Party secretary picked up the phone and told his personal secretary in the outer room not to put through any calls that morning as he had urgent business, then went to the cupboard and brought out the first of many bottles of plum brandy. The stories told by the game-wardens, and listened to with approval by the Party officials, gave me a sense that Tito was rather resented in Titovo Užice:

A Spaniard came here and shot a small bear. You are only allowed one, so he went back to Spain to practise for a week and returned, fired at a bear and missed. He went back to Spain for another week's practice, came back and this time got a shot at a group of three bears huddled close together to make a perfect shot. He missed them all.

A German came here, a very rich man. He booked a whole hotel to himself and they say he brought a waiter down from Belgrade. But it rained the whole week he was here so he never got a shot. People said to him, 'You can buy anything but good weather.'

In 1970 a capitalist shot a champion bear weighing 410 kilos. It took thirty people to haul it out of the ravine where it had fallen. He was so excited that he wouldn't have the skin treated here so it went bad and was ruined.

One hunter was so excited after firing that he had to walk around for twenty minutes to calm himself down before going to see the body. He was frightened of getting too excited and having a heart attack.

I can't understand why these people want to come here and kill a bear. They arrive in a plane or car. They stay in a hotel. They don't belong here. And all they have to do is pull the trigger . . . They go through the forest seeing nothing, hearing nothing, smelling nothing around them. Their faces are all tense. They have a strange look in their eyes. They're interested in only one thing – to kill.

After a morning devoted to bears and plum brandy, the Party secretary invited me to a lunch attended by dozens of veterans of the 'Red Republic' who carried on drinking toasts and making speeches into the late afternoon.

Tito failed to attend the celebrations to mark the twenty-fifth anniversary of the Battle of Sutjeska. His absence slightly saddened the proud survivors, including the Englishman Bill Deakin, who bore a wound from the shell that also hit Tito. The gorge that the Partisans had to cross, before climbing a mountain under intense bombing and shelling, is awesome even in peacetime. Even those who survived the battle were never the same again. 'We went for thirty-seven days without food,' said one man, Nikola Vjestica, 'without food for human beings. We ate animal food such as leaves, grass and bark. My memory has gone now. I can't remember the names of my old comrades. It's not because of my age but because of the suffering we went through.'

The veterans all accepted that Tito had valid reasons for not attending the celebrations. The truth was probably that he did not want to upset the Croats by going to what was virtually an all-Serbian gathering. The character of these Partisans came out in the story told to me by Milica Dragović, who was wounded twenty-three times in the war:

I first saw Comrade Tito in May 1942 at my home at Žablak in Montenegro. I was a shepherdess, aged seventeen, and I had just been made the secretary of our local Communist Party. There was a secret meeting at which we were all making reports on the strength of the enemy in the district. I noticed a stranger at the back of the room and afterwards I asked the senior comrade who it had been. He wouldn't tell me because we weren't supposed to know people's names. But I went on teasing him and because I was a young girl he told me. 'That was Comrade Tito.' My legs shook because I'd heard of Comrade Tito, of how he loved the working class and the peasants . . . The second time I saw Comrade Tito was one year later, here at Sutjeska. I was a courier and I was taking a message into the mountains. I saw a man on a horse who was wearing breeches, a fur hat, a pistol bandolier and carrying a sub-machine-gun. He was staring through his binoculars and suddenly he shouted at us to get down. I lay on the ground with the sun warm on my neck and the bombs crashing all around. I lay with my head in my hands until the Stukas were gone and I looked up and saw the same man. He had got off his horse but was still standing. I recognised Comrade Tito.

It was there at the Battle of Sutjeska in June 1943 that the Communist functionary Josip Broz was at last transformed into the legendary Tito. In the summer of 1971, a Hollywood crew arrived in Yugoslavia to make a film called *The Battle of Sutjeska*, with Tito played by the Welsh actor Richard Burton. The Titos entertained Burton and his wife Elizabeth Taylor during part of their stay in the country, and Burton's diary gives us a rare account of their private life:

August 2nd. Were it not actually for E's delight in the power and glory of it all, I would cut and run – so great is the strain of boredom – especially the interminably translated conversation. Both T and Madame Broz tell long stories which they don't allow the interpreter to interrupt . . . Madame has a very penetrating voice, which after a time becomes very tiresome.

There were occasional bright moments, Tito in English: 'I was very glad when my grandmother died.' E: 'Why?' Tito: 'Because she stopped beating me.' E: 'That was an awful thing to say.' Tito: 'She was small but she was strong and she was always angry.'

He met Churchill who was in the vicinity on Onassis's yacht. Winston C accepted a very small whisky. Tito had his usual big one. 'Why so small a portion?' asked Tito, 'you taught me to drink large ones.' 'That was when we both had power said Winston C. Now I have none and you still have yours.'

Tito seems to have told Burton a number of tall stories. He said he never permitted the shooting of German prisoners and did not drink alcohol during the Second World War. Burton failed to spot that this contradicted the conversation with Churchill. The actor also got the impression that the dictator never met any 'ordinary Joes' and felt that he was surrounded by 'an atmosphere of dread'.

However, Burton never heard a bad word said about Tito: 'I asked
Branka, a veteran Slav actor, why nobody, but simply nobody ever
spoke ill of Tito. Was it caution or fear perhaps? Branka said it was
neither. Tito was still a father figure to the older generation . . .
and to the younger generation there had never been any other
President.'[1]

Richard Burton had found Jovanka tiresome and so, increasingly, did Tito. This was observed by Sir Fitzroy Maclean, who
saw his old friend often during the 1970s. When Tito was in
Washington during the last leg of a world tour, he was persuaded
by Sir Fitzroy to fly up to Canada to accept an honorary doctorate
at Dalhousie University. The next day Maclean joined Tito and
Jovanka on the private plane for the flight on to London. He later
described the journey to his biographer:

> I was trying to keep awake, trying to hoist in what he was saying
> in Serbo-Croat, and generally doing my best. Tito remonstrated
> with his wife for standing up and gazing out of the window.
> 'There's nothing there but sea,' he said. 'No, there's the whole of
> Nova Scotia,' she said. Then she said to me pointedly, 'He likes
> being right.' I thought, what a mistake to make. Breakfast arrived
> and Tito looked at his watch and said, 'Seven a.m. Canada time,
> that's one a.m. London time. Time for a whisky.' Enormous
> breakfasts of scrambled eggs and large measures of whisky were
> produced. Soon Mrs Tito was at it again. 'That's your second
> whisky,' she said. I thought again, you're making a fatal mistake.
> Sure enough, soon afterwards Mrs Tito disappeared or, rather,
> was 'administratively reabsorbed'.[2]

When the diplomatic community observed that Jovanka no longer
attended official or private functions with Tito, the CBS television
company asked Maclean to raise the matter with Tito in an
interview. Maclean refused, but the question was put to Tito by
Walter Kronkite. Quite unabashed, Tito replied that at eighty-five
his nerves were still quite strong but not strong enough to endure
his ex-wife's nagging. In a country worried about the nationalities

problem, Tito's treatment of Jovanka was seen by some as a threat to her fellow Serbs in Croatia.

Sir Fitzroy Maclean has given us some of the last good anecdotes from Tito's life, concerning Margaret Thatcher and the Prince of Wales. When the then Opposition leader visited Yugoslavia soon after a trip to China, Tito talked of that country, then engrossed in controversy over Madam Mao. 'Of course,' said Tito, looking Mrs Thatcher straight in the eye, 'I don't believe in women interfering in politics.' Mrs Thatcher snapped back: 'I don't interfere in politics. I am politics.' According to Sir Fitzroy, Tito was delighted, and after that the two of them got on well. Tito was not above teasing royalty. When Sir Fitzroy accompanied Prince Charles on his official visit to Yugoslavia, he took Tito some of his celebrated MacPhunn malt whisky. At the official reception Tito served Chivas Regal to the disappointment of the Prince, who accosted him: 'Can't we broach some of Fitzroy's malt?' 'Oh no,' replied Tito, 'we keep that for special occasions.'[3]

Tito fell ill early in January 1980, and was taken to hospital in Ljubljana where surgeons amputated first one and then the other leg. He was visited by his sons and by Jovanka, who was evidently deeply upset. Apparently at his own request, Tito was nursed through his last illness by Roman Catholic nuns, giving rise to speculation that all along he had been a religious believer. People recalled his remark to a Church official in 1945, 'I, as a Catholic . . .' Djilas has written that Tito would not rule out the idea of immortality. Tito was kept alive by the doctors until 4 May, as if the country was dreading his departure. His funeral was attended by old comrades-in-arms such as Deakin and Maclean, as well as by Margaret Thatcher, now the Prime Minister, Brezhnev of the Soviet Union, the Vice-President of the United States (President Carter was criticised for not attending in person), and many Third World leaders, including the tearful Kenneth Kaunda. Tito's body was placed in a mausoleum near to his home in the Dedinje suburb of Belgrade.

17

Reassessments
of Tito

Just as the doctors kept Tito alive for months after his span was over, so his successors invoked Tito's memory in the hope of holding the country together. The veneration of Tito, which had begun spontaneously in the mountains of Bosnia in 1943, was kept going during his lifetime by formal events such as the relay race run on his birthday (or putative birthday), by teaching about him in schools, and by slogans, songs and the omnipresent portraits in offices, shops and cafés. Tito himself had never allowed the veneration to turn into idolatry, such as that surrounding Hitler, Stalin and Mao Zedong. He did not have temples built to himself; he did not address the equivalent of a Nuremberg rally; he was always relaxed and affable in his private conversation. In the series of television talks he gave in the 1970s, Tito came across as a kindly great-uncle, not as a god-king. It was only after his death that the veneration of Tito became a cult, inviting his help from beyond the grave to preserve Yugoslavia. The collective leadership – sometimes laughingly known as 'Tito and the eight dwarfs' – dreamed up the preposterous slogan, 'After Tito – Tito!'

Every year for a decade, on 4 May at 3.05 p.m., the sirens wailed all over the country and people were meant to observe a two-minute silence. The army laid wreaths on the tomb of the man they still described as 'our supreme commander'. As late as 1989 a veterans' organisation nominated him for a fourth award of People's

Hero. A special law was passed in 1984 to lay down heavier punishment for those found guilty of insult to Tito's memory. The number of 'Tito's towns' was raised to eight to include not only the six republics but the 'autonomous regions' of Vojvodina and Kosovo. Scores of publications came out after Tito's death to honour his life.

This cult of Tito has been compared with the adulation of Kemal Atatürk, the founder of modern Turkey, whose mass-produced statues remain a popular icon almost sixty years after his death. His successors established the Atatürk cult in the hope of keeping alive his secular, European ideas against an Islamic counter-attack. Moreover Atatürk stood for specifically Turkish nationalism against the claims of the Greeks, Arabs, Armenians, Kurds, Slavs and other ethnic groups in the former Ottoman Empire. Because it is rooted in Turkish national pride, the Atatürk cult has flourished. Because there was no equivalent pride in Yugoslavia, the cult of Tito faded.

It was partly as a reaction to this posthumous cult that many writers on Yugoslavia started to question or even debunk Tito's reputation. In *Tito: The Story from Inside*, Milovan Djilas mars a characteristically brilliant book with uncharacteristically sour and peevish comments. Djilas, the puritan, once more voices his disapproval of Tito's elegant lifestyle but this time loses his sense of proportion. He calls Tito 'the most extravagant ruler of his time', although, as has already been pointed out, he was quite content to live off the Karadjeordjević legacy. Like Ceauşescu in Romania and Marcos in the Philippines, Tito borrowed extravagantly from the International Monetary Fund (IMF), but unlike the others he let the rest of the country share in the spoils. All Yugoslavia joined in the spending spree during the 1970s.

In *Tito: The Story from Inside*, Djilas returns once more to Tito's weakness for flashy suits, uniforms, medals and other adornments to his person. But Tito himself acknowledged this not very serious vanity. Many Yugoslav men share the Italian concern for *bella figura*, as was observed by Rebecca West in *Black Lamb and Grey Falcon*. She described the young bucks of Dalmatia as 'very handsome, with that air of unashamed satisfaction with their own good looks, which one finds only where there is very little homosexuality'.[1]

Again Djilas suggests that Tito, the standard-bearer of Yugoslavia's proletariat, felt ashamed of his humble background: 'He also suffered because of his mutilated finger: the tip of his index finger on his left hand was caught in a machine when he worked as a mechanic. It was as if he bore the mark that he had not risen above the level of a worker.'[2] Yet, as I had heard at Kraljevica, Tito stayed in touch with his former workmates and, far from being ashamed of his early life as a metalworker, he boasted about it.

Djilas is still more unfair when he says that during the war Tito 'had an overwhelming concern for his personal safety'.[3] Nobody else who knew him questioned Tito's courage. It is true that towards the end of the war, when Tito commanded a very large army, he established his staff headquarters in caves at Jajce, Drvar and Vis; but such precautions would be normal for any military leader. Nobody would suggest that Winston Churchill feared for his personal safety because he worked from a bunker in Whitehall. When King David wanted to lead his troops into battle, the people of Israel said to him: 'Thou shalt not go forth . . . thou art worth ten thousand of us: therefore now it is better that thou be ready to succour us out of the city.' (2 Samuel 18:3.)

Djilas even presents as vices what most of us would regard as amiable characteristics. Tito would not sign death warrants, says Djilas, because he felt that in this way 'death would not be inevitable'. When Tito, on leaving for Italy during the war, entrusted his horse to the care of a colleague, Djilas says that he thought more of his horse than of his suffering Partisans. At another point, Djilas says of Tito:

Precisely because of the secondary importance he assigned to other areas – to the economy, to culture, to sport and so on – in relation to the primacy of pure power, pure politics, these and other areas avoided dogmatism and oppression, and developed partial independence.[4]

This is a roundabout way of saying that Tito was tolerant. A real dictator, a Hitler or Stalin, imposes his will on every aspect of human life – the economy, culture and sport included. To explain what he calls Tito's 'sense of danger', Djilas writes:

> Tito's personality thrived on the heat of the moment, yielding readily, instinctively to fresh impressions, but was far too rash in situations of unexpected or drastic change. People like Tito do not always weigh things or think them through. They blend frenzy and fortitude, exactitude and recklessness.[5]

Some might think that Djilas was here describing himself rather than Tito. In at least one situation of unexpected and drastic change – the Hungary crisis of 1956 – Tito was right and Djilas was wrong, as Djilas himself admitted later.

Some critics suggested that even during his lifetime Tito did not care about the future of Yugoslavia. In *The Improbable Survivor*, the first of two biographical studies of Tito, Stevan K. Pavlowitch alleges that during the 1970s Tito stripped the Party of some of its ablest members, then goes on to say: 'This was intended both to prevent a struggle for the succession and anyone ever again wielding such power as he had – in order to keep his achievements and his memory intact and unique.'[6] Now, as we have seen, Tito's sacking of so many able leaders, as well as his failure to groom a strong successor, were largely imposed by the nationalities problem. Was Tito so vain that he wanted the country to perish with him, just as a brahmin insists that his widow must burn with him on the funeral pyre? The surest way to preserve Tito's memory and achievement was to preserve Yugoslavia.

Stevan Pavlowitch, a lecturer at Southampton University, is among those who blame the British, and in particular Fitzroy Maclean, for giving support to Tito both during and after the war.

In the bibliographical note to *Tito*, published in London in 1992, Pavlowitch recommends to his readers Stephen Clissold's *Whirlwind*, then goes on to warn: 'Other British general wartime eyewitness accounts of Tito's "rise to power" are too romantic and uncritical to be listed here. While they are of great use to the scholar, they are of no help to most readers.'[7] In this cursory manner, Pavlowitch dismisses, without even naming, Fitzroy Maclean's *Eastern Approaches* and *Disputed Barricade*, although he commends the same author's *Josip Broz Tito – A Pictorial Biography* as a 'nicely produced photograph album'.[8]

The same hostility to Maclean is found in the memoirs of some of the British who fought on the side of Mihailović during the war, in particular Michael Lees. They accused him not only of bringing Tito to power in the first place, but then, in the 1950s, of shoring up and financing his Communist regime. Books such as *Eastern Approaches* are blamed by Pavlowitch for the fact that 'Tito had been fully re-glamorised with the British public through the medium of war-time connections'.[9] The publication during the 1970s and 1980s of Evelyn Waugh's letters and diaries gave new ammunition to the opponents of Maclean and Tito, as did the revelation by Christopher Booker and others that Yugoslav refugees forced back from Austria by the British in 1945 were slaughtered by the Partisans.

Because of the wartime connection, the British have always had a particular interest in Yugoslavia, but tend to confuse its politics with their own. So it was that in the 1980s enmity towards Tito, and even towards the idea of Yugoslavia, was taken up by an element of the British Right. These were the journalists and academics who backed the then Prime Minister Margaret Thatcher in opposition to Communism in eastern Europe, and in opposition to federalism in western Europe. They denounced Yugoslavia both as a Communist state and as an example of an unworkable, artificial federation, a microcosm of the proposed European Community. This group blamed Maclean not only for having installed Tito in power but for having resurrected the 'Versailles state' of Yugoslavia. They blamed Britain, first for having betrayed the Serbs in

the Second World War, and later for its unwillingness to recognise
Croatia.

While Tito came under attack from the Thatcherite polemicists,
his stock continued to rise among historians of the Second World
War. The publication of Ultra, the intercepts of the German coded
dispatches, vindicated Churchill's decision to back the Partisans.
Because of Ultra, Churchill would have supported Tito even against
the advice of Fitzroy Maclean. By autumn 1943, the Partisans were
by far the most powerful force against the Germans, and would
have taken power in Yugoslavia with or without the help of Britain.
As Fitzroy Maclean himself admits, he played only a minor role in
Tito's rise to power; but he played that role honourably and
correctly. As Maclean's biographer Frank McLynn says: 'Some of
the finest academic historians have gone on record as stating that
the Maclean policy on Yugoslavia was the correct one: Elisabeth
Barker, Ralph Bennett, F. H. Hinsley, Sir William Deakin, Mark
Wheeler, Hugh Seton-Watson. Who is there of this stature on the
revisionist side?'[10]

While British intellectuals debated Tito's reputation, the Yugoslavs were faced with the legacy of his foreign loans. In 1983 the
government tried to stave off bankruptcy by virtually placing itself
in the hands of the International Monetary Fund (IMF) and ceding
control of debts and credits. By the middle of 1984, inflation stood
at 62 per cent; the standard of living had fallen by 30 per cent since
Tito's death; the unemployed made up 15 per cent of the workforce, with half of them under the age of twenty-four. When I had
first gone to Belgrade in 1953, the most valuable note was the red
100 dinars, showing the rugged features of Alija Sirotanović, a
Bosnian miner who had exceeded his norm and become a 'Hero of
Labour'. According to Der *Spiegel* magazine, Sirotanović was now
an embittered alcoholic; and in 1987, in Belgrade, the waitress
asked 'one million and seven dinars' for a coffee, referring to notes
in various stages of worthlessness. The restrictions on foreign
credit had not affected the bookshop near the Moskva Hotel, where
I saw five tables stacked with Penguin editions of P. G. Wodehouse,

apparently bought in bulk from London, and now selling at prices reduced by inflation to only a tenth of their British value.

Scandal surrounded the National Bank, the oil corporation, the railways and even the efforts to sell Tito's yacht. In Bosnia, in 1987, a number of senior Party officials went to prison over a scandal involving a string of factory farms called Agro-Komerc. They had issued false promissory notes for a project involving a billion US dollars, 100,000 jobs and countless beasts and poultry. The money was gone, the workers were sacked and some of the creatures were dead, although in the end Agro-Komerc survived. In that same year, 168 strikes were recorded, a high proportion of them in Croatia.

The situation was not as bad as it seemed to foreign observers, looking at Yugoslavia in terms of their own social system. In spite of its Communist ideology, Yugoslavia was a remarkably free-market state, with only a small bureaucracy, and virtually no welfare system. It was not, for instance, like Britain, where more than five million people work in the public sector and five million more depend on the state for 'income support' and other benefits. Because there was no dole, most of the sacked workers travelled abroad as *Gastarbeiter*, took casual jobs or went to stay with their relatives. There was a healthy drift back from the cities into the countryside and agriculture. New brick houses were built through-out the Šumadija district, as people from Belgrade went back to producing plums and pigs. The large and ever-increasing class of self-employed, or 'independents', continued to flourish. On the island of Hvar in the mid-1980s, I met a restaurant owner who earned so much during the six holiday months that he spent the remaining six in California. Most Yugoslavs regretted the high-borrowing, high-spending 1970s, but knew that they now had to be prudent. The only people suffering real privation were those in the cities who had no relations left in the countryside.

Although a socialist state in the sense that most of its enterprises were owned by the workers, Yugoslavia was not 'left wing' in the way the term is now used in the West. Nobody thought that the State had a right or duty to interfere on behalf of some 'underprivi-

leged' interest group such as the unemployed, the ethnic minorities, working mothers, single parents or putative victims of child
abuse. There was socialism but not much sociology in Yugoslavia.
It had almost entirely escaped the three popular Western causes of
multiracialism, women's rights and homosexual equality. The first
of these was irrelevant in a country that did not encourage
immigration. The other two causes did not take hold in a country
enjoying a good relationship between the sexes. 'It was strange, it
was heart-rending,' Rebecca West wrote in the 1930s, 'to stray into
a world where men are still men and women still women.'[11]

Because of their sociological outlook on life, most Western
visitors failed to understand a country steeped in a sense of family,
tradition, history and religion, all of which they themselves had
abandoned. For this reason, they failed to notice the tremors along
the fault-lines dividing the Orthodox Catholics and Muslims. A
poignant example of this can be found in *The Rough Guide to
Yugoslavia*, published in 1985 to accompany a BBC series of
television travel films presenting the world to the young of Britain.
The authors, Martin Dunford and Jack Holland, have dedicated
their book to 'the continuation of a free, non-aligned and socialist
Yugoslavia'. Although they noted that homosexual behaviour was
still illegal in four of the six republics, the authors approved of
most of the things they observed, such as 'a waning of worship –
today it's mostly the old who fill the churches and mosques'. They
cannot have seen the Masses celebrated at Zagreb Cathedral, which
was packed each Sunday with young men and women. They cannot
have noticed much in Zagreb: 'Once a hotbed of Croat nationalism
and capital of the wartime puppet state of Pavelić, it's widely
regarded as the cultural and artistic heart of Yugoslavia, and
though all Serb–Croat differences have long since been resolved,
there's a Croat disdain of Belgrade that still persists.'[12]

Such a misunderstanding should not be blamed on the authors'
youth, but on the prevailing attitudes of the BBC. The Welsh
archaeologist Arthur Evans was twenty-four when he published the
first of his wonderful books on Bosnia-Hercegovina in the 1870s.
But Evans, although himself a freethinker and liberal, understood

the power over the human heart of history and religion. It was these things, not the collapse of Communism or Tito's economic mistakes, that led to the breakup of Yugoslavia during the 1990s. Although the origins of the disaster lie buried deep in the Balkan past, I have tried to relate what happened to three different phenomena that emerged in 1981, the year after Tito's death. There was first a revolt by the Albanians in Kosovo, the ancient holy place of the Serbs. A book published in Zagreb revived the controversy over the wartime role of Archbishop Stepinac. And at Medjugorje (pronouned Med-joo-gor-ye), a village in Hercegovina where the Franciscans have one of their monasteries, six young people claimed to have heard and seen the Virgin Mary.

18

Towards Disaster
in Serbia

There was a saying in Belgrade not long after the death of Tito: 'The Slovenes have got his collection of vintage cars, the Croats have got his yachts, and we've got his carcass.' This Serb resentment dated back to the early 1970s, when Tito had sacked the 'liberal', reform-minded Communists, and further annoyed the nationalists by giving autonomous status to Vojvodina and Kosovo. After Tito's death, the Serbian Party continued to persecute dissident liberals and would not even reduce the teaching of Marxism in schools and at Belgrade University. At the same time, the government came down hard on even the slightest manifestation of Serbian nationalism, such as singing 'Far Away by the Sea', the lament for the army during the First World War.

In the aftermath of the purge in 1972, obedience to the Party, or 'moral-political suitability', became once more a necessary requirement for any career in business, the media or education. Dissidents called this process 'negative selection' since it meant that careerists and dogmatists rose to the top. A typical product of this system was Slobodan Milošević, the future leader of Serbia. A Montenegrin by ancestry, Milošević was born and grew up in the Serbian town of Požarevac, where both his father and mother were schoolteachers. Young Slobodan was a conscientious pupil, wearing a carefully pressed dark suit to school; he avoided all sports and kept his own company. However, at high school he met his future wife

Mirjana Marković, who was from one of the leading Communist families and was at that time training for her career as a teacher of Marxist sociology. A peculiar double tragedy cast a shadow over an otherwise tranquil youth. When Milošević was at university, his father committed suicide, as did his mother eleven years later.[1]

Milošević began his career in business, becoming director first of a factory and then of a leading bank, a job that took him on frequent visits to the United States. He also moved rapidly to the summit of power, being appointed head of the Belgrade Party in 1984 and of the Serbian Party in 1986. Although he was now an important man in the grey bureaucratic world of post-Tito politics, Milošević was ignored or despised by the public in Serbia. His subsequent transformation into the hero of many Serbs, and a figure of loathing outside the country, was almost entirely due to the crisis in Kosovo.

Edward Gibbon, in *The Decline and Fall of the Roman Empire*, had dwelt on the catastrophic significance of the Battle of Kosovo, at which 'the league and independence of the Sclavonian tribes was finally crushed'. During the next five centuries under Ottoman rule, the Serbs never forgot the fateful anniversary on St Vitus's Day. Bards sang of it to the tune of a one-string fiddle; churchgoers prayed for the soul of Duke Lazar and other fallen heroes; the children learned that on Vidovdan no cuckoo sings, and that during the hours of darkness the rivers run red with blood.[2]

On 28 June 1889, the fifth centenary of the battle, the inhabitants of the new Kingdom of Serbia were able to mark the occasion in freedom, but millions of co-religionists lived under the Ottoman or Habsburg empires. In 1912, in the first of the Balkan wars, the Serbs finally won back Kosovo Polje, the whole army kneeling to kiss its soil, but they lost it again to the Germans and Austrians three years later. When the Germans and the Italians invaded in April 1941, the Royal Yugoslav Army was everywhere in retreat except in Kosovo, from which it launched an attack on Albania. As a punishment to the Serbs, the Axis conquerors permitted Albania to occupy Kosovo for the rest of the war. Afterwards, the new Communist government in Tirana did not press for sovereignty over Kosovo, even though the Albanians were in the majority. Tito's relations with Albania, and in particular his decision to send in two divisions of Yugoslav troops, was one of the points at issue with Stalin in 1948. As soon as the break occurred, the Tirana regime became the most virulent foe of Tito. The Albanians not only sealed the Yugoslav frontier, but frequently sniped at people across it.

Tito went out of his way to help and develop the backward region of Kosovo, and came to be seen by Albanians there as an ally against the Serbs. Towards the end of the 1960s, the bulk of the federal budget for underdeveloped regions was transferred from Bosnia-Hercegovina and Macedonia to Kosovo, so that during the 1970s federal aid provided almost three-quarters of Kosovo's budget and investment. Under the new constitution of 1974, the region acquired autonomous status inside Serbia, and with it the power to borrow abroad. The existing college at Priština was given university status, as well as permission to bring in lecturers from Albania proper, all of whom were advocates of a union with the fatherland. By 1981, the city of Priština had 51,000 students, so that one person in three was in full-time education.

Thanks to federal aid and their natural fecundity, the Albanians in Kosovo increased during the two decades before 1981, from 67 per cent to 77 per cent of the population. The number of Serbs over the same period fell by 30,000.[3] The sacking of the Serb police chief Ranković may have encouraged the growth of Albanian militancy, even triumphalism, for during the 1970s there were stories of Serbs being harassed into departure. Then, in March 1981, Albanian discontent exploded in riots at Priština University, and spread throughout Kosovo, leaving nine dead and more than two hundred injured. This was the start of the decade in which would be celebrated the sixth centenary of the Battle of Kosovo.

Both the federal and the republican governments were loath to clamp down on Albanian nationalism, for fear of being accused of Serbian brutality, especially since the Albanians had sympathy in the outside world. Thanks to two decades of emigration, there were hundreds of thousands of Kosovo Shiptars in Germany,

Belgium, Switzerland and the United States, as well as in north-western Yugoslavia. Like those who remained in Kosovo, they were good linguists, persuasive talkers, and always ready to tell sympathetic journalists an account of their suffering under the Serbian regime. Some of these stories were doubtless true. However, foreign observers failed to notice the fact that, although the Serbs were supposed to be the oppressors, they themselves were departing from Kosovo, complaining about the destruction of property, the desecration of graves and many assaults and rapes. Between 1981 and 1987, there was a further net emigration of Serbs from Kosovo of 30,000, leaving those who remained constituting only 10 per cent of the population.

In April 1987 some 60,000 Serbs in Kosovo signed a petition calling upon the Belgrade government to stop what they called a 'genocide', and when the police arrested one of the protest leaders in Priština, violent clashes took place and were seen on television throughout Yugoslavia. Serb fear and anger were still further inflamed by a brutal remark from the leading Albanian Communist in the province, Fadil Hoxha. To someone who had complained of the numerous rapes of Serbian women in Kosovo, Hoxha retorted with what he meant as a joke, that if more Serb women were prostitutes, there would not be so many rapes.

It was at this point that Milošević for the first time took up the cause of the Kosovo Serbs. He flew down to Priština in September 1987 and told a gathering there: 'No one is going to beat you again.' In the view of an unsympathetic but very perceptive observer, Aleksa Djilas:

> Milošević's sympathy for the plight of the Serbs in Kosovo was genuine. He is not simply a monster only interested in power, as many of his opponents characterise him. Yet other leading communists were also interested in resolving the Kosovo problem. The difference was that Milošević found the strength to overcome the fear of the masses, so characteristic of any entrenched bureaucrat. Above all, he succeeded because he

understood the power of fear and knew how to use it for his own purposes.

The mass movement of Kosovo Serbs developed spontaneously. It was not openly anti-Communist, though it could easily have become so. Milošević only gradually overcame his caution and started supporting it, but he was nonetheless the first leading Communist to do so.

With the help of the party-controlled media and the party machinery, he soon dominated the movement, discovering in the process that the best way to escape the wrath of the masses was to lead them. It was an act of political cannibalism. The opponent, Serbian nationalism, was devoured, and its spirit permeated the eater. Milošević reinvigorated the party by forcing it to embrace nationalism.[4]

After his vow at Priština, the now famous Milošević went back to Belgrade to take control of the government of Serbia. On 23 September 1987 all Yugoslavia watched on live television a gathering of the Serbian Communist Party in which most speakers devoted themselves to the ethnic problems of Kosovo. After more than twenty hours of debate, the former leaders were thrown out because they had not defended the Serbs. During the winter of 1987–8 Milošević quietly purged the Serbian Communist Party of liberals, federalists, believers in 'Brotherhood and Unity', and even some of the Croats and Slovenes working in Belgrade. Milošević and his followers took over Serbian television, *Politika* (the principal morning newspaper), and *NIN* (the most intelligent magazine), converting them all into organs of Serbian nationalism. The Serbian Writers' Club became the centre for the revision of literature and history, giving proper attention again to the time before the Second World War and even before Yugoslavia. A former Partisan general, Dobrica Ćosić, the author of several historical novels, praised the Kingdom of Serbia at the time of the Balkan wars.

Although Milošević played on the fears of millions of simple Serbs in the countryside, he ran into fierce opposition in Belgrade itself. The anti-Communist democrats, the liberal Communists and all those who feared the disintegration of Yugoslavia found themselves lumped together as dissidents. The atmosphere of Belgrade in December 1987 was patriotic and angry, with more than a hint of police repression. The traditional Gypsy bands, consisting of a fiddle, a bass and a squeeze-box, that toured the bars in the evening were now playing old favourites from the First World War such as 'March on the Drina' and 'Far Away by the Sea'. The Milošević press was starting to publish supplements, books and magazines on Serbia's struggle against the Turks from Kosovo down to the Balkan wars. The newspapers and television broadcasts ranted about the fresh Albanian demonstrations in Kosovo, and welcomed the sending of 3,000 federal militia.

For the first time since I had known Belgrade, I was warned by friends against careless talk in public places, and still more on the telephone. People were even keeping their voices down in the café of the Moskva Hotel. Outside the hotel, one of the dissidents selling the student magazines said he had twice been arrested and was now out of a job. This man, who was in his forties, said he was thinking of leaving Serbia for one of the more enlightened republics, and eighteen months later I met him again in Zagreb, selling his dissident magazines in the tunnel beneath the railway station. When I asked him what were his politics, he once more replied simply 'Communist'. Friends I had known for thirty years were talking of going to Slovenia or even to the United States, to escape what they called a 'Fascist' regime.

The atmosphere in Kosovo was still more depressing. When Rebecca West visited Priština in the 1930s, she found a dusty village where there was nothing to eat but chicken and rice. Now, thanks to the subsidies from the rest of Yugoslavia, it had become a teeming, garish city, under a pall of thin brown smoke from the local industrial chimneys. Besides building apartment blocks to contain the Albanian baby boom, the city fathers had squandered money on hideous, gimcrack prestige projects, such as a public library built to look like a mosque, and an office block in the shape of a giant bicycle rack. The walls of the bedrooms in the newly erected Grand Hotel were eaten away as though by rats, and the buttons had disappeared from the tenth-floor lifts, so that guests who did not want to risk pressing a live wire had to make their way down by the stairs in the dark. Ravens wheeled over the crumbling banks and shopping centres, as they once had done over Kosovo Polje, sated with human flesh. Dogs howled all night and at dawn there came the amplified, electronic scream of the muezzin, from concrete mosques.

In spite of the 3,000 militiamen recently brought in to keep the peace, the Albanians in Priština seemed at ease. When I asked at the Belgrade Restaurant whether they did not object to the name of the capital of their oppressors, they grinned and said: 'Everyone comes here. It's "Brotherhood and Unity" . . . Other nations hate us because we have so many children. They say the population will be too large in fifty years. All of us here have at least five, or as many as ten, brothers and sisters. We don't care. We don't care what happens in fifty years. What matters to us is honour (*besa*). If someone comes to our home, he is treated like a brother. No one can harm him. We would rather die than let anything happen to him.'

Tito was still a hero to the Albanians in Priština, so that his picture was found in every shop as it no longer was in Belgrade. Already Albanians were looking to Croats like Tito for help against their traditional foe, the Serbs. Albanian patriotism was open, even triumphalist. I saw an example of this one Sunday afternoon when the peace was shattered as a motorcade, honking horns and waving the national flag (a black, two-headed eagle on a scarlet back-ground), passed up and down the main street of Priština. It was part of a wedding feast for one of the Communist bigwigs. Roused from a siesta, I went to the only one of the three nearby cinemas that did not seem to be showing a pornographic film. The film began as a thriller set on a transcontinental express, but soon turned into an orgy in which two bandits simultaneously raped and sodomised one of the women passengers, as the audience roared Albanian words of approval.

One of the first Serbs I met in Kosovo showed me a typewritten poem beginning: 'Where once there used to be Serbs there are now militia . . .' He took me to see the Field of Blackbirds, now criss-crossed by electricity pylons and fringed by industrial chimneys. As this was December I did not see the famous red peonies, said to have taken their colouring from the blood of the fallen, like the poppies in Flanders. On the side of the Serbian Museum I read the verse in which Duke Lazar warned of the shame that would befall him:

> Who is Serb and of Serbian blood
> But did not come to Kosovo Field . . .

would have no child of his heart, whether male or female, no red wine, nor white wheat.

The Serbs were still the majority in the village of Kosovo Polje, now a suburb of Priština, although even there the Albanians were building a mosque. The Serbs I talked to believed that the Shiptars were trying to drive them out to take their property. 'You've seen my home,' one of them told me, 'it's a decent place for me and my wife and two children. If the Albanians take over, there'll be three or four of them to a room. It's disgusting, uncivilised.' Many Serbs were willing to leave if only they could get a fair price for their house and land, but the law forbade them to leave without making a sale. If they left, they left everything. One man asked if Britain would give him political asylum, then added that he would happily go to a Serbian town like Kraljevo or Kragujevac, if he could only sell his home.

One afternoon I went to a party to bid farewell to a pair of Serb newly-weds, off to Australia not just for their honeymoon but for a life in exile. To the clatter and hammer and surge of the squeeze-box and band, the guests joined in the kolo, their arms on each other's shoulders, jigging and bouncing, straight-backed and heads held high, as their feet in the circle moved through the twinkling, intricate steps. Later they sang some of the old Serb songs, though not 'Far Away by the Sea', which was banned as chauvinistic in

Kosovo. Never have I attended such a dismal wedding feast, for a young couple leaving their homeland for ever.

Before leaving Kosovo I went to Gračanica to see the exquisite church founded in 1313 by Saint Milutin, the Serbian king, whose wife Simonida is also shown in one of the murals there. These Serb warrior-saints, kings, despots and emperors, together with biblical figures, spring from the faded walls with a soaring grace that recalls El Greco, himself a painter of the Byzantine school.

A churchwarden told me about Saint Milutin the King, as he is known. 'His first wife was Bulgarian and his second wife was Greek, so they say from Carigrad' – Tsar City, as the Serbs called Constantinople and still call modern Istanbul. The monastery was now in the care of Serbian nuns who managed a farm with its own tractor and lorry as well as horses and carts. As I was leaving, the abbess charged out of the farmhouse in a temper and started to scream at me; these women are widely renowned for fierceness. From the other direction an elderly nun was driving a flock of sheep, whacking their sides with a switch as a small dog yelped in excitement. She smiled and told me not to worry about the abbess, then talked for a bit about the farm and its problems. The local authorities claimed some of their hay, and they no longer took their produce to market in Priština. Some years ago the Albanians had taken the cheese off the stall and trampled it in the mud.

In the following year, 1988, Milošević took over the Serbian Presidency and continued to play on his countrymen's character-istic persecution mania. He never attacked or abused the Albani-ans, nor later the Germans, Croats and Muslim Slavs, since Serbian persecution mania is rooted in fear rather than hatred. Even in private conversation, one rarely hears from a Serb any animosity to a people in general. Over and over again one hears that 'the Albanians and the Croats hate us, but we don't hate them' or: 'All the world hates us, us and the Jews.'

Milošević is a poor public speaker, almost as poor as Tito, and he is certainly not a rabble-rouser. However, by playing on fear, he succeeded in drawing a million people to one of his rallies in New Belgrade in October 1988. A partly orchestrated but largely spontaneous cult began to develop, accompanied by songs and jingles:

> Slobodan, they call you freedom,
>   you are loved by big and small.
> So long as Slobo walks the land,
>   the people will not be in thrall.[5]

Or another song I found quoted in a Zagreb magazine:

> So we may live in unity, Slobodan help us.
> So we may live in unity, Serbia help us.
> Slobodan, dear brother, your brothers beg you,
> Help us, brother Slobo, for we cannot hold out any longer.
> Our ancestors perished on Kosovo Field,
> As we shall, if needs be, for Serbia.
> Persecution never ceases against us, your brothers and sisters;
> Help us, brother Slobo, you are our father and mother.
> As long as there are Serbs, so will Kosovo be ours.
> Kosovo, our homeland is taken away.

Early in 1989, the bicentenary of the French Revolution and also the beginning of the end of Communism in Europe, a Belgrade publishing house brought out a volume of speeches and interviews given by Milošević. Aleksa Djilas, after remarking upon the narrow intellectual horizon and limited vocabulary of the pieces, points out that the chapter headings are reminiscent of Mao Zedong's *Little Red Book*: 'The difficulties are neither unexpected nor insurmountable', 'The future will still be beautiful, and it is not far away'. The author's use of military terms such as 'mobilisation', 'battle' and 'war' give an aggressive tone to his message. To quote Aleksa Djilas again: 'This ponderous text seemed to be very much in harmony with the author's large photograph on the book's cover. He appears stiff, inhibited, hierarchical – almost robot-like.'

In Croatia, the newspapers raged at Milošević and in particular

at his handling of the Kosovo crisis. Cartoonists depicted him as
'Slobito' (Mussolini) or 'Stalošević' (Stalin). The Croat party organ
Vjesnik, reviewing the book of collected speeches, attributed his
slogan 'Serbia will be a state or she will be nothing' to Hitler's
supposed statement that 'Germany will be a world power or she
will be nothing'. In fact it was Marshal Pilsudski who coined this
phrase with respect to Poland in 1918. In February 1989 collections
were made at offices and factories in Croatia in support of Albanian
miners on strike underground at Mitrovica in Kosovo. When the
Serbian government did away with autonomy for Kosovo and
Vojvodina, angry crowds in Croatia replied by attacking cars with
Serbian number-plates. In March 1989 fresh riots broke out in
Kosovo, leaving twenty dead and more than a hundred wounded.

Arriving in Belgrade in March 1989, I found the atmosphere of
the city strangely familiar from Trotsky's description during the
first Balkan War in 1912. He had seen in the stationers' shops
symbolic battle pictures of powerful horses smashing the Turkish
ranks. In front of a flower shop, crowds of reservists pressed
forward to read the latest reports from the front . . . He saw the
18th Regiment marching to war in their khaki uniforms and *opanki*
with green sprigs in their caps. He was shocked by the scandal in
the boulevard press and made fun of the foreign correspondents,
stealing each other's stories in the café of the Moskva Hotel.

Seventy-seven years later, the off-duty soldiers in khaki outnumbered civilians in cafés along Terazije and the other main streets,
as they quietly chatted and sipped their beer, watching the girls go
by in promenade or on roller-skates. Patriotic music blared from
the street loudspeakers. Stationers' shops were filled with pictures
and books extolling the heroes of Kosovo, the Balkan wars and the
greater ordeal of 1914–18. Groups of civilians and reservists pressed
in front of the electronic shops to watch the latest news from
Kosovo on the display TV sets. Just as in 1912 the Serbs rallied
behind the cunning Prime Minister Pašić, whom Trotsky despised,
so now they rallied behind Milošević, whose sulky features glow-
ered from thousands of posters, over the old Partisan slogan 'Death
to Fascism, Freedom to the People'.

The Belgrade press was just as malicious as it had been in Trotsky's time; the *Evening News* alleged that a woman journalist working for Belgrade TV, who also suffered from Aids, had gone to bed with fifteen of her male colleagues. Articles on Albanian heroin trading shared space with such matters as 'How to lengthen your penis'. The Moskva Hotel, which somehow had survived the bombardments of two world wars, was once more the headquarters of foreign journalists hoping to pick each other's brains. The elderly orchestra in the café, which normally stuck to Lehar and Puccini, was trying its hand at military music such as 'March on the Drina'. Over the noise, a Montenegrin was lecturing me on the Albanians: 'We've treated them too well in the past. We gave them a university. We poured money into Kosovo, more than a million dollars a day. And now they shoot our militiamen.'

Although Milošević still described himself as a Communist, and although his wife was a university lecturer in Marxist sociology, his political platform was pure Serbian nationalism, such as Trotsky encountered in 1912. There was a striking example of this in March 1989, when *Borba*, the federal Communist Party paper, hostile to Milošević, published a letter from a Croatian reader deploring the anti-German *coup d'état* of 27 March 1941, the provocation that angered Hitler into invading Yugoslavia. The reader saw this as an example of Serbian rashness, which it undoubtedly was. The Milošević newspapers castigated *Borba* for publishing what they called an unpatriotic letter, and went on to praise not only the *coup d'état* of 1941 but Princip's assassination of Archduke Franz Ferdinand, the cause of the First World War.

As well as snarling defiance at Austria and Germany, the Serbs were also warning about the danger from Islam. A Milošević author, Dehan Lučić, published a lurid book of investigative reporting called *Secrets of the Albanian Mafia*, which listed members of the Albanian secret service abroad.[6] According to Lučić, the mafia was smuggling drugs through Belgrade airport to Canada and the United States, remitting the profits to buy out the Serbs in Kosovo. On the strength of an interview with a prostitute in an Istanbul brothel, Lučić claimed that Saudi Arabian money was backing the 'Grey Wolf' Muslim fundamentalists in a bid to bring south-east Europe back into the Turkish empire.

In an interview with *NIN* magazine, Lučić expanded his views on the Muslim peril: 'Albanian criminals through the ages have plundered Orthodox churches, a crime they have justified by a jihad against unbelievers. Turkey, as the Ottoman Empire, tolerated this in order to bring them under its political influence. Today the same role is played by certain pan-Islamic states and their unofficial religious organisations.' The militant Serbs were coming to see themselves as defending not only their own nation but Christendom. 'On Kosovo, just as six hundred years ago, the battle for Europe is being fought,' proclaimed one of the newspapers run by Milošević. The Belgrade government, which for forty years had neglected or even persecuted the Serbian Church, now organised pop concerts to raise the money to build the largest basilica in the Orthodox world. Early in 1989, the authorities made arrangements to transfer the mortal remains of Duke Lazar from Valjevo to Gračanica in Kosovo, stopping at every village on the way, so that the faithful could kiss the urn. The government even hinted that it would give a school holiday for the feast of Saint Sava, the patron saint of the Serbs but not of the Roman Catholic or Muslim Yugoslavs.

Religious weddings were now back in fashion, particularly at the old Synod Church, across the road from the Question Mark inn. Priests in robes of scarlet and gold intoned the prayers as a bass choir in the gallery sang the responses in Old Slavonic. When the time came for the sacrament, the priests put silver crowns on the heads of the bride and groom, who each held two lighted candles as they proceeded round the altar. After drinking deep from the cup of Communion wine, the couple gravely embraced. Even afterwards there was none of the jollity or facetiousness of an English wedding. The king and queen for a day had the look of preparing themselves for a sacrifice rather than marriage. It made me think of the Kosovo poem, 'The Serbian Girl', in which the young woman's lover is killed on the field of battle. Outside the

Synod Church there were notices offering seats on the coaches going to Kosovo for the coming sixth centenary.

At the beginning of April, I set off for Kosovo with a Yugoslav journalist. We stayed overnight at the green and attractive town of Kragujevac, whose principal tourist sight is the mass grave of the 8,000 men and boys shot by the Germans on 20 October 1941. For many years afterwards, the dead were portrayed as Partisan heroes; now, with more justice, the Chetniks were claiming them as their own. The massacre was the major justification for Draža Mihailov-ić's decision not to pursue an all-out war against the Axis. The restaurant where we dined had one of the best Gypsy bands I have ever heard, consisting of five dark and distinguished-looking men in moustaches. Since the executives of the local car-works who were present hailed from all parts of Yugoslavia, the band played the appropriate music, whether a Bosnian love lament, a Slovene jig or a Dalmatian shanty, hinting of salt and fish and wine. The restaurant was a pleasant reminder that ordinary Yugoslavs, as distinct from their politicians, were perfectly able to get on together.

After Kragujevac, we started to climb into the mountains of southern Serbia, towards that border region where Turks and Slavs, Muslims and Christians have fought each other for six hundred years, and where in the Second World War the Chetniks and Partisans fought each other as well as the Axis invaders. Just beyond Kraljevo, we stopped at a café to eat lamb from the spit and hear the talk of the genial landlord: 'There are many Albanians here and Muslim Slavs. We get on fine. In fact I never serve pork or have it cooked in the kitchen because it gives offence to Muslim customers. We've all got to live together, isn't that right? What's happening in Kosovo is not the fault of the Albanians. It's the politicians and the economy. The politicians have given them too many things free and they don't want to work any more.'

The landlord and his friends had certain specific complaints about the Kosovo Albanians. Many with Yugoslav passports had gone to West Germany and then, instead of finding a job, had asked for political asylum: 'The Germans say they will look into the case but meanwhile the Albanians aren't allowed to work, while the German government gives them food and lodging. The Germans work but the Albanians idle. Naturally the Germans are getting fed up with this, for the Albanians aren't real political refugees. They've nothing to fear in this country. Now we're afraid that, in order to keep out these Albanians, the West Germans are going to make all Yugoslavs have a visa.'

A few miles further south we made a detour to visit one of the sacred places of the Serbs. The founder of their medieval empire, Grand Prince Stefan Nemanja (c.1113–99) established a monastery in the remote and beautiful gorge of the River Studenica, at a place that his son Saint Sava described as 'a deserted hunting-ground for wild beasts'. It seemed on an April morning, like an enchanted woodland, overwhelmed by a great profusion of trees, flowers and blossom, the mountain air loud with the sound of insects and birds. The Nemanjas built here the Church of the Virgin with its renowned frescos, a smaller chapel and Serbia's first hospital. This monastery in the mountains remained the religious centre of the Serbs, who had no political capital. The monastery survived the Turkish occupation partly because the Sultans valued it as a place to breed falcons. The Orthodox Church is strongly conservationist. The abbot of Studenica did not want to talk about Kosovo, but he was eager to get our support in opposing the plan for a hydroelectric dam on the river.

The Serbs are ever aware of the damage that man can do to nature. Crossing from Serbia proper to Kosovo province, one finds an ecological ruin. One moment the hills at the side of the road are verdant with dense forest; the next they are bare stone. Perhaps this is proof of the old Serb adage that 'no grass grows where the Turk trod'; it may be a result of Albanian methods of farming and tree-felling, whose dire effects I saw the following year in Albania proper. It provided a gloomy introduction to Kosovo, even before we met the tanks and the truckloads of troops in combat gear.

Priština was a sadder and grimmer place than when I had been there sixteen months earlier. Tanks were parked outside the Grand Hotel. Pinned to the trees in the high street were mourning notices and photographs of the militiamen who had been killed in the fighting.

In the ice-cream parlour behind the Grand Hotel, I talked to a young Serb teacher and her lawyer husband, who dandled the baby as he described the recent confrontation: 'Have you heard about the Albanian girl they're turning into a martyr? She went for a militiaman with one of her stiletto-heeled shoes, trying to put his eye out. She left a big dent in his forehead before he shot her. It was hard for the militia to fire over people's heads but they should have done so . . . I've nothing against Albanians. An Albanian was our best man. I used to go out drinking with another Albanian friend. Now their own people threaten them if they talk to us.'

His wife blamed the trouble on the economy: 'Twenty years ago we were well off. Now we're desperately trying to pay for food and the baby's clothes. We don't have any luxuries. I don't mean a weekend in Paris, we wouldn't dream of that, but a dinner out . . . Once Tito came here when I was a little girl and I was photographed giving him flowers. I was so proud. But the politicians did nothing for us. All they did was build these useless skyscrapers, these shopping precincts all falling to bits and littered with broken bottles. Look at them!'

Most of the guests at the Grand Hotel were army officers, UDBA or Belgrade officials. A Serb who was running an economic enterprise said that he still had Albanian friends and was trying to learn the language, 'though it's a bastard to learn'. He blamed the troubles on the Republic of Albania, which he alleged had 15,000 people living illegally in Kosovo. I got to know one of the few Albanians left in the Kosovo government; he stayed at the Grand for his own protection. He was a brave and decent man who still believed in Yugoslavia, but now he knew that his position was hopeless.

At the end of my stay, I went with the Yugoslav journalist to visit the Gračanica church that soon would be receiving the mortal remains of Duke Lazar. Across the road from the entrance I noticed a new 'Café 1389' and a bookstall selling *The Battle of Kosovo: Myth, Legend and Reality*. Four little Albanian boys were trying to rifle the church letter-box, as we went in search of the abbess. As on my previous visit, she turned out to be in a filthy temper: 'How dare you try to come to someone else's house? Have you no manners? What makes you think you can behave so rudely?' Once more I was rescued by kindly old Sister Jephremia, whom I had seen before with a flock of sheep.

Sister Jephremia took us into the church and allowed us to get a close look at the frescos, which had been very much damaged over the last six centuries. The Turks had defaced some. Peasant women are said to have rubbed off the paint to use as a treatment for eye diseases. By far the worst harm had been done by recent vandals scratching hearts and initials and sometimes even their names with a date. It was only in the last few years that the State had tried to protect this wonderful building. In 1989 the politicians in Belgrade were boasting about their mission to save Christian Europe from Islam, but Sister Jephremia told us a different story:

'The Turks came here in 1389, the year of the Battle of Kosovo. They did some damage then and over the next few hundred years. But they weren't as bad as the Bulgarians who came here. Yes, the Bulgarians were Christians like the Serbs, but they were worse than the Turks. We all know the Turks are our enemies. We have more to fear from our friends behind our backs . . . It was bad for us after the war. They [the Communists] didn't want to let us stay here. They asked why shouldn't they pull the monastery down. They billeted the council here. The head man really hated us, and they desecrated the church.'

When I asked if these people were Serbs or Albanians, Sister Jephremia answered:

'The Serbs were the worst. One Albanian said to me that if anyone treated a mosque like they had treated this church he would have killed him. Then in 1952 the Marshal [Tito] came on a visit here. He was photographed outside, you can see the picture. There was a man here, a learned man who spoke six languages, and he dared to speak to the Marshal. He said the church should be restored, if not for religion, as a historical monument. The Marshal agreed.

'But in that same year they brought the army reserves and put them into the monastery. They forced us out at gunpoint. So we decided to go and protest in Belgrade. We had no help from the Patriarch. It was just our idea. I was very young and naïve and didn't realise what a risk I took, going to see people and protesting. We didn't see Tito but we were received by Ranković. I don't know what he thought of us in our black clothes, but he listened to us. I was so naïve, I didn't realise that they might have killed us. However, I'd have gone straight to heaven. Since then, more sensible people have come into government . . .'

Here Sister Jephremia crossed herself then looked at me with a smile:

'You've been here before, some years ago, I remember.'

'And I remember you. You were driving a flock of sheep.'

'Yes, it was winter. Now the sheep are up in the mountains. But when you were here last, I didn't talk like I've talked today, did I?'

No, she had not. Until this visit it had not occurred to me that in seven centuries Gračanica had never suffered as badly as it did under the Communists after the Second World War. We gave Sister Jephremia some money towards the church, and she in turn gave us two bottles of wine and said she would pray for us.

A few weeks later the mortal remains of Duke Lazar were brought to Gračanica, and then on 28 June 1989, almost a million Serbs gathered at Kosovo Field for the sixth centenary of the battle. By now the fear of the Serbs in Serbia proper had spread to the Orthodox Christians in Croatia and Bosnia-Hercegovina, reviving memories of the Second World War. Because of the self-fulfilling nature of persecution mania, the Serbs in Croatia did in fact start to suffer harassment, especially after the rise to power of Fran jo Tudjman in 1990. And as the reports came back of Serbs being beaten up, their houses burnt and motor cars pushed into the sea, Milošević played on fear to his own advantage. Just as Milošević played on Serb fears, so Tudjman exploited Croat hatred of 'Chetniks'. The two men needed each other to stay in power, and were in fact quite close political friends.

Millions of Serbs were opposed to Milošević and wanted to

remain part of Yugoslavia. The last chance to get rid of him came in March 1991, when a huge crowd gathered in front of the Belgrade TV station, protesting against its use for Milošević propaganda. Since the government had imposed a ban on public meetings in old Belgrade, Milošević sent in tanks and troops who first used tear-gas, then fired on the demonstrators, killing two. After this first rally, organised by the opposition political parties, a larger and separate demonstration began in Marshal Tito Boulevard, now generally known by its nineteenth-century name of Terazije (The Scissors). They kept up a night-and-day vigil similar to the demonstrations the previous year in Beijing's Tiananmen Square. But whereas the Chinese were protesting against the Communist system, the Serbs were denouncing chauvinism and militarism.

By the time I reached Belgrade, the crowd had begun to disperse in a spirit of hope and confidence; Milošević had been forced to sack his placemen on the executive of Belgrade TV, and to stop jamming the Yutel channel from Sarajevo, which gave a news service free from Serb or Croat propaganda. Milošević had also lost control of the main Belgrade paper, *Politika*. Belgrade public opinion praised the moderation and sense of the young protesters. Instead of chanting the old Serbian battle hymns or doggerel complaints of persecution, they called for liberty to the sound of their own Slavonic pop music. Actors and TV presenters, rather than politicians, caught the mood of the crowd. Nor were these people anti-Communist dissidents, such as the world had seen in Russia, China, East Germany and Czechoslovakia. Paradoxically, many of them were looking back to Tito's Yugoslavia as a more tolerant society. Only the old, such as Milovan Djilas, remembered the time when Yugoslavia was an oppressive Communist state.

The demonstrations especially delighted those who still believed in Yugoslavia, standing above national chauvinism. The Zagreb magazine *Danas* hailed what it called a 'velvet Revolution', similar to the recent events in Czechoslovakia. It recounted the touching story that an Albanian baker had handed out free bread and cakes to the young protesters, to show his appreciation of their goodwill.

One of the headlines in *Danas* summed up the situation in Belgrade as 'Milošević on his knees'.

So indeed it seemed at the time. For some days Milošević did not even dare to appear in public. When he tried to stage a counter-rally in New Belgrade, at the place where a million had gathered eighteen months earlier, scarcely 5,000 people turned up, most of them old, dejected and bitter. Many were soldiers and their families living in nearby flats, who feared that the overthrow of Milošević would threaten their jobs, pensions and privileges. The few young men in the crowd looked shamefaced in front of the TV cameras. The vast majority of the city's youth, including the students living in New Belgrade, had come to the old city to join the rally against Milošević and against a war. As someone remarked to me: 'In New Belgrade, age; in Old Belgrade, youth.'

19

Towards Disaster
in Croatia

During a stay in Zagreb in March 1981, I went as usual to visit the twin-spired Gothic cathedral which stands at the foot of the hill in the Upper Town. On this occasion, I was surprised to see a notice on one of the side gates; 'Danger of Death. Entry Forbidden', beneath a skull and crossbones. A similar sign was posted over the north gate, while over the west front hung two metal notices warning of danger of death. Apprehensive, I ventured inside the cathedral and started to read the appeals for money towards the repair and upkeep of this ancient building. Three loose stones had been laid out on the floor to indicate that the trouble lay in the roof and masonry; but the structural weaknesses were hardly unusual and did not seem to constitute a danger of death.

It soon become clear that the skull and crossbones had little to do with the masonry and much to do with the pilgrims kneeling at prayer beside the marble shrine of Cardinal Stepinac, now adorned with a Meštrović statue, bunches of flowers and dozens of lighted candles. The man who had been in Lepoglava prison when I had first come to Zagreb in 1951, and had died under house arrest nine years later, was now a cult as well as a candidate for beatification and sainthood.

This veneration of Stepinac may or may not have been justified but it was scarcely new; so what was the cause of the confrontation? It was common knowledge in Yugoslavia that Tito himself had tried to reach an arrangement with Stepinac after the war; that he only reluctantly ordered the trial; that he wanted Stepinac to go into exile rather than stay under house arrest; and that he permitted the tomb in Zagreb Cathedral. Relations between the Vatican and the Yugoslav state had grown even warmer since Tito's death. In December 1980 the President of the new Presidium met and got on well with Pope John Paul II, inviting him to the tercentenary of the Marian apparitions at Marija Bistrica. Yet three months later Zagreb Cathedral was under siege.

The man responsible for the fresh attack on the Roman Catholic Church, and in particular on the reputation of Cardinal Stepinac, was Jakov Blažević, President of the new Presidium of Croatia and an old Party workhorse who had made his name as the public prosecutor during the trial of Stepinac and others. Like many old politicians, Blažević had recently published his self-congratulatory memoirs, of which the latest volume had just appeared. On 27 January 1981, in a radio broadcast to plug his book, Blažević made an intemperate attack not just on Stepinac but on the Catholic Church, its priests, the laity and especially those 'degenerate' Croats living in exile abroad. On 30 January 800 priests attended a congress to give their unanimous backing to Zagreb's incumbent archbishop, Cardinal Franjo Kuharić. On 10 February, the twenty-first anniversary of Stepinac's death, a congregation of 7,000 attended Mass in Zagreb Cathedral, the building one was supposed to enter in danger of death.

Meanwhile the Croatian Party newspaper *Vjesnik* was serialising Blažević's memoirs, of which I read several instalments during my stay. The book is depressing both in its bigotry and in its stale Marxist jargon. Stepinac is blamed for his kulak origins and for having served in the Austro-Hungarian army, though both things applied also to Tito. The pre-war Peasant Party is given inverted commas, although it enjoyed more public support than the Communists ever did.

In an article that I wrote at the time, I asked the rhetorical question: Why should Stepinac become a figure of conroversy twenty-one years after his death? And does the dispute pose a threat to the Communist system or even to Yugoslavia as a state? The article in which I attempted to answer these questions now strikes me as far too sympathetic towards Stepinac and the Church. Although I remarked that the Archbishop of Sarajevo 'not only condoned but encouraged the massacre of the Serbs in Bosnia-Hercegovina', I wrote of Stepinac: 'To Catholics he became a martyr and even those who disliked Stepinac knew that his crime was not that he fraternised with the fascists but that he refused to fraternise with the Communists.'[2]

At that time I did not know, and perhaps subconsciously did not want to know, the terrible truth about the Croatian Catholic Church. Nor did I understand the extent of the nostalgia for an independent Croatia. After the death of Tito the collective Presidium continued to crack down on nationalism among the Croats as well as among the Serbs, actually arresting the student Dobroslav Paraga during the ceremonies at the time of Tito's funeral. During this and subsequent periods in prison, Paraga was portrayed in the West as an idealistic democrat, but he later emerged as head of the black-uniformed HOS militia and advocate of a Greater Croatia.

In 1981, the year of the government's contretemps with the Catholic Church, ex-General Tudjman was once more in trouble. Becoming frustrated by his enforced silence in Yugoslavia, Tudjman decided to air his views in a book published in English in the United States.[3] As a punishment for the views expressed, Tudjman was sentenced to three years in prison in Yugoslavia and five years of loss of freedom to publish, but nonetheless was acclaimed as a hero and martyr by Croats in the diaspora. Like all Tudjman's writing, *Nationalism in Contemporary Europe* is turgid, pedantic and always ambiguous, so it is never quite clear if he is voicing his own or somebody else's opinion. This is what he says of the Independent State of Croatia (NDH):

[It] was at first the main obstacle to both the Chetnik movement with its plans for the re-establishment of a Karadjeordjević, unitary Yugoslavia and to the Partisan movement with its programme of creating a new quite different Yugoslavia on federal principles. However, the notion of the NDH as a lasting solution offering them their own state was soon fundamentally undermined in the eyes of the Croat people by Pavelić's territorial concessions to Italy and his vassal-like attitude towards Germany, and in particular by the methods of the Ustasha movement's fascist reign.[4]

Needless to say, the NDH was not an obstacle to, but the principal cause of, the Chetniks and Partisans, who in 1941 were defending their lives rather than planning a post-war constitution for Yugoslavia. It is true that many Croats, notably Archbishop Stepinac, grieved over the cession of land to Mussolini, but far from having a 'vassal-like attitude towards Germany', Pavelić shocked his ally by launching a reckless and vicious attack on the Serbs.

Tudjman goes on to justify the inclusion of Bosnia-Hercegovina within the NDH 'on the basis of a common history and the fact that they constituted a geo-political whole'. He admits that 'the Serbian Orthodox population constituted a plurality (about 44 per cent) while the Croatian Catholics made up only about 23 per cent of the population and the Moslems 33 per cent'. (Tudjman refers to the pre-war population, before the massacre of the Serbs reduced their percentage of the total.) However, Tudjman then tries to redress the balance by saying that, although the Serbs were the largest single group, 'they were in the minority compared with the ethnically largely identical Catholic and Moslem population'. On the next page Tudjman develops this racial theory, based on the writings of Starčević and Pavelić: 'An objective examination of the numerical composition of the population of Bosnia-Hercegovina cannot ignore that the majority of the Moslems is in its ethnic character and speech incontrovertibly of Croatian origin.'[5] This is the shaky ground for Tudjman's claim that Bosnia-Hercegovina belongs to Croatia.

With regard to Jasenovac and the other concentration camps, Tudjman employs an argument dear to defenders of Hitler. He quotes highly inflated estimates of the people who died there, before giving an estimate that is very much too low:

> Year after year for decades now the assertion has been rammed into the heads of the Yugoslav and world public almost every day . . . by means of the media (press, TV and radio), that during the NDH, in just one camp at Jasenovac, there were at least 700,000 men, women and children killed and that they were mostly Serbs . . . it is a historical fact that in the war, in all the camps and prisons, about 60,000 people from the territory of Croatia perished and they were of all nationalities: Croatian anti-fascists, Serbs, Jews, gypsies and others.[6]

Again, this is a specious argument. Jasenovac camp had been so little publicised even in Yugoslavia that I for one had not knowingly heard of it until the late 1980s, when I began to study books on the Independent State of Croatia. The outside world had never heard of Jasenovac.

While playing down the enormity of the crimes committed against the Serbs by the Ustasha, Tudjman plays up the real or imagined slights against the Croats under the Tito regime. He lists a number of prominent 'Communist revolutionaries' who were deposed, including Hebrang, suspected of being a Russian agent, and Večeslav Holjević 'whose main offence was that he fought to keep the International Trade Fair in Zagreb'. Since the Trade Fair remained in Zagreb, perhaps there was some other reason for Holjević's dismissal. Tudjman complains that in 1981 'every one of the nations of the SFRY [Socialist Federal Republic of Yugoslavia] has its own academy of science and arts except the Croats who are obliged to have theirs, the oldest of all, called Yugoslav in accordance with the Strossmayerian integrationist illusion of the last century that the name would be accepted by both the Croats and all the other South-Slav nations.[7] In the tradition of Ante Starčević, the prophet of Croat nationalism a hundred years before, Tudjman rejects the Yugoslav vision of Bishop Strossmayer, and with it the dream of reconciling the Orthodox and Catholic churches.

During the 1980s, two spectres from the Ustasha past returned to haunt modern Croatia. Early in 1986, a group of American Jews succeeded in getting the extradition to Yugoslavia of Andrija Artuković, the former Ustasha Minister of the Interior. Forty years after he made his escape to Ireland, then on to California, the 'Yugoslav Himmler' was put on trial in Zagreb. Since he was ill and virtually senile, Artuković could not give coherent testimony, but his presence alone alarmed the Yugoslav government. During the trial a law was hastily passed whereby anyone who had been accused of genocide could not be buried in consecrated ground, for fear that Artuković might die before sentence was passed and become the focus of a martyr's cult.[8] In May 1986 he was sentenced to execution by firing-squad but remained in prison until his death from natural causes in January 1988.

Another ghost from the Independent State of Croatia was Kurt Waldheim, the former Secretary-General of the United Nations and now the President of Austria. There were rumours in the Western press that during the Second World War Waldheim had acted disreputably while serving in Yugoslavia, although there were no specific charges. In fact he had been a German intelligence officer attached to Army Group 'E' in Banja Luka, some twenty miles from Jasenovac. In 1942 he had taken part in the action against the Serbs in the Kozara region in which tens of thousands were killed and the rest taken off to the death camp. For this campaign and his other services to the NDH, Waldheim was awarded the Silver Medal of the Crown of King Zvonimir by Ante Pavelić. In his *Wehrmacht* reports, Waldheim made constant reference to the Ustasha 'cleansing' of Serbs in Bosnia-Hercegovina, though forty years later he called this 'humanitarian resettlement'.[9]

Austria became an important patron of Franjo Tudjman, when he was free to travel abroad in 1987. In western Europe, Canada and the United States, Tudjman made many valuable friends in the exiled Croat communities who later would give him financial, diplomatic and public-relations support towards his election campaign. Meanwhile Tudjman finished writing his most ambitious book, published in Zagreb in 1989 as *Bespuća povijesne zbiljnosti*.[10] As far as one can make any sense of his rambling and turbid thought processes, Tudjman appears to be saying that violence and genocide are the mainsprings of human behaviour: 'Whenever a movement, people, state, alliance, or ideology faces an adversary that threatens its survival or the establishment of its own supremacy, everything possible will be done, and all means available used, to subdue or destroy the opponent. In such confrontations, nothing but the risk of self-destruction precludes a resort to genocide.'[11]

A new and disturbing feature of *Bespuća* is Tudjman's apparent obsession with the Jews and his conviction that they are a 'genocidal' people. Like many revisionist writers on Hitler's policy towards the Jews, Tudjman is careful to sound objective and non-judgemental:

> The idea of the world mission of the German 'Herrenvolk', seen as the highest race, was also based on the assumption of a 'final solution' of the Jewish question, meaning that the Jews were meant to disappear definitively from German and European history. An explanation of this should probably be sought – in addition to historical roots – in the fact that German imperialism, for geopolitical reasons, was primarily directed towards the domination of Europe. As such, Hitler's 'new European order' could be justified by the need both to remove the Jews (more or less undesirable in all European countries), as well as to correct the Versailles (French-English) wrong.[12]

Tudjman describes with apparent approval the plan to send the Jews of Europe to Madagascar, which failed when Hitler's armies became bogged down in Russia: 'As such, during the third year of the Second World War [1942], the leadership of the Third Reich proceeded with the idea of the 'Final Solution' – i.e. the exclusion of Jews from German and European life by way of gradual extermination.'[13]

Tudjman delves into the Old Testament to prove his thesis that for the Jews, 'genocidal violence is a natural apparition, in line with man and his social nature . . . Violence is not only permissible, it is advisable; moreover it is in accord with mighty Jehovah's words; it is to be used whenever necessary for the revival or renewal of the kingdom of the chosen people . . .' From the Old Testament, Tudjman turns to the treatment of Palestinian Arabs in modern Israel: 'After all that it endured in history, especially its terrible suffering during the Second World War, the Jewish people will, within a very short time, initiate such a cruel genocidal policy, which can be justifiably called "Judeo-Nazism".' Then Tudjman adds: 'And all this is happening in the mid-1980s when world Jewry goes on having to remind us of its victims during the "holocaust", even by trying to prevent former Secretary-General Kurt Waldheim from being elected President of Austria!'[14]

One eerie chapter of *Bespuća* suggests that the Jews helped to run Jasenovac concentration camp. Ignoring the great mass of published testimony on Jasenovac and the other camps in the complex, Tudjman relies on just two witnesses, Vojislav Prnjatović of Sarajevo and Ante Ćiliga, a former Croatian Communist. The first of these is quoted at great length in the two volumes of documentation in Antun Miletić's book on Jasenovac, which do not however contain the passage cited by Tudjman to the effect that the day-to-day management of the camp, including the purchase of food supplies, was left to a group of 'free prisoners', all of whom were Jews. Tudjman quotes Prnjatović as saying: 'The free prisoners do not live within the camp itself, but in the town of Jasenovac, in private flats, to which they can also bring their families. As such, they live together with their families freely in Jasenovac. Unfortunately this is only the case for Jews.'[15] On the evidence of Prnjatović, Tudjman says that because the Jews came early they managed to grab the important jobs in the prison hierarchy, intriguing against the other prisoners so that the Serbs, besides suffering at the hands of the Ustasha, 'suffer as well at the hands of the Jews'. Tudjman then quotes Prnjatović: 'The Jew remains a Jew, even in the Jasenovac camp. In the camp they kept all their defects except that they were more visible. Selfishness, craftiness, unreliability, stinginess, deceit and secrecy are their main characteristics.' Tudjman then adds his own comment:

> This judgement of Prnjatović's seems exaggerated, one might even say that it is anti-Semitic in character, but other witnesses speak in a similar way. Some of the Jewish camp officials were even armed and took part in the killings. What is more, Jews to a large extent ran the 'selection process', i.e. they chose which prisoners would be liquidated and they even partly handled the executions.

The other main witness quoted by Tudjman is Ćiliga, who says that the Jews ran the camp 'from the highest to the lowest of positions – from the manager down to the cowherd, except for rare exceptions'. Ćiliga is quoted as saying that Jews joined with the Ustasha in murdering Gypsies in order to steal their gold. Again, quoting at times from Ćiliga, Tudjman offers his own startling explanation of why the Jews were favoured at Jasenovac:

> The fact that the camp's management was left to the Jews was in contradiction with the official anti-Semitism of Pavelić's regime, which Hitler had bound him to. This is because, in one way or another, 'basically Pavelić's party was philosemitic, specifically it was the "Jewish Party" among the Croats', also because Jews 'were the least important and least dangerous opponents in Croatia'.[16]

It is true that some of the Ustasha leaders had Jewish blood, or like Pavelić, married a partly Jewish wife. But 'philosemitic' they were not.

At the elections held in Croatia in April 1990, Tudjman was given an overwhelming mandate to lead his country to independence from Yugoslavia. Neither during the election campaign nor in a subsequent referendum did Tudjman offer assurances to the Orthodox population, most of them in the old Military Frontier or on the Adriatic coast. In August of that year the Serbs in Knin armed themselves and took control of the town, effectively cutting the main road and railway link between Zagreb and the sea. The strategic importance of Knin had been understood by Emperor Diocletian, who built his palace at nearby Split; it was one of the towns where the kings of Croatia held occasional court in the tenth and eleventh centuries. Later it served as a base to the *Uskok* ('Escaper') brigands who preyed on the Venetians along the Dalmatian coast. In 1877 Knin was a haven for Orthodox refugees from Bosnia-Hercegovina and also a base for the *Manchester Guardian* correspondent Arthur Evans. He called the locals a 'wild Morlach population – robbers driven seaward from the interior, pirates driven inland from the sea, repressed and corrupted later by Turkish, Venetian and Austrian despotism'.[17]

Although the people of Knin call the region the Krajina (Frontier), it was never actually part of the old Austrian *Militärgrenze*. During the Second World War, Knin was the base for the Orthodox priest and Chetnik commander Duke Momčilo Djujić, who led his army to Italy in 1945. They eventually settled in Britain, so that in August 1990 events at Knin were followed with great anxiety by the 40,000 Krajina Serbs living in West London and several provincial cities. Delegations from Knin arrived at a Serb bed-and-breakfast house on Holland Park Avenue; a shop in Queensway that specialises in bullet-proof vests was soon to do good business with British Serbs preparing to return to see their relatives in Krajina.

In October 1990 I went to Zagreb to write about the return of the huge equestrian statue of Governor Jelačić, removed from its plinth by the Communists in 1947. Even three weeks before the official ceremony, Jelačić Square, as it was once more called, was gripped by high excitement. Curious bystanders, rather like those who gawp for hours at bulldozers excavating a building site, stared at the plinth, without even reading the notices on the railing that gave an outline of the career of Baron Joseph Jelačić von Buzim (1801–59). In the revolutionary year of 1848, when Jelačić was governor both of the Military Frontier and of civilian Croatia, he led an army of *Grenzer* to put down rebellions first in Hungary and then in Vienna. As a reward from the Habsburg Emperor, Jelačić got his title, the statue and even a march in his honour by Johann Strauss, though this was never as popular as the 'Radetzky March', named after the brute who crushed the rebellion in Italy. The bookshops in and around Jelačić Square showed portraits of him, and coloured contemporary prints of the *Grenzer* in Hungary and Vienna, shaggy mustachioed giants in breeches and sandals, leaning on long-barrelled guns and no doubt dreaming of plunder.

Like many nations that try to invent or improve their history, the Croats had got it all slightly wrong. In the first place Jelačić was a blundering general who failed to defeat the Magyar rebellion and had to retire to Vienna to crush the virtually unarmed students. Jelačić and Radetzky may have been heroes in Zagreb and at the Habsburg court, but they were hated by liberals and nationalists in the rest of Europe for having opposed Kossuth in Budapest and Garibaldi in Rome. The 'Croatians', as the *Grenzer* were called, had long been feared for their valour in war and pitiless rape and slaughter of the civilians, as Thackeray noted in *Esmond*, his novel set at the time of the Duke of Marlborough's campaigns. From 1848, the 'Croatians' shared with the Cossacks of Russia a reputation as foes of freedom.

There was also the irony, seemingly lost on the people of Zagreb, that *Grenzer* 'Croatians' were almost all Orthodox Christians, and therefore what they would now call 'Serbs'. As I have pointed out in an earlier chapter, Jelačić was a proto-Yugoslav and an admirer of Serbia, then struggling for its independence from Turkey. During the crisis of 1848, Jelačić played host to the Orthodox Patriarch Rajačić, then leading a Serb revolt against Hungary.[18]

On the Sunday after I arrived in Zagreb, the great bronze statue was brought down the hill from the northern suburb where it had been stored, accompanied by a joyful throng including a choir in folklore costumes and horsemen and horsewomen dressed as hussars. As the crowd approached the golden Madonna and Child in front of the twin-towered Zagreb Cathedral, all the bells burst out in a jubilant peal, and the priests and nuns came out into the street to clap and cheer. The statue and the procession at last reached Jelačić Square, where a bigger crowd was already refreshing itself from barrels of white wine.

Throughout the following week, in cafés and bars and on the open streets of the fine old city centre, I listened to yells and roars of Croatian chauvinists, for such people seldom speak in anything less than a bellow. A young man clutching an eight-foot medieval Croatian banner, which threatened to smash the ceiling lamp, implored me to 'tell the people of England that Serbs are primitive, savage, warmongering, idle and Balkan'. 'Look what the Serbs have done to the Albanians in Kosovo,' was another refrain. 'We welcome Albanians here as friends.' When my article later appeared in the *Independent Magazine,* the photograph of the crowd showed two men waving the blood-red Albanian flag with a black, two-headed eagle.

The Serbs at Knin were by definition both Chetniks and Bolsheviks. When I suggested that the Serbs might entertain genuine fears for their safety, I found myself shouted down. A schoolmaster I met became incandescent with fury when I suggested that Serb and Croat were much the same language. The Croat chauvinism, the obsession with ancient flags and battles, was still more depressing than the Serb equivalent I had listened to in Belgrade the previous year, because it was much more aggressive. It was only occasionally comic. 'Who invented the Zeppelin? A Croat! Who invented the ball-point pen? A Croat! Who invented the rotating magnetic field? A Croat!' This was a reference to Nikola Tesla, later denounced as a Serb from the Krajina.

Some of the conversations were not at all funny. On two occasions, groups of Croats expressed their support for the IRA and, when I objected, said that the British were just as bad as the Serbs. In a police bar, I was plied with drink by detectives who said that they no longer had to look out for terrorists, since 'they are all in Belgrade'. In fact the Ustasha who murdered the Yugoslav diplomat in Stockholm, and may have blown up a Yugoslavian airliner, were said to be back in Croatia and in favour. Some of the revellers seemed anxious to make my flesh creep. 'In the war we were up to our knees in blood,' said an elderly Croat from Bosnia, 'and this time it'll be up to our necks.' A young man said proudly that World War Three could well begin in Yugoslavia, just as the First World War had done.

On the square in front of Zagreb Cathedral, Albanians and Gypsies were selling umbrellas, knives of the sort once carried by the Ustasha, and 'God and Croatia' T-shirts. At Mass on Sunday morning, which I heard in the overspill congregation, Cardinal Kuharić called on the worshippers to remember the Church's 1,300-year history. In the clerical press, he denounced the Serbian Orthodox Bishop of Croatia for having said that his flock were living in fear of persecution and death. A few months later Cardinal Kuharić told the London *Times* that only a 'handful' of Serbs were killed in the wartime Independent State of Croatia.[19]

In the subsequent article that I wrote for the *Independent Magazine*, I tried to explain why the Serbs in Croatia were apprehensive, why they were remembering the massacres that occurred during the Second World War, but nevertheless I ended on a foolishly optimistic note: 'Yet for various reasons, I think there is small chance of the horror repeating itself. The Ustasha were able to seize power in 1941 only because of the German occupation . . . The Serbs at Knin and throughout Croatia can still rely for protection on the largely Serb-officered army of Yugoslavia.'[20]

During the winter of 1990–1, Tudjman made final plans for a declaration of independence, at first intended for 10 April, the fiftieth anniversary of the founding of the Pavelić Independent State of Croatia. He now had the unofficial backing of the Slovenes (who also were planning independence), Austria, Hungary and most important of all the Vatican. Although the governments of the European Community and the United States were still committed to the integrity of Yugoslavia, much of their press and public opinion, especially in Germany, was now sympathetic to the Croatian cause. At the time of the breakup of the Soviet Union, Tudjman was able to make an analogy between Croatia and the Baltic states, hoping to free themselves from alien 'Bolshevik' rule.

Tudjman continued to benefit from the ever more brutal and truculent statements from Belgrade.

The only obstacle to Tudjman's progress towards independence was raised by the demonstrators in Belgrade in March 1991, and the seeming likelihood of Milošević's downfall. For if their principal bogyman vanished why should the Croats demand independence? According to the *Guardian* correspondent Ian Traynor, sometime in late March or early April 1991, Milošević and Tudjman 'got together secretly over whisky and cigars' to discuss the partition between them of Bosnia-Hercegovina, as had been done by the Serb and Croat politicians in 1939.[21] Whether or not this meeting took place, the student riots in Belgrade had upset Tudjman's plan for a declaration of independence on 10 April, and the date was put back to June.

Meanwhile, In May 1991 Tudjman accepted an invitation to London to get the public seal of approval from Margaret Thatcher who, though no longer Prime Minister, was nevertheless by far the most respected politician in western Europe, if not the world. In turn, Mrs Thatcher saw in the furtherance of an independent Croatia the means of revenging herself on her enemies in the Conservative Party, as well as stopping the drift towards a federal Europe. She hoped that the break-up of Yugoslavia would demonstrate the futility of the federal system, as well as dividing the European Community. The mainly Thatcherite Centre for Policy Studies invited President Tudjman to London on 7 May, to give a speech, later published in an extended version as 'Croatia at the Crossroads: In Search of a Democratic Confederacy'.

According to his host, Lord Griffiths of Fforestfach, during his visit President Tudjman had useful discussions with the Foreign Secretary Douglas Hurd and 'a long, informal talk' with Mrs Thatcher before making his speech, 'which was widely reported by the national press and relayed to television programmes throughout Europe'. Connoisseurs of Tudjman's writing recognised his obscure but slightly menacing turn of phrase and his weird interpretation of history, as in his references to Winston Churchill:

History teaches us that in this world there can be no good without evil, and no light without darkness; there can be no heavenly splendour without the baseness of the Devil, and no freedom without repression . . . Not even at the height of her mighty kingdom, during the Middle Ages, did Croatia initiate wars of conquest. Based on the historic tradition of Croatian statehood, the Independent State of Croatia was established during World War II within the frame of Hitler's New European Order . . . Winston Churchill was deeply aware of the irreconcilable national, as well as the cultural and social, division within Yugoslavia. Based on the experience of the British in Balkan politics, an agreement was reached with Stalin in 1944, negotiating a fifty-fifty division of the spheres of influence in the geopolitical region. This agreement by itself acknowledged the deep, historical, political and cultural divisions between the two areas; on the one hand, the Western-oriented, Christian, Croatian-Slovenian region, and on the other hand, the Eastern-oriented Byzantine and Orthodox regions of Serbia, Montenegro and Macedonia.[22]

Needless to say, Churchill had no such understanding of Yugoslavia. His fifty-fifty deal with Stalin concerned the balance of influence between Russia and the West, not the geographical border inside Yugoslavia. As Churchill knew, in two world wars the Serbs were allies of the Western powers France and Britain, while Croatia aligned with the Central powers of Germany and Austria-Hungary.

An explanatory gloss to the sayings of Dr Tudjman was given by Norman Stone, Professor of Modern History at Oxford, and Mrs Thatcher's main adviser on European affairs:

Most Croats, like their neighbours in Slovenia, now wish to break with Yugoslavia and join 'Europe' in association with Austria. Official 'Europe' does not care for this, the Parliament in Strasbourg declaring that the unity of Yugoslavia is a *desideratum sine qua non*, of aid from 'Europe'. They are out of their minds, as they usually are.

Professor Stone went on to say that President Tudjman, in spite of his faulty English and his obscure grievances, was 'the Boris Yeltsin of Yugoslavia, both its destroyer and its hope'. He continued:

> However, the grievances are real enough, expressed in the interior, mainly in Zagreb, Croatia's capital – by the way, a splendid city, a little Vienna. If you are a Croat brought up in European fashion, you do not greatly like modern Yugoslavia. Your chances of a job in the State machine are not very good. The language may be more or less the same but the mentality of the Serbs, the dominant people, is very, very different.

He then turned his attention to the First World War, which, he argues, was caused when the Archduke Franz Ferdinand was shot 'by a Serbian nationalist who was actually aiming at someone else' – a startling new theory about the murder – before proceeding:

> Dr Tudjman, with his broken English, nevertheless addresses three great European matters. There is first of all the end of the First World War. Then there is the end of Communism. And then there is the end of the European Community . . . What we are talking about is the end of the First World War – that extraordinary moment when we created artificial states that are now being destroyed from within. This is happening in Iraq, it is happening in the Soviet Union, and it is also happening in Yugoslavia . . . Yugoslavia was set up to stop predatory Germans. The Germans are now not predatory. We can therefore allow an independent Croatia.[23]

Fortified by the support of the 'Iron Lady' and her spokesman Professor Stone, President Tudjman returned to Zagreb to prepare for the declaration of independence, now fixed for 25 June 1991.

20

Towards Disaster in Bosnia-Hercegovina

In the early evening of 24 June 1981, six children of Medjugorje in western Hercegovina returned from the hillside where they tended sheep and claimed to have seen a great light and the Virgin Mary. Next day the four girls and two boys, whose ages ranged from eleven to seventeen, went back to the hillside and, once more, said that they saw the Virgin. This time their report was taken seriously by the adults of Medjugorje and, in particular, by the Franciscan friars whose number included the parish priest. The date of this second sighting, 25 June 1981, is now the accepted start of the Medjugorje apparitions, and ten years later it was chosen for the announcement of an independent Croatia, the act that started the civil war.

On the third day, a crowd of thousands of curious locals gathered to climb the hillside with the six who, once more, said that they saw Our Lady. News of the apparitions spread through western Hercegovina, quickly reaching the ears of the civil and church officials in Mostar, capital of the province. The police arrested and later imprisoned two of the friars, while the six young seers were questioned at length by doctors, psychiatrists and the Roman Catholic Bishop of Mostar, Monsignor Pavao Žanić. When the authorities stopped the meetings on the hillside, the six young people met instead in a small side chapel of Medjugorje's new and hideous twin-towered church.

All six described seeing a beautiful woman in her early twenties, wearing a blue dress and white veil, with pale cheeks, blue eyes and dark hair, crowned with stars, which is how she appeared in the wax statuette which was made for the parish church. It is a poor work of art, resembling Snow White in the Walt Disney film and still more closely the girl in the advertisements for the local Sarajevo beer. However, unlike Saint Bernadette, who detested the famous statue in the grotto at Lourdes, the seers were pleased with it.

Soon the witnesses also heard the voice of the apparition, who described herself as 'the Blessed Virgin Mary' and sometimes as 'the Queen of Peace', always speaking in 'pure Croatian' rather than Serbo-Croat. Once she appeared with the infant Jesus in her arms and on other occasions the witnesses touched her dress. According to Dr Rupčić, a sympathetic chronicler of the appar- ition, one of the girl witnesses saw the Devil. 'He promised me something very nice. When I answered "no" he vanished. The Virgin then told me that he always tried to lead astray true believers . . . When Joseph [the parish priest] was in prison, the Virgin showed him to us. It was like the films. We saw heaven and hell . . . just flames and people there weeping, some with horns or tails or four legs. God help them.'[1] Two of the six told Dr Rupčić they planned to adopt a cloistered life; three were uncertain and one girl said that she intended to marry, as later she did. At the end of his book, Dr Rupčić added a list of fifty people who claimed to have had a miraculous cure after a visit to Medjugorje. A former sufferer from multiple sclerosis even expressed her feelings in verse:

> From Zagreb to Lipik Spa,
> Without the Virgin I was not cured.
> At Medjugorje Church with two towers,
> There one must go and pray!
> Virgin of Peace I thank thee for all!
> I had been ill since childhood,
> The Virgin of Peace has healed me.[2]

When I visited Medjugorje in April 1984 it had not yet won the international fame that later turned it into a place of pilgrimage second only to Lourdes. Our party of twelve assembled at Heathrow Airport without the chanting of hymns and wearing of badges normal with pilgrims to Lourdes or Fátima or Jerusalem. We had read reports published by earlier pilgrims that groups had been turned back from Yugoslav airports when it was found they were heading for Medjugorje, that hotel and tourist agency employees might denounce us to the government, and that in Medjugorje itself we should 'beware people who look out of place in or around the church and ask a lot of seemingly friendly questions'. These warnings were justified, though it has to be said that the Yugoslav government was behaving no more harshly at Medjugorje than had the French at Lourdes or the Portuguese who dynamited the church at Fátima.

Since we were being discreet on a flight of the Yugoslav airline JAT, our party of pilgrims did not make each other's acquaintance until Dubrovnik, where we were spending the night. The party included a lively group of Irish from Bedford, three middle-aged ladies from Guernsey and Peter, a serious and ascetic Indian whose father had been an Anglican clergyman. 'He was broken-hearted when I converted to Roman Catholicism,' Peter told me, 'and since than I have known sorrow and misfortune in a temporal sense, but I have never for one moment regretted conversion.' As Chaucer had understood so well, any group of pilgrims is bound to include, besides the pious, the tourists such as the Wife of Bath, who spent the money left by her husbands on journeys to Canterbury, Rome and even Jerusalem.

It was a pleasant journey by private bus from Dubrovnik to Mostar, where we were all staying for five days. The party exchanged good Irish jokes, recited Hail Marys and capped each other's adventures:

In France, as we were on the way to Lourdes, we were in a natural disaster after a flood of sixteen inches of rain. There were

cars piled up like garbage cans with cocks of hay on top of them
. . . In the Holy Land we went to Masada, the place where the
Israeli officers go to swear their oath of allegiance, like the Nazis
in the 1930s . . . Last year we were in Garabandel in Spain. It's
much more primitive than here in Bosnia-Hercegovina. Did you
see the film on Garabandel? It's only an amateur job but you see
the children flying through the air . . . Of course there's no
hardship these days in a pilgrimage. It's not like it was for Saint
Malachy who went down twice to Rome.

Only a few months earlier, the media had given enormous publicity
to the Winter Olympics at Sarajevo but none to events at Medjugorje. Remarking on this, one of the Irish pilgrims exclaimed,
'Doesn't it show that Satan controls the media, which made such a
fuss of the Games when the Queen of Heaven's appearing just
down the road?'

From Mostar I made several visits into the harsh and virtually
treeless district round Medjugorje (the village's name means
'between the mountains'). The six young witnesses were always
described in the press as shepherds and shepherdesses but, as I
knew from my travels in eastern Hercegovina, sheep were no
longer important in agriculture. For anyone with the energy to
remove the surface rock, there is plenty of good red earth round
Medjugorje for growing the vines, tobacco and fruit for which the
region is known. However, the major providers of wealth are the
thousands of men who have gone to work in Germany, Sweden or
Belgium, then come back to set themselves up as 'independent'
mechanics, electricians, lorry drivers or café keepers, always with
a plot of land on the side. 'We don't live badly at all at Medjugorje,'
said one of the several motor mechanics, then grinned to show that
they lived very well. Three miles away at the town of Čitluk there
were banks, a department store, a hunters' club and fine new
villas.

Because the authorities wanted to discourage pilgrims, in 1984
Medjugorje had no hotel or even a boarding-house, while the only
amenities were a bar, a hot-dog stall and one public lavatory
consisting of three sheds with doors that did not shut and three

holes in the earth surrounded by flies and excrement. Although they were not allowed to exploit the pilgrim trade, the people of Medjugorje were in the grip of a building boom, as could be seen from the half-finished villas and farmhouses, the higgledy-piggledy piles of bricks and stone, and hundreds of yards of drainpipe waiting to be laid.

Even if we had not been warned of the tension at Medjugorje, our group of pilgrims would soon have noticed the police cars, the helicopter chattering overhead and the surly plainclothes men. We gave a lift to a woman whose brother, the parish priest at Medjugorje, was still in prison for 'harmful political activities'. His sentence was halved when Bishop Žanić of Mostar reached an agreement with the authorities to stop pilgrims going to the hillside where the Virgin first appeared.

In spite of the Bishop's injunction, our group went straight to the slope of boulders and jagged stones which even Saint Malachy would have had to admit was heavy going. The children who first saw the apparition felt they were 'carried up' the miraculous hillside. To me it was hard work, though not as bad as for those who had to be hauled to the spot where the Virgin appeared. To add to the penitential character of the hillside, the witnesses or the friars had let it be known that staring into the sun was an aid to godliness, or so it was thought by some credulous pilgrims. Yugoslav newspapers rightly warned of the danger of eye damage and sunstroke.

On the way back from the hillside, an eighty-two-year-old woman begged for money because, so she told me, she and her husband had never had children. Begging like this is almost unheard of in Yugoslavia, especially in a village as rich as Medjugorje. A little later another old woman offered delicious red wine from her vineyard, then rather pointedly asked us to pay for it; this, again, is unusual in Yugoslavia.

The six young witnesses did not accept gifts of money or anything else. When an Italian pilgrim asked to buy an intercession one of the friars answered caustically that the Virgin Mary did not answer requests; she merely demanded prayer, fasting and penance. According to the witnesses, the Virgin had asked for a rosary of seven Our Fathers, Hail Marys and Glory Bes, as well as the Creed, amounting to three and a half hours, almost all of which was spent by the congregation on their knees. Apart from those who had found a pew with a padded rail, the pilgrims knelt throughout on the stone floor of a church whose atmosphere is generally cold and damp. At times the Protestant voice in me would ask if Roman Catholics ever got off their knees. What with the clambering over boulders, the rain and the constant kneeling, I left Medjugorje feeling less fit than when I arrived. One of the Irishmen said that the spicy mixed grill he had eaten in Mostar had made every bone in his body ache.

When I got back from Medjugorje, I felt unable to say if the apparitions were genuine. It was clear that pilgrims such as the cheerful Irish people with whom I travelled got spiritual benefit from the experience. From what I saw of the six young witnesses, both at Medjugorje and in a later video film, they struck me as normal, frank and, in several cases, engaging personalities. However, they could have been under the influence of the friars, who gave a bullying, brutal impression. One of them, in my presence, scolded a peasant woman for saying that I spoke Serbo-Croat: 'There's no such language!' I knew that the friars and the witnesses had irritated the secular clergy of Hercegovina as well as the Bishop of Mostar, Monsignor Žanić.

By the end of the 1980s, the Medjugorje phenomenon was attracting millions of pilgrims, especially from Ireland and Italy and even such distant countries as the Philippines and Mexico. Although most visitors trusted the seers, a few were critical of the character of the friars. For instance the English writer Richard Bassett, a Roman Catholic who has lived in Croatia and speaks the language, noticed the interest of the monks in attractive female pilgrims. One friar, who had begged off meeting a pious enquirer because he was 'going to Mostar', spent that evening closeted with an Austrian lady for what the boarding-house keeper described as 'two hours of spiritual instruction'.[3]

The main opposition to the Franciscans at Medjugorje came not from the Communist government but from the diocesan clergy. Since 1950, the Bosnia-Hercegovina Franciscans had fought off attempts by the Church to take back parishes held by the Order for hundreds of years. The apparition at Medjugorje was widely seen in the Church as one more ploy in the old Franciscan struggle for power and patronage. A small minority of the Franciscans themselves, the overwhelming majority of the diocesan priests and above all the Bishop of Mostar, Pavao Žanić, denounced the Medjugorje seers as frauds, liars or dupes of the friars. In the pamphlet *Medjugorje*, published in Mostar in 1990, Bishop Žanić says that at first, when the Communists were persecuting the friars, the 'seers' and even the pilgrims, he defended them but never believed in the apparitions. He accuses one Franciscan, Tomislav Vašić, of masterminding the seers and getting 'the Virgin' to utter attacks on himself and messages of support for Vašić and two sacked Franciscans. One of those friars was Ivica Vega.

> Due to his disobedience, by an order of the Holy Father the Pope, he [Vega] was thrown out of his Franciscan religious order OFM by his General, dispensed from his vows and suspended 'a divinis'. He did not obey this order and he continued to celebrate Mass, distribute the sacraments and pass the time with his mistress . . .
>
>   It is unpleasant to write about this, yet it is necessary in order to see who Our Lady is speaking of.
>
>   According to the diary of Vicka [Vicka Ivanković, the leading seer] and the statements of the 'seers', Our Lady mentioned thirteen times that he [Vega] is innocent, and that the Bishop is wrong. When his mistress, Sister Leopolda, a nun, became pregnant, both of them left Medjugorje and the religious life and began to live together near Medjugorje where their child was born. Now they have two children. His prayerbook is still sold in Medjugorje and beyond in hundreds of thousands of copies.[4]

In the summer of 1990, the Bishop of Mostar took his pamphlet to Rome to try to convince the Pope of the fraudulent nature of

Medjugorje. However, by then the Croats had voted to power a government loyal to Medjugorje and its Croatian Virgin. The declaration of independence on 25 June 1991 was timed for the tenth anniversary of the apparitions. This coincidence later became the proudest boast of the Medjugorje Franciscans.

Few foreign pilgrims to Medjugorje realised the long Franciscan connection with Bosnia-Hercegovina. The friars first went there in 1260 to stamp out the Bogomil heresy. After the Turkish conquest of 1463, the Franciscans signed an agreement by which, in return for helping to keep down the troublesome Orthodox Christians, they were exempt from poll tax and also given the right to carry arms. During more than four centuries of Ottoman rule, the Franciscans were the auxiliaries of the Slav Muslim ruling class, and lived in some kind of harmony with the other two religions. In 1877 the *Manchester Guardian* correspondent Arthur Evans saw a friar joining the Orthodox peasants in one of their village revels: 'I was a little surprised and not a little amused to see his Reverence bustle out, form a ring for the national "kolo" dance, seize two buxom lasses by the waist, and join as lustily as his ecclesiastical vestments would allow, in the merry-go-round.'5 From *The Red Knight*, the volume of Serbian women's songs collected by Vuk Karadjić in the nineteenth century, we learn that Orthodox women sometimes regarded Franciscans as more than dancing partners:

> The friar tripped on a sod and fell.
> He broke the prick that f. . . s so well.
> Married or betrothed, the women
> gathered round and stared at him!
> 'Oh, our c. . . s' pride, oh holy friar,
> Is this a sign of heaven's ire!'6

Relations between the Franciscans and the Orthodox turned sour during the twentieth century. After the murder of Archduke Franz Ferdinand in 1914, some of the friars encouraged the hanging of Serbs by Catholic lynch mobs, though Bishop Mišić of

Mostar called for toleration. When Stepinac was made Archbishop-Coadjutor of Zagreb in 1934, he applied to join the Franciscan Third Order. The General of the Order, Father Leonardo Bello, visited Zagreb in September of that year to assist at the celebration of the 700th aniversary of the Franciscans in Croatia. On 29 September, in the presence of a large congregation in the Franciscan church, he vested the new Archbishop-Coadjutor with the scalpel and girdle of the Franciscans, 'a public witness of Stepinac's desire to identify himself with the ideal of poverty and to assume the burdens of his office in the spirit of patience and humility which St Francis typified'.[7]

It was partly out of respect for the Order that, both before and during the Second World War, Stepinac tried to promote the canonisation of Nikola Tavelić, a fourteenth-century friar who had served in Bosnia-Hercegovina, trying to stamp out heresy. Archbishop Stepinac was also very attached to belief in the Virgin Mary as 'Queen of Croatia', and leader of its crusade against heresy and schism. His colleague Ivan Šarić, the Bishop of Sarajevo, linked the name of the Mother of God to his own Ustasha brand of religious nationalism. Soon after the establishment of the Independent State of Croatia, his diocesan paper *Katolički Tjednik* (11 May 1941) said in a leading article:

> Above the new, young and free Croatia, the image of the Virgin Mother, the beautiful shining image has appeared in the heavens as a sign – *signum in cielo*. The Lady comes to visit her Croatia, within her maternal mantle she wishes to enfold her young, reborn Croatia exactly in the thousandth year of the Catholic Jubilee. Again she descends on the flags of our freedom to occupy her ancient place; in order to protect us and to defend us as she did at the time when our Bans and Princes went into battle under the flag bearing her image.[8]

In two earlier chapters of this book, I have tried to convey the enormity of the crimes committed during the Second World War by members of the Franciscan Order. Some of the very worst took place in western Hercegovina, close to Medjugorje. In the astounding letter to Archbishop Stepinac written in August 1941, the then Bishop of Mostar described among other atrocities how the Ustasha had brought 'six waggons full of mothers, girls and children under eight to the station of Surmanci, where they were taken out of the waggons, brought into the hills and thrown alive, mothers and children, into deep ravines'.[9] Those ravines are less than two miles from Medjugorje. We do not know if the friars at Medjugorje took part in the murder but three of them, all sworn Ustasha, died fighting alongside the German SS at Široki Brijeg near the end of the war. The names of the three Franciscan Ustasha from Medjugorje are now on a plaque in honour of those who died fighting the Communists.[10]

Mostar itself was the epicentre of horror in Bosnia-Hercegovina from 1941 to 1945, as it was to become once more half a century later. It was during a fortnight in Mostar during the summer of 1991 that I came to see the love and veneration of Tito among those who longed for the preservation of Yugoslavia. It is there that I bring to an end the story of Tito's triumphs and ultimate, tragic failure.

Even before reaching Mostar during an overland journey back from Albania, I met many Yugoslavs who did not join in the nationalistic madness. As ever, the Montenegrins took an Olympian view of everyone living closer to sea level. The young woman who showed me round the museum at Cetinje, pointing out with pride the flag riddled by 396 bullet holes, said: 'We were the first independent state in the Balkan peninsula, the first one with links with Europe. We were the only one that Europe had even heard of. Now we're the only part of Yugoslavia that is calm. We don't want to go into the army reserve. My husband says he would go right away if Yugoslavia was attacked by the Germans or the Albanians, but he doesn't want to fight the Croats or Slovenes. Only a few years ago he was in the army with these people. He ate and drank with them. Why should he fight them?' She showed me a photograph in the museum of some Montenegrin Chetniks, once vilified as Fascists and collaborators: 'Some people now say they were right all along. I don't know about that. Personally I have always been a great admirer of Josip Broz Tito. And the greatest day of my life was two years ago when they brought back the body of King Nikola, our king.'

After five days in the most tranquil part of Yugoslavia – there was even a Montenegrin pacifist movement, almost a contradiction in terms – I took a bus down the coast to Dubrovnik in Croatia. When I had first gone there during the off-season of April 1954, as Yugoslavia was just beginning to open its doors to the West, the city was busy and cheerful in comparison with what I saw in July 1991, when I encountered no other foreigner. On that first occasion a smiling young woman had come up and asked me to marry her, so that she might live abroad. Now the whole population was facing exile. Even the physical safety of Dubrovnik depended on maintaining the 'open city' status granted by Tito in 1968, the year he closed the naval and army bases there. A few weeks later, the Croat military rearmed Dubrovnik, which then came under attack from the Yugoslav Navy and Serb forces inland. At my favourite café-restaurant near the market, I saw that they still had Tito's portrait instead of the red-and-white chequerboard flag and other Croatian insignia. The manageress explained that they were 'Orthodox from Bosnia'.

A Bosnian journalist in the café in Dubrovnik told me that Pavao Žanić, the Bishop of Mostar, was still incensed by the friars at Medjugorje but now had to hold his tongue for fear of the Tudjman regime. Only the day before, the Croats had flown the Italian Prime Minister, Giulio Andreotti, to pay his respects to the 'Queen of Peace' at Medjugorje, a visit that doubtless helped to stiffen the Roman Catholic vote back home. Going by bus from Dubrovnik to Mostar and heading upstream along the River Neretva, I looked with a feeling of horror towards the limestone hills of western Hercegovina, the scene of the Medjugorje apparitions, and tens of thousands of murders fifty years ago.

Seven years earlier I had stayed in the Bristol Hotel on the right, or western, bank of the river, but this time I took a room in the Neretva Hotel, on the other side of the green torrent. Only now did I understand that the river divided Mostar as the Wall had once divided Berlin, with Roman Catholics making up approximately one-third of the western side but a mere 5 per cent of the largely Muslim, but partly Orthodox, east. Western Hercegovina, with its abundance of red-and-white chequerboard flags, its Ustasha graffiti and rabidly anti-Serbian press, was ready and eager to join a Greater Croatia. The Orthodox in the countryside of eastern Hercegovina were just as keen to get the help of Serbia and Montenegro. Already the Bosnian Serbs were engaged in a shrill propaganda campaign against the elected President, Alija Izetbegović, branding him an Islamic fundamentalist. Although Izetbegović was a pious Muslim, I could not believe that this sensible man could hope to enforce Koranic law on his easy-going countrymen. He feared and detested both Milošević and Tudjman, comparing the choice between them to that between leukaemia and a brain tumour. The confrontation in Mostar was so intense and so depressing that I decided to stay only one or two days, but on the first evening I stumbled and broke an ankle, so I was stuck there for a fortnight.

Since it was nearly two weeks before I could hobble even as far as the bridge, my impressions of Mostar this time were limited to the Neretva Hotel. It was the hottest month of the year in the hottest town in Europe; however, a clump of trees and a gurgling fountain created an impression of coolness at the outdoor café. At least twice a day, jets of the Yugoslav air force buzzed over the town and the Croat positions to the west, and several times at night I heard automatic fire. Throughout the time I was there, I half expected the start of the civil war that broke out the following April, first with a Serb bombardment and then a prolonged Croat assault on the east bank.

The café of the Neretva was the meeting-place of a number of middle-aged or elderly Muslim gentlemen, joking over their coffee, brandy or fresh lemonade. One of them, let us call him Murat, spoke to me as the nearest muezzin bellowed the midday call to prayer: 'You mustn't get the impression that we're like your Bradford Muslims. We don't burn books, we marry women from

other religions, and many of us are drunk from morning till night.'
Murat detested Milošević and the Bosnian Serb leader Radovan
Karadžić: 'He's a Montenegrin psychiatrist. What more can you
say against a man?' He dreaded a repetition of 1941, when the
Croats murdered the Serbs and the Serbs revenged themselves on
the Muslims: 'My uncle had his throat cut by a Chetnik, who later
became a Partisan National Hero. In fact he's living only a few
doors from me now.' However, Murat acknowledged that all the
Bosnians were one people and raged against those Westerners who
talked about 'ethnic' differences: 'It's rubbish to say we're three
nations here in Bosnia. In all the old families here in Mostar you
have Muslims, Orthodox and Catholics together. We're just three
different kinds of the same shit.'

Another regular at the café was a former UDBA, or secret police,
chief, a rugged ex-Partisan from a Muslim family, a man with a
good sense of humour, but now pessimistic:

> The situation is worse now than it was before the war started in
> 1941. Before the war we all lived together OK. Then the Ustasha
> came and took many Serbs. The rest were saved by the Commu-
> nists. About 30 per cent of the Muslims here became Commu-
> nists, especially the children of good families. About 80 per cent
> of the Serbs joined the Communists; the rest may have joined the
> Chetniks. About 5 per cent of the Croats were Communists,
> others were Ustasha, but most of them concentrated on just
> surviving. After the war, the Serbs and Croats at first did not
> come back to Mostar. Now the Croats are back in force, about
> 20,000 of them, almost all in the north-west of town.

Twice I met the *Oslobodjenje* correspondent Mugdim Karabeg.
In spite of his Muslim name, he had passed through an ecumenical
childhood, typical of a generation caught up in the Second World
War:

> I was first brought up as the only Muslim child in a Roman
> Catholic village in Slavonia, where the priest befriended me,

taught me the catechism and gave me the first-name Slobodan. Then I went to school in Trebinje, in eastern Hercegovina, where they were mostly Serbs. When I came back to my place of origin, Mostar, the Muslims gave me the name Mugdim. Until about five years ago, nobody bothered what religion you were.

The newspaper *Oslobodjenje* was now the moderate voice of the largely Muslim centre parties, opposed to the Croat as much as the Serb fanatics. Both Christian extremist groups hated *Oslobodjenje* and tried to prevent its sale. They gave a hard time to its correspondent Mugdim, as he recounted to me:

For months there have been three or four barricades on the road to Nevesinje – that's the Serb town east of here. These barricades are manned by youngsters with automatic weapons and slivovitz on their breath. They insist on searching my car and insult me because of my Muslim name. The Serbs there are cutting down the forests and stealing quantities of wood but the Serb police won't prosecute . . . When I go to the Croat towns and villages in western Hercegovina, the people there say they want to hang Milošević and Marković, that's the best politician we have. [Ante Marković, a Croat, was federal Prime Minister, striving to hold the country together.]

Mugdim talked with deep emotion about the Ustasha massacres in 1941:

The Ustasha, including Franciscans, came over from Italy in 1938 and 1939, to draw up a plan for the massacre of the Serbs, as soon as they came to power. They examined which were the deepest quarries and crevices in which to throw them.
  In the first wave, starting on Vidovdan, 28 June 1941, they killed at least 10,000 Serbs round here. They ripped open the wombs of pregnant women, caught babies on bayonets, gouged people's eyes out . . . Unfortunately there were some Muslim rabble (*ološ*) who joined in killing the Orthodox so that many

Serbs in eastern Hercegovina took a terrible revenge, massacring
Muslim villages . . . Some of the worst Chetniks came from
Hercegovina . . . We are a people here of the hot sun and the dry
rocks, a mountain people, a people who have lived for centuries
only praying for rain, an irrational, mythic people . . . What is
happening in the Krajina and Slavonia is nothing compared to
what will happen in Hercegovina if the fighting starts . . .

Do you know the worst thing? That the Roman Catholic
Church has never admitted what happened in 1941, and never
apologised for the things that were done by the Franciscans. For
throwing people into ravines. How could they do those things?
To babies, to beautiful young girls, to old women? The Roman
Catholic Church, the Pope, should now make an apology but
they have said nothing.

The following weekend, the head of the Serbian Orthodox
Church, Patriarch Pavle, came to Hercegovina to give a Christian
burial to the remains of the many thousands murdered fifty years
earlier, including the women and children hurled screaming over
the side of a precipice near Medjugorje. One of the few survivors,
now a university lecturer, blamed the crimes partly on 'Croatian
separatists wanting to break away from their brother Yugoslavs',
and partly on 'a large and universal Church, which wants to further
spread its power, the number of its believers, and the territory it
controls'.[11]

The following week, I wrote about this for a London Sunday
newspaper, quoting as well the Bishop of Mostar's terrible letter of
1941 and the verdict of Carlo Falconi in *The Silence of Pius XII*:
'Only in Croatia was the extermination of at least half a million
human beings due more perhaps to hatred of their religion than of
their race, and was sacrilegiously bound up with a campaign for
rebaptism.' As Hubert Butler found when he wrote of these things
in Ireland, forty years earlier, 'nobody in the British Isles . . . ever
commented on it, quoted from it, or wrote to me to enquire how I
had secured it'.[12]

In so far as the English newspapers mentioned the massacres

fifty years earlier, they tended to blame the Serbs for 'raking up the past'. One correspondent seemed to think that the victims were Roman Catholics. In the *Spectator* a woman remarked sarcastically that the Serbs were now so paranoiac, they even believed that the Vatican was against them. A few weeks after my article, the Roman Catholic Archbishop of Zagreb, Cardinal Kuharić told the London *Times* that only a 'handful' of Serbs were killed in the Independent State of Croatia.

Seven years earlier, when I stayed in the Bristol Hotel on the western side of the river, I could see on the mountains opposite the slogan: 'Tito, We Love You' ('Tito, Volimo Te'). I found it absurd and rather disgusting. Now I saw that someone had added the word 'Peace' ('Mir'), and somehow I found the slogan pleasing. Like most of the regulars in the Neretva café, Murat spoke with affection of Tito, both as a man and as a politician: 'You'll hear young people say how much better off they were under the Communists, and it's true. In England, you may have a very big salary but you'll still have to choose between taking a beach or a skiing holiday. Here even a primary school teacher could take both, and have a car and second home. Of course it was all on credit and came from borrowing from the international banks. But people lived well, especially if they had relatives in the country.'

When the Italian army went back into Bosnia-Hercegovina in 1941 to stop the Ustasha persecution, thousands of Serb women and children gathered in Mostar to offer a posy of flowers to the Italian commander, begging him for continued protection. Fifty years later it seemed once more to be the women and young who wanted peace and toleration. The girl receptionist at the Neretva Hotel, who had worked in London and Rome but hoped to continue living in Mostar, kept lecturing me on the views of the young as opposed to those of people of my generation:

You hear people say how awful it was under the Communists. It was wonderful under the Communists! The hotels were full. Everyone could travel around the country or go abroad.

People of different religions were friendly with each other. My father is Serb and my mother is Croat. My best friend is Muslim. My nearest neighbours are Muslims, and next to them are Serbs. Why should I fight these people? Like most of my friends, I only wish the Communists were back!

During my second week in Mostar, the children started collecting signatures for peace, either on sheets of foolscap paper or in their exercise books. Since there were more collectors of signatures than there were people to sign, the very few customers in cafés like the Neretva were much in demand. There was a solemn little Croat girl in a bonnet who asked me so many times that I started to sign the names of my friends in England. Some of the male Yugoslavs muttered that 'peace is for women and children', but nevertheless they signed.

On the day before I was ready to leave, tens of thousands of young people and children marched to a Mostar sports ground to hold a rally for peace. Some came on foot, some by car, scooter or bicycle, but almost all of them carried the two symbols of peace: the red, white and blue flag of Yugoslavia superimposed by a Communist red star, and Tito's portrait. The memory stays with me of one platoon of boys and girls, scarcely old enough to be born when Tito died, who carried his picture above their heads as they solemnly marched, their little arms swinging and little knees rising to stamp the roadway; and as they marched they chanted and piped the old cry of the Partisans: 'Tito is ours, and we are Tito's' ('Tito je naš i mi smo Titovi'). The slogan that forty years ago I had found repulsive and totalitarian now charmed and moved me. In all the years I had known Yugoslavia under the rule or influence of Josip Broz Tito, I never dreamed I should live to see him leading a children's crusade. Watching that pitiful, doomed procession, I felt overwhelmed by dread of the coming disaster.

Epilogue

Although this book was written in 1993, I ended the story of Tito's Yugoslavia in August 1991, before the outbreak of full-scale war, and before the international recognition of Slovenia and Croatia dashed all hope of preserving a South Slav federation. However I like to think that this book may have helped readers to understand the tragic events of the last five years in the light of earlier conflicts, such as the Bosnia-Hercegovina Crisis of 1875–78, the First World War that followed the Sarajevo assassination in 1914, and the hideous carnage during the Second World War in the Independent State of Croatia.

The first warning shots in the present conflict were fired in the *Krajina*, or Military Frontier, region of Croatia, which Arthur Evans described in 1877 as 'containing the most warlike and not the least civilised part of its population . . . peopled by what is in fact a separate and purely Serbian nationality'. In 1941, the Ustasha launched their campaign to remove the Orthodox Serbs from Croatia by converting a third, expelling a third and killing a third. Though many Serbs around Knin became royalist Chetniks, their fellows in Slavonia joined Tito's Partisans. When the Communist leaders in 1943 discussed the constitution of postwar Yugoslavia, they overruled the suggestion by Moša Pijade, of forming a series of semi-autonomous Serb enclaves in Croatia. These Serb enclaves round Knin and in western and eastern Slavonia took up arms in 1991, as they had threatened to do in

1971. In eastern Slavonia, the Serbs used artillery of the former Yugoslav army to batter the town of Vukovar into surrender. This, and the shelling of the suburbs of Dubrovnik (although not, as it turned out, the old city centre), aroused world opinion against the Serbs and in favour of recognition for Slovenia and Croatia. The support given by Germany and Austria to their wartime ally Croatia fuelled Serb fears of a new 'Drang nach Osten' or 'drive to the East'.

When the rest of Europe rather reluctantly followed the lead of Germany in recognising Croatia, the Muslims in Bosnia-Hercegovina found themselves in a dire predicament. They formed a plurality, not a majority of the population, and were overwhelmingly concentrated in cities and towns. The Orthodox, or Serbs, who made up a third of the population, owned nearly two-thirds of the land, while the Catholics, or Croats, owned virtually all the land in western Hercegovina and in districts of central Bosnia. The independent state of Bosnia-Hercegovina, which came into being in 1992, could be described as a string of towns encircled by hostile countryside. Moreover, the country Muslims around Bihac, where Tito established his government in 1942, had made a local alliance with the Serbs against the Sarajevo government.

As soon as fighting began in Bosnia-Hercegovina in April 1992, the Serbs and Croats rushed to consolidate and expand what they regarded as their rightful territory. The Serbs, as if programmed by history, resumed their struggle against the South Slav converts to Islam, begun at Kosovo in 1389, and celebrated by Petar Njegoš, the Montenegrin poet:

> So tear down minarets and mosques,
> Kindle the Serb yule logs
> And paint the Easter eggs.

In Banja Luka the Serbs not only destroyed all but one of the fifteen mosques, but beat, imprisoned, starved or murdered thousands of Muslims before expelling most of them from their ancient homeland. Having convinced themselves that the Bosnian government wanted to introduce Islamic fundamentalism, the Serbs rampaged through eastern Bosnia, where Chetniks had slaughtered thousands of Muslims at Foča and Goražde in 1941. A wartime letter from a Chetnik commander (though probably not by Mihailović, as the signature purports), in which the author recommends 'cleansing' non-national elements to create an 'ethnically pure, great Serbia', was seized upon by an American public relations company, acting on behalf of the Bosnian government, to accuse the Serbs of 'ethnic cleansing'.

Since the warring parties in Bosnia-Hercegovina were ethnically identical, the phrase 'ethnic cleansing' was meaningless when applied to what was in fact a religious conflict; however it had the desired effect of branding the Serbs as 'racist' and anti-semitic, therefore condemning them in the eyes of the Jewish community in the United States of America and Europe. This was a welcome but undeserved propaganda bonus for President Tudjman of Croatia, whose attitude to the Jews is made clear in his book *Wastelands*.

In his articles for the *Manchester Guardian*, in 1877, Arthur Evans reported that 250,000 Orthodox refugees had been driven from Bosnia-Hercegovina and that 50,000 had died from cold, disease and starvation; he also alleged that many Orthodox women had suffered 'the usual fate' from Muslim soldiers. The number of refugees in recent years has been no higher proportionately to the size of the population, but the Muslims have suffered as much as, or more than, the Serbs. This time, the Serbs were widely accused of raping Muslim women, and once again the alleged attacks were denounced in the House of Commons.

Evans described how after the Montenegrins captured the Slav Muslim town of Nikšić, there was 'hardly a house that had not been struck by a shell, and it is not by any means safe to knock too hard on a friend's door when paying a visit'. Later, the Montenegrins hauled their twelve-and-a-half-pounder guns into Bosnia-Hercegovina, to shell the Muslims there. More than a

hundred years later, the Montenegrin psychiatrist Radovan Karadjić ordered his Bosnian Serbs to employ their much larger
weapons against the city of Sarajevo. The Bosnian government
and Croatian forces have also shelled or mortared those parts of
the city mainly inhabited by the Serbs. A former British Army
officer, Rod Thornton, who had studied Serbo-Croat in Sarajevo
for six months shortly before the war, rejoined his regiment for a
year in Bosnia and later described the artillery warfare there:

> On returning to Sarajevo as a soldier, I noticed that the buildings
> which had taken the brunt of the shelling were the gleaming,
> newly-built, architecturally monstrous show-pieces that had
> mostly sprung up prior to the 1984 Winter Olympics. The
> Oslobodenje tower was a mere stump, the Privedna Banka and
> its copper-coloured glass was no more.
>
> Other new structures had similar damage while the buildings
> standing on either side of them had been barely scratched. The
> blue-windowed twin skyscrapers next to the Holiday Inn had,
> due to their proximity to the hotel and the Press inside, escaped
> relatively lightly (they were still standing). On asking the Serb
> gunners on the hills why they picked out these particular
> buildings, the age-old rural/urban conflict . . . became apparent.
> The vast majority of these men were from villages around
> Sarajevo. To them it did not matter who lived in the city – Serb,
> Muslim, or Martian – they just wanted to pound it and
> everything in it . . . especially its symbols, the brash, colourful
> modern eyesores . . . It made no difference that places like the
> Oslobodenje tower and the futuristic TV mast had long since
> been reduced to piles of rubble – they continued to pump shell
> after shell into what remained. I myself spent one afternoon
> watching the shelling of both these structures. Over 150 shells
> were fired at objects that were empty of people and had already
> been completely destroyed. It was sheer vandalism.

Like several military observers, Thornton suggests that the
Bosnian government used artillery or mortar fire to discredit the
Serbs in the eyes of the outside world:

The airport, for instance, where many UN soliders have died, has been closed more often due to direct government fire than Bosnian Serb fire. The periodic ceasefires, likewise, do not conform to the perceived pattern. All, during my time in the city, were broken by the government forces.

The British troops billeted in Sarajevo . . . were accommodated in a barracks in the Old Town. The courtyard of the building next door happened to be the site of some of the government's heavy mortars. The ceasefires and the days of relative calm would come to an end as these mortars began firing at the blocks of flats in the Serb-held suburb of Grbavica. Before long the answering fire would come in from the Serbs and Sarajevo would be back to 'normal' . . .

Once, in the street outside our barracks, I met one of the government soldiers and asked him rather pointedly why his side was breaking the ceasefires. They had orders, he said. Sarajevo was too quiet: to stay at the centre of the world's attention it needed to be its 'normal' self – it needed to be shelled.

Sometimes the shelling would be nothing to do with the Serbs; the Croats would be bombarding the Muslim sector and vice-versa.

South Slav Journal, Volume 15, No 3–4

Mostar, the capital of Hercegovina, whose atmosphere in the summer of 1991 I tried to convey in this book's final chapter, was first bombarded by the Serbs in April the following year, and in 1993 came under prolonged bombardment by the Croats, who finished off the destruction of the old Muslim town by smashing the Turkish bridge on the River Neretva. The Muslim friend, referred to as 'Murat', who was by this time a refugee in London, said that the loss of the bridge had grieved him more than the death of his own mother a few weeks earlier. It seemed to him the end of a centuries-old civilisation.

The Croats of western Hercegovina have taken on the mantle of the Ustasha, whose massacre of the Serbs in 1941 was denounced by the then Bishop of Mostar, Alojzije Misic. In 1993

they attacked the Muslims of Mostar, beating, starving and
murdering them with the same ferocity that the Serbs had shown
to the Muslims of Banja Luka. The Croats of Hercegovina
inspired the massacre of the Muslims in the central Bosnian
region around Gornji Vakuf, an atrocity witnessed by troops of
the British peace-keeping force. These extremist Croats, who
favour a merger in a revived Great Croatia, have all along had the
support of the Franciscan Order, now once more at odds with the
diocesan clergy. At the village of Medjugorje, where the Franciscans have continued to promote the cult of Marian apparitions,
the local women sat down in the road to stop a UN convoy taking
food to the starving Muslims of Mostar. In 1994, the new Bishop
of Mostar renewed the plea to the Vatican made by his predecessor Monsignor Zanić, to stop the Franciscans promoting
claims for the Medjugorje apparitions.

The Roman Catholic Bishop of Banja Luka, Franjo Komarica,
whose predecessor during the 1960s preached reconciliation with
the Orthodox church, spoke up for the Muslims in 1992, and
shamed the Serb authorities into relaxing their persecution. In
May 1995, when Serb refugees from Croatia attacked Catholic
churches and homes in the Banja Luka region, Monsignor
Komarica went on hunger strike. Yet he denounced talk of a
Great Croatia, and remained true to the ideal of a Bosnia-
Hercegovina in which all three religions would co-exist, 'like a
garden full of different flowers', as he was fond of saying.

During the first Bosnia-Hercegovina crisis of 1875–78, the
statesmen of Europe, including our own Disraeli and Gladstone,
were thoroughly versed in the history of the region. They understood that religious conflict between the South Slav Orthodox
Christians, Roman Catholics and Muslims carried the risk of
involving the mighty champions of these faiths, respectively
Russia, Austria-Hungary and the Ottoman Empire. The same
was true of the statesman who managed to keep the peace in
1908, after the Habsburg annexation of Bosnia-Hercegovina. The
Sarajevo assassination of 28th June, 1914 led to the First World
War and then the collapse of the Austro-Hungarian, Russian,

German and Ottoman empires. When the Ustasha murdered King Alexander of Yugoslavia in 1934, the statesmen of Europe once more ensured that Europe did not become involved in the feud between Serbs, Croats and Muslims.

When the latest Bosnian crisis exploded in 1992, the statesmen of Europe seemed unaware of the ancient religious differences in the Balkans, preferring to talk instead of 'ethnic' or 'racial' conflict. The then US president, George Bush, acknowledged tacitly that the Balkans were not in the American sphere of interest or understanding, and should be left to the Europeans. He decided against sending American troops, and welcomed the large British and French contribution to a United Nations peace-keeping force. Cyrus Vance, an American representing the UN, and Lord Owen, representing the European Union, were given the diplomatic task of negotiating a peace, or at least a series of ceasefires.

The neutral attitude of the Vance-Owen team and the generals commanding the UN forces infuriated the international Press, who were by now demanding punitive action against the Serbs. In the summer of 1992, Bill Clinton, the Democrat candidate for the US presidency, accused Milošević of 'crimes against humanity' and demanded the use of American air power. On becoming president in 1993, Clinton refused support to a new Vance-Owen peace plan, and said that what was at stake in Bosnia was 'standing up against the principle of ethnic cleansing'.

As America sought a Bosnian settlement that would at the same time punish the Serbs, other outside powers began to take an interest in the conflict. Germany and Austria continued to back the Croats, their allies in two world wars. Iran and other Muslim states were sending arms and supplies to the Bosnian government, whose army was stiffened by more than a thousand Afghan guerillas. In Russia, both the nationalists and the Communists called on Yeltsin to help their old allies the Serbs. When NATO launched an air attack on the Bosnian Serbs in 1995, relations between the USA and Russia were at their worst since the Cold War. Clinton's aggressive policy succeeded in tipping the military balance against the Serbs, forcing them to peace talks at Dayton, Ohio, in November 1995. As I write this, agreement has just been reached on a plan that appears to divide up Bosnia between Serbia and Croatia, with peace guaranteed by 60,000 NATO troops. The man who initialed the draft agreement on behalf of the Bosnian Serbs was the same Belgrade politician, Slobodan Milošević, whom Clinton had accused of 'crimes against humanity' in 1992.

Milošević's opposite number, President Tudjman of Croatia, was ready in 1995 to show off the might of his army, funded by German money and trained by former United States officers. In the first week of May, his troops invaded and soon over-ran the Serb enclave of western Slavonia, driving its people in flight over the River Sava. Among the small towns captured by the Croats was Jasenovac, the site of the main Ustasha extermination camp from 1941–45. As it happened, the last Commandant of Jasenovac, Dinko Šakić, had only recently come back to Croatia from exile in Australia. In an interview with the Zagreb *Magazin* (February 1995), Šakić spoke of his time at Jasenovac:

> I regret that we hadn't done all that is imputed to us, for had we done that then, today Croatia wouldn't have had problems, there wouldn't have been people to write lies. I am proud of what I did. If I was offered the same duty today I would accept.

Asked why he had not returned to Croatia sooner, Šakić replied: 'It was not out of concern for myself, or fear, but in order not to make problems for the President [Tudjman] and the government, for some people could have used my presence . . . to accuse that the head of Jasenovac, a war criminal, walks the streets of Zagreb.'

The activities of Šakić have been described in some of the documents cited in *Koncentracioni Logor Jasenovac 1941–1945*. Another Jasenovac guard, Ljubo Miloš has told how in April 1945 he and Šakić worked to remove the evidence of the killing at this and other neighbouring camps. They dug up mass graves and tried to cremate the remains. Newly-killed prisoners were usually thrown into the Sava with weights attached to them, or with their bellies cut open so that they would not float to the surface. Although Miloš was caught by the Partisans, to whom he gave this testimony, Šakić escaped along with many Ustasha, shortly before VE Day, 8th May, 1945.

President Tudjman was one of the foreign heads of state invited to London to celebrate the fiftieth anniversary of VE Day. On Saturday 6th May, 1995, Tudjman was a guest at a banquet given by the Queen at the Guildhall. His neighbour at dinner, the Liberal Democrat politician Paddy Ashdown, asked Tudjman during the course of the evening how he thought Bosnia-Hercegovina would be divided. Tudjman sketched on the back of Ashdown's menu a rough map showing Bosnia-Hercegovina split between the Serbs and Croats, on something not dissimilar to the arrangement agreed at Dayton, Ohio. He went on to explain that such a division had been agreed four years earlier with Milošević, who, he added, was 'one of us'. When Ashdown asked what would be the role in Bosnia of the Muslim leader, Alija Izetbegović, Tudjman dismissed him as 'a fundamentalist and an Algerian'. Six months later, Tudjman, Milošević and Izetbegović were filmed shaking hands with each other after the initialling of the treaty at Dayton, Ohio.

In August 1995, Tudjman ordered his army to clear the Serbs from their largest remaining enclave in Croatia, with its capital at Knin. After a massive shelling of Knin itself, the Croats occupied the enclave, brushing aside the UN peace-keeping force. Some 150,000 Serbs fled east across Bosnia in a pathetic convoy to Serbia. In four years Tudjman had achieved what his predecessor Pavelić had failed to do – to drive almost all the Serbs from Croatia.

November 1995

Notes

1 The History of the South Slavs

To understand the troubles of modern Yugoslavia, there is still no better introduction than Edward Gibbon's *The Decline and Fall of the Roman Empire*, especially the volumes describing the time from the coronation of Charlemagne in AD 800 to the fall of Constantinople in 1453. Gibbon explains how the barbarian hordes from Asia and north-east Europe, including the South Slavs, first tried to destroy the remains of the Roman Empire, were slowly Christianised and finally came to continue the ancient civilisations. The last part of the book is largely taken up with the three-way conflict between the Orthodox Church, the Catholic Church and Islam, a conflict that continues to this day in Bosnia-Hercegovina. Gibbon's eighteenth-century humanism serves as an antidote to the modern Marxist and sociological schools of history, which vainly try to interpret Yugoslavia in terms of class or race. Two hundred years after the death of Gibbon, we see he was right to suggest that 'history is little more than the register of the crimes, follies and misfortunes of mankind'.

The early history of the South Slav peoples is thin on fact but rich in fantasy. Modern Croat nationalists may exalt the power and majesty of their kingdom, which lasted from 925 to 1102, yet Vjekoslav Klaić, in *Povijest Hrvata*, his history of the Croats from 641 to the mid-sixteenth century, devotes less than 50 pages out of more than 2,000 to this kingdom. Little about it is really known. We are better informed on the medieval Serbs because their kingdom, or empire, started after that of the Croats had ended. The first history of the Serbs, by the great German historian Leopold von Ranke, is still the best. There are good essays by William Miller on the medieval Serbian empire and on Bosnia before the

Turks. The two books on Bosnia by Arthur Evans remain the best in English about the South Slavs. In his very long introduction to *Through Bosnia and the Herzegovina on Foot*, Evans provides a masterly study of medieval Bosnia and the Bogomil heretics, based largely on the ecclesiastical records. No other writer, before or since, has grasped the huge significance of the Bogomils in the religious disputes of Europe. A brilliant study of the Bosnian Muslims by Husein Ćišić was published in Sarajevo in 1991, just before the destruction of the civilisation he loved. A cynical but entertaining view of the Ottoman Empire is found in *Turkey in Europe* by 'Odysseus'.

Among background books on the history of the South Slavs, Rebecca West's *Black Lamb and Grey Falcon* is best known and still worth reading, especially on art, architecture and the remote regions like Macedonia. Some object to her anti-Habsburg, anti-Croat and pro-Serb bias. (Perhaps I should mention that Rebecca West is no relation.) J. A. Cuddon's *Companion Guide to Yugoslavia* covers the same ground, is less pretentious but more learned. Useful books for understanding the Serbian Orthodox Church are Anne Kindersley's *The Mountains of Serbia* and Timothy Ware's *The Orthodox Church*.

The fullest study of the Serb-Croat 'nationalities problem' is Ivo Banac's *The National Question in Yugoslavia*. Aleksa Djilas's *The Contested Country: Yugoslav Unity and Communist Revolution, 1919–1953* shrewdly debunks the claims of the Serb and Croat chauvinists and gives a good history of the 'Illyrian' idea.

1 Edward Gibbon, *The Decline and Fall of the Roman Empire* (London, 1813), vol. 11, p. 176.
2 Vjekoslav Klaić, *Povijest Hrvata* (Zagreb, 1975), vol. 1, p. 180.
3 Gibbon, *Decline*, vol. 11, p. 180.
4 Ibid. pp. 236–7.
5 Arthur Evans, *Through Bosnia and the Herzegovina on Foot* (London, 1876), p. xxxv.
6 Ibid. p. xxxvi.
7 Ibid. p. xxxix.
8 Ibid.
9 Gibbon, *Decline*, vol. 11, p. 446.
10 Ibid. p. 450. Gibbon's story is too good to be true. Bajazet called off his invasion of Europe to meet a threat to Asia Minor.
11 Ibid. vol. 10, p. 188.
12 J. A. Cuddon, *The Companion Guide to Yugoslavia* (London, 1974), pp. 342–4.

13 Evans, *Through Bosnia*, p. lxi.

14 Quoted by Ivo Banac, *The National Question in Yugoslavia* (Ithaca, NY, 1984), p. 58.

15 Aleksa Djilas, *The Contested Country: Yugoslav Unity and Communist Revolution, 1919–1953* (Cambridge, Mass., 1991), pp. 20–1.

16 Banac, *The National Question in Yugoslavia*, p. 60.

17 Djilas, *The Contested Country*, p. 192, n. 15.

18 Elinor Murray, *Despalatović Ljudevit Gaj and the Illyrian Movement* (Boulder, Colo., 1975), p. 132. For Jelačić's friendly relations with the Serbs, see also Auguste Picot, *Les Serbes d'Hongroi* (Prague, 1873), pp. 241–3.

19 Gibbon, *Decline*, vol. 10, p. 197.

20 Arthur Evans, *Illyrian Letters* (London, 1878), p. 90.

21 Ibid.p. 200.

22 Joan Evans, *Time and Change* (London, 1943), p. 223.

23 Arthur Evans, *Illyrian Letters*, p. 227.

24 Ibid. pp. 23–4.

25 Ibid.p. 66.

26 Ibid. pp. 68–9.

27 Ibid.p. 230.

2 Youth

Tito's autobiography, as told to Vladimir Dedijer in the early 1950s, remains the principal source of information about his early life. His various biographers, and those such as Stevan K. Pavlowitch who have written critical interpretations of Tito's career, have relied on Dedijer's book and found it revealing. In a series of TV interviews in the 1970s, Tito gave a franker account of his early life but did not substantially change his story. In Chapter 16 I describe some visits I have made to places that feature in Tito's youth.

There is a huge mass of literature on the events leading up to the First World War and the emergence afterwards of new states such as Yugoslavia. Arthur J. May's *The Hapsburg Monarchy 1867–1914* and *The Passing of the Hapsburg Monarchy 1914–1918* are especially to be recommended since the author understands the aspirations of the South Slavs but does not take sides between the Serb and Croat nationalists. The British historian R. W. Seton-Watson and his son, Hugh, were often accused of a sentimental belief in 'Versailles states' such as Czechoslovakia and Yugoslavia but, unlike their critics, they knew and understood these countries.

1 Vladimir Dedijer, *Tito Speaks: His Self-Portrait and Struggle with Stalin* (London, 1953), p. 3.
2 Stevan K. Pavlowitch, *Tito: Yugoslavia's Great Dictator. A Reassessment* (London, 1992), p. 98.
3 Dedijer, *Tito Speaks*, p. 4.
4 Ibid.p. 5.
5 Ibid.
6 Ibid.p. 6.
7 Ibid.p. 9.
8 Ibid.p. 8.
9 Ibid.p. 9.
10 Ibid.p. 11.
11 Ibid. pp. 11–12.
12 Ibid.p. 11.
13 Ibid.p. 13.
14 R. W. Seton-Watson, *Absolutism in Croatia* (London, 1912), p. 3.
15 Dedijer, *Tito Speaks*, p. 19.
16 Ibid.p. 20.
17 Ibid.p. 22.
18 Ibid.p. 23.
19 Ibid.
20 Ibid. pp. 23–4.
21 Ibid.p. 25.
22 Leon Trotsky, *The Balkan Wars, 1912–13*, trans. Brian Pearce, ed. George Weissman and Duncan Williams (New York, 1984), pp. 61–3
23 Ivo Banac, *The National Question in Yugoslavia* (Ithaca, NY, 1984), p. 294.
24 Viktor Novak, *Magnum Crimen: Pola vijeka klerikalizma u Hrvatskoj* (Zagreb, 1948), p. 31.
25 Quoted in Arthur J. May, *The Passing of the Hapsburg Monarchy 1914–1918* (2 vols., Philadelphia, 1966), vol. 1, p. 43.
26 Ibid.p. 100.
27 Ibid.p. 115.
28 Dedijer, *Tito Speaks*, p. 26.
29 Ibid.
30 Ibid.p. 28.
31 Ibid.p. 29.
32 Ibid. pp. 28–9.
33 Ibid. pp. 29–30.
34 Ibid.p. 30.
35 Ibid.

36 Dedijer, *Tito Speaks*, p. 32.
37 Stevan K. Pavlowitch, *The Improbable Survivor: Yugoslavia and its Problems, 1918–1988* (London, 1988), p. 35.
38 Dedijer, *Tito Speaks*, pp. 34–5.

3 The Making of a Communist

Vladimir Dedijer's *Tito Speaks* remains the principal source for this chapter. But it was during the 1930s that Tito first met the man who was to become his principal chronicler, disciple and finally critic, Milovan Djilas. The various memoirs written by Djilas after his disgrace in 1954 constitute one of the great autobiographies of the twentieth century, and by far the best account of the Communist movement by one who took an active role in it. They also contain the most revealing account of modern Yugoslav history and of its principal figure, Tito. Although Djilas himself played a major role as one of Tito's lieutenants, and later quarrelled bitterly with his friends, he never allows his personal feelings to interfere with the testimony in his books. Most of his memoirs appeared abroad during the lifetime of Tito and many other former Communist colleagues, but although Djilas was often attacked for disloyalty or even hypocrisy, he was scarcely ever questioned on points of fact.

1 Arthur J. May, *The Passing of the Hapsburg Monarchy 1914–1918* (2 vols., Philadelphia, 1966), vol. 2, p. 679.
2 Stevan K. Pavlowitch, *Tito: Yugoslavia's Great Dictator. A Reassessment* (London, 1992), p. 96.
3 Vladimir Dedijer, *Tito Speaks: His Self-Portrait and Struggle with Stalin* (London, 1953), p. 36.
4 Ibid. p. 37.
5 Ibid. pp. 38–9.
6 In his essay 'The Medieval Serbian Empire', published soon after the First World War, William Miller wrote: The conquests of the Tsar Stephan Dushan in Macedonia have been invoked as one of the Serbian claims to that disputed land; whereas no Englishman of today has been known to demand a large part of France on the ground that it belonged to the English Crown in the reign of Dushan's contemporary, Edward III.' William Miller, *Essays on the Latin Orient* (Cambridge, 1921), p. 441.
7 Quoted in May, *The Passing of the Hapsburg Monarchy*, vol. 1, p. 42.
8 Viktor Novak, *Magnum Crimen: Pola vijeka klerikalizma u Hrvatskoj* (Zagreb, 1948), p. 266. Although Tito does not mention in his

memoirs the strong anti-Italian feeling in Yugoslavia during the
1920s, this hatred was remarked on by many foreign observers. The
Scottish adventurer and diplomat R. H. Bruce Lockhart, who worked
as a banker in central Europe after the First World War, spent much
time fishing in Slovenia: 'As the wine was passed round, tongues were
unloosed, and I heard horrible tales of Slovene persecution by the
Italians in Istria and the other parts of Slovenia which Italy had
acquired under the rapacious Peace Treaty ... Today, Italian
Imperialism has done more to weld Croats, Slovenes and Serbs into
one Yugoslav nationality than the wisest statesman could have done in
fifty years.' R. H. Bruce Lockhart, *Retreat from Glory* (London,
1934), pp. 288–9.

9 Dedijer, *Tito Speaks*, pp. 49–50.
10 Ibid. pp. 63–8.
11 Stella Alexander, *The Triple Myth: A Life of Archbishop Alojzije
Stepinac* (Boulder, Colo., 1987), p. 52. Alexander Solzhenitsyn, in
The Gulag Archipelago, named the people responsible for organising
the White Sea and Moscow canal projects, without pointing out that
they were mostly Jewish.
12 Alexander, *The Tuple Myth*, p. 25.
13 Dedijer, *Tito Speaks*, pp. 98–100.
14 See Milovan Djilas, *Memoir of a Revolutionary*, (New York, 1973). A
recent author, Pero Simić, in his book *Kad, Kako i zašto je Tito
postavljen za sekretara CK KPJ* (Belgrade, 1989), has set out to
explain how Tito rose to power in the Yugoslav Communist Party. He
shows that Tito accepted Stalin's accusations against Milan Gorkić,
but gives no evidence of Tito's complicity in the frame-up.
15 Dedijer, *Tito Speaks*, pp. 112–13.
16 Milovan Djilas, *Memoir of a Revolutionary*, p. 259.
17 Ibid. p. 302.
18 R. W. Seton-Watson, *R. W. Seton-Watson and the Yugoslavs:
Correspondence 1906–41* (2 vols., London, 1979), vol. 2, p. 97.
19 R. W. Seton-Watson, from a lecture given in 1931 and reprinted in
Studies in History (Oxford, 1966).
20 Fikrita Jelić-Butić, *Ustaša i Nezavisna država Hrvatske 1941–1945*
(Zagreb, 1977), p. 214. Stella Alexander was not given permission by
the Communist authorities to see Stepinac's diaries, which are here
quoted by an approved Yugoslav historian.
21 Dedijer, *Tito Speaks*, p. 131.
22 Ibid. p. 134.
23 Ibid. p. 138.

4 Wartime

1 Hubert Butler, *The Sub-prefect Should Have Held His Tongue and Other Essays* (London, 1990), p. 285.
2 Carlo Falconi, *The Silence of Pius XII*, trans. Bernard Wall (London, 1970), p. 13.
3 Jonathan Steinberg, 'The Roman Catholic Church and Genocide in Croatia, 1941–45', paper delivered at a conference at University College, London, on 20 January 1992, to mark the fiftieth anniversary of the Wannsee Conference.

5 The Ustasha Terror

There is no book in any language giving a comprehensive history of the Independent State of Croatia. My own account in this and subsequent chapters is based on various books dealing with different aspects of the regime. By far the most important of these is Viktor Novak's immense *Magnum Crimen*, published in Zagreb in 1948, and recently reprinted. It has never been translated from the Serbo-Croat, even in an abridged form, and it was virtually suppressed in Yugoslavia when Tito was attempting to appease the Croatian Catholic Church. The author was a Catholic Croat, a believer in Yugoslavia but not a Marxist.

Two Croatian historians, Fikrita Jelić-Butić and Bogdan Krizman, have written a number of books on the NDH, based on the archives. Another historian, Antun Miletić, has gathered together a mass of documents on the NDH concentration camps and the massacre of the Muslims in the NDH, which was carried out mostly by the Serbian Chetniks. There are several accounts of the NDH by Germans and Italians. The most famous of these was by the journalist Curzio Malaparte who claimed that, during an interview, Pavelić had shown him a basketful of eyes gouged from the heads of Serbs. Although few people questioned this episode in Malaparte's book *Kaputt*, it seems that the author was actually embellishing some of the stories circulating about the Ustasha. By far the best account of the NDH by an Axis observer is that of Glaise von Horstenau, the German Plenipotentiary General, whose diaries appeared in the 1980s, edited by Peter Broucek. Von Horstenau was an Austrian in the old Habsburg tradition, who hated the Ustasha and seems to have tried to save the lives of the Serbs, if not the Jews. He was also a good writer and sharp, even sardonic, judge of character.

Since Britain and the United States were at war with the Independent State of Croatia, there are no eyewitness accounts of the NDH in English.

The first British officers to be dropped into Yugoslavia during the war went into Serbia and Montenegro. By the time that Fitzroy Maclean and others joined the Partisans in Bosnia, the NDH had lost control over much of its own territory. Few of these officers had the inclination or time to find out what had happened under the Ustasha as early as 1941. The exception to this was Stephen Clissold, who had lived in Zagreb before the war, had joined the Allied military mission and after the war served in the British Embassy in Belgrade. His excellent book *Whirlwind*, published in 1949 and describing Tito's rise to power, gives the first account in English of the Ustasha regime and how it drove the Serbs into joining the Partisans.

The Irish scholar and amateur archaeologist Hubert Butler spent much of the 1930s living in Russia, the Baltic States, Austria and Croatia. Soon after the Second World War he returned to Zagreb, interviewed Archbishop Stepinac in prison and searched through the archives of the NDH and the Catholic Church as well as the newspapers. Over the next forty years, Butler published a number of essays about the NDH in Irish magazines and collected volumes. These essays did not appear in Britain till 1990, the year of Butler's death at the age of ninety. Although his book *The Sub-prefect Should Have Held His Tongue and Other Essays* was much admired by the critics, they concentrated attention on what he wrote about Ireland, ignoring his essays on Croatia, which had not yet come into the news. Butler's writings on Yugoslavia are so understanding and prophetic that one can only regret that he did not devote a whole book to the subject.

During the 1950s, a few anti-Catholic polemicists seized on events in the NDH to abuse the Catholic Church as a whole. Among these was Edmond Paris who published, first in French, a book that was later published in English as *Genocide in Satellite Croatia 1941–45*. It was subsequently reprinted by a Protestant publisher in the US as *Convert or Die . . .*, with a blood-red cover showing a man kneeling at gunpoint in front of a priest. In spite of this lurid presentation, Paris's book is based on careful research, much of it from *Magnum Crimen*. He relies to a great extent on the testimony of Serbs who fled Yugoslavia after the war. However, their testimony bears out what we know of the Ustasha massacres from German, Italian and Yugoslav government sources.

In 1970 an English translation appeared of Carlo Falconi's *The Silence of Pius XII*, the first account of the Vatican's attitude to the wartime genocide that takes in the NDH as well as the Third Reich. Then, in 1979, Cambridge University Press published Stella Alexander's *Church and State in Yugoslavia since* 1945, whose opening chapter has a very good summary of the religious conflict there during the Second World War. Alexander later suplemented this valuable book with *The Tuple Myth*, a life of Archbishop Stepinac.

Shortly before the most recent conflict in Yugoslavia, the Cambridge historian Jonathan Steinberg published an excellent book on the impact on various countries in Europe, including the NDH, of Hitler's plan to exterminate the Jews. Although Steinberg does not read Serbo-Croat, he has put the story together from the Italian and German archives. His book *All or Nothing* and his essay 'The Roman Catholic Church and Genocide in Croatia, 1941–45', delivered on the fiftieth anniversary of the Wannsee Conference, offer further horrific evidence as to the character of the Ustasha regime. They also serve as a tesimony to the courage and decency of the Italian soldiers and civilians who saved the lives of tens of thousands of Jews and Serbs.

1 Hubert Butler, *The Sub-prefect Should Have Held His Tongue and Other Essays* (London, 1990), p. 258.
2 Viktor Novak, *Magnum Crimen: Pola vijeka klerikalizma u Hrvatskoj* (Zagreb, 1948), p. 754.
3 Aleksa Djilas, *The Contested Country: Yugoslav Unity and Communist revolution, 1919–1953* (Cambridge, Mass., 1991), p. 114.
4 Ladislaus Hory and Martin Broszat, *Der Kroatische Ustascha-Staat, 1941–1945* (Stuttgart, 1964), p. 97.
5 Butler, *The Sub-prefect*, p. 283. Butler had set out to discover how and why Artuković hid out for a year in Ireland after the war.
6 Edmond Paris, *Genocide in Satellite Croatia, 1941–45* (Chicago, 1961), p. 83.
7 Milovan Djilas, *Rise and Fall* (London, 1985), p. 49.
8 Butler, *The Sub-prefect*, p. 227.
9 Novak, *Magnum Crimen*, p. 607.
10 Ibid.p. 603.
11 Ibid.p. 605.
12 Paris, *Genocide*.
13 Novak, *Magnum Crimen*, pp. 550–2.
14 Ibid.p. 835.
15 Stella Alexander, *The Tuple Myth: A Life of Archbishop Alojzije Stepinac* (Boulder, Colo., 1987), pp. 63–4.
16 Novak, *Magnum Crimen*, p. 32.
17 Ibid. pp. 555–6.

18 Ibid.p. 557 n.
19 Ibid. pp. 557–8. This translationis from Butler, *The Sub-prefect*, p. 278.
20 *Katolički Tjednik*, 11 May 1941; quoted in Paris, *Genocide*, p. 64.
21 Novak, *Magnum Crimen*, pp. 566–71, 969; Butler, *The Sub-prefect*, pp. 258–9.
22 Novak, *Magnum Crimen*, pp. 572–3.
23 Ibid.p. 646.
24 Ibid. pp. 697–8.
25 Paris, *Genocide*, p. 59.
26 Ibid.
27 Butler, *The Sub-prefect*, pp. 288–9.
28 Paris, *Genocide*, p. 80.
29 Novak, *Magnum Crimen*, p. 651.
30 Ibid.p. 654.
31 Ibid.p. 705; *Hrvatska Krajina*, 16 May 1941.
32 Butler, *The Sub-prefect*, pp. 285–6; Novak, *Magnum Crimen*, pp. 1061–2.
33 Stella Alexander, *Church and State in Yugoslavia since 1945* (Cambridge, 1979), p. 32; Butler, *The Sub-prefect*, p. 275.
34 Butler, *The Sub-prefect*, p. 282.
35 Fikrita Jelić-Butić, *Ustaša i Nezavisna država Hrvatske 1941–1945* (Zagreb, 1977), pp. 200–1.
36 Milovan Djilas, *Wartime* (New York, 1977), p. 12.
37 Paris, *Genocide*, p. 59.
38 Hory and Broszat, *Der Kroatische Ustascha-Staat*, p. 101.
39 Alexander, *Church and State*, p. 23.
40 Jonathan Steinberg, *All or Nothing* (London, 1990), pp. 57, 63–4.
41 Paris, *Genocide*, p. 100.
42 Novak, *Magnum Crimen*, p. 652.
43 Falconi, *The Silence of Pius XII*, trans. Bernard Wall (London, 1970), p. 382.
44 Most of my information about Djujić and his followers comes from Krajina Serbs now living in London.
45 Fikrita Jelić-Butić, *Četnici u Hrvatskoj, 1941–1943* (Zagreb, 1985), p. 29.
46 Steinberg, *All or Nothing*, pp. 29–30.
47 Ibid.p. 31.
48 Ibid.p. 38.
49 Paris, *Genocide*.
50 Paris, *Genocide*.
51 Stevan K. Pavlowitch, *Unconventional Perceptions of Yugoslavia, 1940–45* (New York, 1985).

6 First Clashes with the Chetniks

From the opening of the Partisan campaign in 1941, Milovan Djilas was one of Tito's close colleagues and comrades-in-arms. His subsequent book *Wartime* is therefore a major historical document as well as a powerful work of autobiography. As always, Djilas struggles to be fair to the man whose later enmity caused him sorrow and disappointment. In spite of his disenchantment with Communism, Djilas never regretted his role as a Partisan general. Nor does he try to conceal his errors of judgement, such as his handling of the rebellion in Montenegro in 1941. In writing of this and another controversial episode, the loss of the wounded at Sutjeska in 1943, Djilas is clearly brooding over his own failure, more than thirty years later. We can also sense from Djilas's account that he was more than partly to blame for the quarrel with Moša Pijade that had a disastrous denouement in 1954. It is part of Djilas's charm as a writer that often he shows himself in a poor and even ridiculous light. One gets the impression from Djilas's own accounts of their conversations that Tito and Ranković were amused as well as occasionally vexed by his Montenegrin stubbornness and impetuosity. Because he is such a good writer and an unrivalled source of information, Djilas may at times seem to be taking over from Tito as central character in the story. Perhaps this is as it should be. Although Tito was always in command and although he relied for advice more on Kardelj and Ranković, he took his inspiration from younger romantics like Djilas and Ivo Lola Ribar. Ribar's death in 1943 and Djilas's defection in 1954 deprived Tito of much of his purpose in life. And in spite of the quarrel, Djilas has lived to become the last and greatest of those who made Tito's Yugoslavia.

1 Vladimir Dedijer, *Tito Speaks: His Self-Portrait and Struggle with Stalin* (London, 1953), p. 143.
2 Ibid.p. 146.
3 Milovan Djilas, *Wartime* (New York, 1977), p. 8.
4 Ibid. pp. 23–4.
5 Ibid.p. 37.
6 Ibid.p. 81.
7 Stevan K. Pavlowitch, *Yugoslavia* (London, 1971), p. 122.
8 Dedijer, *Tito Speaks*, p. 149.
9 Milovan Djilas, *Wartime*, p. 103.
10 Dedijer, *Tito Speaks*, p. 158.
11 Milovan Djilas, *Wartime*, p. 97.
12 Ibid.p. 91.
13 Ibid. pp. 93–102.

14 Dedijer, *Tito Speaks*, p. 165.
15 Ibid.p. 170.
16 Milovan Djilas, *Wartime*, p. 119.
17 Ibid.p. 99.
18 Ibid.p. 120.
19 Dedijer, *Tito Speaks*, p. 174.
20 Milovan Djilas, *Wartime*, p. 139. Vladimir Dedijer and Antun Miletić, the editors of the book of documents *Genocid nad Muslimanima*, 1941–1945 (Sarajevo, 1990), give an appendix with a list of the names of 3,525 Muslims allegedly killed by the Chetniks in the Foča district during the period of 1941–2, plus a further 55 killed by persons unknown. The corresponding figures for Muslims allegedly killed by the Chetniks and persons unknown in the district of Goražde, also in eastern Bosnia, are 1,365 and 71 respectively. Most of the documents reprinted by Dedijer and Miletić were kept in the Sarajevo library destroyed in 1992 by artillery fire from latter-day Chetniks. I have not been able to find any statistics or even estimates on the number of Slav Muslims killed by the Chetniks in southern Serbia and Montenegro. Muslims have told me that the worst Chetnik atrocities took place in the Sandjak region of Serbia.
21 Dedijer and Miletić (eds.), *Genocid nad Muslimanima*, pp. 25–31. This is the first use I have found of the term 'ethnic cleansing', recently taken up by the foreign press. Only a Serb or Croat nationalist of the most purblind sort could see the Muslim Slavs as a different ethnic group.
22 Milovan Djilas, *Wartime*, pp. 139–40.
23 Ibid.p. 174.
24 Ibid.p. 54.
25 Ibid.p. 173.
26 Ibid. pp. 175–6.
27 Ibid.p. 176.

7 The Long March

1 Milovan Djilas, *Wartime*, (New York, 1977), p. 188.
2 Ibid.p. 205.
3 Ibid.p. 211.
4 Ibid.p. 198.
5 Ibid.p. 205, quoting Josip Broz Tito, *Borba za oslobodjenje Jugoslavije* (Belgrade, 1947), pp. 138–9.

6 Stevan K. Pavlowitch *The Improbable Survivor: Yugoslavia and its Problems, 1918–1988* (London, 1988), p. 37.

7 Milovan Djilas, *Wartime*, p. 212. For a sympathetic account of Nazor, see Hubert Butler's essay 'Nazor, Oroschatz and the Von Berks' in *The Sub-prefect Should Have Held His Tongue and Other Essays* (London, 1990).

8 Information from Krajina Serbs now living in London.

9 Peter Broucek (ed.) *Ein General in Zwielicht: Die Erinnerungen von Edmund Glaise von Horstenau* (3 vols., Vienna, 1988), vol. 3, p. 153.

10 Vlatko Maček, *In the Struggle for Freedom* (University Park, Pa., 1957), p. 234.

11 Maček, *In The Struggle*, p. 245.

12 Antun Miletić, *Koncentracioni logor Jasenovac* (2 vols., Belgrade, 1986), vol. 1, p. 334. This collection of documents is well edited by Miletić, with proper references, a commentary and many reproductions of the originals. Vladimir Dedijer's *The Yugoslav Auschwitz and the Vatican*, trans. Harvey Kendall (Buffalo, NY, 1992) is confused, rambling and very exaggerated. It does not give references, although most of these could probably be traced to Miletić's book. The Croatian historian Franjo Tudjman, the President of his country since 1990, has given what might be called a 'revisionist' version of what went on in Jasenovac and the other camps of the NDH. This is discussed in Chapter 19.

13 Milovan Djilas, *Wartime*, p. 210.

14 Edmond Paris, *Genocide in Satellite Croatia, 1941–45* (Chicago, 1961), p. 137.

15 Viktor Novak, *Magnum Crimen: Pola vijeka klerikalizma u Hrvatskoj* (Zagreb, 1948), p. 649 n.

16 Paris, *Genocide*, p. 149.

17 Novak, *Magnum Crimen*, pp. 677–8.

18 Stevan K. Pavlowitch, *Unconventional Perceptions of Yugoslavia, 1940–45*, (New York, 1985), based on interviews in Australia with Rapotec, now a distinguished artist. (Also see Stella Alexander, *The Tuple Myth: A Life of Archbishop Alojzije Stepinac* (Boulder, Colo., 1987), p. 92.)

19 Alexander, *The Triple Myth*, p. 91.

20 Butler, *The Sub-prefect*, p. 288.

21 Novak, *Magnum Crimen*, p. 966.

22 Ibid. p. 890.

23 Paris, *Genocide*, pp. 177–8; Carlo Falconi, *The Silence of Pius XII*, trans. Bernard Wall (London, 1970), p. 314.

24 Falconi, *The Silence*, p. 315–16.
25 Jonathan Steinberg, *All or Nothing* (London, 1990), pp. 43–4.
26 Mario Roatta, *Otto Milioni di Baionette* (Verona, 1946), p. 177.
27 Steinberg, *All or Nothing*, pp. 45–7.
28 Miletić, *Koncentracioni logor Jasenovac*, vol. 1, pp. 170–2.
29 Broucek, *Ein General*, vol. 3, p. 165. Glaise von Horstenau describes a lunch he attended at which Hitler harangued the guests, including Pavelić, on the iniquity of the Jews. Afterwards von Horstenau remarked to a colleague: 'It would be great if the Führer were ever to hear that the man sitting opposite him has a half-Jewish wife, whose sister has also married a Jew.' (Ibid.p. 208.)
30 Ibid.p. 168.
31 Ibid.p. 167.

8 The Fourth and Fifth Offensives

1   Vladimir Dedijer and Antun Miletić (eds.), *Genocid nad Muslimanima, 1941–1945* (Sarajevo, 1990), p. 254.
2   Vladimir Dedijer, *The War Diaries* (London, 1990), entries for 3 December 1942, and 30 January and 14 February 1943.
3   F. W. Deakin, *The Brutal Friendship* (London, 1962), p. 99.
4   Ibid.p. 190.
5   Dedijer and Miletić (eds.), *Genocid nad Muslimanima*, pp. 161–2, 200–1.
6   Ibid. pp. 195–6.
7   Mišo Leković, *Martovski Pregovori* (Belgrade, 1985), p. 35.
8   Ibid. pp. 26–7.
9   Milovan Djilas, *Wartime* (New York, 1977), p. 220.
10 Deakin, *The Brutal Friendship*, pp. 184–5.
11 Ibid. pp. 183, 199.
12 Dedijer, *War Diaries*, entry for 6 March 1943.
13 Milovan Djilas, *Wartime*, p. 230.
14 Ibid. pp. 231–2.
15 Ibid. pp. 236–40.
16 Ibid. pp. 242–3.
17 William Hoettl, *The Secret Front: The Story of Nazi Espionage* (London, 1953), pp. 170–2.
18 Milovan Djilas, *Wartime*, p. 243. This woman may have been Tito's common-law wife, Herta Hass. Djilas would have refrained from mentioning her in a book published during Tito's life. In the memoir of Tito published after his death, Djilas mentions that Herta was one

of the exchanged prisoners whom he brought back to the Partisans from Sarajevo. He did not break the news to her in advance that Tito now had another mistress, Zdenka. Apparently Tito himself explained that the relationship was finished. Djilas liked Herta as much as he disliked Zdenka.

19 Glaise von Horstenau disapproved of Archbishop Stepinac because the latter had changed allegiance during the First World War, deserted from the Austro-Hungarian Army and joined one of the Yugoslav brigades on the Salonica front.

20 Peter Broucek (ed.), *Ein General in Zwielicht: Die Erinnerungen von Edmund Glaise von Horstenau* (3 vols., Vienna, 1988), vol. 3, p. 35.

21 Hoettl, *The Secret Front*, p. 42.

22 Milovan *Djilas, Wartime*, p. 244.

23 Ibid.p. 246.

24 Dedijer and Miletić (eds.), *Genocid nad Muslimanima*, p. 362.

25 Milovan Djilas, *Wartime*, p. 248.

26 Ibid.p. 256.

27 Vladimir Dedijer, *Tito Speaks: His Self-Portrait and Struggle with Stalin* (London, 1953), pp. ix–xii.

28 Milovan Djilas, *Wartime*, p. 300.

29 Dedijer, *Tito Speaks*, p. 195.

30 Milovan Djilas, *Wartime*, p. 303.

31 Ibid., p. 302.

32 Ibid.p. 310.

33 Ibid.p. 326.

34 Ibid.p. 330.

35 Ibid. pp. 332–8.

9 The Triumph of the Partisans

For the first and last time in the story of Tito, some of the most revealing sources are in English. Many of the British people involved in Yugoslavia from 1943 until the end of the war afterwards published their reminiscences. They included such famous authors as Evelyn Waugh and Winston Churchill. The two books of memoir by Sir Fitzroy Maclean, the head of the British military mission to Tito, are excellent both as history and as entertainment. Maclean's biographer Frank McLynn has done thorough and comprehensive research into Britain's role in Yugoslavia during the war. His findings vindicate the decision to back Tito. He also understands that the British had little influence on the outcome of Yugoslavia's civil war.

1 Peter Broucek (ed.), *Ein General in Zwielicht: Die Erinnerungen von Edmund Glaise von Horstenau* (3 vols., Vienna, 1988), vol. 3, pp. 38–9.

2 Fitzroy Maclean, *Eastern Approaches*, (London, 1949), pp. 402–3.

3 Maclean's biographer believes that he was not 'as ignorant of Ultra as (according to the rules) he should have been . . .' (Frank McLynn, *Fitzroy Maclean* (London, 1992), p. 217).

4 Ralph Bennett, *Ultra and Mediterranean Strategy, 1941–1945* (London, 1989), p. 338.

5 Ibid.p. 343.

6 Ibid.p. 347.

7 Fitzroy Maclean, *Disputed Barricade* (London, 1957), p. 233.

8 Ibid.p. 233; Milovan Djilas, *Wartime* (New York, 1977), p. 348.

9 Maclean, *Disputed Barricade*, p. 233.

10 McLynn, *Fitzroy Maclean*, pp. 158–9.

11 Ibid. pp. 157–61.

12 Quoted in ibid. p. 162.

13 Phyllis Auty and Richard Clogg (eds.), *British Policy towards Wartime Resistance in Yugoslavia and Greece* (London, 1975), pp. 75–6; see also Milovan Djilas, *Wartime*, p. 251.

14 Milovan Djilas, *Wartime*, p. 346.

15 Vladimir Dedijer, *Tito Speaks: His Self-Portrait and Struggle with Stalin* (London, 1953), pp. 203–4.

16 Milovan Djilas, *Wartime*, p. 356.

17 Ibid.

18 Dedijer, *Tito Speaks*, pp. 204–5.

19 Milovan Djilas, *Wartime*, p. 363.

20 Dedijer, *Tito Speaks*, pp. 244–6.

21 Milovan Djilas, *Wartime*, 359–62.

22 Bennett, *Ultra*, p. 347.

23 Milovan Djilas, *Conversations with Stalin*, trans. Michael B. Petrovich (London, 1962), p. 103.

24 McLynn, *Fitzroy Maclean*, pp. 185–7.

25 Ibid.p. 187.

26 For Farish's final report, see Michael Lees, *The Rape of Serbia* (New York, 1990), pp. 288–92.

27 McLynn, *Fitzroy Maclean*, p. 189.

28 Stella Alexander, *Church and State in Yugoslavia since 1945* (Cambridge, 1979), p. 18.

29 Lees, *The Rape of Serbia*, pp. 300–2.

30 Viktor Novak, *Magnum Crimen: Pola vijeka klerikalizma u Hrvatskoj* (Zagreb, 1948), pp. 1033–4.

31 Ibid.p. 1000.

32 Carlo Falconi, *The Silence of Pius XII*, trans. Bernard Wall (London, 1970), pp. 371–2.

33 McLynn, *Fitzroy Maclean*, pp. 202–7. Apparently Ultra gave advance warning of the German attack, but this was not passed on to the British at Drvar, for fear of revealing that the code had been cracked.

34 Dedijer, *Tito Speaks*, p. 218.

35 Ibid.p. 219.

36 *The Diaries of Evelyn Waugh*, ed. Michael Davie (London, 1976), p. 571.

37 Ibid. pp. 571–2; David Pryce-Jones, *Evelyn Waugh and his World* (London, 1973), p. 135.

38 F.O. 371/48910, Captain Evelyn Waugh to Brigadier Maclean, 30 March 1945. (Quoted by Anthony Rhodes, *The Vatican in the Age of the Dictators, 1922–1945* (London, 1973), p. 328.)

39 McLynn, *Fitzroy Maclean*, p. 212.

40 Ibid.p. 195.

41 Ibid.p. 214.

42 Maclean, *Disputed Barricade*, p. 275.

43 Martin Gilbert, *Road to Victory: Winston S. Churchill, 1941–1945* (London, 1986), p. 890.

44 McLynn, *Fitzroy Maclean*, pp. 215–16.

45 Ibid.p. 217.

46 Ibid.p. 219.

47 Dedijer, *Tito Speaks*, p. 231.

48 Ibid.p. 233.

49 Ibid.p. 234.

50 Milovan Djilas, *Conversations with Stalin*, p. 82.

51 Novak, *Magnum Crimen*, pp. 1038–9.

52 McLynn, *Fitzroy Maclean*, p. 234.

10 Power

Milovan Djilas is once more the most important source on Tito and Yugoslavia from 1945 until his own fall from power in 1954. His memoirs include *Rise and Fall, Conversations with Stalin* and *Tito*.

1 *Official History of the Second World War*, vol. 4, part 3.

2 Milovan Djilas, *Rise and Fall* (London, 1985), pp. 41–2.

3 Ibid. pp. 20–2.

4 Interview with George Seldes, editor of *In Fact*, 22 November 1948.

5 Milovan Djilas, *Rise and Fall*, p. 15.
6 Ibid.p. 16.
7 Ibid.p. 14.
8 Milovan Djilas, *Tito: The Story from Inside* (London, 1981), p. 141.
9 Ibid.p. 143.
10 Ibid. pp. 142–3.

11 Settling Scores

Britain was largely responsible for forcing at least 30,000 Yugoslavs to return to their deaths at the hands of Tito's Partisans. Britain was also largely responsible for *not* sending back Ustasha war criminals such as Ante Pavelić. Thanks to the secrecy of the British government, both these shameful matters are still obscure. Some writers on the forced repatriations to Yugoslavia and the Soviet Union have been carried away by indignation, and muddied the issue with wild allegations. I have relied mostly on Cowgill *et al., The Repatriations from Austria in 1945: The Report of an Inquiry*, One of the three authors of this report, the journalist Christopher Booker, pursued his inquiries further and wrote his own separate book, which has not yet been published. He concludes that most of the Yugoslavs were shot on the orders of Tito, after a vengeful speech at Ljubljana.

A Yugoslav historian, Bogdan Krizman, has written a book on the Ustasha in exile, *Pavelić u bjekstvu*, and their activities are also mentioned by Antun Miletić in his books on Jasenovac concentration camp. Hubert Butler made a special study of the escape of Andrija Artuković, the 'Yugoslav Himmler'. The Australian broadcaster Mark Aarons's *Sanctuary: Nazi Fugitives in Australia* describes in chilling detail the activities of the Ustasha in Australia, supplementing an earlier book by three other authors on the clandestine element in Australian politics, *Rooted in Secrecy*. Aarons also collaborated with John Loftus, a former attorney with the US Justice Department, to write *Ratlines*, the story of the escape of Nazi and Ustasha criminals after the Second World War. Many Ustasha war criminals and their friends and relations are now back in Croatia.

1 Stevan K. Pavlowitch, *Yugoslavia* (London, 1971), p. 177 n.
2 The pro-Serb Michael Lees also served on the commission.
3 Anthony Cowgill, Lord Brimelow and Christopher Booker, *The Reparations from Austria in 1945: The Report of an Inquiry* (London, 1990), p. 14.
4 Ibid.p. 41.

5 Ibid.p. 44.

6 Ibid. pp. 81–2.

7 Interview with Christopher Booker.

8 *Globus*, 22 May 1992.

9 Mark Aarons and John Loftus, *Ratlines* (London, 1991), pp. 273–4.

10 *Globus*, 22 May 1992.

11 Croat Franciscans helped to arrange the escape of the German war criminal Klaus Barbie. See Aarons and Loftus, *Ratlines, passim*.

12 Bogdan Krizman, *Pavelić u bjekstvu* (Zagreb, 1986), p. 143.

13 See the essay 'The Artuković File' in Hubert Butler's *The Sub-prefect Should Have Held His Tongue and Other Essays* (London, 1990).

14 Mark Aarons, *Sanctuary: Nazi Fugitives in Australia*, (Melbourne, 1989), p. 251. Apparently Luburić and the more extreme Ustasha broke away when Pavelić started to talk terms with *émigré* right-wing Serbs, trying to agree on a frontier between the two nations.

15 Milovan Djilas, *Rise and Fall* (London, 1985), p. 42.

16 Ibid. pp. 55–6.

17 Ibid.p. 38.

18 Ibid. pp. 36–7.

19 Butler, *The Sub-prefect*, p. 227.

20 Stella Alexander, *The Triple Myth: A Life of Archbishop Alojzije Stepinac* (Boulder, Colo., 1987), p. 117; Milovan Djilas, *Rise and Fall*, p. 39.

21 Alexander, *The Triple Myth*, p. 121.

22 Ibid.p. 133.

23 Ibid.p. 130.

24 George Selde, *Witness to a Century* (New York, 1987), p. 432. George Seldes, a veteran newspaper reporter of left-wing but anti-Stalinist views, had got to know Vladimir Dedijer and through him obtained an interview with Tito in November 1948, published in Seldes's radical magazine *In Fact: An Antidote for Falsehood in the Daily Press*. In 1950 Seldes went on holiday to Dubrovnik. Tito summoned him to Zagreb and plied him with questions about the American press's treatment of the Stepinac trial: 'How powerful is the Roman Catholic Church in the United States?' 'Why is the whole American press against Yugoslavia, while in the Catholic countries, such as Spain and Italy, it's not?' 'Do the American people know that Stepinac is just as guilty as Hitler of genocide?' Seldes adds a postscript to his account of meeting Tito: 'Of all the world political leaders, noted and notorious, or all the prominent men I ever met, good or evil, dictators and presidents, newsmakers all of whom I had

the good or bad fortune to interview and in whose countries I
sometimes lived for years, the one I knew longest was Benito
Mussolini, 1919 to 1925. In 1919 and 1920 we worked together on an
equal basis. I thought we were friends – did he not address me as *caro
collego*, "dear colleague", and sometimes call me "caro Giorgio"? In
1924 when I finally got an official interview with him, he pretended
we had never met. Tito talked to me as a friend.' (*Witness to a
Century*, pp. 427–34.)

25 Alexander, *The Triple Myth*, p. 163.
26 *Spectator*, 4 April 1981.
27 Alexander, *The Tuple Myth*, p. 217.
28 Butler, *The Sub-prefect*, p. 285.
29 Ibid. pp. 271–83.

12 The Quarrel with Stalin

The story of Yugoslavia's break with the Soviet Union is told in the
greatest of all Milovan Djilas's books, *Conversations with Stalin*, sup-
plemented by some of his later memoirs when he was able to mention
politically delicate matters. With the opening up of the Moscow files to
foreign scholars – at a price – we may get to know how the Russians
regarded their conversations with Tito. Already one of the Russian
newspapers has published a story on how Stalin sent SMERSH assassins
to Italy in the hope of getting to Yugoslavia and killing Tito.

1 Milovan Djilas, *Conversations with Stalin*, trans. Michael B. Petrovich
   (London, 1962), p. 56.
2 Ibid. p. 59.
3 *Borba*, 12 December 1944; quoted in Stephen Clissold, *Djilas: The
   Progress of a Revolutionary*, (London, 1983), p. 138.
4 Milovan Djilas, *Conversations with Stalin*, p. 70.
5 Ibid. p. 88.
6 Ibid. pp. 101–3.
7 Milovan Djilas, *Rise and Fall* (London, 1985), p. 78.
8 Ibid. pp. 77–81.
9 Ibid. p. 85.
10 Ibid. p. 92.
11 *Borba*, 28 May 1945; quoted in Milovan Djilas, *Rise and Fall*, p. 91.
   It was in the same speech that Tito demanded punishment for the
   anti-Communists sent back by the British from Austria.
12 Milovan Djilas, *Rise and Fall*, p. 92.

13 Milovan Djilas, *Conversations with Stalin*, p. 127.
14 Ibid. pp. 129–30.
15 Ibid. pp. 139–40.
16 Ibid. pp. 140–6.
17 Milovan Djilas, *Rise and Fall*, p. 162.
18 Milovan Djilas, *Conversations with Stalin*, pp. 157–8.
19 Ibid. pp. 157–65.
20 Ibid.p. 168.
21 Milovan Djilas, *Rise and Fall*, p. 173.
22 Vladimir Dedijer, *Tito Speaks: His Self-Portrait and Struggle with Stalin* (London, 1953), pp. xiii–xv.
23 Milovan Djilas, *Rise and Fall*, p. 182.
24 Ibid.p. 185.
25 Ibid. pp. 184–6; Dedijer, *Tito Speaks*, pp. 350–1.
26 Milovan Djilas, *Rise and Fall*, p. 200.
27 Ibid.
28 Ibid.p. 201.
29 Ibid. pp. 228–9.
30 Ibid. pp. 216–19.
31 Duncan Wilson, *Tito's Yugoslavia* (Cambridge, 1979), p. 62.
32 Milovan Djilas, *Rise and Fall*, p. 250.
33 Barbara Tuchman, *The March of Folly: From Troy to Vietnam* (London, 1984), p. 304.

13 Titoism

Milovan Djilas's quarrel with Tito is really the leitmotiv of all his remarkable volumes of memoir. It is told in most detail in *Rise and Fall*. Stephen Clissold's excellent *Djilas: The Progress of a Revolutionary* offers us many additional insights. Clissold was an assistant lecturer at Zagreb University in the late 1930s, joining the staff of the Consulate, and later Maclean's military mission. After the war he served in the British Embassy in Belgrade. He was remarkably free from the querulous spirit that characterised the British, as well as the Serbs and Croats, involved in Yugoslavia during and after the war.

1 Milovan Djilas, *Tito: The Story from Inside* (London, 1981), pp. 145–8; *idem, Rise and Fall* (London, 1985), p. 278.
2 Milovan Djilas, *Tito*, pp. 148–9.
3 Milovan Djilas, *Rise and Fall*, pp. 268–9.
4 Ibid. pp. 278–80.

5 *The Letters of Evelyn Waugh*, ed. Mark Amory (London, 1980), p. 395. Evelyn Waugh wrote letters protesting about the Tito visit to the *New Statesman*, the *Spectator* and *The Times*.

6 Quoted by Milovan Djilas in an obituary in the *Sunday Times*, 11 May 1980.

7 Milovan Djilas, *Rise and Fall*, p. 286.

8 Vladimir Dedijer, *Tito Speaks: His Self-Portrait and Struggle with Stalin* (London, 1953), pp. 418–33.

9 Milovan Djilas, *Tito*, pp. 65–6.

10 Milovan Djilas, *Rise and Fall*, pp. 335–6.

11 Milovan Djilas, *Tito*, pp. 65–6.

12 Milovan Djilas, *Rise and Fall*, p. 334.

13 Stephen Clissold, *Djilas: The Progress of a Revolutionary* (London, 1983), p. 232.

14 Milovan Djilas, *Rise and Fall*, p. 323.

15 Ibid. pp. 324–5.

16 Ibid. p. 337.

17 Ibid. p. 340.

18 Ibid. p. 341.

19 Milovan Djilas, *The Unperfect Society: Beyond the New Class* (London, 1969), pp. 17–18.

20 *Borba*, 20 December 1953; quoted in Clissold, *Djilas*, p. 236.

21 *Borba*, 22 December 1953; quoted in Clissold, *Djilas*, p. 237.

22 Quoted in Clissold, *Djilas*, pp. 238–9.

23 *Borba*, 24 December 1953; quoted in Clissold, *Djilas*, p. 239.

24 *Borba*, 27 December 1953; quoted in Clissold, *Djilas*, pp. 239–40.

25 Clissold, *Djilas*, p. 244.

26 Ibid. pp. 245–6.

27 Milovan Djilas, *Rise and Fall*, pp. 354–5.

28 Clissold, *Djilas*, 247–8.

29 Milovan Djilas, *Rise and Fall*, p. 360.

30 Clissold, *Djilas*, pp. 249–51.

31 Ibid. p. 231.

32 Ibid. p. 256.

33 Milovan Djilas, *Tito*, p. 133.

34 When I sprang this story on Djilas, rather unfairly, during a TV interview in 1968, he said that he could not remember the incident, but that though he had been stern he had never been cruel. In his book *Rise and Fall*, Djilas returned to this incident: 'Meanwhile in *Borba* – was it in 1945 or 1946? – I attacked the courts for delivering too lenient a verdict against some small-time swindler ... The

wretched swindler was given a death sentence; fortunately, he was not executed, I heard. From the standpoint of ideology and revolutionary morality, I was right, but the consequences for order and legality were catastrophic.' (*Rise and Fall*, pp. 17–18.)

35 Vladimir Dedijer, *Novi prilozi za biografiju druga Tita* (Rijeka, 1981), p. 627.

36 Milovan Djilas, *Rise and Fall*, p. 382.

37 Clissold, *Djilas*, p. 290.

14 Yugoslavia's Place in the World

After 1954, and the fall from grace of both Djilas and Dedijer, we no longer have any firsthand account of Tito's personal and political life. The rest of his circle seem to have had no taste for writing their memoirs. Of Tito's three main biographers, only Fitzroy Maclean kept up his friendship. For Tito's reaction to the Hungary crisis of 1956 and the Czechoslovakia crisis of 1968, we have to depend on the secondhand estimates of politicians such as Khrushchev, diplomats such as Mičunović and journalists who reported on these events. During the 1960s and early 1970s, I had the good fortune to travel a lot on journalistic assignments, some of them in Yugoslavia, neighbouring countries and areas of the Third World where Tito was highly regarded.

1 Milovan Djilas, *Conversations with Stalin*, trans. Michael B. Petrovich (London, 1962), p. 112.

2 Nikita Khrushchev, *Khrushchev Remembers* (London, 1971), pp. 375–6.

3 Veljko Mičunović, *Moscow Diary*, trans. David Floyd (London, 1980), p. 61.

4 Timothy Ware, *The Orthodox Church* (London, 1993), p. 157.

5 Mičunović, *Moscow Diary*, p. 61.

6 Stephen Clissold, *Djilas: The Progress of a Revolutionary* (London, 1983), p. 269.

7 Milovan Djilas, *Rise and Fall* (London, 1985), pp. 118–19.

8 I quoted this remark in a *Sunday Times Magazine* article on Tito published later in 1968.

9 Clissold, *Djilas*, p. 301.

10 Ion Pacepa, *Red Horizons* (London, 1988), p. 345.

11 Barbara Tuchman, *The March of Folly: From Troy to Vietnam* (London, 1984), p. 304.

12 Richard West, *The White Tribes Revisited* (London, 1978), pp. 8–9.

13 Stevan K. Pavlowitch, *Yugoslavia* (London, 1971), p. 226.

15 The Return of the Nationalities Problem

1 Stevan K. Pavlowitch, *Yugoslavia* (London, 1971), p. 288 n. He cites the estimates given in I. Hamilton, *Yugoslavia – Patterns of Economic Activity* (New York, 1968), and Fritz Hondius, *The Yugoslav Community of Nations* (The Hague and Paris, 1968).

2 Antun Miletić, *Koncentracioni logor Jasenovac* (2 vols., Belgrade, 1986), vol. 1, p. 170.

3 Hubert Butler, *The Sub-prefect Should Have Held His Tongue and Other Essays* (London, 1990), pp. 271–303.

4 Anne Kindersley, *The Mountains of Serbia* (London, 1976), pp. 10, 100.

5 Ibid.p. 142.

6 Duncan Wilson, *Tito's Yugoslavia* (Cambridge, 1979), p. 180.

7 Pavlowitch, *Yugoslavia*, pp. 317–18.

8 Wilson, *Tito's Yugoslavia*, pp. 203–4.

9 Sava Bosnić, 'The Political Career and Writings of Franjo Tudjman', *South Slav Journal*, 14/1–2. Professor Bosnić's article also appeared as a booklet, *Franjo Tudjman: Une carrière ambiguë* (Lausanne, 1993).

10 Joan Coxsedge, Ken Caldicott and Gerry Harant, *Rooted in Secrecy: The Clandestine Element in Australian Politics* (Melbourne, 1982), pp. 43–59; Mark Aarons, *Sanctuary: Nazi Fugitives in Australia* (Melbourne, 1989). Mystery still surrounds the JAT aeroplane disaster. It has been alleged that the aircraft had illegally crossed Czechoslovak territory and was brought down by the Warsaw Pact defences. The Belgrade government did not want to admit that aircraft of the national carrier were vulnerable to sabotage. The Western press and police showed no interest in the affair.

11 Husein Ćišić, *Bosanskohercegovački Muslimani i bosanska autonomija* (Sarajevo, 1991).

12 Stella Alexander, *Church and State in Yugoslavia since 1945* (Cambridge, 1979), pp. 124–7.

13 Pavlowitch, *Yugoslavia*, p. 316.

14 Alexander, *Church and State*, pp. 244–5.

15 Mugdim Karabeg in conversation with the author in 1991.

16 *Observer Magazine*, 30 March 1980.

16 The Final Years

1 Melvyn Bragg, *Rich: The Life of Richard Burton* (London, 1988).

2 Frank McLynn, *Fitzroy Maclean* (London, 1992), p. 360.

3 Ibid. pp. 361–2.

17 Reassessment of Tito

1 Rebecca West, *Black Lamb and Grey Falcon* (2 vols., London, 1942), vol. 2, p. 215.
2 Milovan Djilas, *Tito: The Story from Inside* (London, 1981), p. 8.
3 Ibid.p. 12.
4 Ibid. pp. 69, 132.
5 Ibid.p. 25.
6 Stevan K. Pavlowitch, *The Improbable Survivor: Yugoslavia and its Problems, 1918–1988* (London, 1988), p. 26.
7 Stevan K. Pavlowitch, *Tito: Yugoslavia's Great Dictator. A Reassessment* (London, 1992), p. 111.
8 Ibid.p. 112.
9 Ibid.p. 61 n.
10 Frank McLynn, *Fitzroy Maclean* (London, 1992), pp. 259–60.
11 Rebecca West, *Black Lamb*, vol. 1, p. 215.
12 Martin Dunford and Jack Holland, T*he Rough Guide to Yugoslavia* (London, 1985), p. 37.

18 Towards Disaster in Serbia

1 Aleksa Djilas, 'Profile of Slobodan Milošević', *Foreign Affairs* (Summer 1993). Djilas refers to Slavoljub Djukić's *Kako se dogodio vodja: Borba za vlast u Srbiji posle Josipa Broza* (Belgrade, 1992).
2 Velemir Vesović (ed.), *Kosovska bitka: Mit, legenda i stvarnosti* (Belgrade, 1988), p. 17.
3 Stevan K. Pavlowitch, *The Improbable Survivor: Yugoslavia and its Problems, 1918–1988* (London, 1988), p. 84.
4 Aleksa Djilas, 'Profile of Slobodan Milošević', p. 84.
5 Quoted in ibid.
6 Dehan Lučič, *Tajne Albanske Mafije* (Belgrade, 1989).

19 Towards Disaster in Croatia

1 Jakov Blažević, *Mač a ne mir* (3 vols., Zagreb, 1980), vol. 3.
2 Richard West, 'Cathedral: Keep out!', *Spectator*, 4 April 1981.
3 Franjo Tudjman, *Nationalism in Contemporary Europe* (Boulder, Colo., 1981).
4 Ibid.p. 106.
5 Ibid. pp. 113–14.

6 Ibid. pp. 162–3.

7 Ibid. p. 117

8 Hubert Butler, *The Sub-prefect Should Have Held His Tongue and Other Essays* (London, 1990), p. 303 n.

9 Robert Fisk, 'Jasenovac', *Independent*, 15 August 1992.

10 Franjo Tudjman, *Bespuća povijesne zbiljnosti: Rasprava o povijesti i filosofiji zlosilje* (Zagreb, 1990). The title, like much of the contents of the book, is obscure and vaguely sinister. The first part has been variously translated as 'Impasses', 'Confusion' or 'Wilderness' of 'Historical Reality'. The subtitle means 'A Discussion of History and of the Philosophy of Bad Force'. Slobodan Despot, who has translated from English into French Sava Bosnić's essay on Tudjman, has this to say about the title: '*Zlosilje*, le mot utilisé dans le sous-titre, n'est pas d'usage courant et n'a pas de traduction précise. Les notions de "violence mauvaise", "mal violent" et "génocide" en sont des approximations aussi (in) adéquates les unes que les autres. Le vocabulaire de l'auteur comprend beaucoup de termes de ce genre, qui sont peut-être des creations personnelles, car ils figurent dans aucun dictionnaire publié en Croatie.' ('*Zlosilje*, the word used in the subtitle, is not in current usage and has no precise translation. The notions of "evil violence", "violent evil" and "genocide" are approximations of equal (in) adequacy. The author's vocabulary includes many terms of this kind, which are perhaps personal inventions, because they do not appear in any dictionary published in Croatia.') Since Tudjman's book has become the subject of much international argument, discussed by the Presidents of Israel and the United States, it is worth noting the further remarks of Slobodan Despot: 'Semblable remarque peut-être faite sur le mot *bespuća*, restitué par *déroutes, impasses* ou *dérives* au gré des traducteurs. En fait il s'agit d'un mot signifiant à peu près "étendues sans bornes" ou "terres desertes", mais que l'auteur utilise dans un sens manifestement transposé et métaphorique.' In my own translations, based on those of various students of Tudjman's style, I have tried to avoid giving precision to words and phrases that are obscure, perhaps intentionally so.

11 Ibid. p. 161.

12 Ibid. p. 149.

13 Ibid. pp. 152–3.

14 Ibid. pp. 172, 160.

15 Ibid. p. 315.

16 Ibid. pp. 318–9.

17 Arthur Evans, *Illyrian Letters* (London, 1878), p. 4.
18 Auguste Picot, *Les Serbes d'Hongroi* (Prague, 1873), pp. 241–3.
19 *The Times*, 25 August 1991.
20 *Independent Magazine*, 16 November 1990.
21 *Guardian*, 30 June 1993.
22 Franjo Tudjman, 'Croatia at the Crossroads: In Search of a Democratic Confederacy', lecture delivered at the Centre for Policy Studies, 7 May 1991.
23 *Sunday Times*, 12 May 1991. When Professor Stone says that the Archduke Franz Ferdinand was shot 'by a Serbian nationalist who was actually aiming at someone else', he may be thinking of Princip's second shot, aimed at the Governor of Bosnia, which killed instead the Archduchess Sophie. Princip expressed regret for this at his trial. Far from being a 'Serbian nationalist', Princip belonged to the Mlada Bosna (Young Bosnia) movement of Orthodox, Roman Catholic and Muslim radicals hoping to build a Yugoslavia. Princip refused to describe himself as a Serb at his trial.

20 Towards Disaster in Bosnia-Hercegovina

1 Ljudevit Rupčić, *Gospina Ukazanja u Medjugorju* (Samobor, 1983), pp. 45–6.
2 Ibid.p. 117.
3 Richard Bassett, *Balkan Hours* (London 1990), p. 90.
4 Pavao Žanić, *Medjugorje* (Mostar, 1990). This pamphlet was published in English.
5 Arthur Evans, *Illyrian Letters* (London, 1878), p. 66.
6 Vuk Karadjić, *The Red Knight*, trans. Daniel Weissbort and Tomislav Longinović (London, 1992), p. 53.
7 Stella Alexander, *The Tuple Myth: A Life of Archbishop Alojzije Stepinac* (Boulder, Colo., 1987), pp. 26–7.
8 Edmond Paris, *Genocide in Satellite Croatia, 1941–45* (Chicago, 1961), p. 64.
9 See Ch. 5.
10 Information from Andrew Brown of the *Independent*, who visited Široki Brijeg in 1993.
11 *Oslobodjenje*, 5 August 1991.
12 'Yugoslavia needs the Pope' and 'Christian foes kept apart by Muslims', *Sunday Telegraph*, 11 August 1991.

Bibliography

(Place of publication is London unless otherwise indicated.)

Aarons, Mark, *Sanctuary: Nazi Fugitives in Australia* (Melbourne, 1989)
—— and Loftus, John, *Ratlines* (1991)
Alexander, Stella, *Church and State in Yugoslavia since 1945* (Cambridge, 1979)
—— *The Tuple Myth: A Life of Archbishop Alojzije Stepinac* (Boulder, Colo., 1987)
Amory, Mark (ed.), *The Letters of Evelyn Waugh* (1980)
Auty, Phyllis, *Tito: A Biography* (1970)
—— and Clogg, Richard (eds.), *British Policy towards Wartime Resistance in Yugoslavia and Greece* (1975)
Banac, Ivo, *The National Question in Yugoslavia* (Ithaca, NY, 1984)
Bassett, Richard, *Balkan Hours* (1990)
Behschnitt, Wolf Dietrich, *Nationalismus bei Serben und Kroaten* (Munich 1980)
Beloff, Nora, *Tito's Flawed Legacy: Yugoslavia and the West, 1939–1984* (1985)
Bennett, Ralph, *Ultra in the West* (1979)
—— *Ultra and Mediterranean Strategy, 1941–1945* (1989)
Blažević, Jakov, *Mač a ne mir* (3 vols., Zagreb, 1980)
Bosnić, Sava, *Franjo Tudjman: Une carrière ambiguë*, trans. Slobodan Despot (Lausanne, 1993)
Bower, Tom, *The Pledge Betrayed* (1981)
Bragg, Melvyn, *Rich: The Life of Richard Burton* (1988)
Broucek, Peter (ed.), *Ein General in Zwielicht: Die Erinnerungen von Edmund Glaise von Horstenau* (3 vols., Vienna, 1988)
Butler, Hubert, *The Sub-prefect Should Have Held His Tongue and Other Essays* (1990)

Čerović, Božo, *Bosanski Omladinci i Sarajevski atentat* (Sarajevo, 1930)
Ćišić, Husein, *Bosanskohercegovački Muslimani i bosanska autonomija* (Sarajevo, 1991)
Clissold, Stephen, *Whirlwind: An Account of Marshal Tito's Rise to Power* (1949)
—— *Djilas: The Progress of a Revolutionary* (1983)
Cowgill, Anthony, Brimelow, Lord, and Booker, Christopher, The *Repatriations from Austria in* 1945: *The Report of an Inquiry* (1990)
Cox, Geoffrey, *The Race for Trieste* (1977)
Coxsedge, Joan, Caldicott, Ken, and Harant, Gerry, *Rooted in Secrecy: The Clandestine Element in Australian Politics* (Melbourne, 1989)
Crankshaw, Edward, *The Fall of the House of Habsburg* (1963)
Cuddon, J. A., *The Companion Guide to Yugoslavia* (1974)
Cvijić, J., La Péninsule balkanique (Paris, 1918)
Davidson, Basil, *Partisan Picture* (1946)
Davie, Michael (ed.), *The Diaries of Evelyn Waugh* (1976)
Deakin, F. W., *The Brutal Friendship* (1962)
Dedijer, Vladimir, *Tito Speaks: His Self-Portrait and Struggle with Stalin* (1953)
—— *The War Diaries* (1960)
—— *Sarajevo* 1914 (1967)
—— *Novi prilozi za biografiju druga Tita* (Rijeka, 1981)
—— *The Yugoslav Auschwitz and the Vatican*, trans. Harvey Kendall (Buffalo, NY, 1992)
—— and Miletić, Antun (eds.), *Genocid nad Muslimanima,* 1941–1945 (Sarajevo, 1990)
Despalatović, Elinor, *Ljudevit Gaj and the Illyrian Movement* (Boulder, Colo., 1975)
Djilas, Aleksa, *The Contested Country: Yugoslav Unity and Communist Revolution,* 1919–1953 (Cambridge, Mass., 1991)
——'Profile of Slobodan Milošević', *Foreign Affairs* (Summer 1993)
Djilas, Milovan, *The New Class* (1957)
—— *Conversations with Stalin*, trans. Michael B. Petrovich (1962)
—— *The Unperfect Society: Beyond the New Class* (1969)
—— *Wartime* (New York, 1977)
—— *Rise and Fall* (1985)
—— *Tito: The Story from Inside* (1981)
—— *Memoir of a Revolutionary* (New York, 1973)
Dunford, Martin, and Holland, Jack, *The Rough Guide to Yugoslavia* (1985)
Evans, Arthur, *Through Bosnia and the Herzegovina on Foot* (1876)

—— *Illyrian Letters* (1878)

Evans, Joan, *Time and Change* (1943)

Falconi, Carlo, *The Silence of Pius XII*, trans. Bernard Wall (1970)

Gibbon, Edward, *The Decline and Fall of the Roman Empire* (1813)

Gilbert, Martin, *Road to Victory: Winston S. Churchill, 1941–1945* (1986)

Glendinning, Victoria, *Rebecca West: A Life* (1987)

Hašek, Jaroslav, *The Good Soldier Švejk* (1973)

Hoettl, William, *The Secret Front: The Story of Nazi Espionage* (1953)

Hervat, Joža, and Stambuk, Zdenka (eds.), *Dokumenti o protunarodnom radu i zločinima jednog dijela katoličnog klera* (Zagreb, 1946)

Hory, Ladislaus, and Broszat, Martin, *Der Kroatische Ustascha-Staat, 1941–1945* (Stuttgart, 1964)

Irby, A. P., and Mackenzie, G. Muir, *Travels in the Slavonic Provinces of Turkey-in-Europe*, (2 vols. 1877)

Ivanovic, Vane, *LX: Memoirs of a Jugoslav* (1977)

Jelić-Butić, Fikrita, *Ustaša i Nezavisna država Hrvatske 1941–1945* (Zagreb, 1977)

—— *Četnici u Hrvatskoj, 1941–1943* (Zagreb, 1985)

Karadjić, Vuk, *The Red Knight*, trans. Daniel Weissbort and Tomislav Longinović (1992)

Khrushchev, Nikita, *Khrushchev Remembers* (1971)

Kindersley, Anne, *The Mountains of Serbia* (1976)

Klaić, Vjekoslav, *Povijest Hrvata* (5 vols. Zagreb, 1975)

Kranjcevic, Ivan, *Uspomene jednog učesnika u Sarajevskom atantatu* (Sarajevo, 1954)

Krizman, Bogdan, *Pavelić izmedju Hitlera i Musolinija* (Zagreb, 1980)

—— *Ustaše i treći Reich* (2 vols., Zagreb, 1983)

—— *Pavelić u bjekstvu* (Zagreb, 1986)

Lees, Michael, *The Rape of Serbia* (New York, 1990)

Leković, Mišo, *Martovski Pregovori* (Belgrade, 1985)

Lockhart, R. H. Bruce, *Retreat from Glory* (1934)

Lučić, Dehan, *Tajne Albanske Mafije* (Belgrade, 1989)

Maček, Vlatko, *In the Struggle for Freedom* (University Park, Pa., 1957)

Maclean, Fitzroy, *Eastern Approaches* (1949)

—— *Disputed Barricade* (1957)

—— *Josip Broz Tito: A Pictorial Biography* (1980)

McLynn, Frank, *Fitzroy Maclean* (1992)

Malaparte, Curzio, *Kaputt* (1946)

Martin, David, *Patriot or Traitor: The Case of General Mihailović* (Stanford, Calif., 1978)

—— *The Web of Disinformation* (New York, 1991)

May, Arthur J., *The Hapsburg Monarchy 1867–1914* (2 vols., Cambridge, Mass., 1951)
—— *The Passing of the Hapsburg Monarchy 1914–1918* (Philadelphia, 1966)
Mičunović, Veljko, *Moscow Diary*, trans. David Floyd (1980)
Miletić, Antun, *Koncentracioni logor Jasenovac* (2 vols., Belgrade, 1986)
Miller, William, *Essays on the Latin Orient* (Cambridge, 1921)
—— *The Ottoman Empire and its Successors* (1936)
Murray, Elinor, *Despalatović, Ljudevit Gaj and the Illyrian Movement* (Boulder, Colo., 1975)
Neubacher, Hermann, *Sonderauftrag Südost: 1940–1945* (Göttingen, 1956)
Novak, Viktor, *Magnum Crimen: Pola vijeka klerikalizma u Hrvatskoj* (Zagreb, 1948)
'Odysseus' (Sir Charles Eliot), *Turkey in Europe* (1908)
Official History of the Second World War
Pacepa, Ion, *Red Horizons* (1988)
Paris, Edmond, *Genocide in Satellite Croatia, 1941–45* (Chicago, 1961)
Parrott, Cecil, *The Bad Bohemian* (1978)
Pavlowitch, Stevan K., *Yugoslavia* (1971)
—— *Unconventional Perceptions of Yugoslavia, 1941–45* (New York, 1985)
—— *The Improbable Survivor: Yugoslavia and its Problems, 1918–1988* (1988)
—— *Tito: Yugoslavia's Great Dictator. A Reassessment* (1992)
Picot, Auguste, *Les Serbes d'Hongroi* (Prague, 1873)
Pryce-Jones, David, *Evelyn Waugh and his World* (1973)
Ranke, Leopold von, *The History of Serbia* (1853)
Rhodes, Anthony, *The Vatican in the Age of the Dictators, 1922–1945* (1973)
Roatta, Mario, *Otto Milioni di Baionette* (Verona, 1946)
Rothenberg, Gunther, *The Austrian Military Border in Croatia 1522–1747* (Urbana, Ill., 1960)
—— *The Military Border in Croatia, 1740–1881* (Chicago, 1966)
Rupčić, Ljudevit, *Gospina Ukazanja u Medjugorju* (Samobor, 1983)
Seldes, George, *Witness to a Century* (New York, 1987)
Seton-Watson, Hugh, *The East European Revolution* (1956)
—— *Eastern Europe between the Wars: 1921–1941* (1967)
Seton-Watson, R. W., *Absolutism in Croatia* (1912)
—— 'The Role of Bosnia in International Politics, 1875–1914' in *Studies in History* (Oxford, 1966)

—— *R. W. Seton-Watson and the Yugoslavs: Correspondence 1906–41* (2 vols., 1979)

Simić, Pero, *Kad, kako i zašto je Tito postavljen za sekretara CK KPJ* (Belgrade, 1989)

Steinberg, Jonathan, *All or Nothing* (1990)

Sykes, Christopher, *Evelyn Waugh* (1975)

Temperley, H. W., *History of Serbia* (1917)

Tito, Josip Broz, *Borba za oslobodjenje Jugoslavije* (Belgrade, 1947)

Trotsky, Leon, *The Balkan Wars, 1912–13*, trans. Brian Pearce, ed. George Weissman and Duncan Williams (New York, 1984)

Tuchman, Barbara, *The March of Folly: From Troy to Vietnam* (1984)

Tudjman, Franjo, *Nationalism in Contemporary Europe* (Boulder, Colo., 1981)

—— *Bespuća povijesne zbilnosti: Rasprava o povijesti i filosofiji zlosilje* (Zagreb, 1990)

Vesović, Velemir (ed.), *Kosovska bitka: Mit, legenda i stvarnosti* (Belgrade, 1988)

Ware, Timothy, *The Orthodox Church* (1993)

West, Rebecca, *Black Lamb and Grey Falcon* (2 vols., 1942)

West, Richard, *The White Tubes Revisited* (1978)

Wilson, Duncan, *Tito's Yugoslavia* (Cambridge, 1979)

Woolf, R. L., *The Balkans in our Time* (Cambridge, Mass., 1956)

Zilliacus, Konni, *Tito of Yugoslavia* (1952)

Index